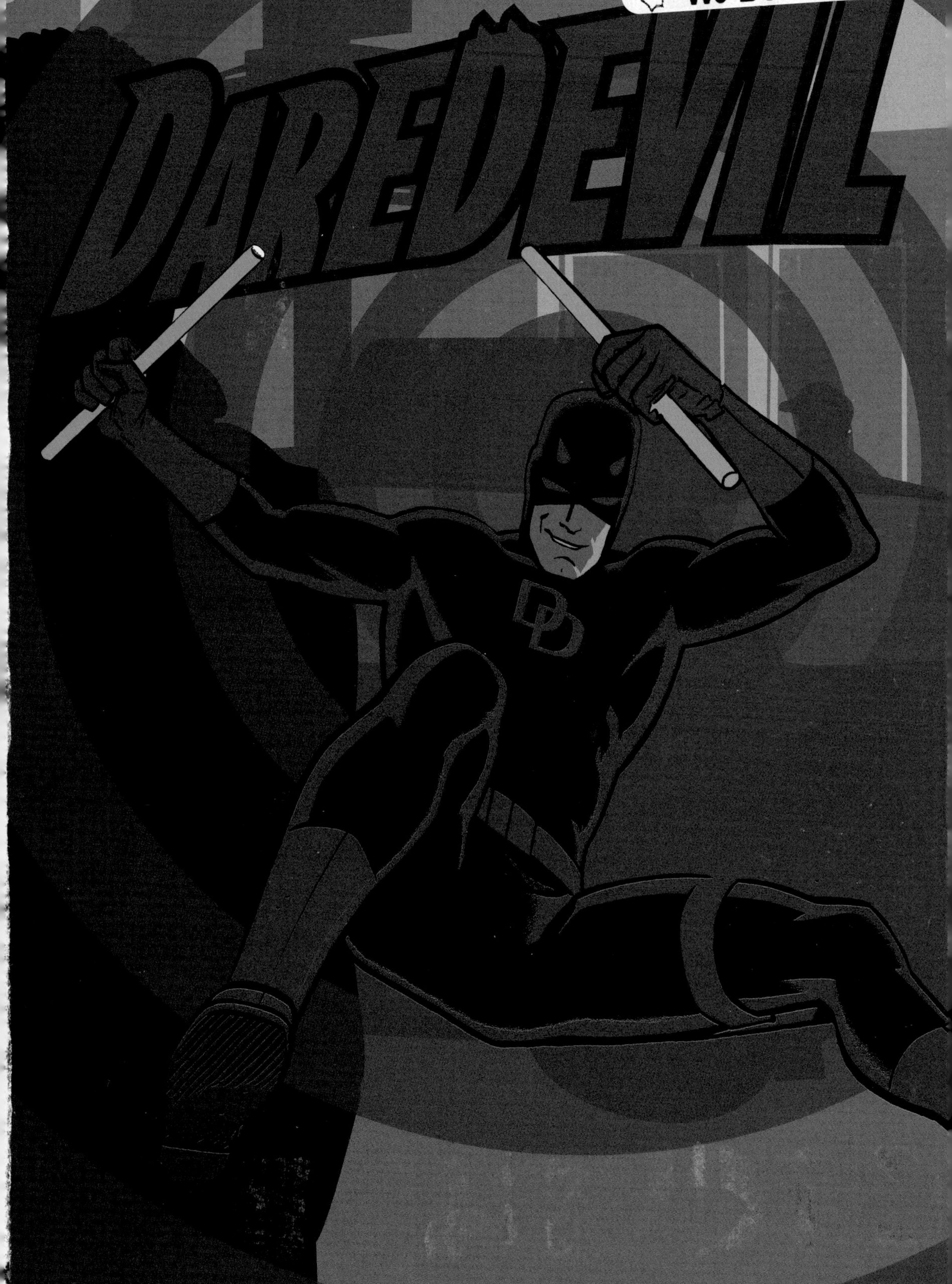
DAREDEVIL
DD

DAREDEVIL VOL. 1: DEVIL AT BAY. Contains material originally published in magazine form as DAREDEVIL #1-5 and #0.1. First printing 2014. ISBN# 978-0-7851-5411-2. Published by MARVEL WORLDWIDE, INC., a subsidiary of MARVEL ENTERTAINMENT, LLC. OFFICE OF PUBLICATION: 135 West 50th Street, New York, NY 10020. **Printed in the U.S.A.** ALAN FINE, EVP - Office of the President, Marvel Worldwide, Inc. and EVP & CMO Marvel Characters B.V.; DAN BUCKLEY, Publisher & President - Print, Animation & Digital Divisions; JOE QUESADA, Chief Creative Officer; TOM BREVOORT, SVP of Publishing; DAVID BOGART, SVP of Operations & Procurement, Publishing; C.B. CEBULSKI, SVP of Creator & Content Development; DAVID GABRIEL, SVP Print, Sales & Marketing; JIM O'KEEFE, VP of Operations & Logistics; DAN CARR, Executive Director of Publishing Technology; SUSAN CRESPI, Editorial Operations Manager; ALEX MORALES, Publishing Operations Manager; STAN LEE, Chairman Emeritus. For information regarding advertising in Marvel Comics or on Marvel.com, please contact Niza Disla, Director of Marvel Partnerships, at ndisla@marvel.com. For Marvel subscription inquiries, please call 800-217-9158. **Manufactured between 8/22/2014 and 9/29/2014 by R.R. DONNELLEY, INC., SALEM, VA, USA.**

10 9 8 7 6 5 4 3 2 1

WRITER
MARK WAID

DAREDEVIL #1-5

ARTIST
CHRIS SAMNEE
COLOR ARTIST
JAVIER RODRIGUEZ
LETTERER
VC'S JOE CARAMAGNA

DAREDEVIL #0.1

ARTIST
PETER KRAUSE
COLOR ARTIST
JOHN KALISZ
LETTERER
VC'S JOE SABINO

EDITOR
ELLIE PYLE
SENIOR EDITOR
NICK LOWE
COVER ARTISTS
CHRIS SAMNEE &
JAVIER RODRIGUEZ

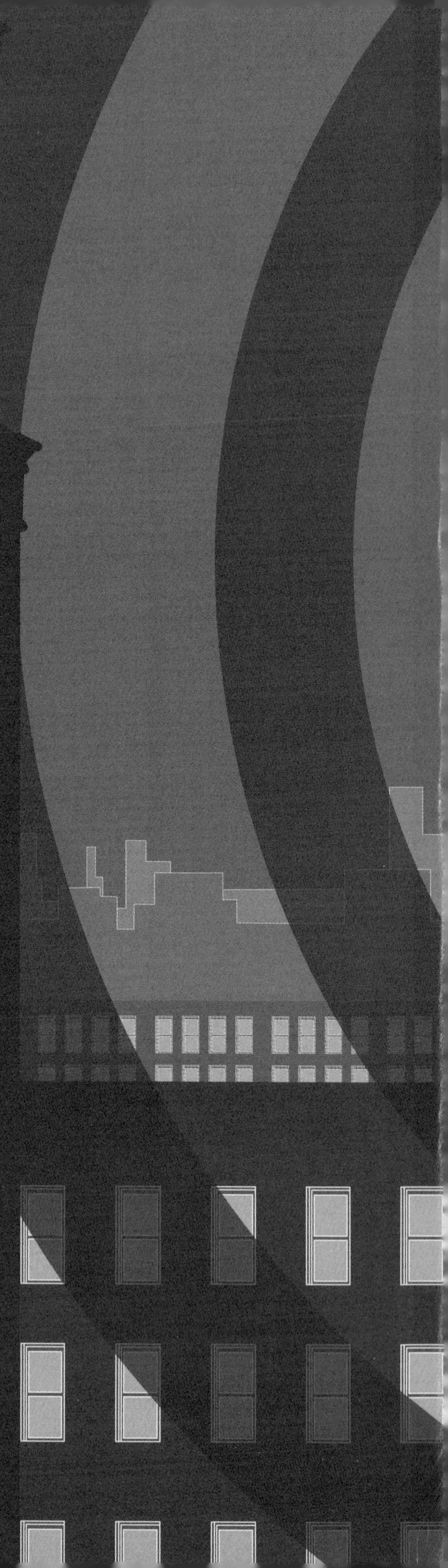

COLLECTION EDITOR
ALEX STARBUCK
ASSISTANT EDITOR
SARAH BRUNSTAD
EDITORS, SPECIAL PROJECTS
JENNIFER GRÜNWALD & **MARK D. BEAZLEY**
SENIOR EDITOR, SPECIAL PROJECTS
JEFF YOUNGQUIST
SVP PRINT, SALES & MARKETING
DAVID GABRIEL
BOOK DESIGNER
NELSON RIBEIRO

EDITOR IN CHIEF
AXEL ALONSO
CHIEF CREATIVE OFFICER
JOE QUESADA
PUBLISHER
DAN BUCKLEY
EXECUTIVE PRODUCER
ALAN FINE

DAREDEVIL: ROAD WARRIOR WAS ORIGINALLY PUBLISHED DIGITALLY AS AN INFINITE COMIC RELEASED WEEKLY BETWEEN *DAREDEVIL (2011) #36* AND *DAREDEVIL (2014) #1*. IF YOU ENJOY THIS PRINTED VERSION, PLEASE CHECK OUT THE INFINITE VERSION ON THE MARVEL COMICS APP.

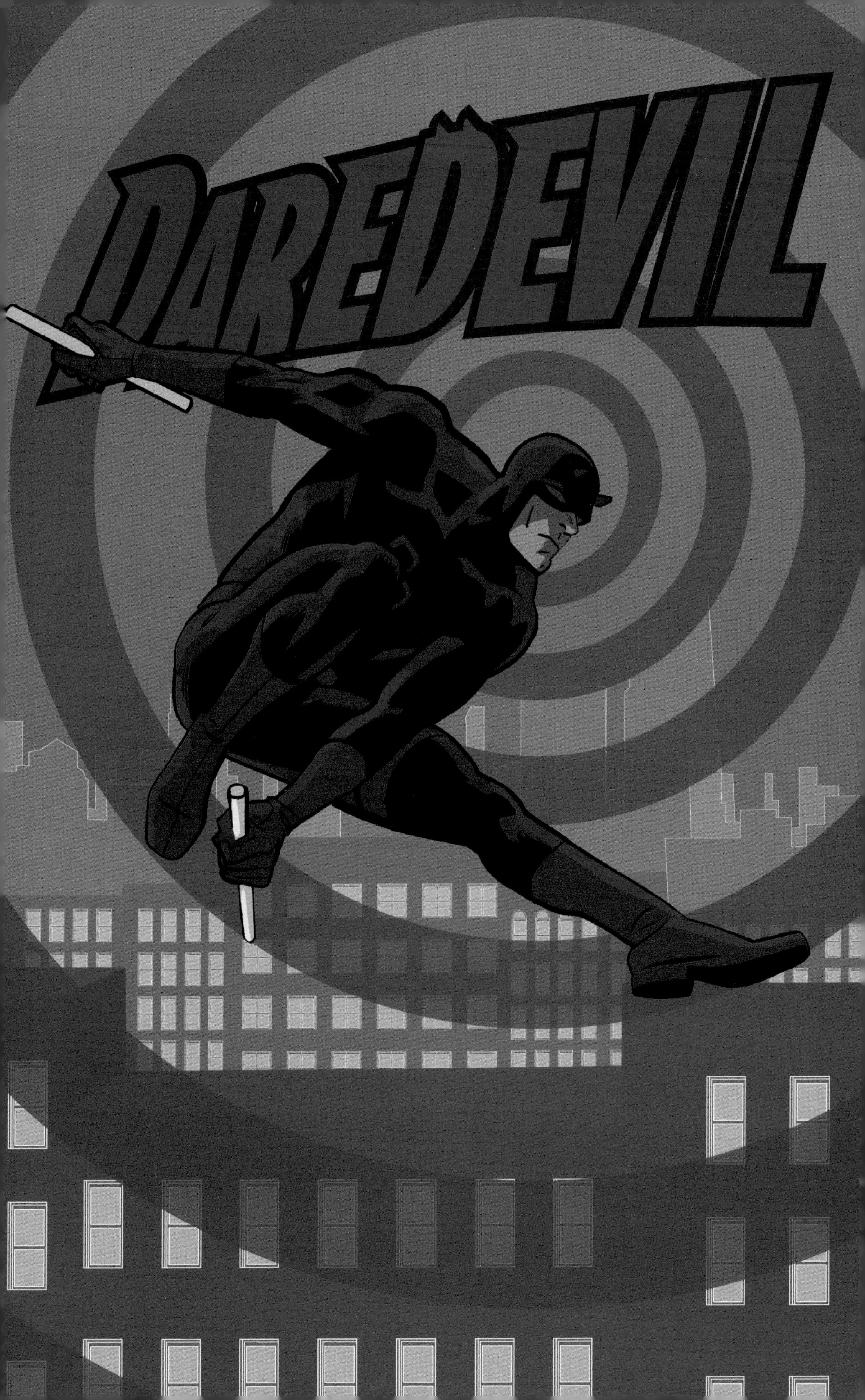
DAREDEVIL

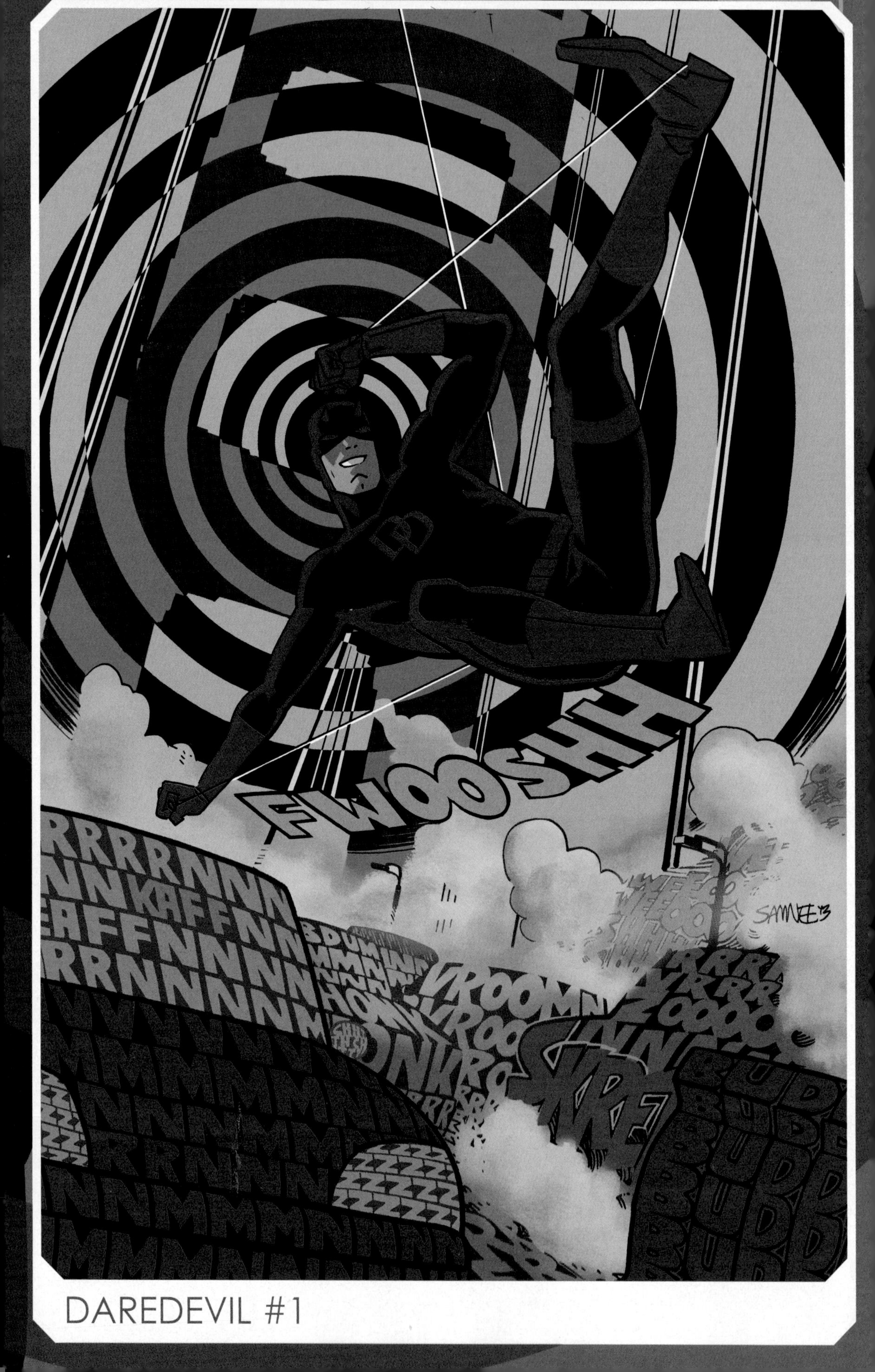
FWOOSH
VROOOM
SAMNEE '13

DAREDEVIL #1

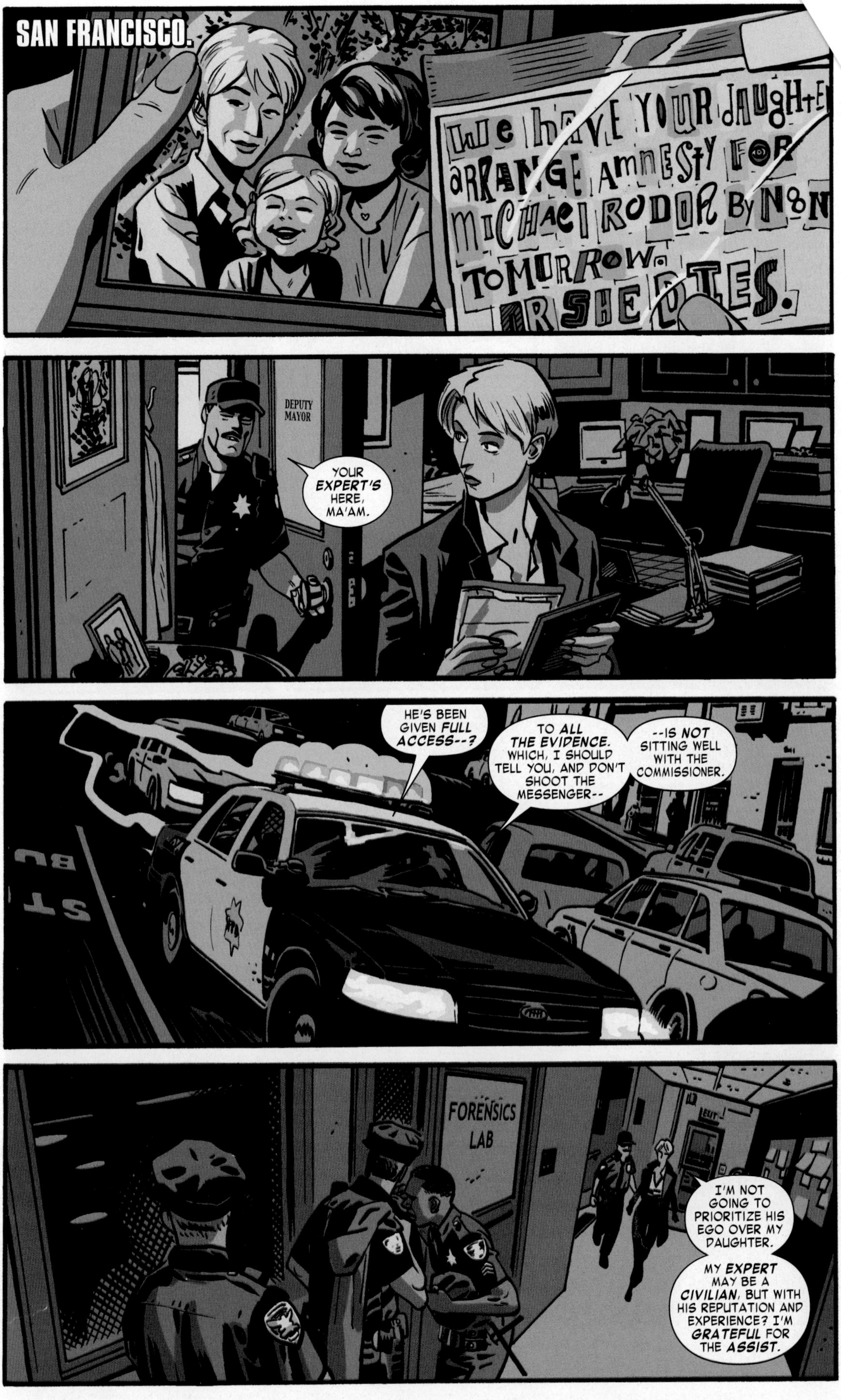
SAN FRANCISCO.
WE HAVE YOUR DAUGHTER
ARRANGE AMNESTY FOR
MICHAEL RODOH BY NOON
TOMORROW.
OR SHE DIES.
DEPUTY MAYOR
YOUR EXPERT'S HERE, MA'AM.
HE'S BEEN GIVEN FULL ACCESS--?
TO ALL THE EVIDENCE. WHICH, I SHOULD TELL YOU, AND DON'T SHOOT THE MESSENGER--
--IS NOT SITTING WELL WITH THE COMMISSIONER.
FORENSICS LAB
I'M NOT GOING TO PRIORITIZE HIS EGO OVER MY DAUGHTER.
MY EXPERT MAY BE A CIVILIAN, BUT WITH HIS REPUTATION AND EXPERIENCE? I'M GRATEFUL FOR THE ASSIST.

WELL? ANY PROG--

QUIET, PLEASE!

THE FLUORESCENT LIGHTS WERE NOISY *ENOUGH.*

GIVE ME THE RAG DOLL AGAIN.

IT HAS NO PRINTS--

IT HAS NO *FINGER*PRINTS. THE *HANDPRINT* IS A *BOUQUET* OF ODORS POINTING TO WHERE THEY'RE HOLDING THE GIRL.

MILDEW. MOLD. BASIDIOMYCOTA FUNGI, THE SORT OF SPORES THAT PROLIFERATE PRIMARILY AT OCEANSIDE.

BRICK DUST. NO--TALCUM POWDER, STALE AS HELL. WEIRD.

PLUS, THE DOLL ITSELF HAS SPONGED UP THE TINIEST TRACE OF SOMETHING ODD BUT FAMILIAR...AEROSOL DISINFECTANT? LIKE ANTIPERSPIRANT, BUT *NOT.*

PLAY THE RECORDING ONE MORE TIME.

MOMMY, HELP ME! MOMMY! ♪TUMP♪ ♪TUMP♪

HEY, GRAB HER--!

♪TUMP♪ ♪TUMP♪ MOMMY, ♪TUMP♪ IT'S *DARK* ♪TUMP♪ AND *COLD* AND ♪TUMP♪ I'M *SCARED!* MOMMY, PLEASE--!

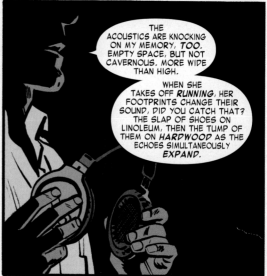

THE ACOUSTICS ARE KNOCKING ON MY MEMORY, *TOO.* EMPTY SPACE, BUT NOT CAVERNOUS. MORE WIDE THAN HIGH.

WHEN SHE TAKES OFF *RUNNING,* HER FOOTPRINTS CHANGE THEIR SOUND, DID YOU CATCH THAT? THE SLAP OF SHOES ON LINOLEUM, THEN THE TUMP OF THEM ON *HARDWOOD* AS THE ECHOES SIMULTANEOUSLY *EXPAND.*

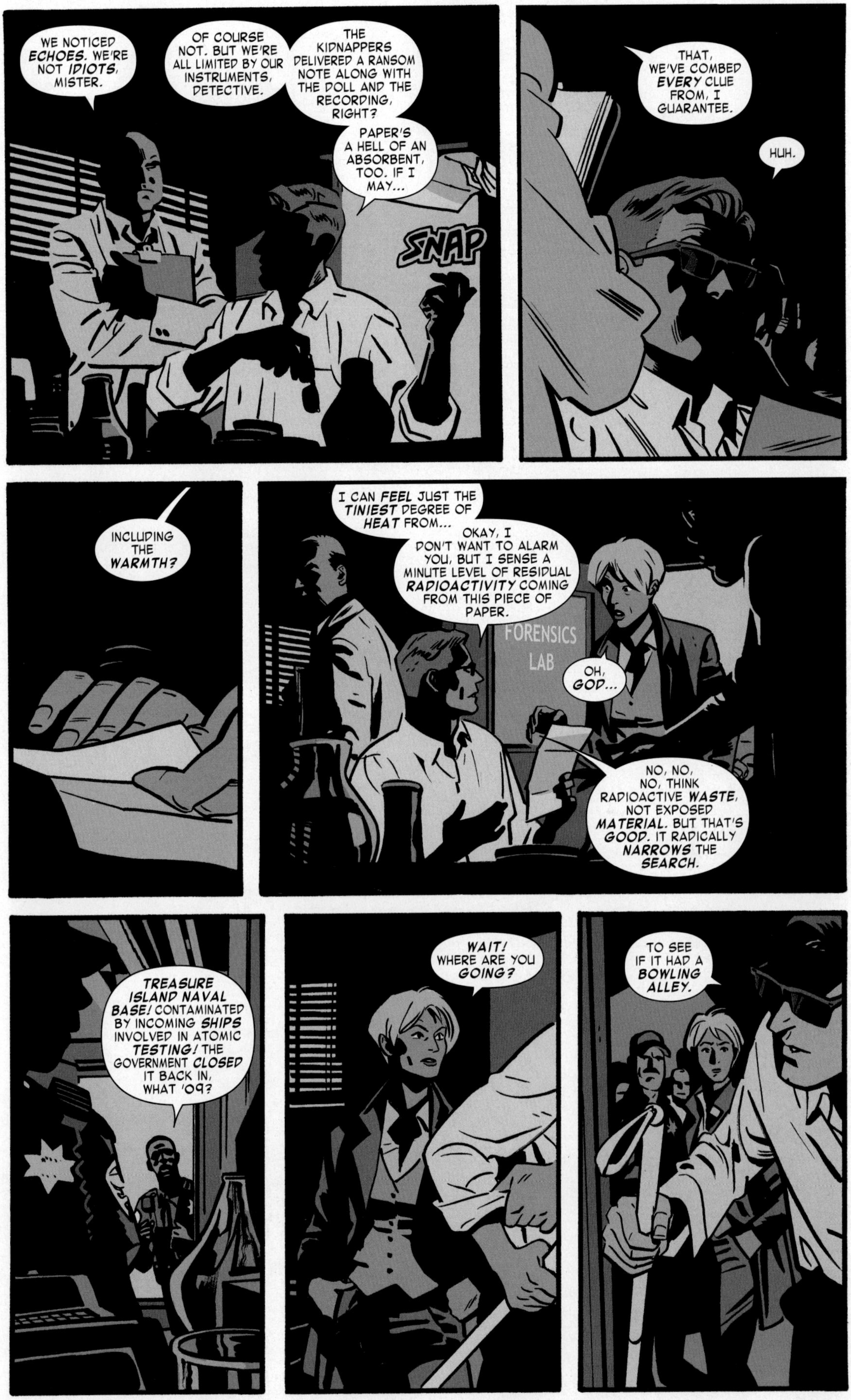
WE NOTICED ECHOES. WE'RE NOT IDIOTS, MISTER.
OF COURSE NOT. BUT WE'RE ALL LIMITED BY OUR INSTRUMENTS, DETECTIVE.
THE KIDNAPPERS DELIVERED A RANSOM NOTE ALONG WITH THE DOLL AND THE RECORDING, RIGHT?
PAPER'S A HELL OF AN ABSORBENT, TOO. IF I MAY...
SNAP
THAT, WE'VE COMBED EVERY CLUE FROM, I GUARANTEE.
HUH.
INCLUDING THE WARMTH?
I CAN FEEL JUST THE TINIEST DEGREE OF HEAT FROM...
OKAY, I DON'T WANT TO ALARM YOU, BUT I SENSE A MINUTE LEVEL OF RESIDUAL RADIOACTIVITY COMING FROM THIS PIECE OF PAPER.
FORENSICS LAB
OH, GOD...
NO, NO, NO, THINK RADIOACTIVE WASTE, NOT EXPOSED MATERIAL. BUT THAT'S GOOD. IT RADICALLY NARROWS THE SEARCH.
TREASURE ISLAND NAVAL BASE! CONTAMINATED BY INCOMING SHIPS INVOLVED IN ATOMIC TESTING! THE GOVERNMENT CLOSED IT BACK IN, WHAT '09?
WAIT! WHERE ARE YOU GOING?
TO SEE IF IT HAD A BOWLING ALLEY.

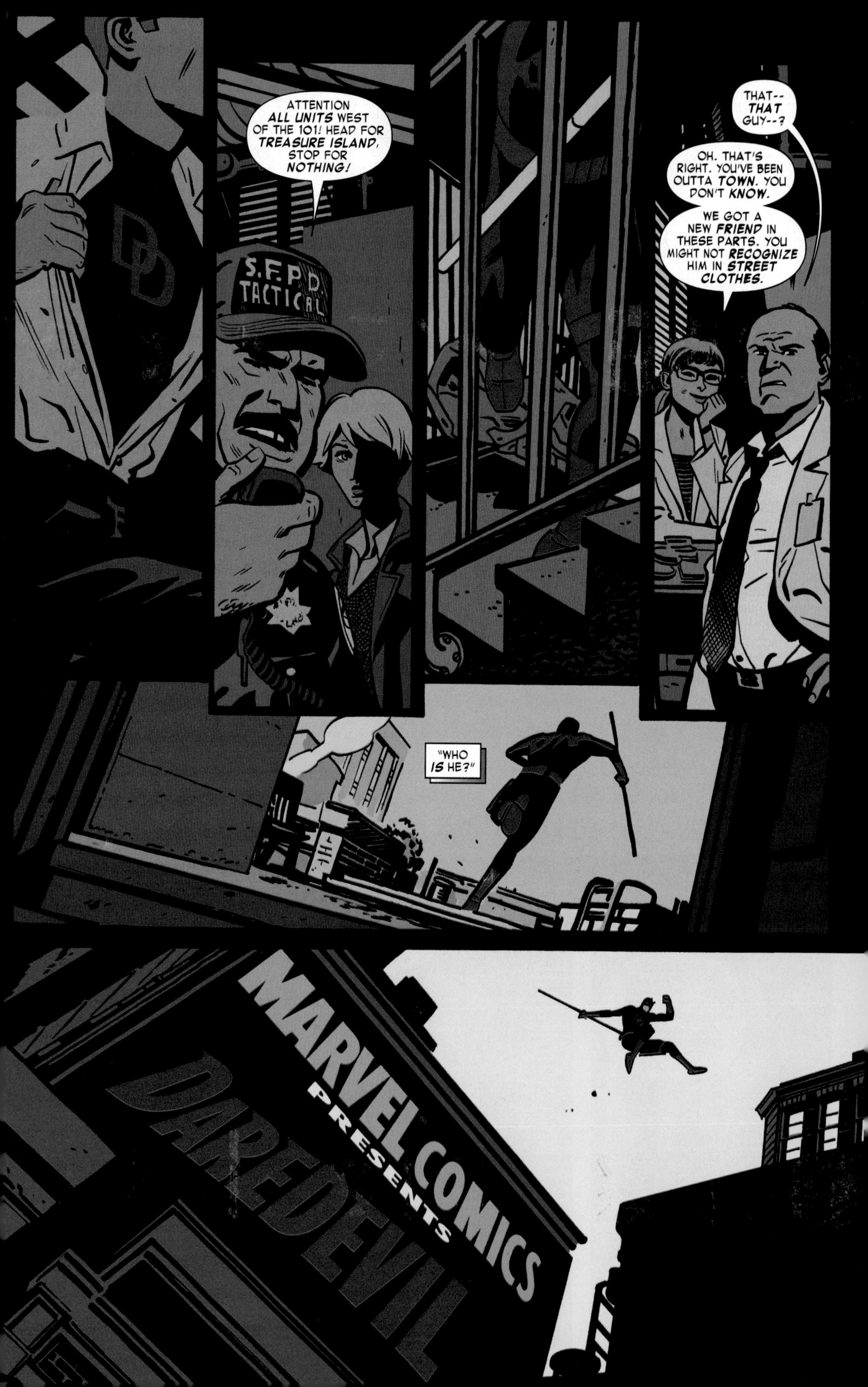
S.F.P.D. TACTICAL
ATTENTION ALL UNITS WEST OF THE 101! HEAD FOR TREASURE ISLAND, STOP FOR NOTHING!
THAT-- THAT GUY--?
OH. THAT'S RIGHT. YOU'VE BEEN OUTTA TOWN. YOU DON'T KNOW.
WE GOT A NEW FRIEND IN THESE PARTS. YOU MIGHT NOT RECOGNIZE HIM IN STREET CLOTHES.
"WHO IS HE?"
MARVEL COMICS PRESENTS
DAREDEVIL

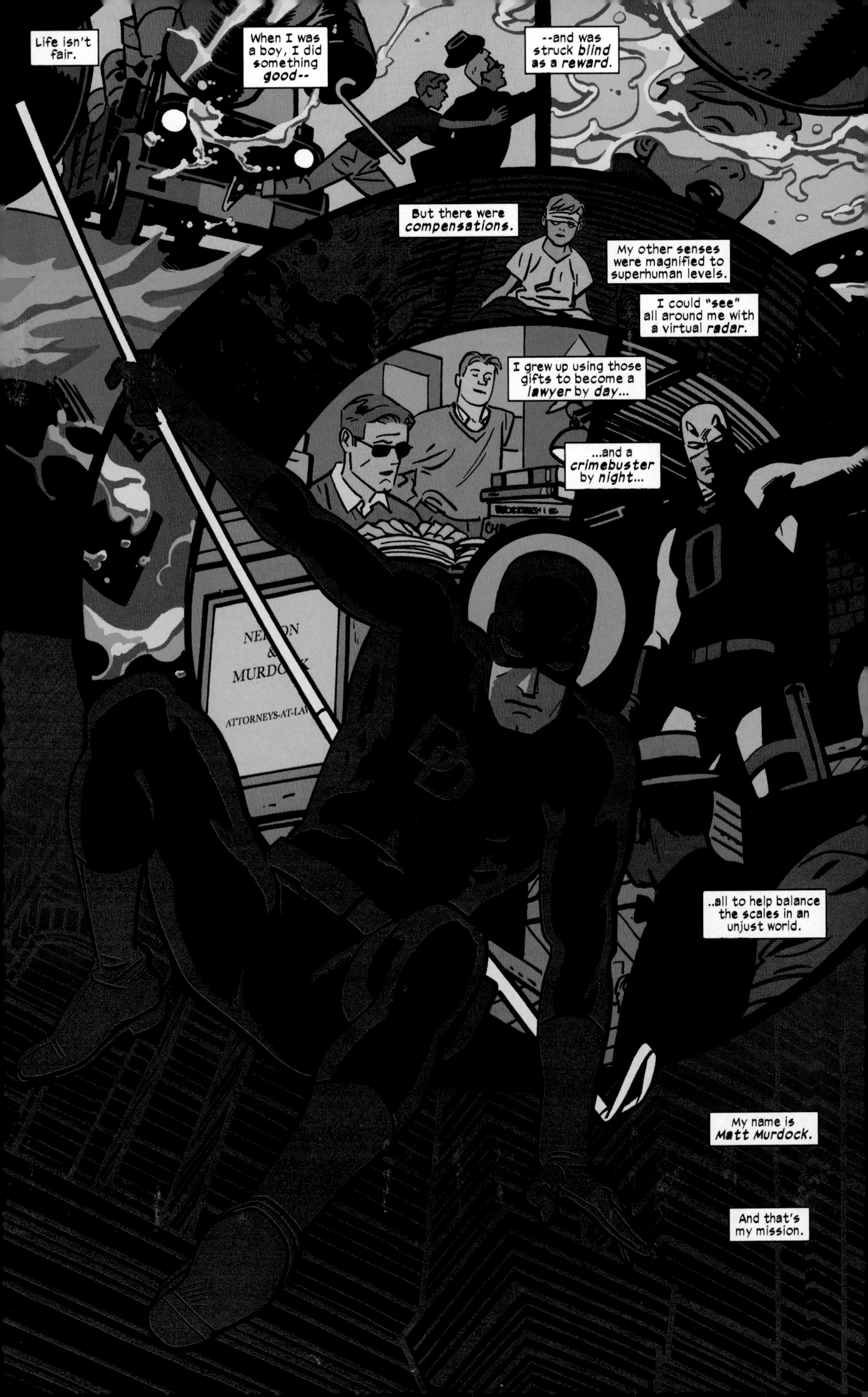
Life isn't fair.
When I was a boy, I did something good--
--and was struck blind as a reward.
But there were compensations.
My other senses were magnified to superhuman levels.
I could "see" all around me with a virtual radar.
I grew up using those gifts to become a lawyer by day...
...and a crimebuster by night...
NELSON & MURDOCK ATTORNEYS-AT-LAW
..all to help balance the scales in an unjust world.
My name is Matt Murdock.
And that's my mission.

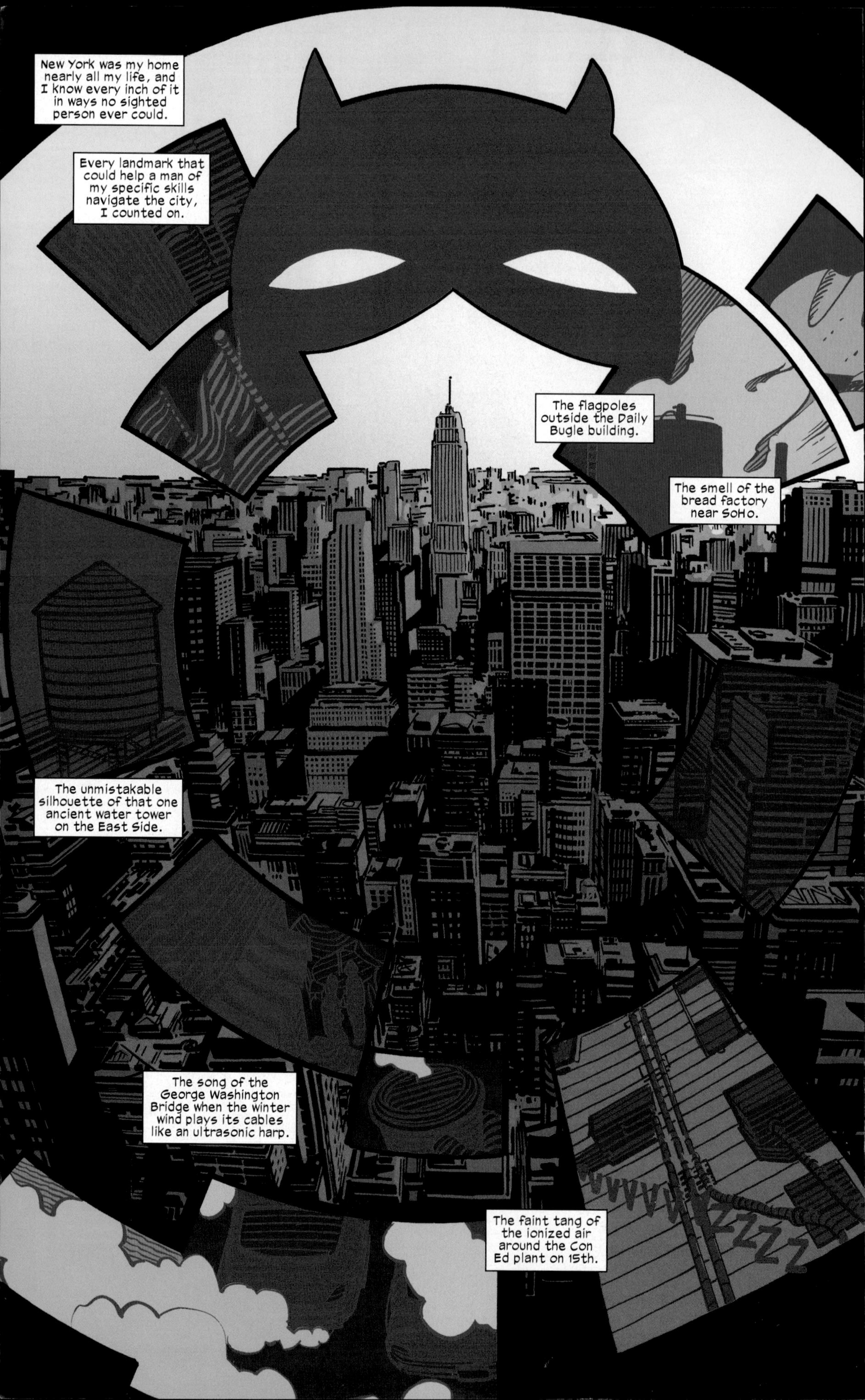
New York was my home nearly all my life, and I know every inch of it in ways no sighted person ever could.
Every landmark that could help a man of my specific skills navigate the city, I counted on.
The flagpoles outside the Daily Bugle building.
The smell of the bread factory near SoHo.
The unmistakable silhouette of that one ancient water tower on the East Side.
The song of the George Washington Bridge when the winter wind plays its cables like an ultrasonic harp.
The faint tang of the ionized air around the Con Ed plant on 15th.

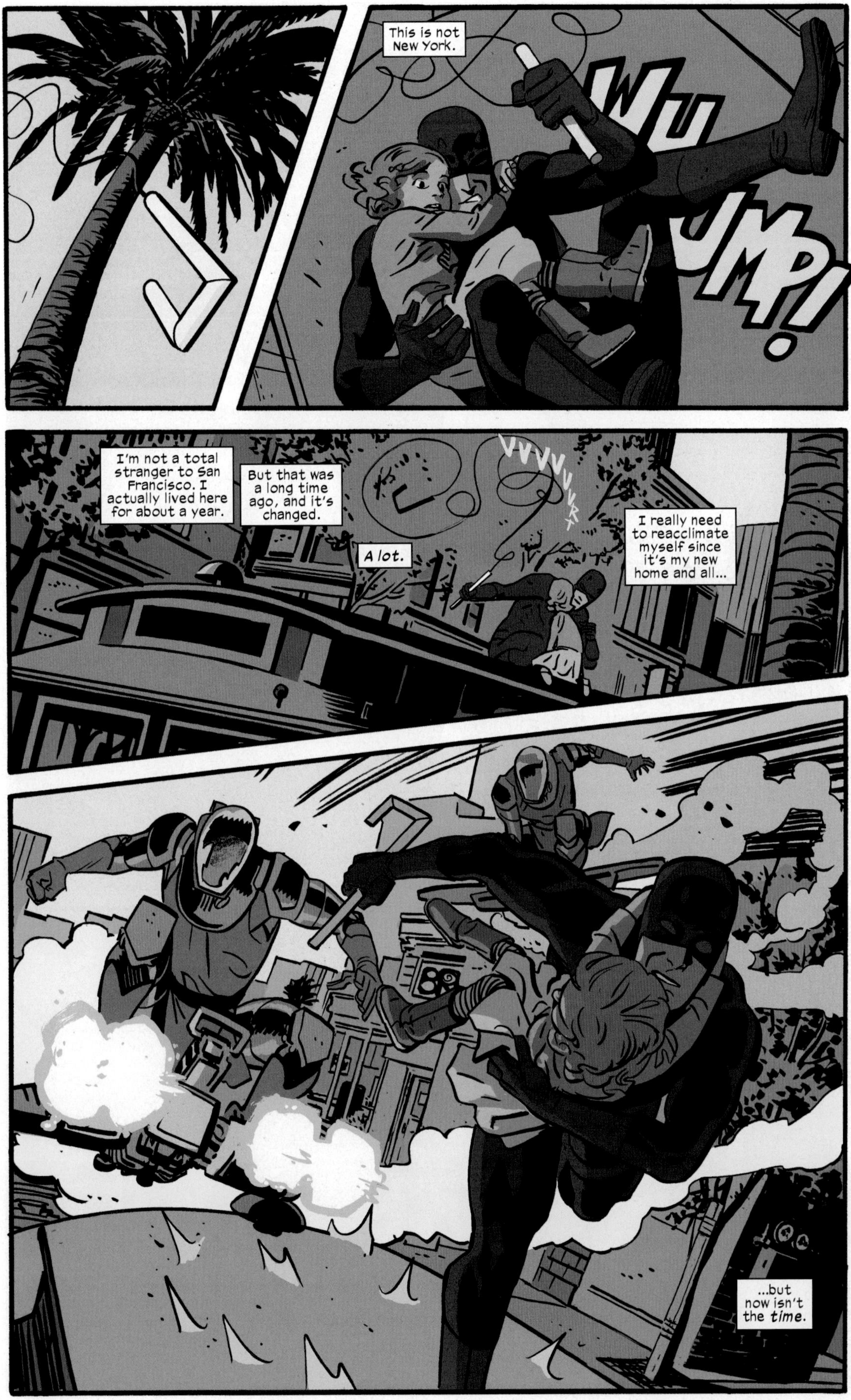
This is not New York.
WUUMP!
I'm not a total stranger to San Francisco. I actually lived here for about a year.
But that was a long time ago, and it's changed.
A lot.
VVVVVVVRT
I really need to reacclimate myself since it's my new home and all...
...but now isn't the *time*.

THE KIDNAPPERS ARE ACTUALLY CHASING YOU? WHO DOES THAT? WHY ARE THEY--?

UNLESS THIS GIRL IS THE SECRET HEIR TO A LOST KINGDOM, WHICH SHE'S NOT, I COULDN'T TELL YOU!

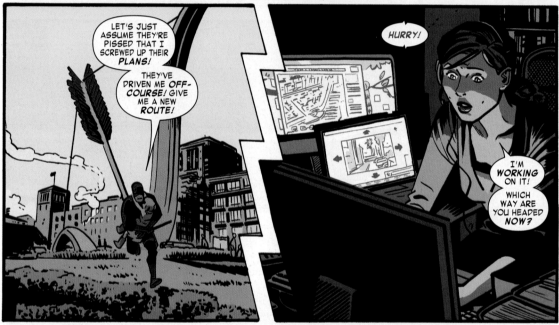

LET'S JUST ASSUME THEY'RE PISSED THAT I SCREWED UP THEIR PLANS!

THEY'VE DRIVEN ME OFF-COURSE! GIVE ME A NEW ROUTE!

HURRY!

I'M WORKING ON IT! WHICH WAY ARE YOU HEADED NOW?

Sun on my left shoulder, ship horns at 3:00...

NORTHWEST!

GOOD! SWING WEST AROUND THE EMBARCADERO CLOCK TOWER!

I tried to cheat the reorientation process by setting up an earpiece comm-link with my let's say "friend" Kirsten McDuffie...

PAF

CLIK

CLIK

CLIK

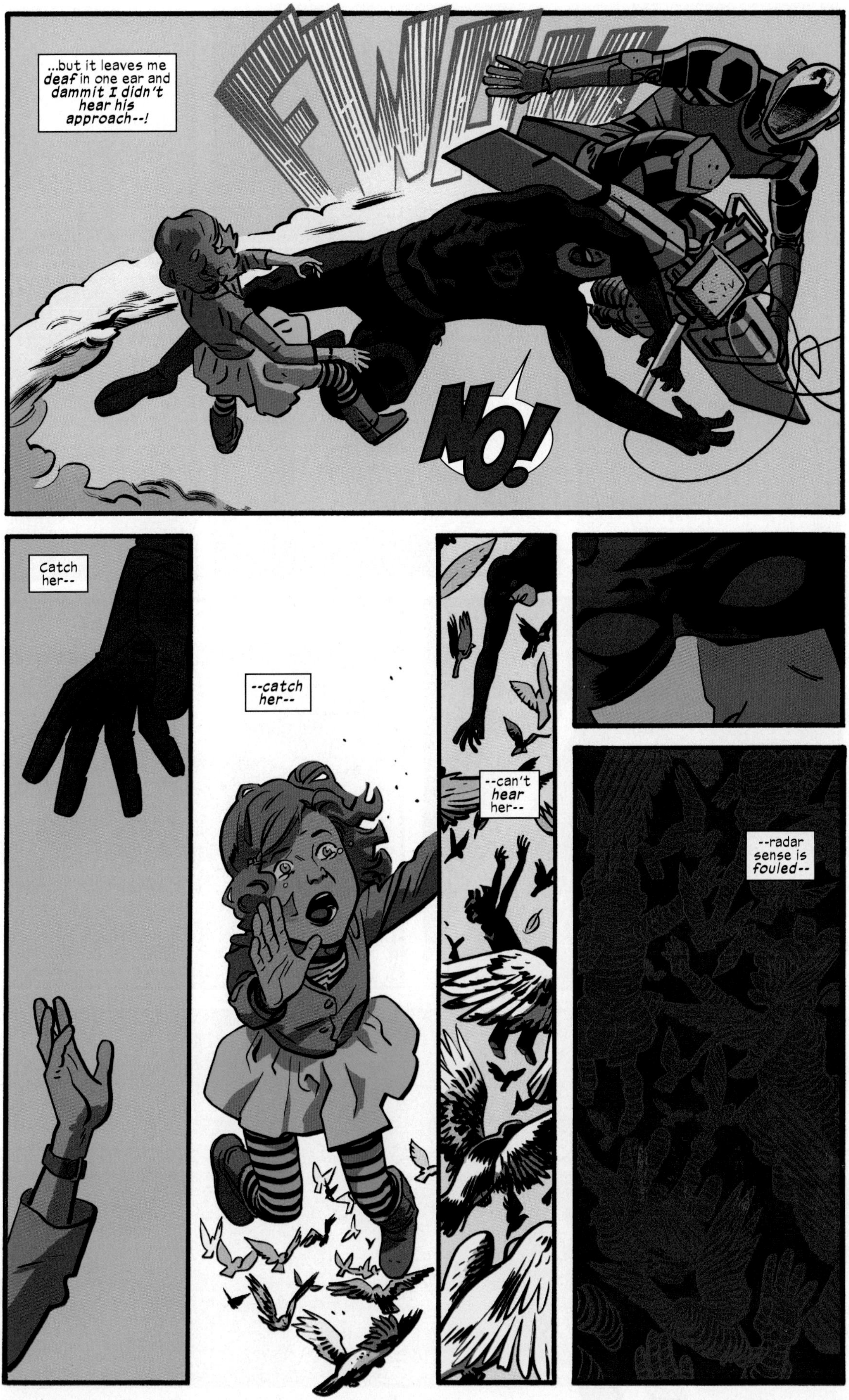
...but it leaves me *deaf* in one ear and *dammit I didn't hear his approach--!*
FWOOM
NO!
Catch her--
--catch her--
--can't *hear* her--
--radar sense is *fouled*--

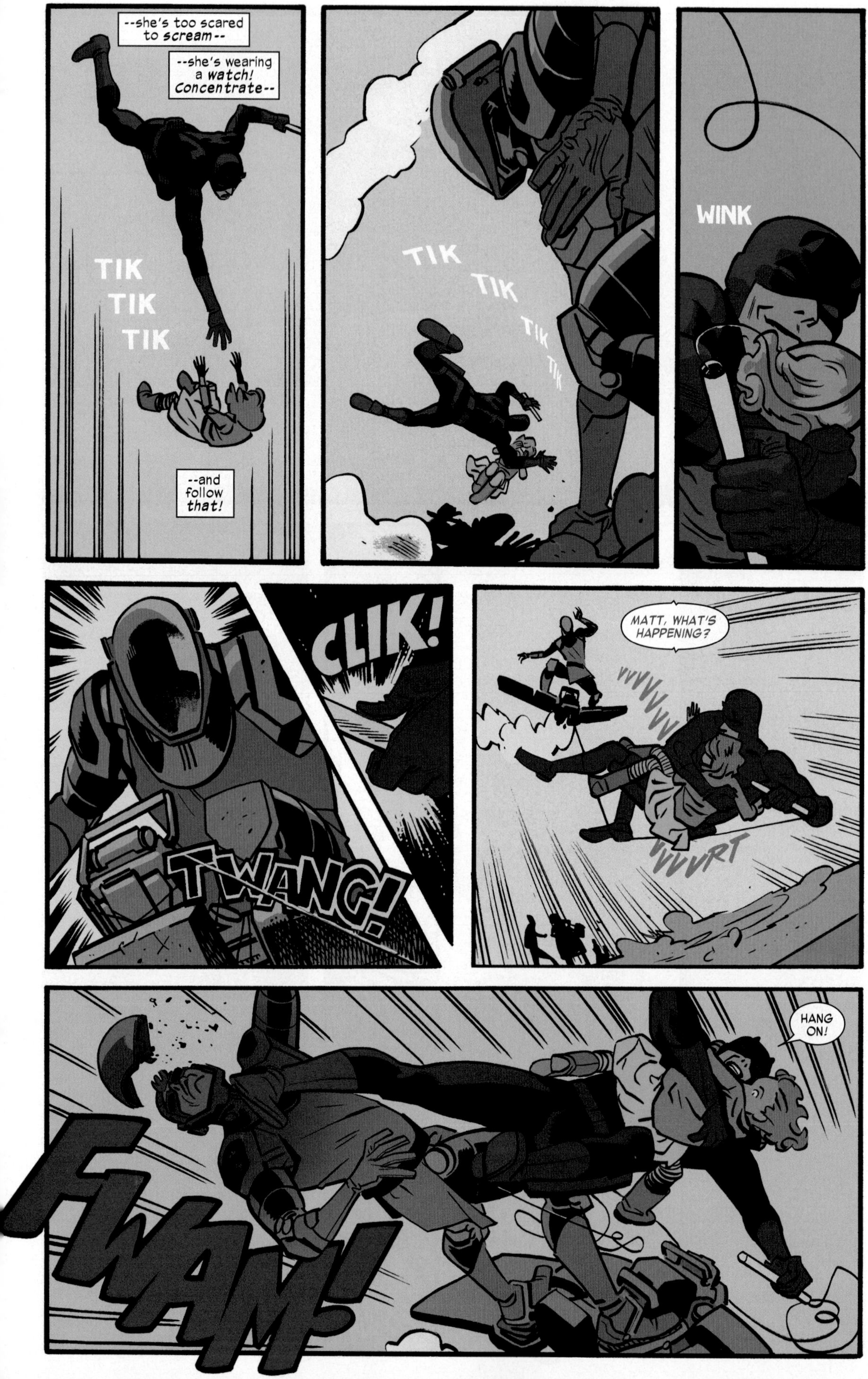
--she's too scared to scream--
--she's wearing a watch! Concentrate--
TIK
TIK
TIK
--and follow that!
TIK
TIK
TIK
TIK
WINK
CLIK!
TWANG!
MATT, WHAT'S HAPPENING?
VVVVVVVV
VVVVRT
HANG ON!
FWAM!

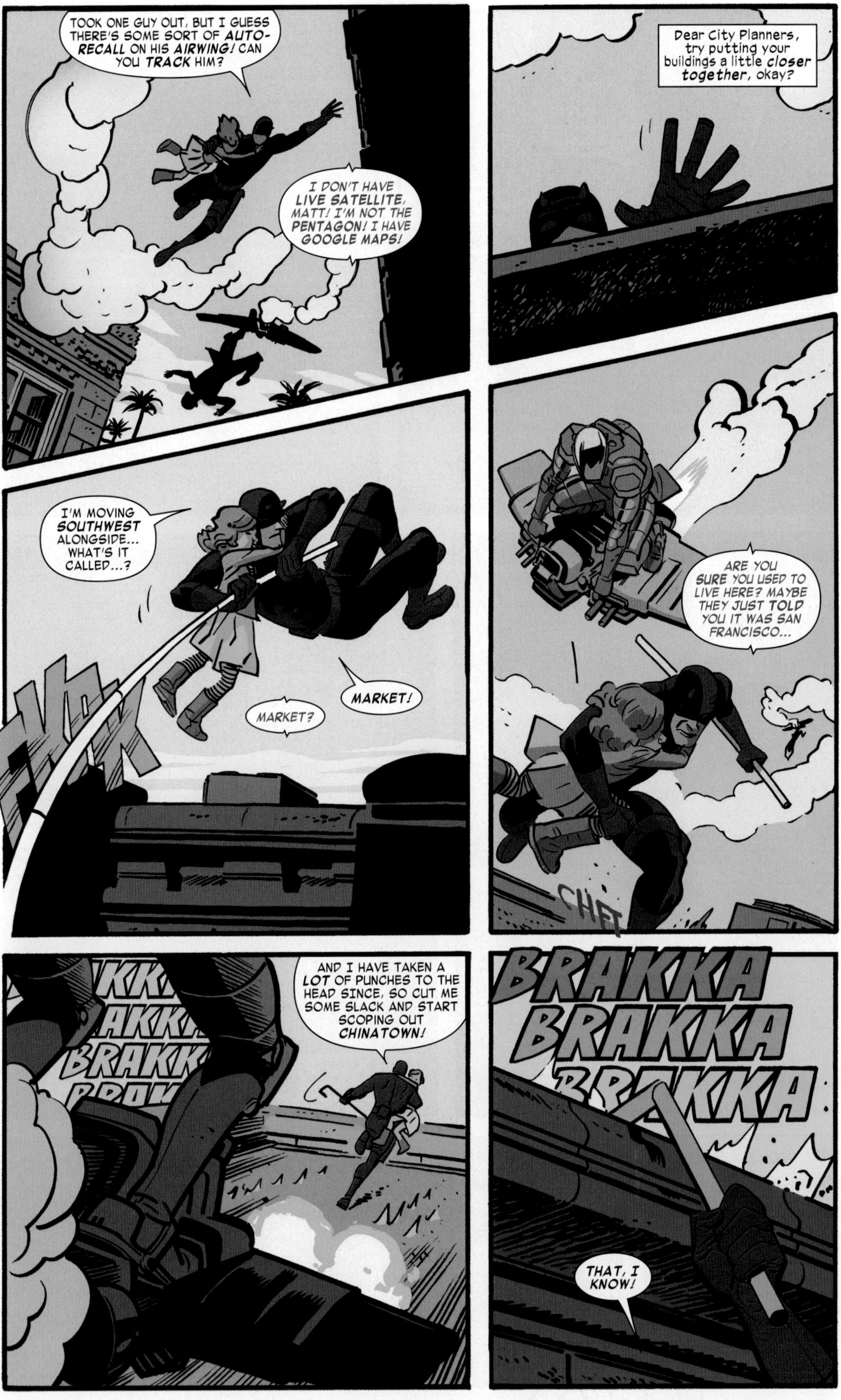
TOOK ONE GUY OUT, BUT I GUESS THERE'S SOME SORT OF AUTO-RECALL ON HIS AIRWING! CAN YOU TRACK HIM?
I DON'T HAVE LIVE SATELLITE, MATT! I'M NOT THE PENTAGON! I HAVE GOOGLE MAPS!
Dear City Planners, try putting your buildings a little closer together, okay?
I'M MOVING SOUTHWEST ALONGSIDE... WHAT'S IT CALLED...?
MARKET?
MARKET!
ARE YOU SURE YOU USED TO LIVE HERE? MAYBE THEY JUST TOLD YOU IT WAS SAN FRANCISCO...
CHFT
AND I HAVE TAKEN A LOT OF PUNCHES TO THE HEAD SINCE, SO CUT ME SOME SLACK AND START SCOPING OUT CHINATOWN!
BRAKKA
BRAKKA
BRAKKA
THAT, I KNOW!

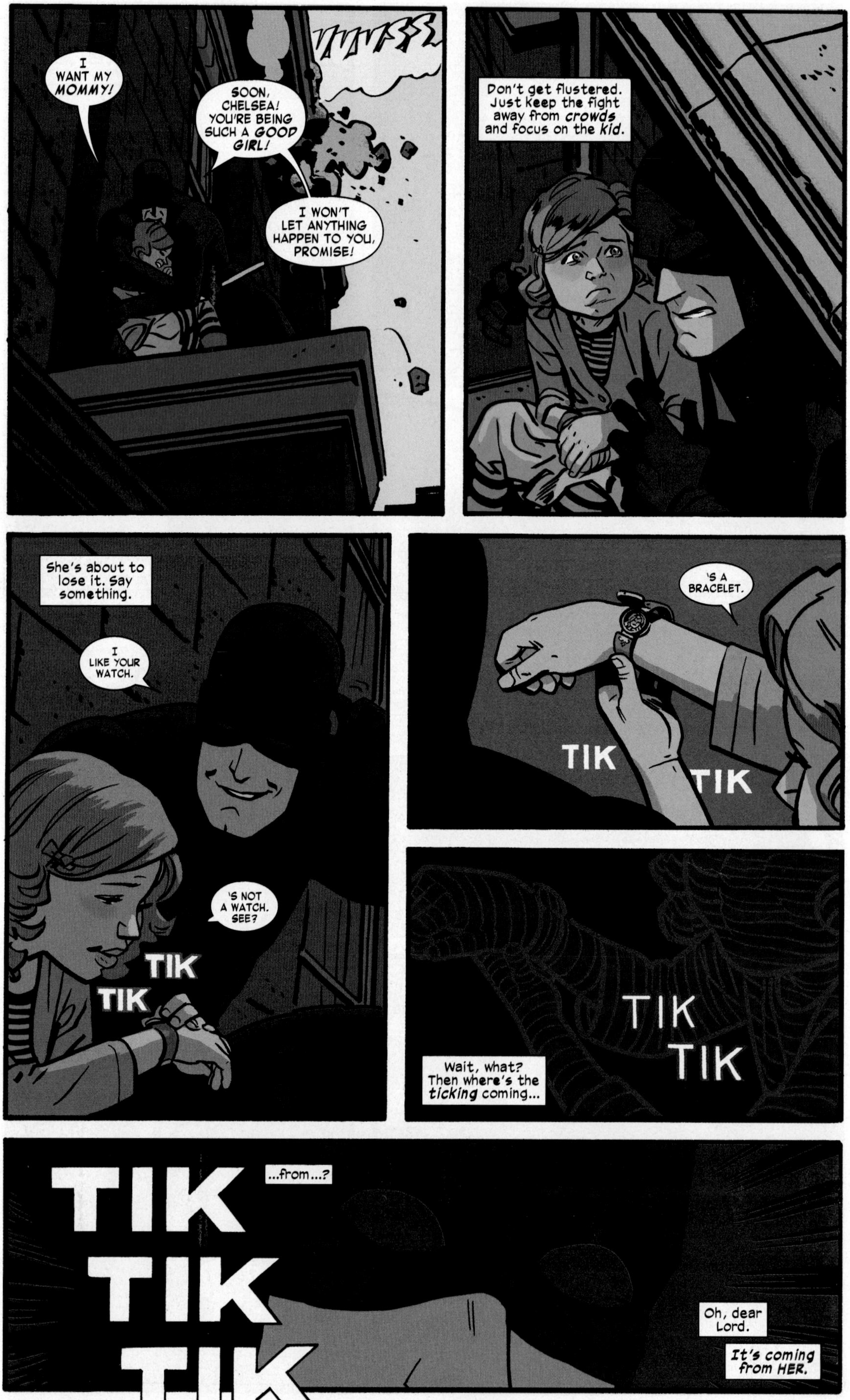

VVVVVSSS
I WANT MY MOMMY!
SOON, CHELSEA! YOU'RE BEING SUCH A GOOD GIRL!
I WON'T LET ANYTHING HAPPEN TO YOU, PROMISE!
Don't get flustered. Just keep the fight away from crowds and focus on the kid.
She's about to lose it. Say something.
I LIKE YOUR WATCH.
'S NOT A WATCH. SEE?
TIK
TIK
'S A BRACELET.
TIK
TIK
TIK
TIK
Wait, what? Then where's the ticking coming...
TIK
...from...?
TIK
TIK
Oh, dear Lord.
It's coming from HER.

Okay. Okay. Okay.

MATT? MATT?

Sorry, sweetie. I hate this, but you shouldn't be *awake* for this next part. *Gentle*...

CLIK

*

NEAREST HOSPITALS! GO!

MATT, ARE YOU HURT?

NO! FIND A HOSPITAL!

WATERFORD HOSPITAL, JACKSON STREET! IT'S--

SINGLE-STORY, RIGHT?

WHAT? MAYBE? WHAT DIFF--

TALLER!

A HOSPITAL! A HOTEL, EVEN! THE TALLER, THE BETTER!

In downtown New York, I could find what I need ten times on every block. Here...

ST. FRANCIS, SOUTHWEST, ON BUSH! VERY TALL! WHAT'S HAPPENING?

THE KIDNAPPERS? THEY PUT SOMETHING INSIDE THE KID THAT HAS TO BE A BOMB!

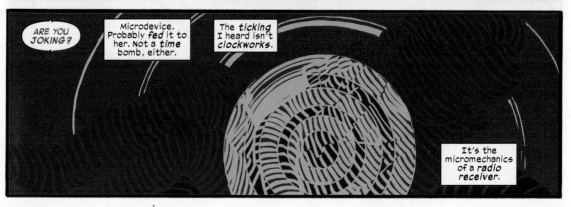

ARE YOU JOKING?

Microdevice. Probably *fed* it to her. Not a *time* bomb, either.

The *ticking* I heard isn't *clockworks*.

It's the micromechanics of a *radio* receiver.

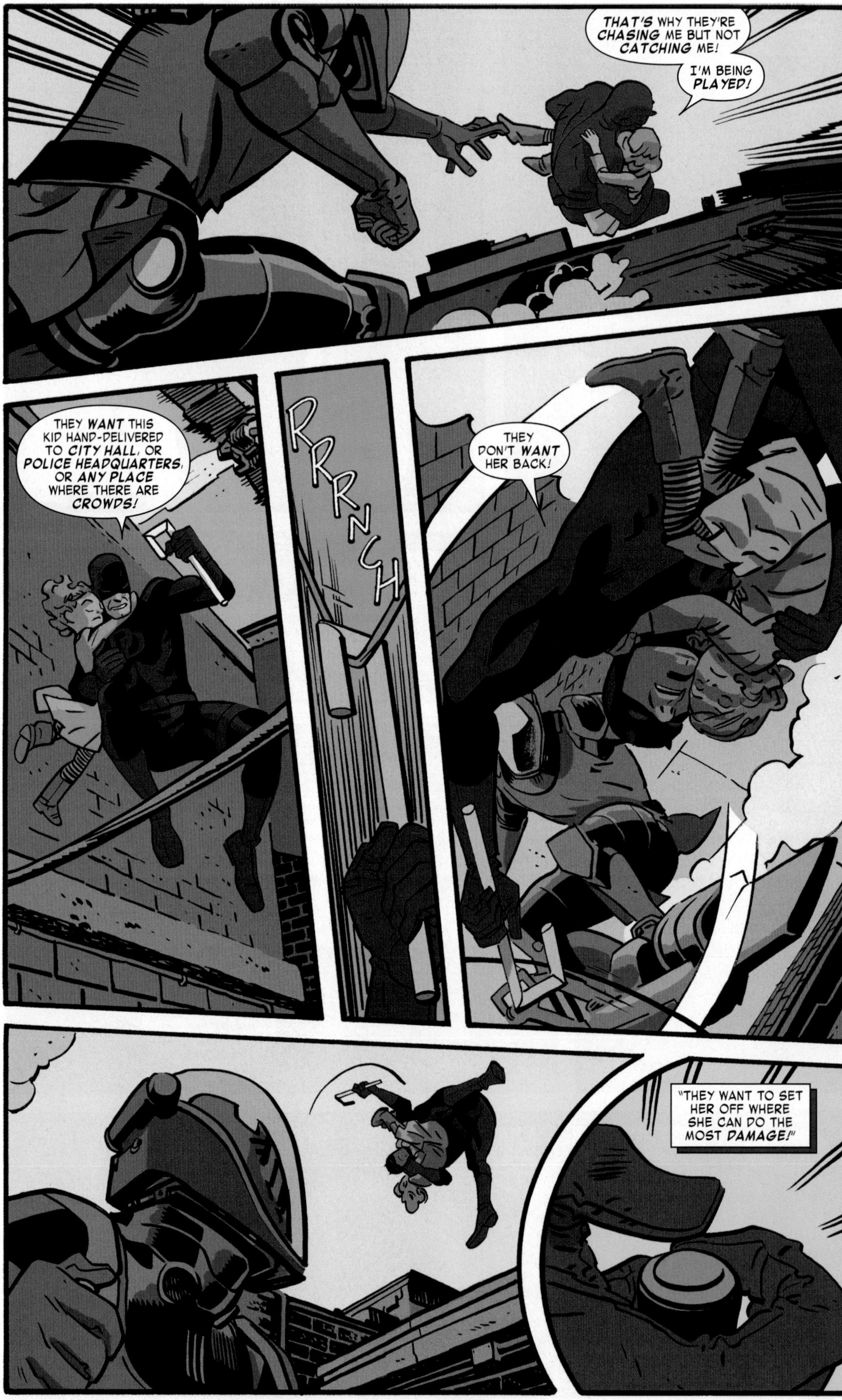
THAT'S WHY THEY'RE CHASING ME BUT NOT CATCHING ME!
I'M BEING PLAYED!
THEY WANT THIS KID HAND-DELIVERED TO CITY HALL, OR POLICE HEADQUARTERS, OR ANY PLACE WHERE THERE ARE CROWDS!
RRRNCH
THEY DON'T WANT HER BACK!
"THEY WANT TO SET HER OFF WHERE SHE CAN DO THE MOST DAMAGE!"

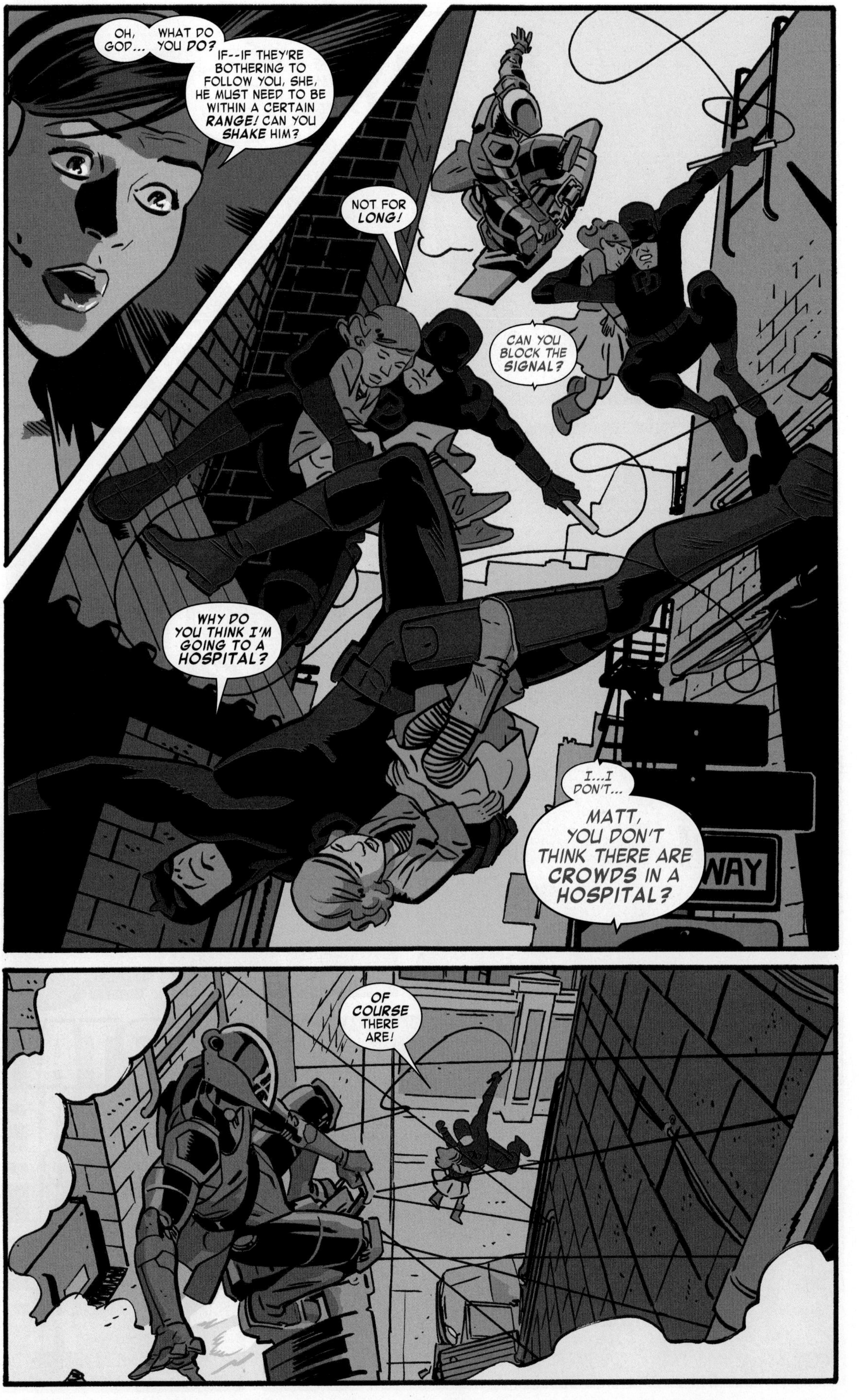
OH, GOD...
WHAT DO YOU DO?
IF--IF THEY'RE BOTHERING TO FOLLOW YOU, SHE, HE MUST NEED TO BE WITHIN A CERTAIN RANGE! CAN YOU SHAKE HIM?
NOT FOR LONG!
CAN YOU BLOCK THE SIGNAL?
WHY DO YOU THINK I'M GOING TO A HOSPITAL?
I...I DON'T...
MATT, YOU DON'T THINK THERE ARE CROWDS IN A HOSPITAL?
WAY
OF COURSE THERE ARE!

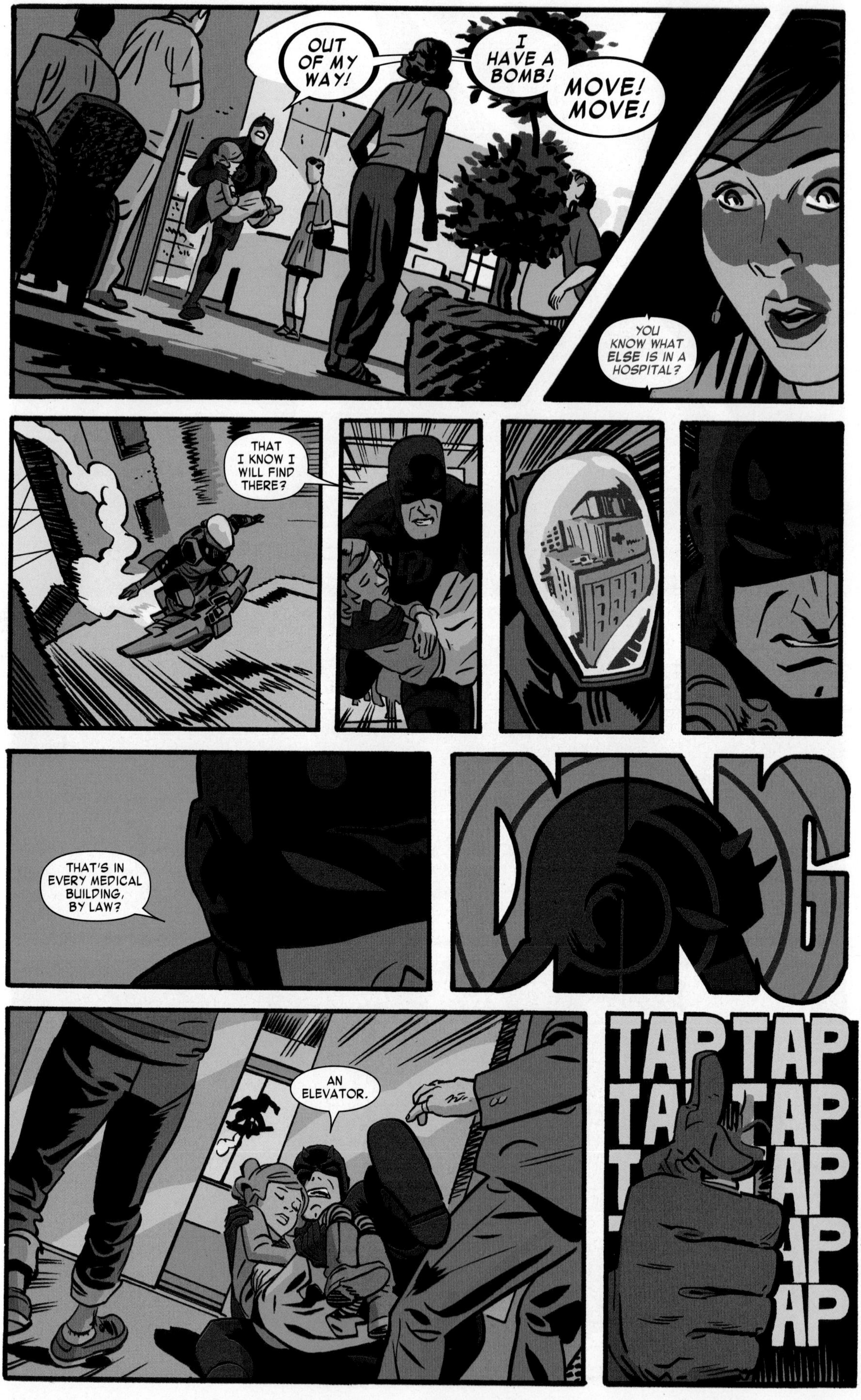
OUT OF MY WAY!
I HAVE A BOMB!
MOVE! MOVE!
YOU KNOW WHAT ELSE IS IN A HOSPITAL?
THAT I KNOW I WILL FIND THERE?
THAT'S IN EVERY MEDICAL BUILDING, BY LAW?
DING
AN ELEVATOR.
TAP TAP
TAP TAP
TAP
TAP
TAP

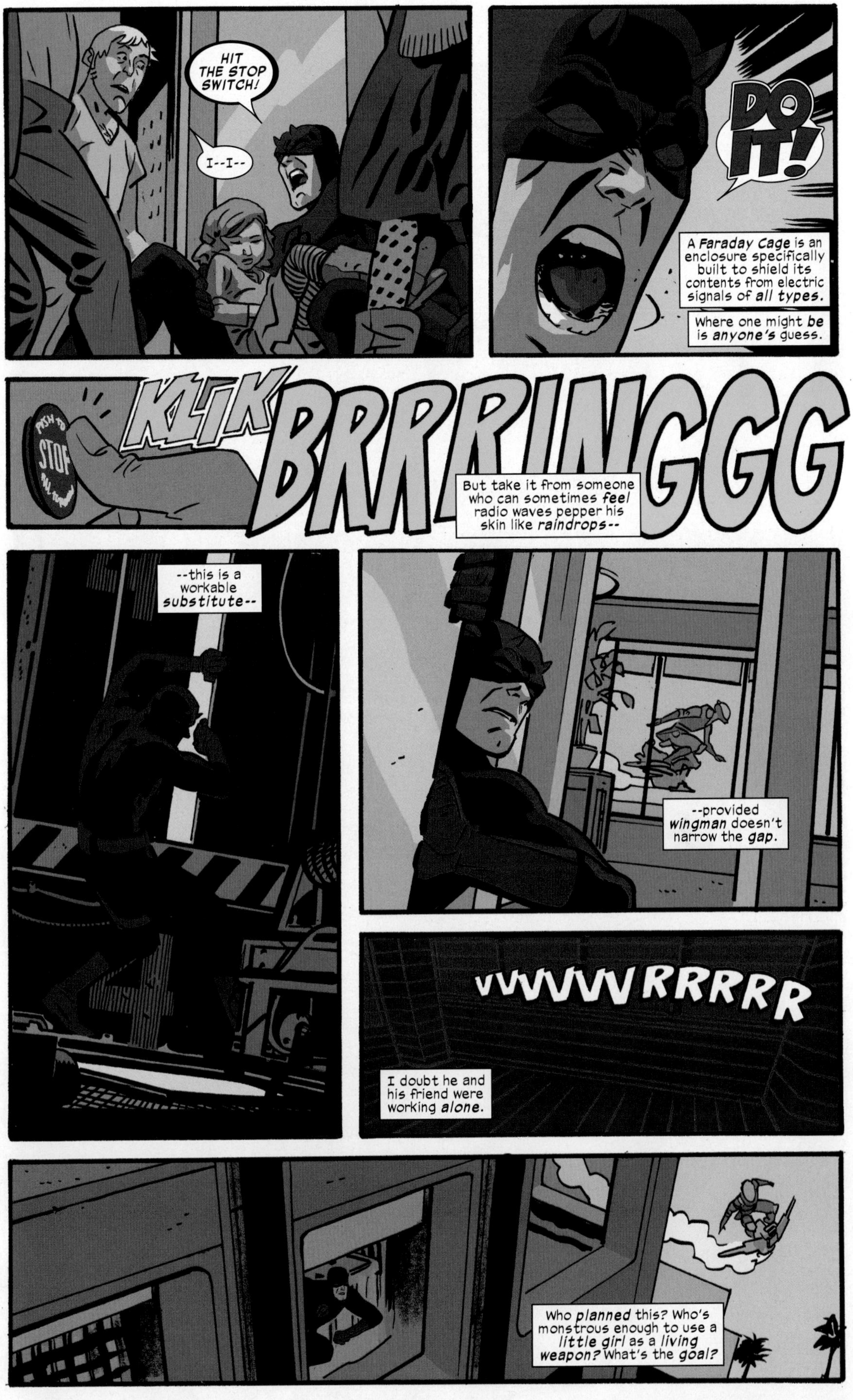
HIT THE STOP SWITCH!
I--I--
DO IT!
A Faraday Cage is an enclosure specifically built to shield its contents from electric signals of all types.
Where one might be is anyone's guess.
KLIK
BRRRINGGG
But take it from someone who can sometimes feel radio waves pepper his skin like raindrops--
--this is a workable substitute--
--provided wingman doesn't narrow the gap.
VVVVVVRRRRR
I doubt he and his friend were working alone.
Who planned this? Who's monstrous enough to use a little girl as a living weapon? What's the goal?

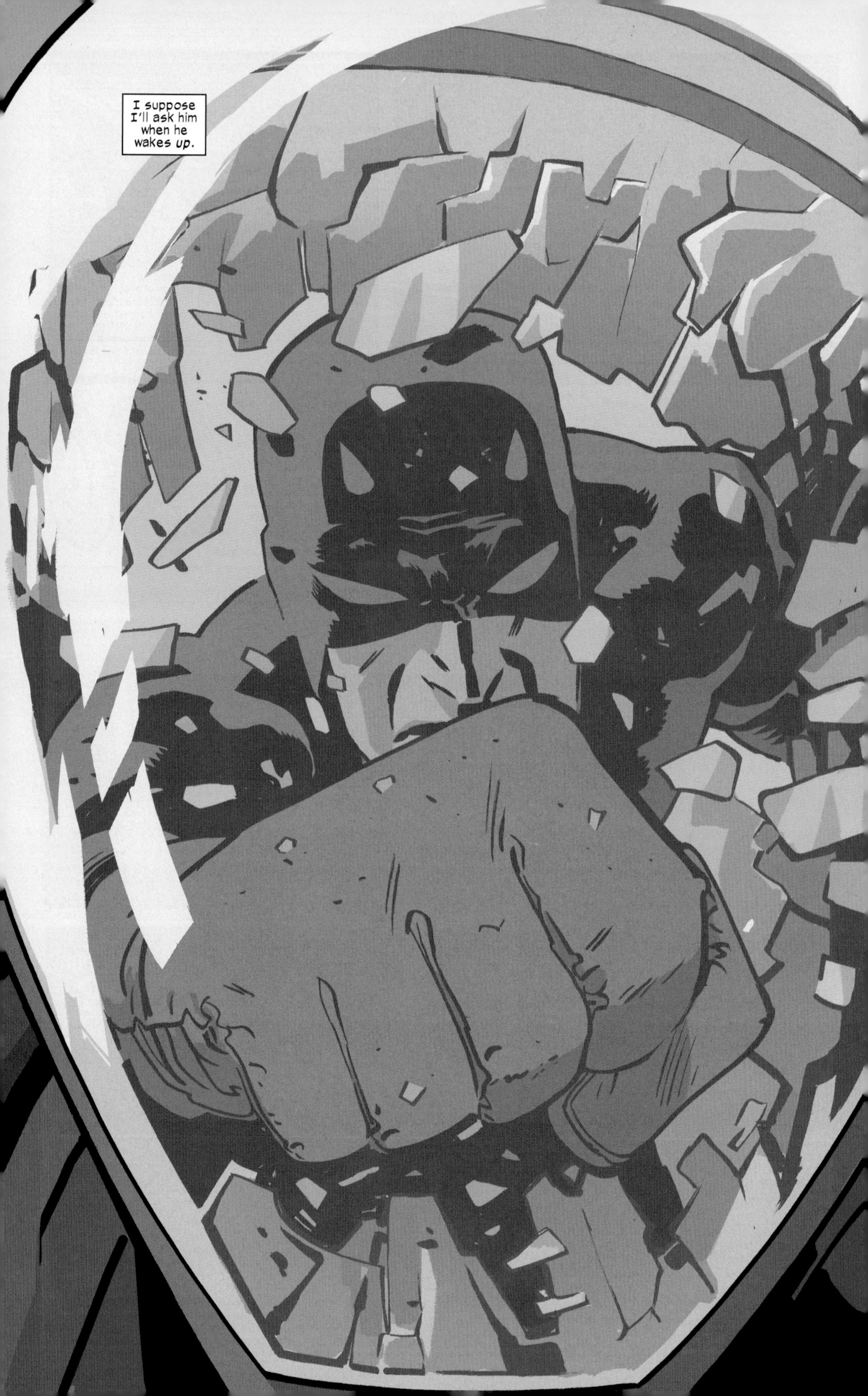
I suppose I'll ask him when he wakes *up*.

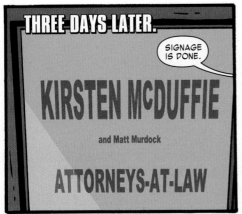

THREE DAYS LATER.

SIGNAGE IS DONE.

KIRSTEN McDUFFIE

and Matt Murdock

ATTORNEYS-AT-LAW

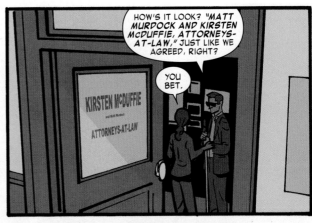

HOW'S IT LOOK? "MATT MURDOCK AND KIRSTEN McDUFFIE, ATTORNEYS-AT-LAW," JUST LIKE WE AGREED, RIGHT?

YOU BET.

AND WE HAVE OUR FIRST VISITOR. INTRODUCE ME.

Gardenia soap and vanilla shampoo. Nicotine gum.

KIRSTEN, MAY I PRESENT DEPUTY MAYOR *CHARLOTTE HASTERT.* CHARLIE, THIS IS *KIRSTEN,* THE CO-BENEFACTOR OF YOUR *REAL ESTATE CONNECTIONS.*

PLEASE. ALL I DID WAS... *REMIND* THE BUILDING OWNER THAT WE'RE NOT... *TOLERANT* OF LEASING DISCRIMINATION IN THIS CITY.

STRANGE HOW SO FEW LANDLORDS WANT TO RENT TO A SUPER HERO WHO GOT HIS OFFICE BLOWN UP EVERY SIX MONTHS EVEN BEFORE HIS IDENTITY WENT PUBLIC.

I WANTED YOU TO KNOW THAT CHELSEA'S FINE NOW. THE DOCTORS REMOVED THE IMPLANT. YOU SAVED HER LIFE.

AND THE KIDNAPPER?

HE'S GIVEN UP NOTHING. HE DOESN'T EVEN SEEM TO KNOW WHAT THE RANSOM DEMAND WAS. TRUST ME, I WON'T LET THAT REST.

WHATEVER WE CAN DO TO HELP.

I LIKE HER.

DIDN'T YOU HAVE A DIFFERENT PARTNER BACK IN NEW YORK, THOUGH?

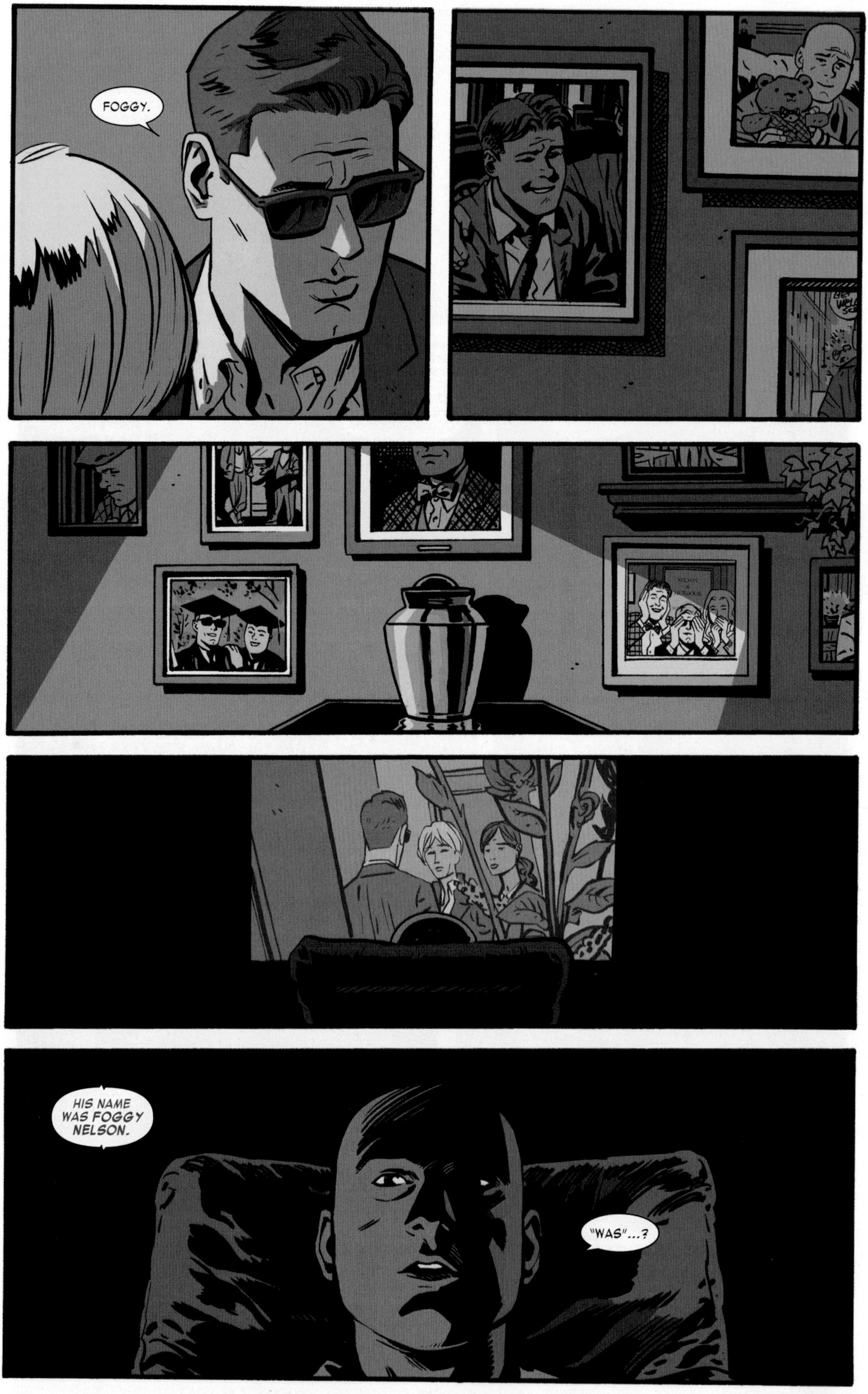
FOGGY.
HIS NAME WAS FOGGY NELSON.
"WAS"...?

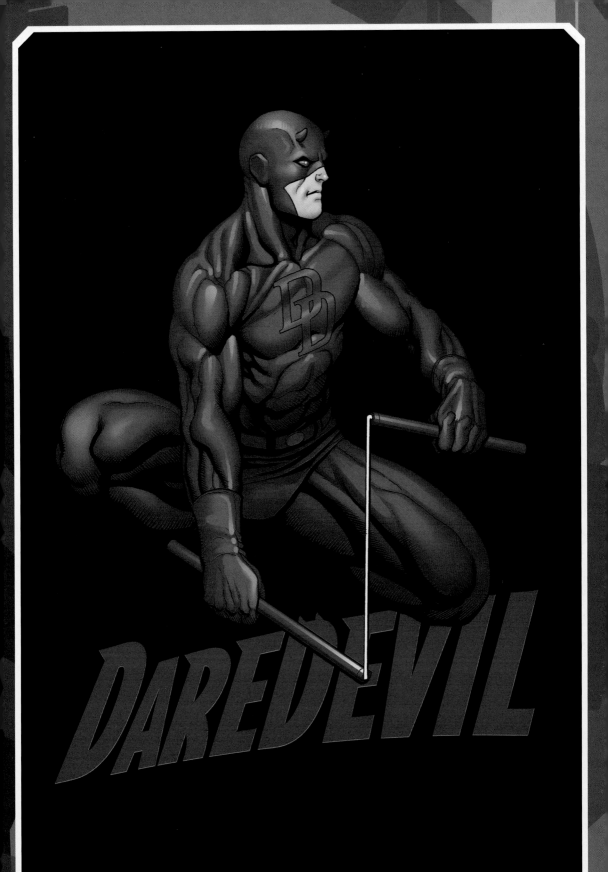

VARIANT BY FRANK CHO DAREDEVIL #2

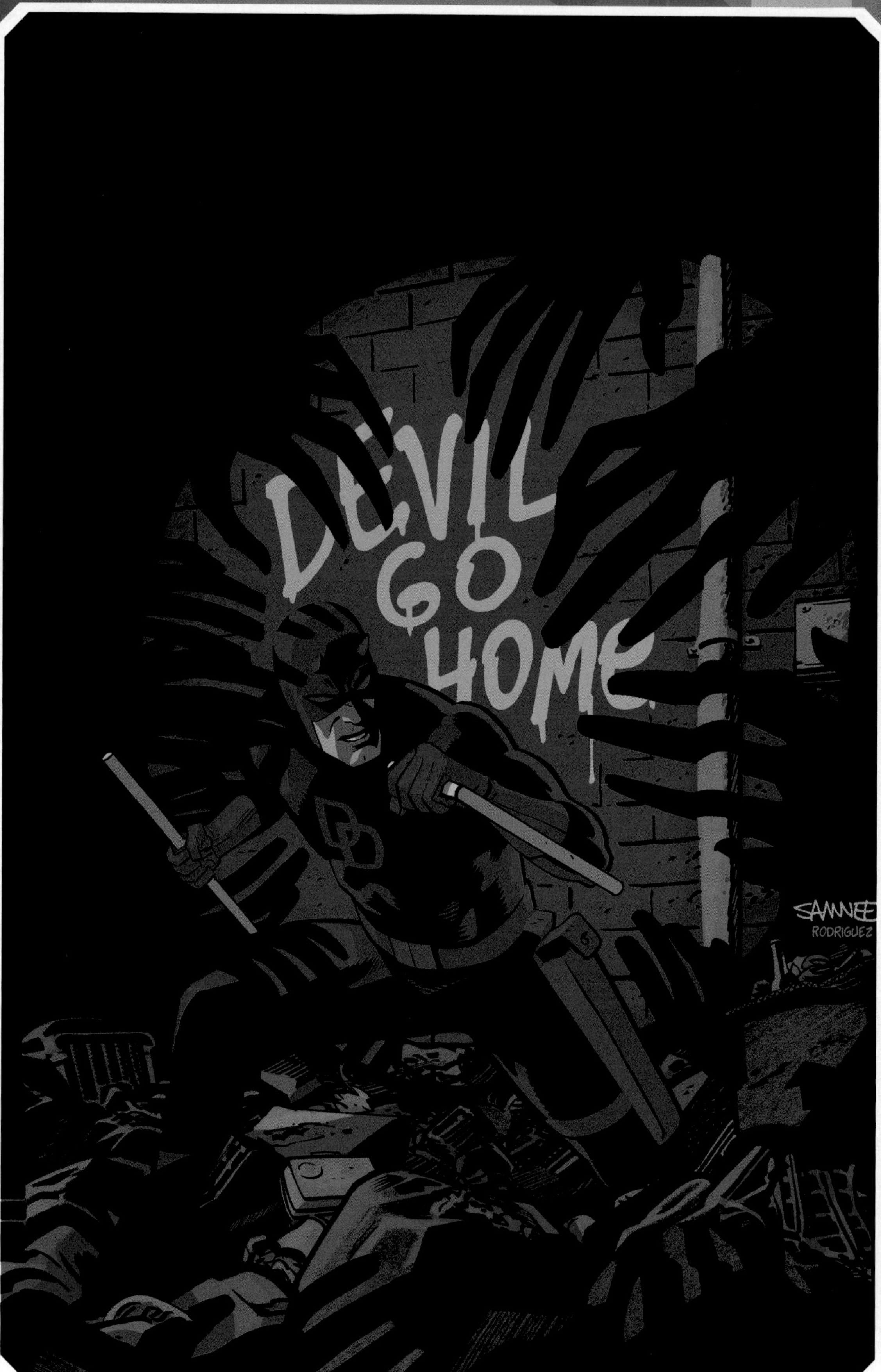
DEVIL GO HOME
SAMNEE
RODRIGUEZ
DAREDEVIL #2

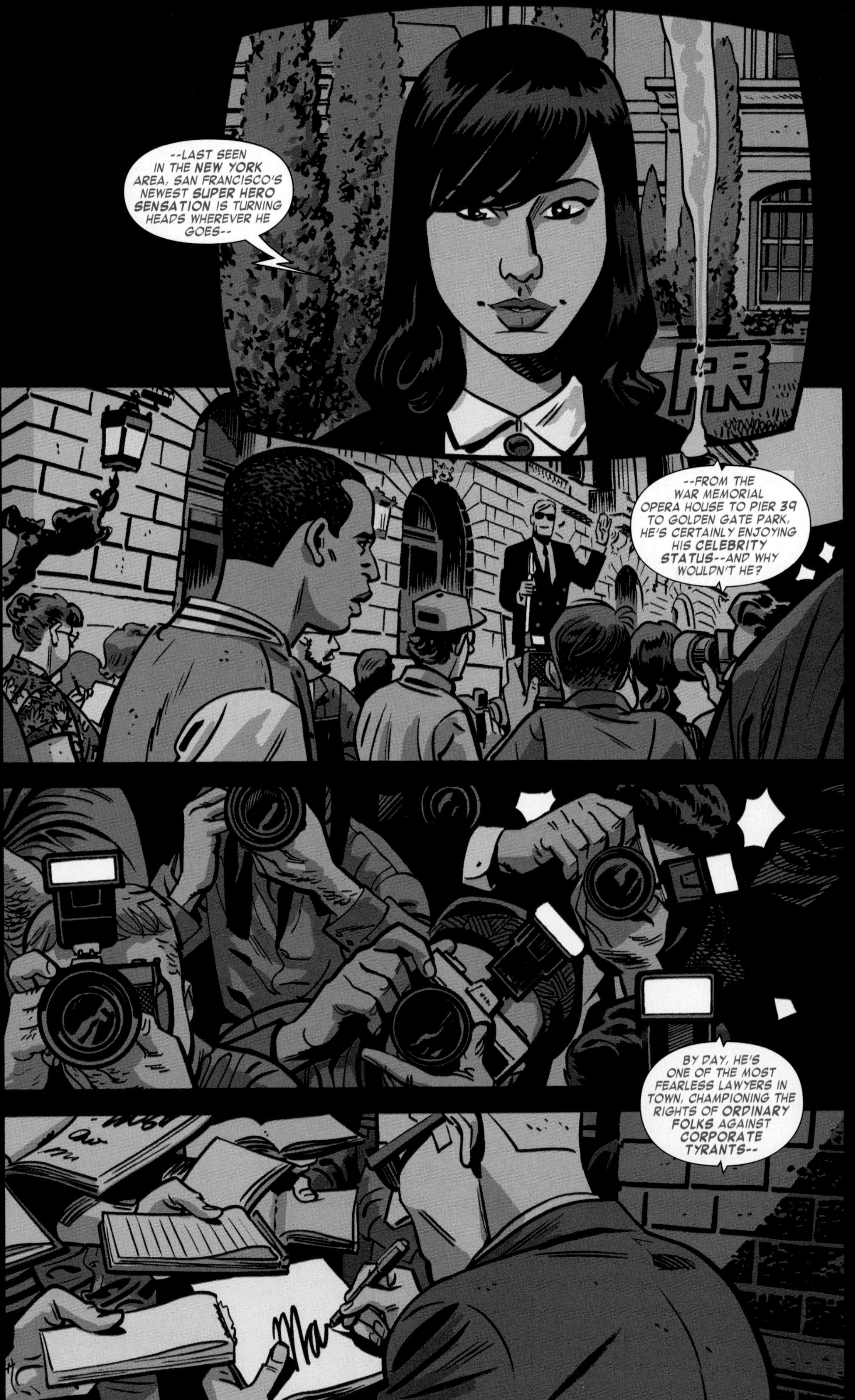
--LAST SEEN IN THE NEW YORK AREA, SAN FRANCISCO'S NEWEST SUPER HERO SENSATION IS TURNING HEADS WHEREVER HE GOES--
--FROM THE WAR MEMORIAL OPERA HOUSE TO PIER 39 TO GOLDEN GATE PARK, HE'S CERTAINLY ENJOYING HIS CELEBRITY STATUS--AND WHY WOULDN'T HE?
BY DAY, HE'S ONE OF THE MOST FEARLESS LAWYERS IN TOWN, CHAMPIONING THE RIGHTS OF ORDINARY FOLKS AGAINST CORPORATE TYRANTS--

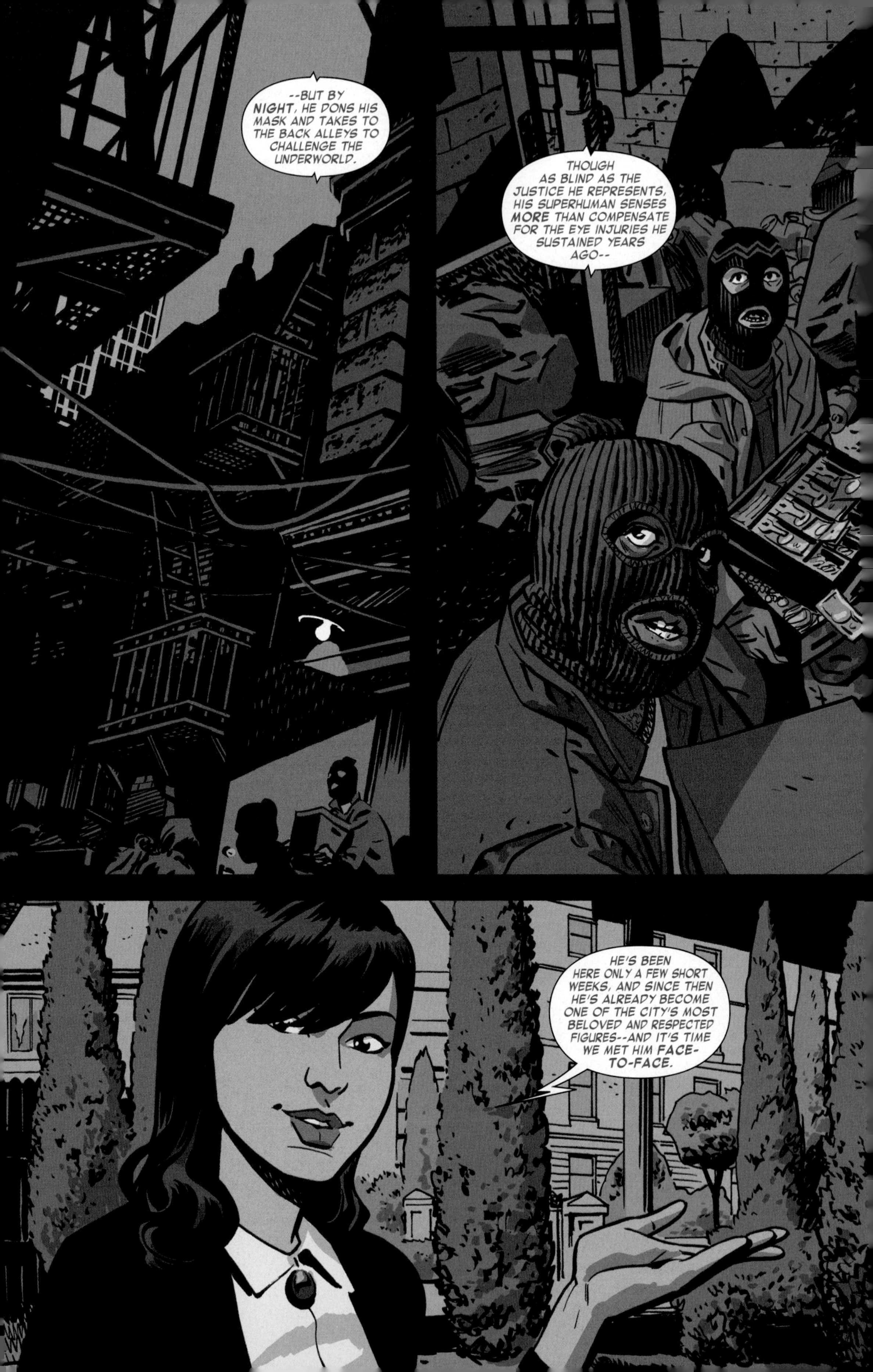
--BUT BY NIGHT, HE DONS HIS MASK AND TAKES TO THE BACK ALLEYS TO CHALLENGE THE UNDERWORLD.
THOUGH AS BLIND AS THE JUSTICE HE REPRESENTS, HIS SUPERHUMAN SENSES MORE THAN COMPENSATE FOR THE EYE INJURIES HE SUSTAINED YEARS AGO--
HE'S BEEN HERE ONLY A FEW SHORT WEEKS, AND SINCE THEN HE'S ALREADY BECOME ONE OF THE CITY'S MOST BELOVED AND RESPECTED FIGURES--AND IT'S TIME WE MET HIM FACE-TO-FACE.

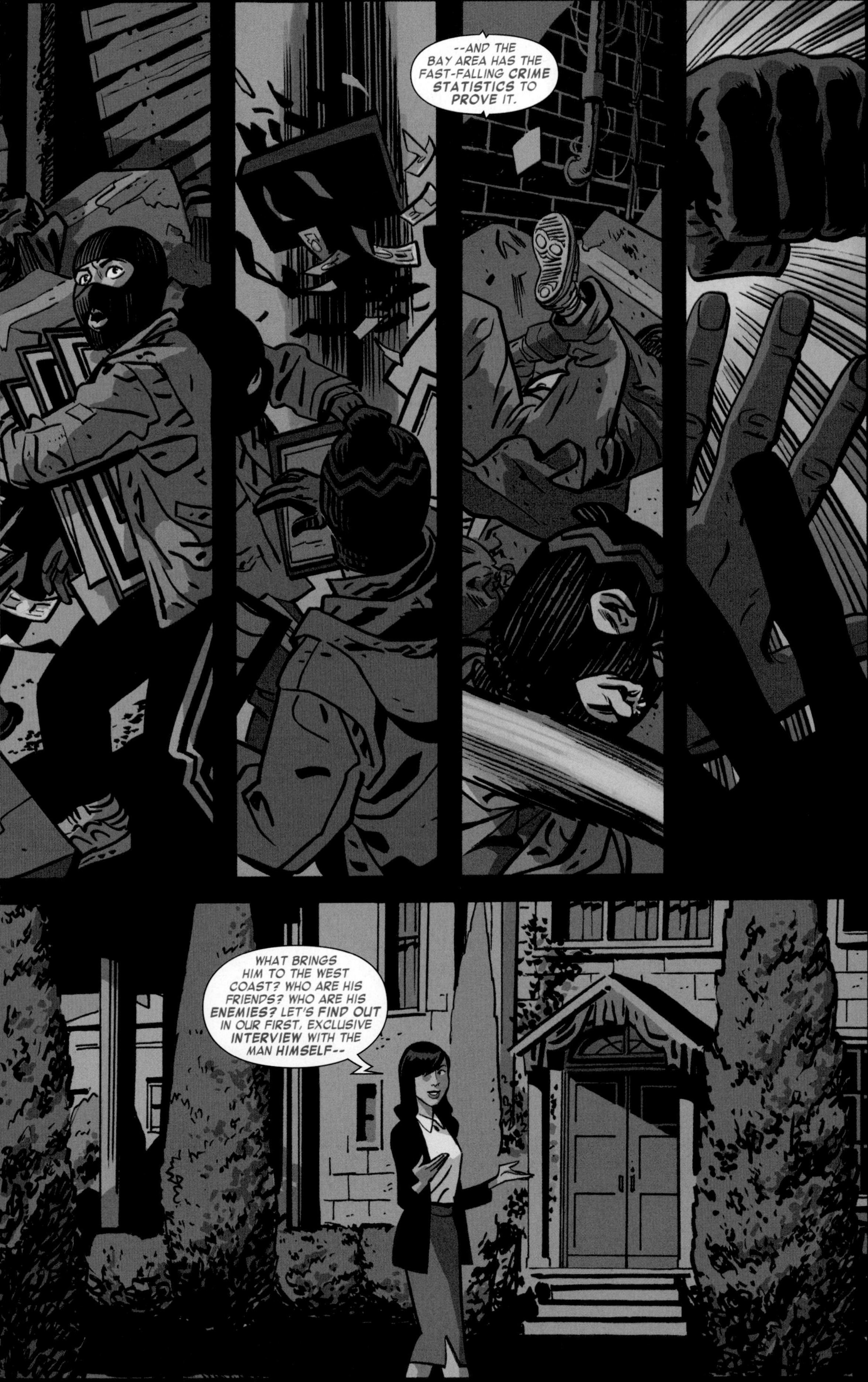
--AND THE BAY AREA HAS THE FAST-FALLING CRIME STATISTICS TO PROVE IT.
WHAT BRINGS HIM TO THE WEST COAST? WHO ARE HIS FRIENDS? WHO ARE HIS ENEMIES? LET'S FIND OUT IN OUR FIRST, EXCLUSIVE INTERVIEW WITH THE MAN HIMSELF--

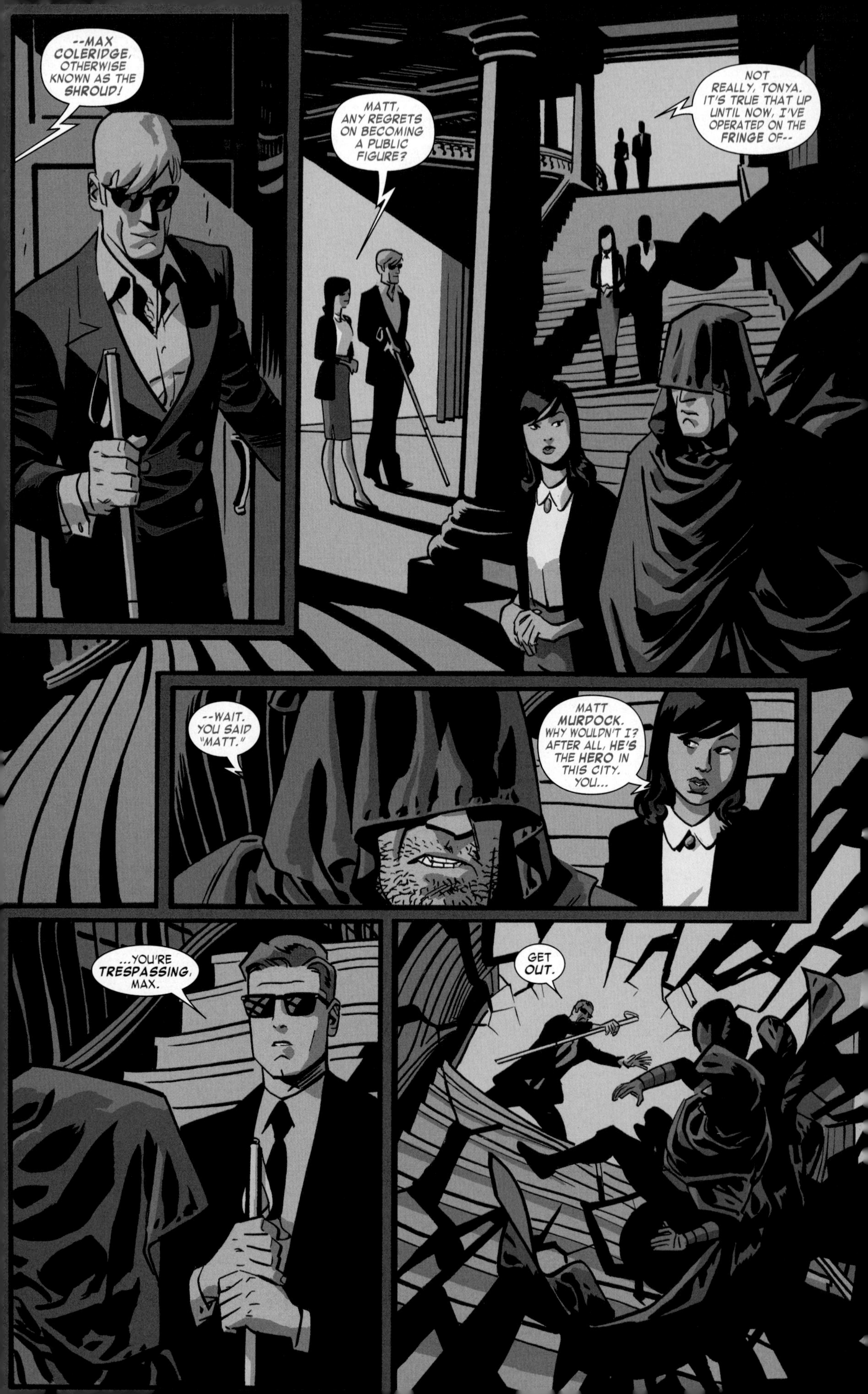
--MAX COLERIDGE, OTHERWISE KNOWN AS THE SHROUD!
MATT, ANY REGRETS ON BECOMING A PUBLIC FIGURE?
NOT REALLY, TONYA. IT'S TRUE THAT UP UNTIL NOW, I'VE OPERATED ON THE FRINGE OF--
--WAIT. YOU SAID "MATT."
MATT MURDOCK. WHY WOULDN'T I? AFTER ALL, HE'S THE HERO IN THIS CITY. YOU...
...YOU'RE TRESPASSING, MAX.
GET OUT.

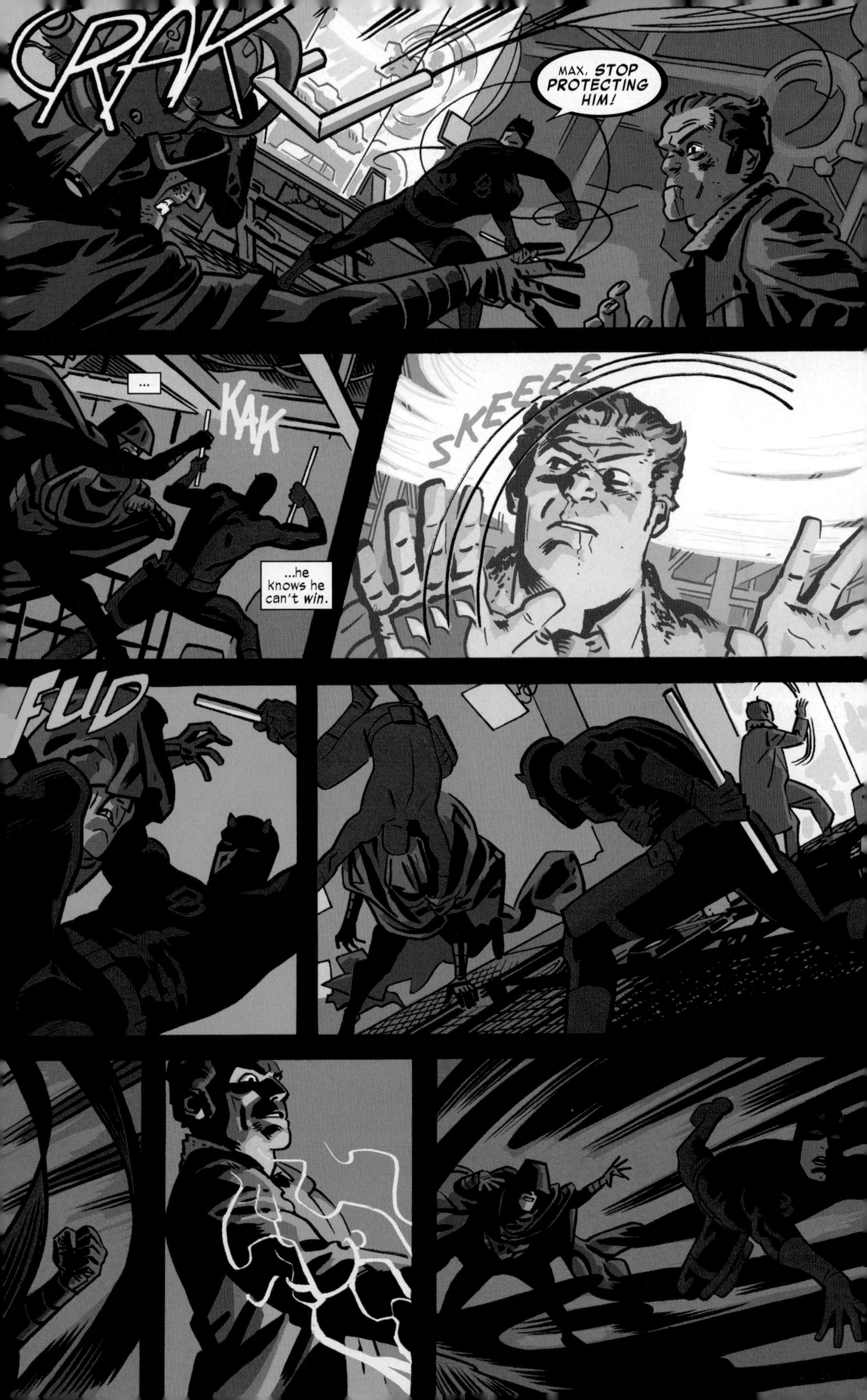
CRAK
MAX, STOP PROTECTING HIM!
...
KAK
...he knows he can't win.
SKEEEEE
FUD

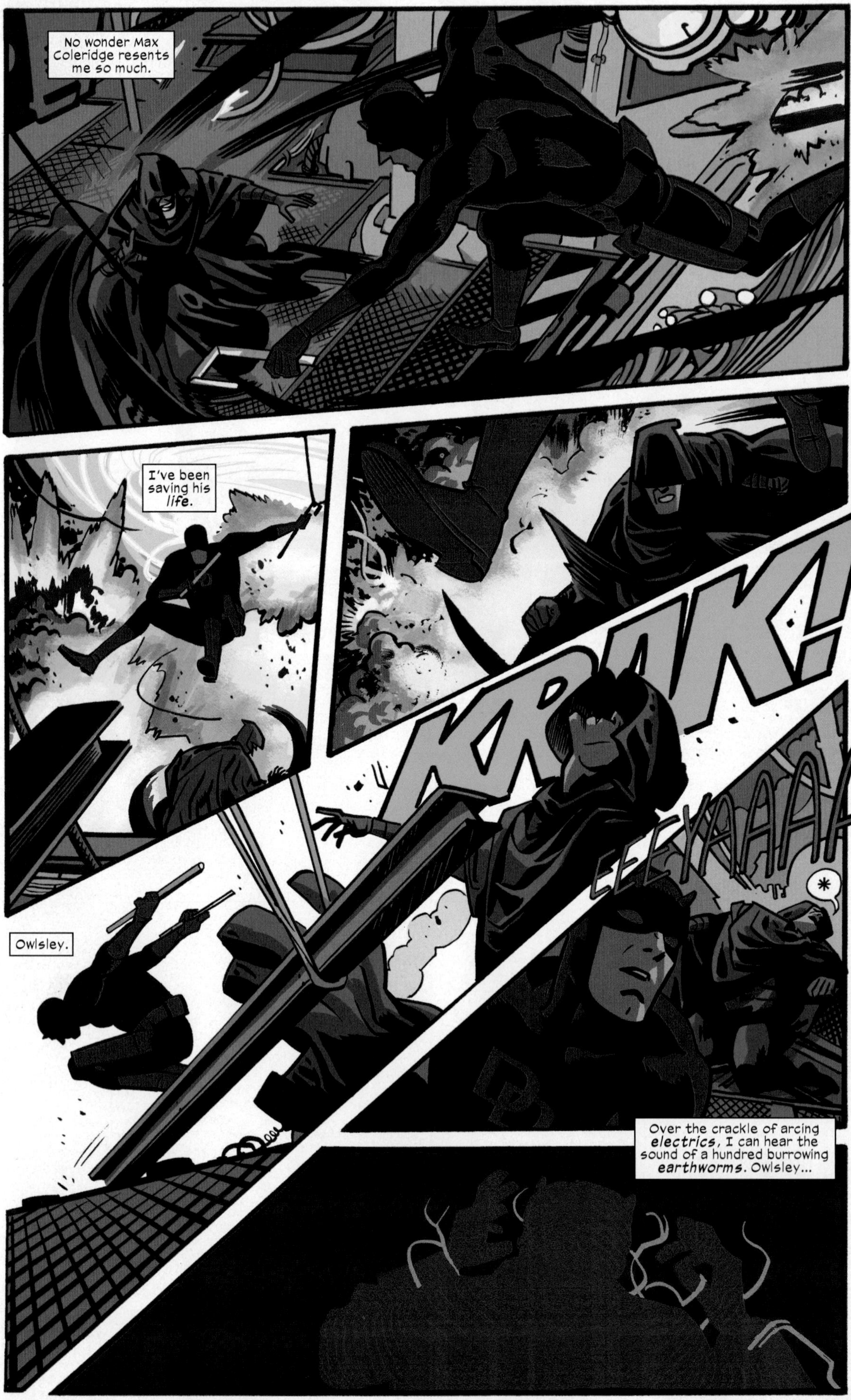
No wonder Max Coleridge resents me so much.
I've been saving his *life*.
KRAK!
EEEYAAAA
*
Owlsley.
Over the crackle of arcing *electrics*, I can hear the sound of a hundred burrowing *earthworms*. Owlsley...

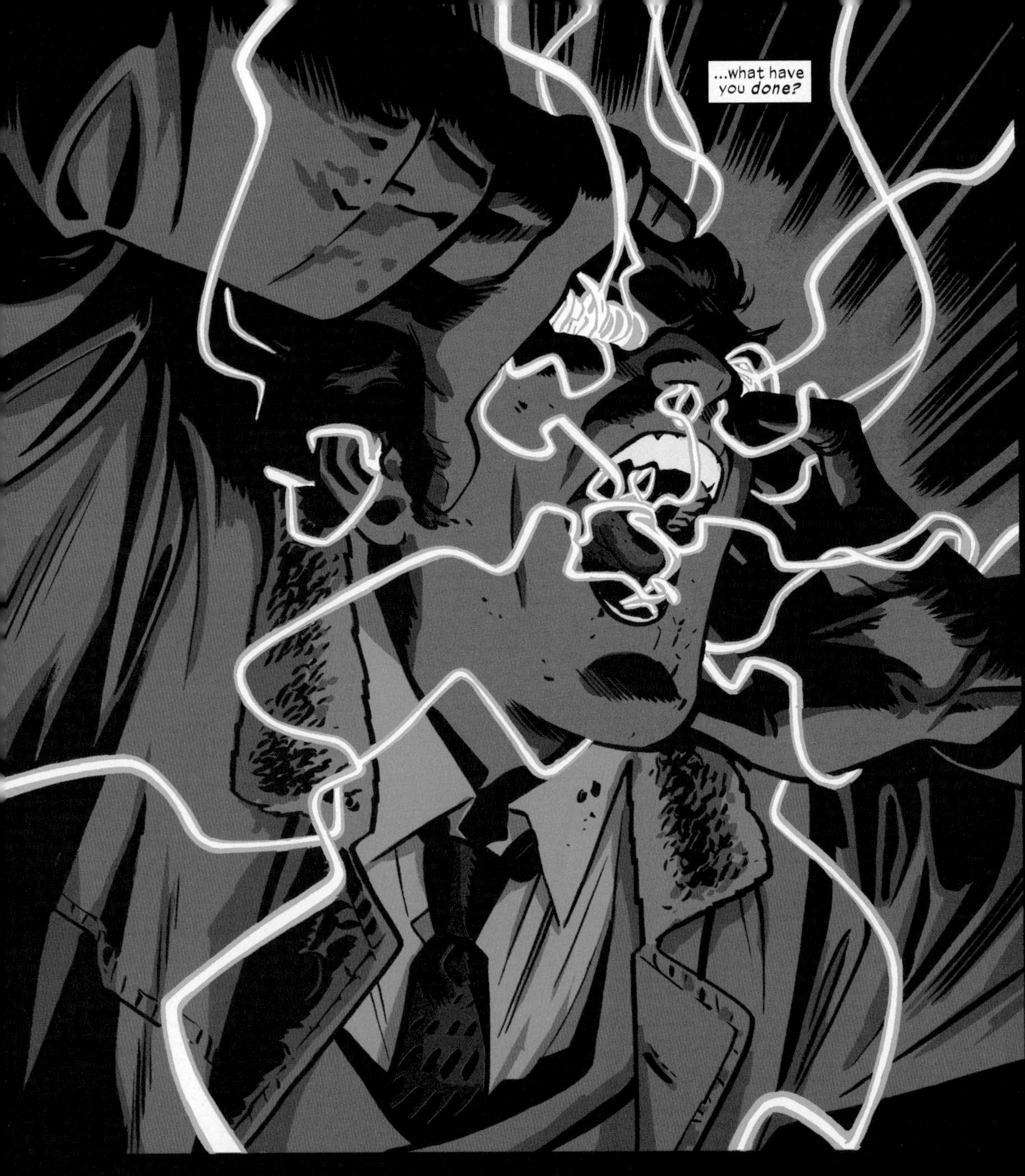
...what have you done?

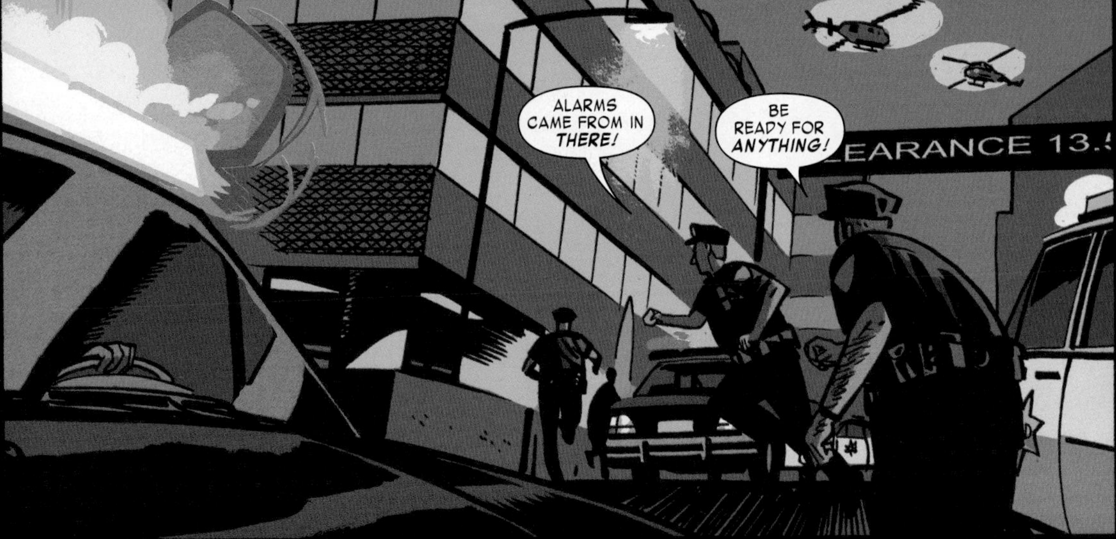
ALARMS CAME FROM IN THERE!
BE READY FOR ANYTHING!
LEARANCE 13.5

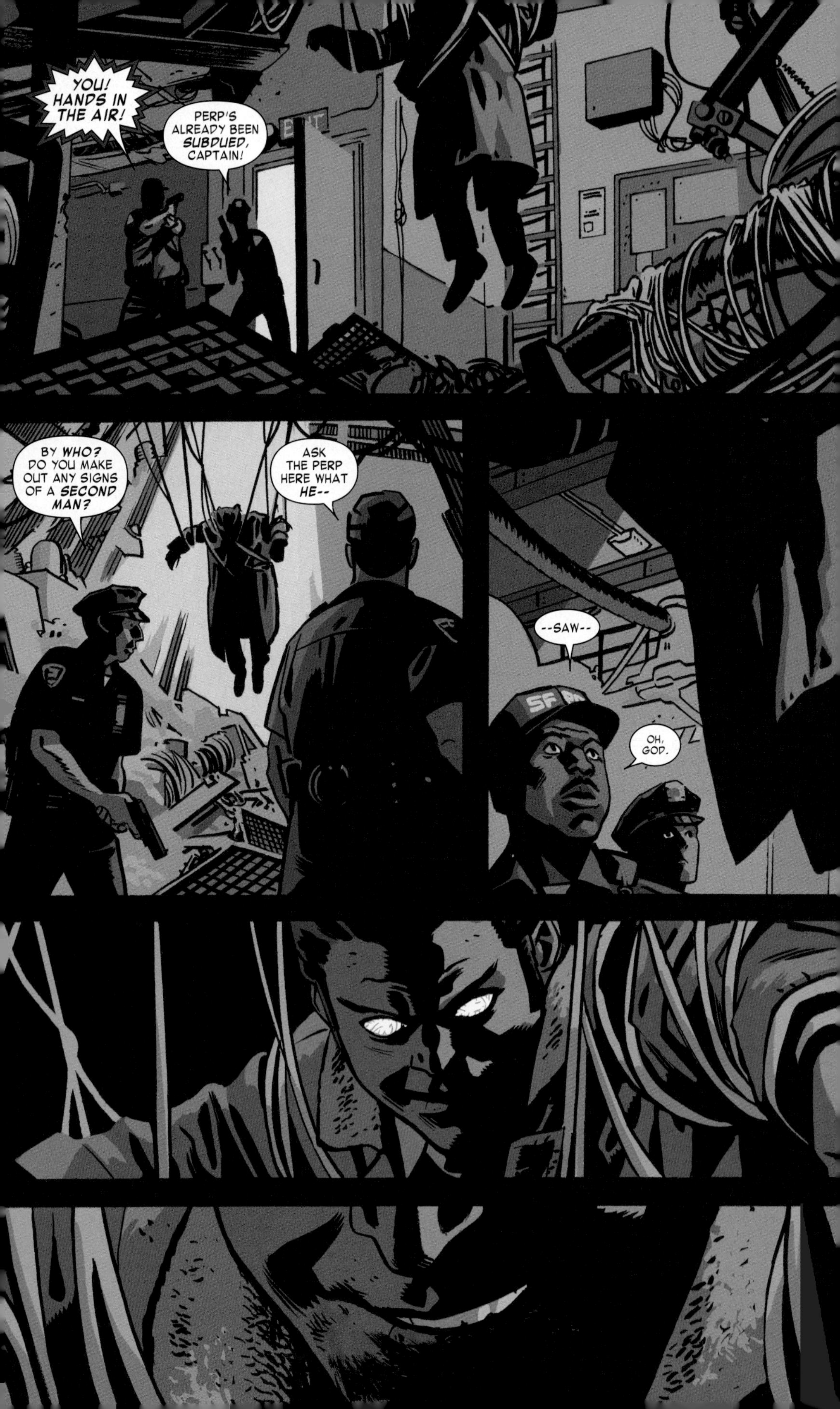
YOU! HANDS IN THE AIR!
PERP'S ALREADY BEEN SUBDUED, CAPTAIN!
BY WHO? DO YOU MAKE OUT ANY SIGNS OF A SECOND MAN?
ASK THE PERP HERE WHAT HE--
--SAW--
OH, GOD.

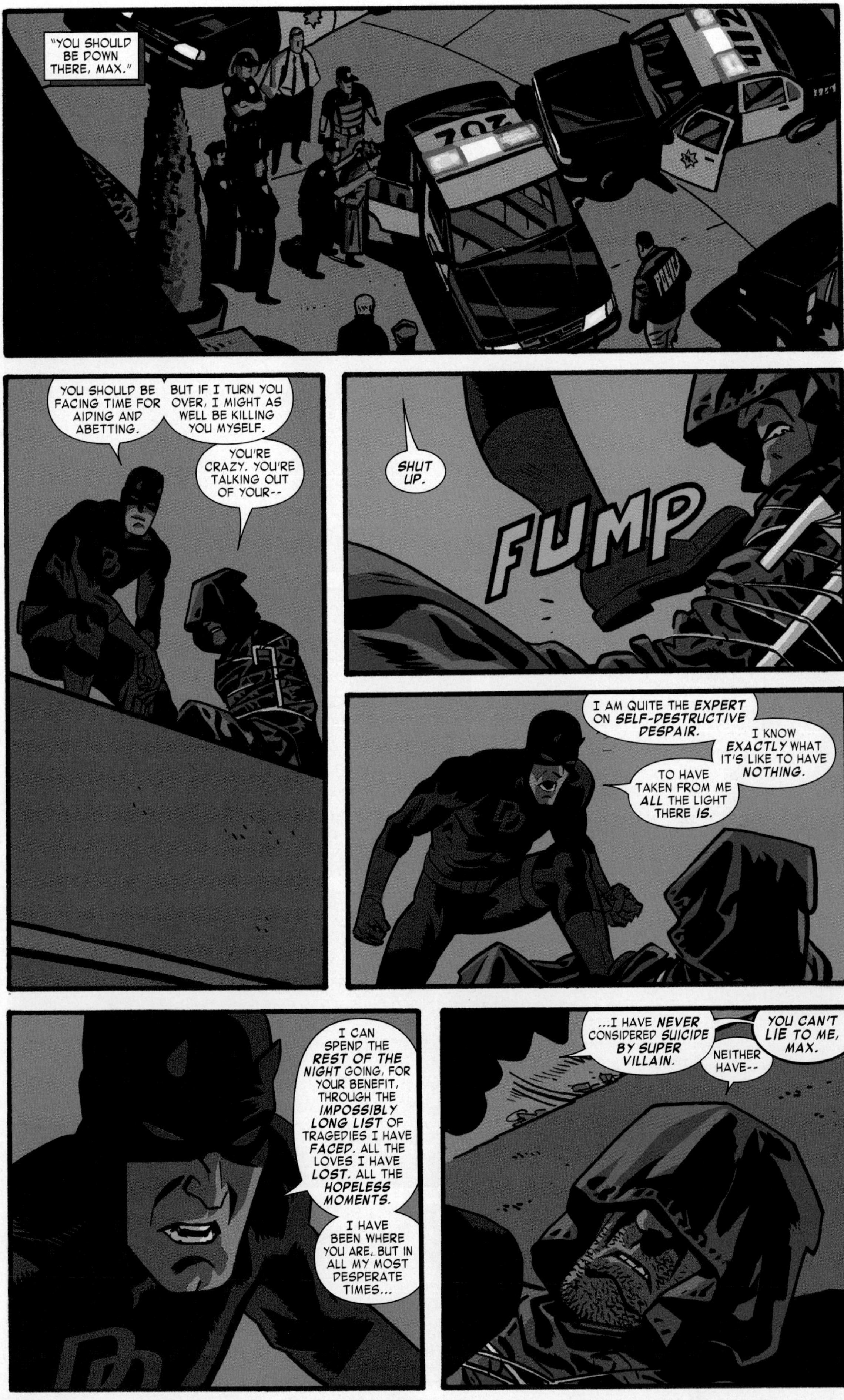
"YOU SHOULD BE DOWN THERE, MAX."
YOU SHOULD BE FACING TIME FOR AIDING AND ABETTING.
BUT IF I TURN YOU OVER, I MIGHT AS WELL BE KILLING YOU MYSELF.
YOU'RE CRAZY. YOU'RE TALKING OUT OF YOUR--
SHUT UP.
FUMP
I AM QUITE THE EXPERT ON SELF-DESTRUCTIVE DESPAIR.
I KNOW EXACTLY WHAT IT'S LIKE TO HAVE NOTHING.
TO HAVE TAKEN FROM ME ALL THE LIGHT THERE IS.
I CAN SPEND THE REST OF THE NIGHT GOING, FOR YOUR BENEFIT, THROUGH THE IMPOSSIBLY LONG LIST OF TRAGEDIES I HAVE FACED. ALL THE LOVES I HAVE LOST. ALL THE HOPELESS MOMENTS.
I HAVE BEEN WHERE YOU ARE. BUT IN ALL MY MOST DESPERATE TIMES...
...I HAVE NEVER CONSIDERED SUICIDE BY SUPER VILLAIN.
NEITHER HAVE--
YOU CAN'T LIE TO ME, MAX.

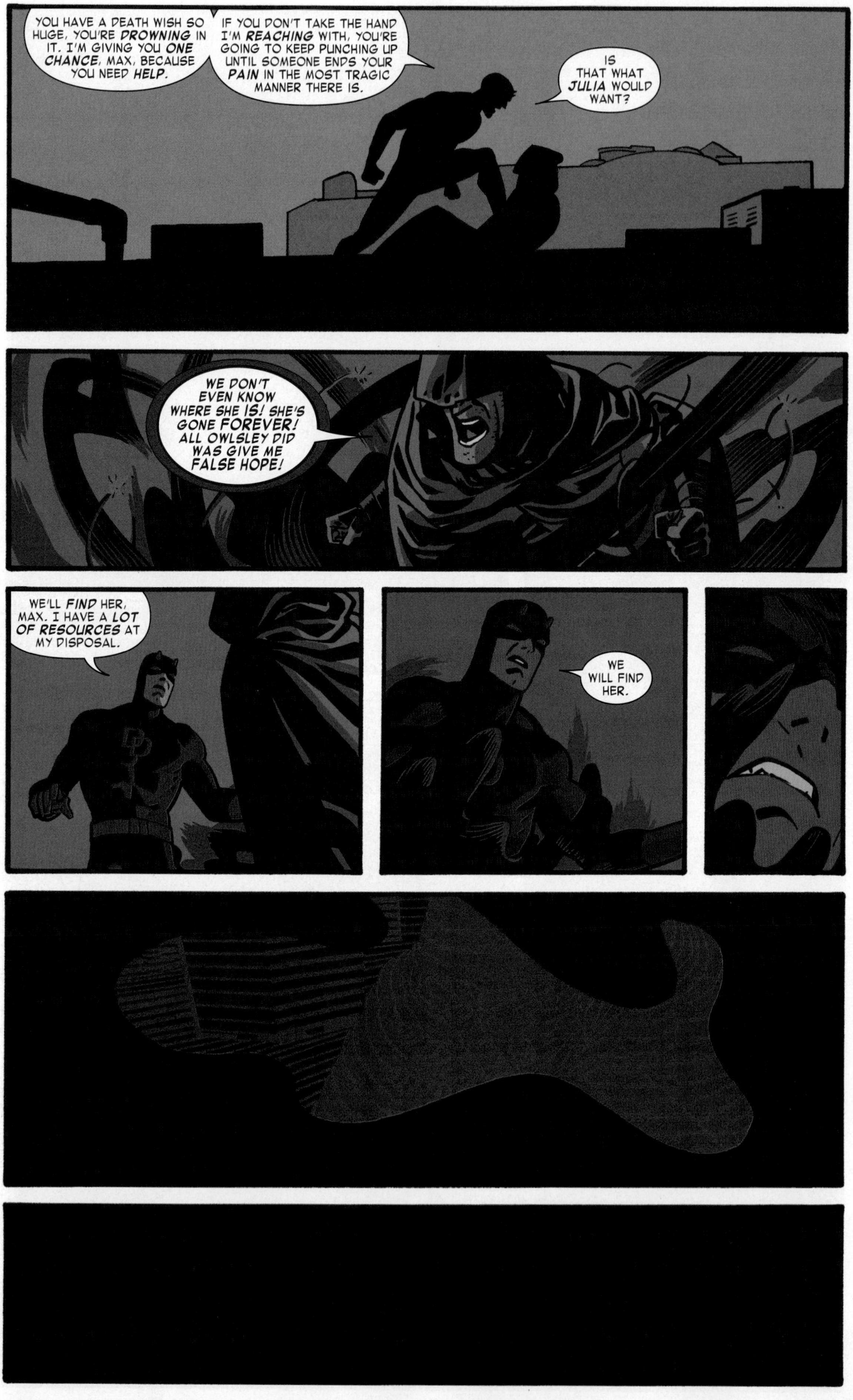
YOU HAVE A DEATH WISH SO HUGE, YOU'RE DROWNING IN IT. I'M GIVING YOU ONE CHANCE, MAX, BECAUSE YOU NEED HELP.
IF YOU DON'T TAKE THE HAND I'M REACHING WITH, YOU'RE GOING TO KEEP PUNCHING UP UNTIL SOMEONE ENDS YOUR PAIN IN THE MOST TRAGIC MANNER THERE IS.
IS THAT WHAT JULIA WOULD WANT?
WE DON'T EVEN KNOW WHERE SHE IS! SHE'S GONE FOREVER! ALL OWLSLEY DID WAS GIVE ME FALSE HOPE!
WE'LL FIND HER, MAX. I HAVE A LOT OF RESOURCES AT MY DISPOSAL.
WE WILL FIND HER.

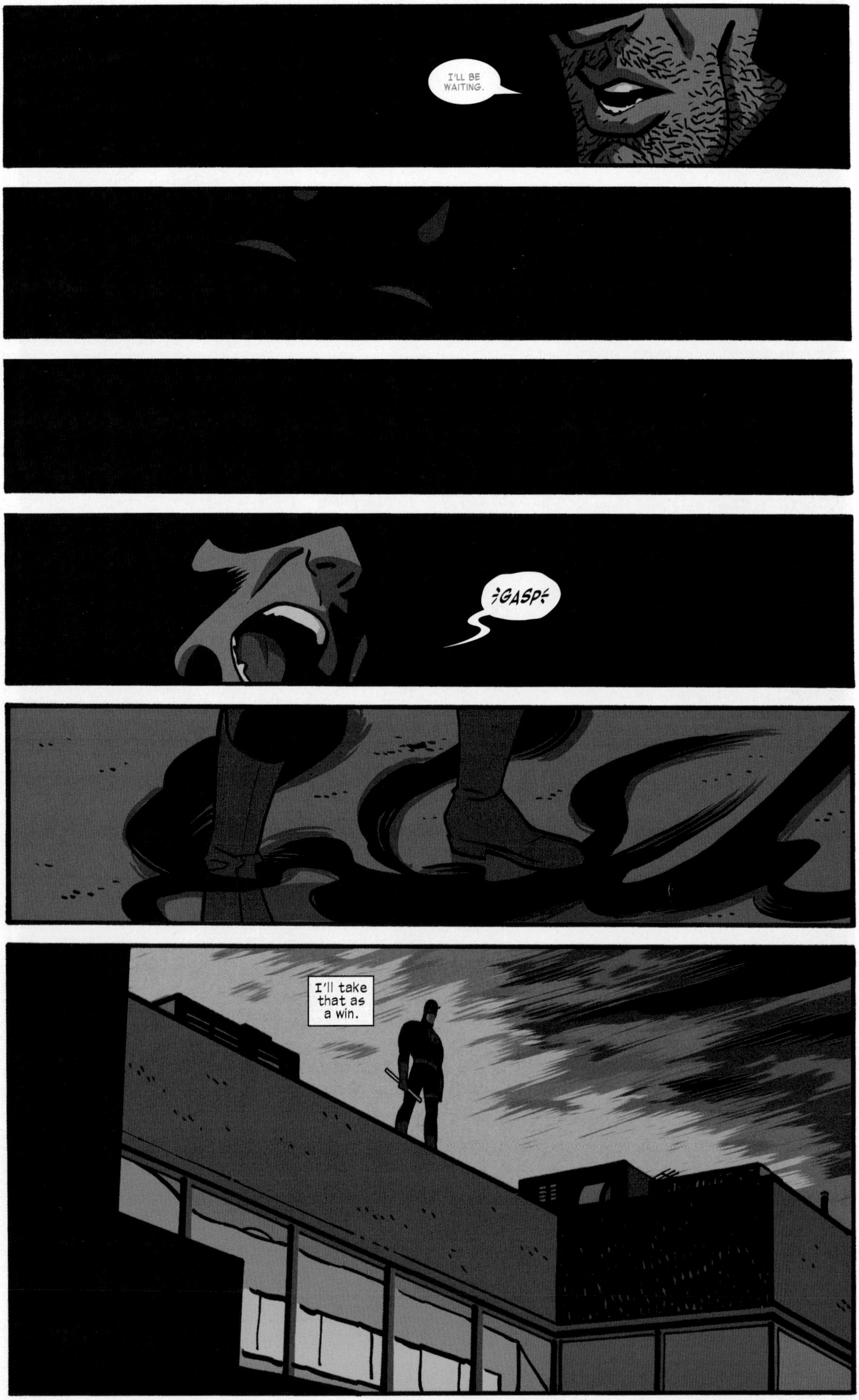
I'LL BE WAITING.
GASP
I'll take that as a win.

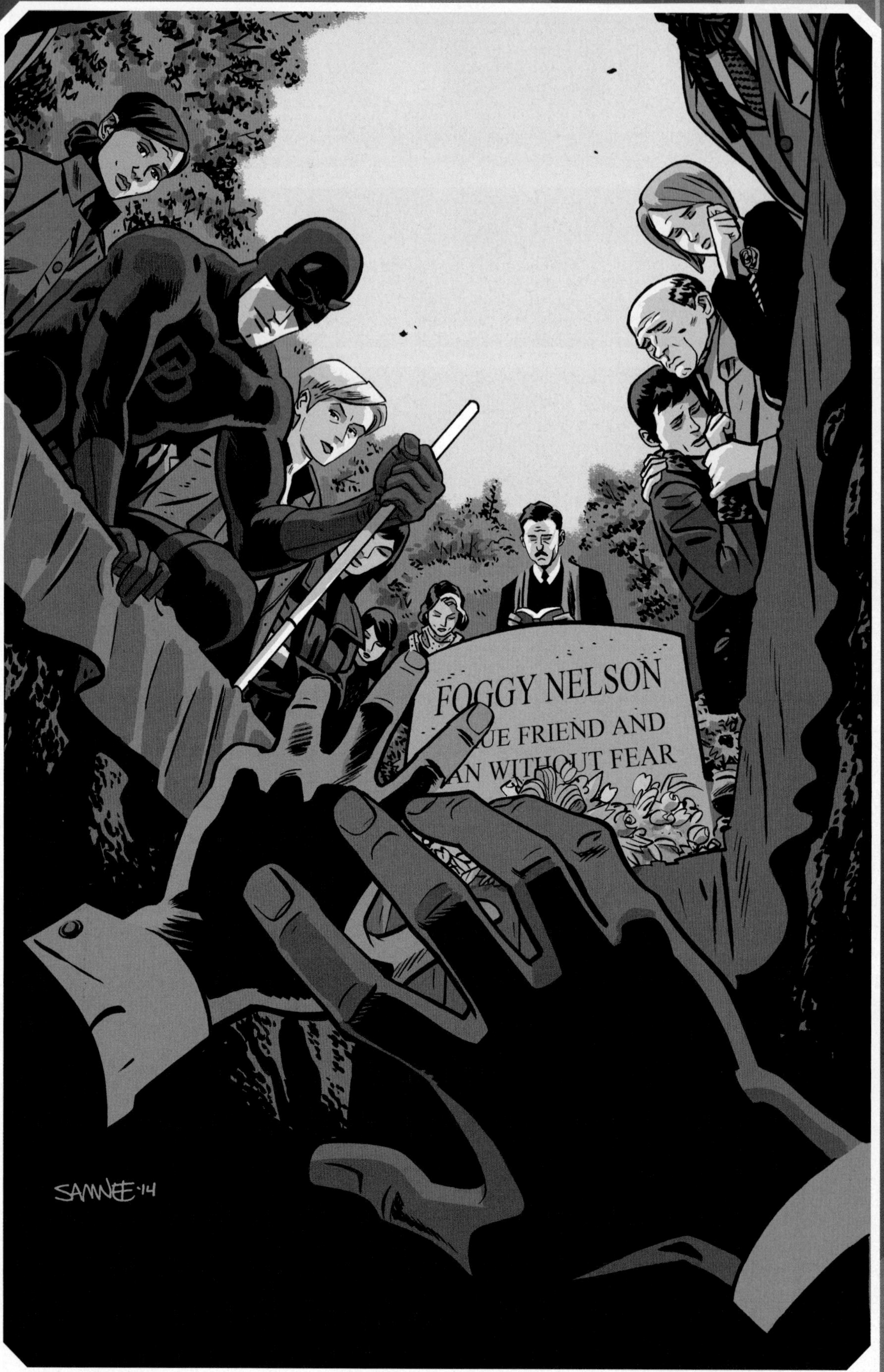
FOGGY NELSON
…UE FRIEND AND
…AN WITHOUT FEAR
SAMNEE·14

DAREDEVIL #5

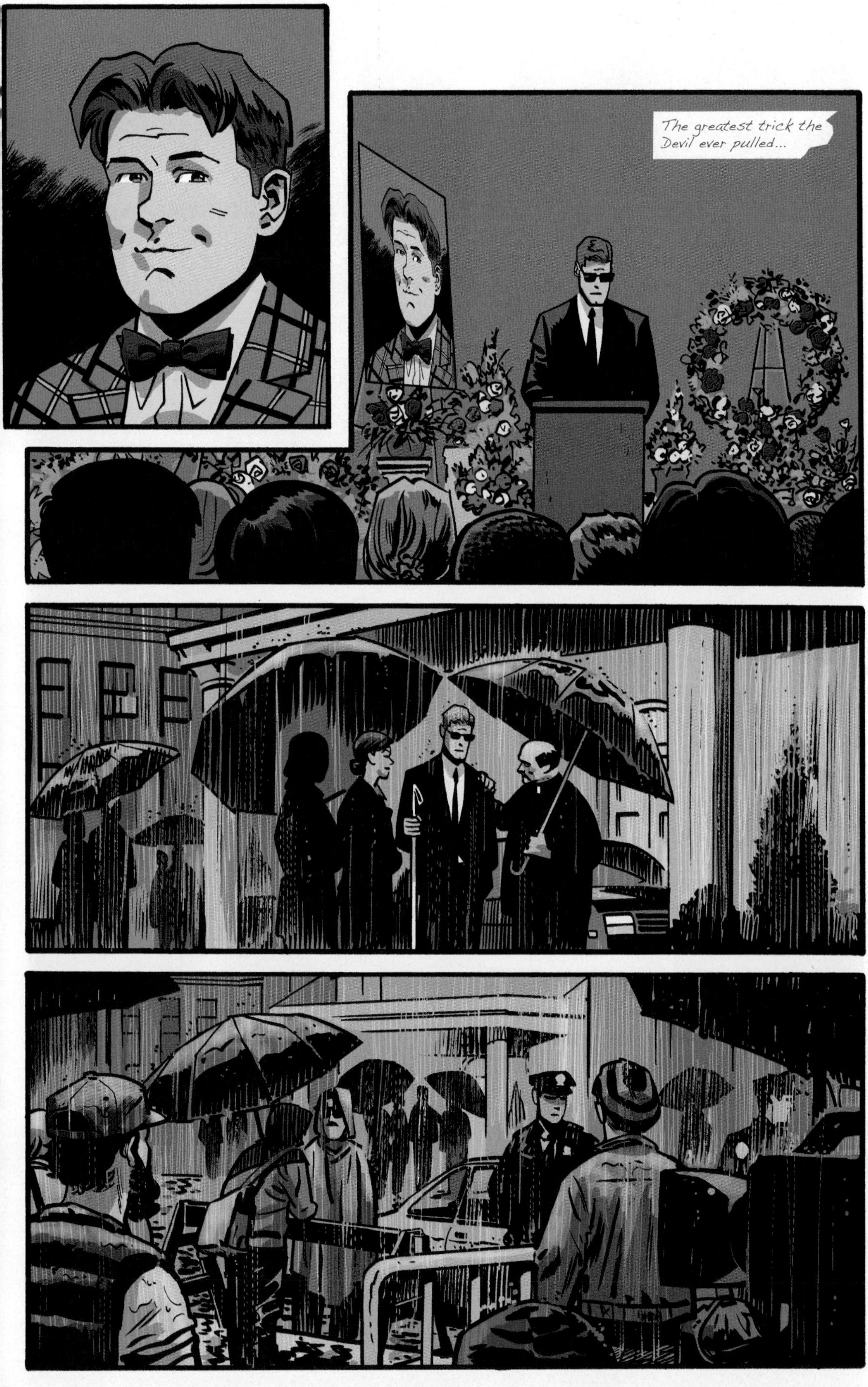
The greatest trick the Devil ever pulled...

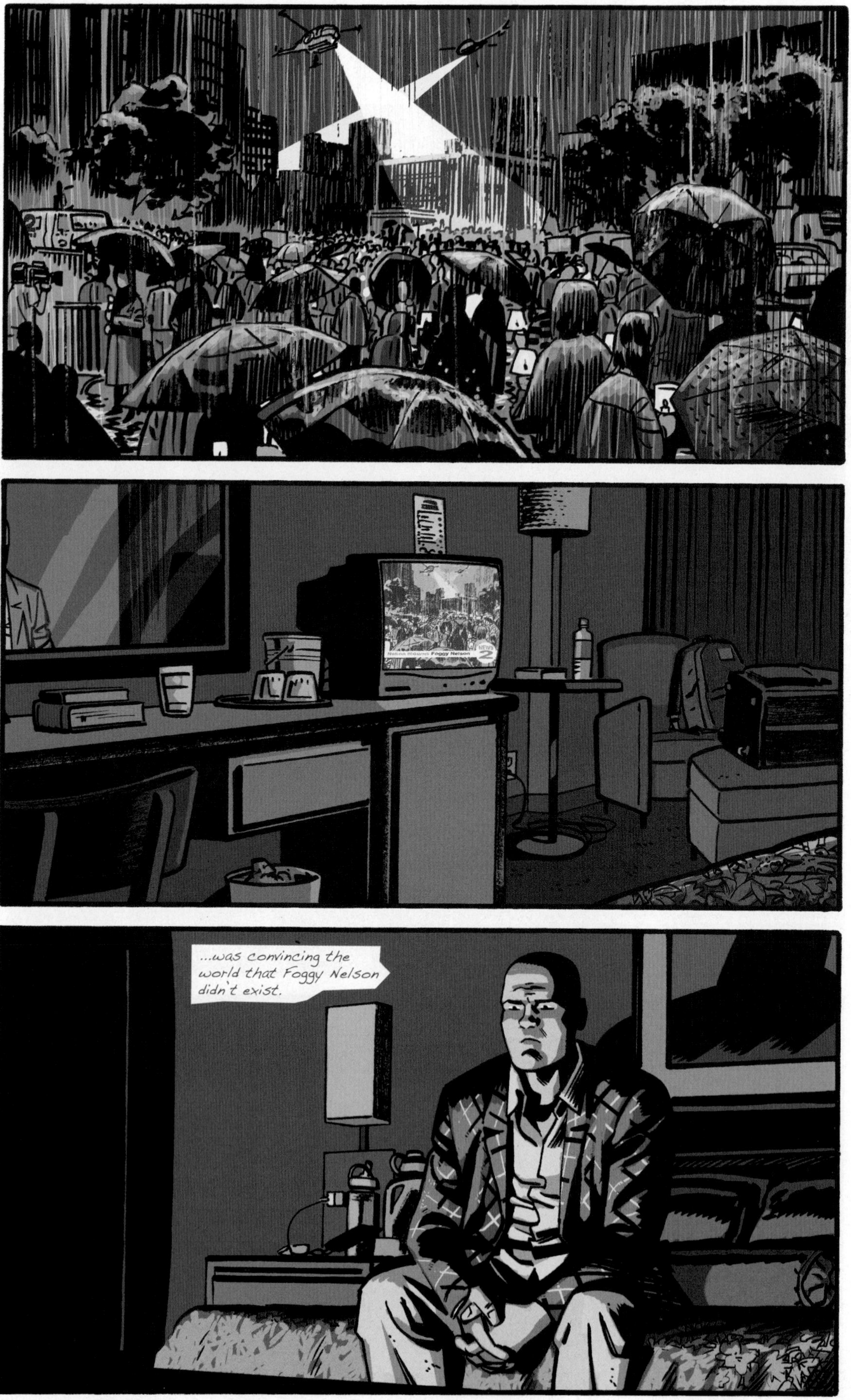
Nation Mourns Foggy Nelson
NEWS 2
...was convincing the world that Foggy Nelson didn't exist.

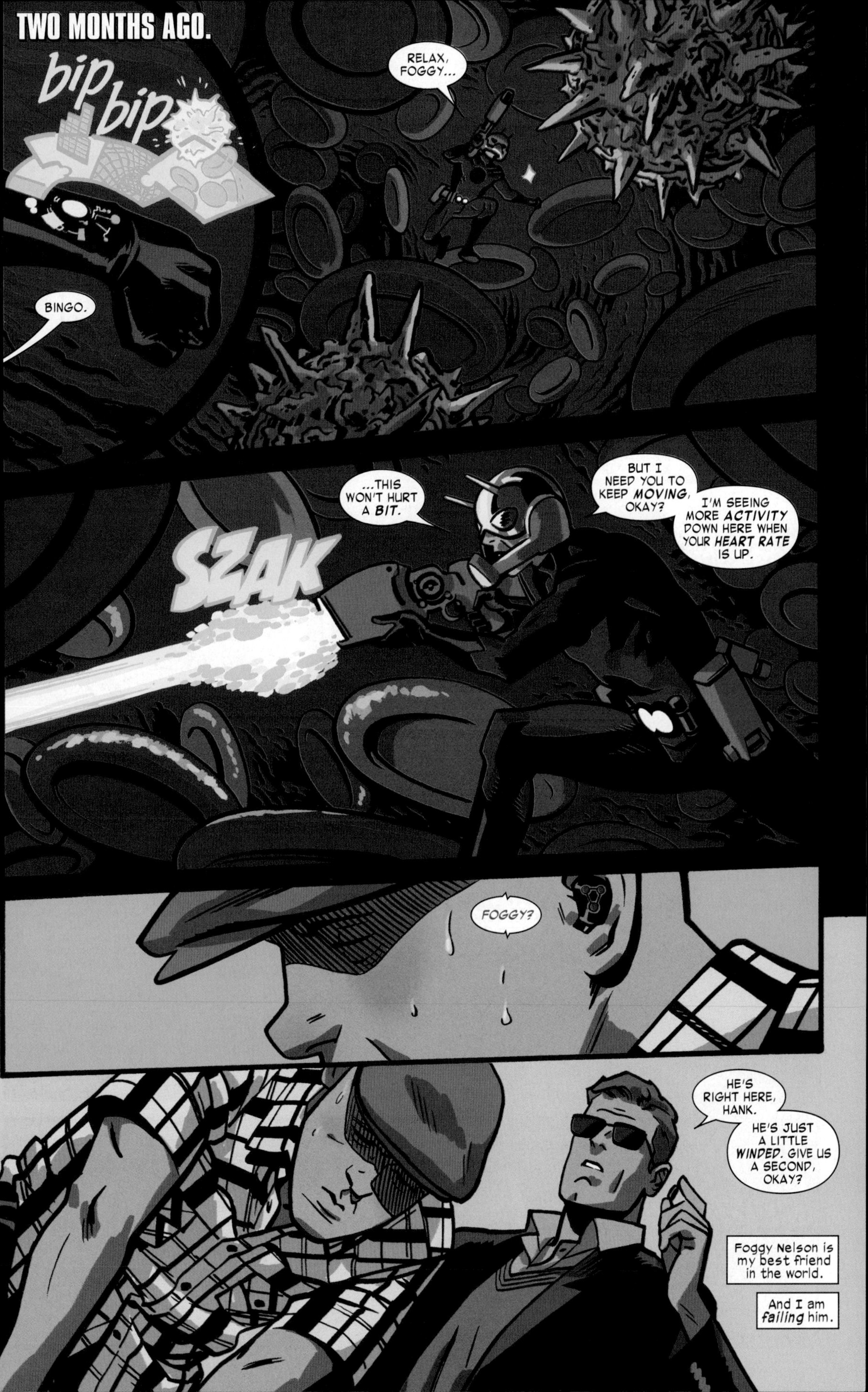
TWO MONTHS AGO.
bip bip
RELAX, FOGGY...
BINGO.
...THIS WON'T HURT A BIT.
BUT I NEED YOU TO KEEP MOVING, OKAY?
I'M SEEING MORE ACTIVITY DOWN HERE WHEN YOUR HEART RATE IS UP.
SZAK
FOGGY?
HE'S RIGHT HERE, HANK.
HE'S JUST A LITTLE WINDED. GIVE US A SECOND, OKAY?
Foggy Nelson is my best friend in the world.
And I am failing him.

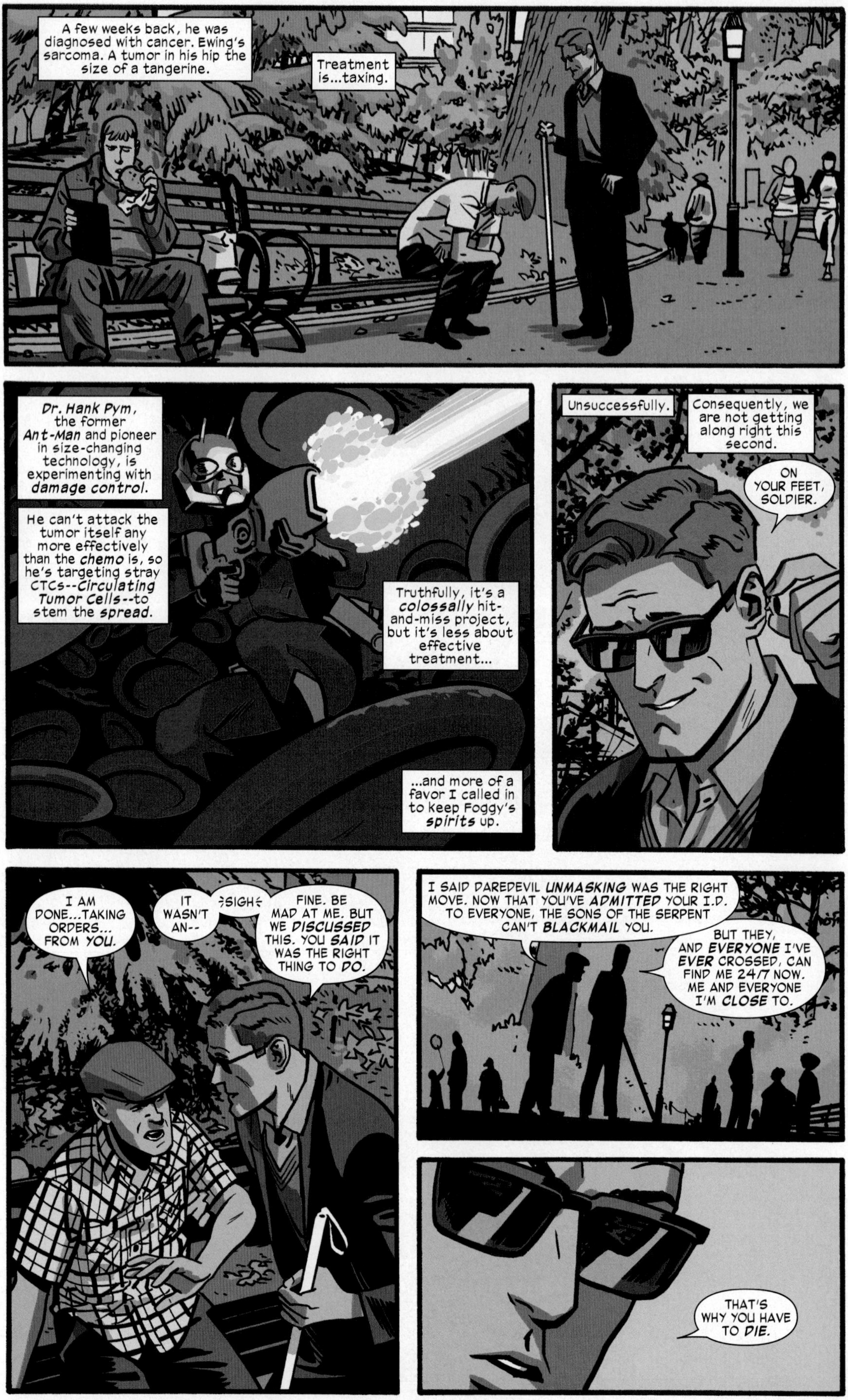
A few weeks back, he was diagnosed with cancer. Ewing's sarcoma. A tumor in his hip the size of a tangerine.
Treatment is...taxing.
Dr. Hank Pym, the former Ant-Man and pioneer in size-changing technology, is experimenting with damage control.
He can't attack the tumor itself any more effectively than the chemo is, so he's targeting stray CTCs--Circulating Tumor Cells--to stem the spread.
Truthfully, it's a colossally hit-and-miss project, but it's less about effective treatment...
...and more of a favor I called in to keep Foggy's spirits up.
Unsuccessfully.
Consequently, we are not getting along right this second.
ON YOUR FEET, SOLDIER.
I AM DONE...TAKING ORDERS... FROM YOU.
IT WASN'T AN--
SIGH
FINE. BE MAD AT ME. BUT WE DISCUSSED THIS. YOU SAID IT WAS THE RIGHT THING TO DO.
I SAID DAREDEVIL UNMASKING WAS THE RIGHT MOVE. NOW THAT YOU'VE ADMITTED YOUR I.D. TO EVERYONE, THE SONS OF THE SERPENT CAN'T BLACKMAIL YOU.
BUT THEY, AND EVERYONE I'VE EVER CROSSED, CAN FIND ME 24/7 NOW. ME AND EVERYONE I'M CLOSE TO.
THAT'S WHY YOU HAVE TO DIE.

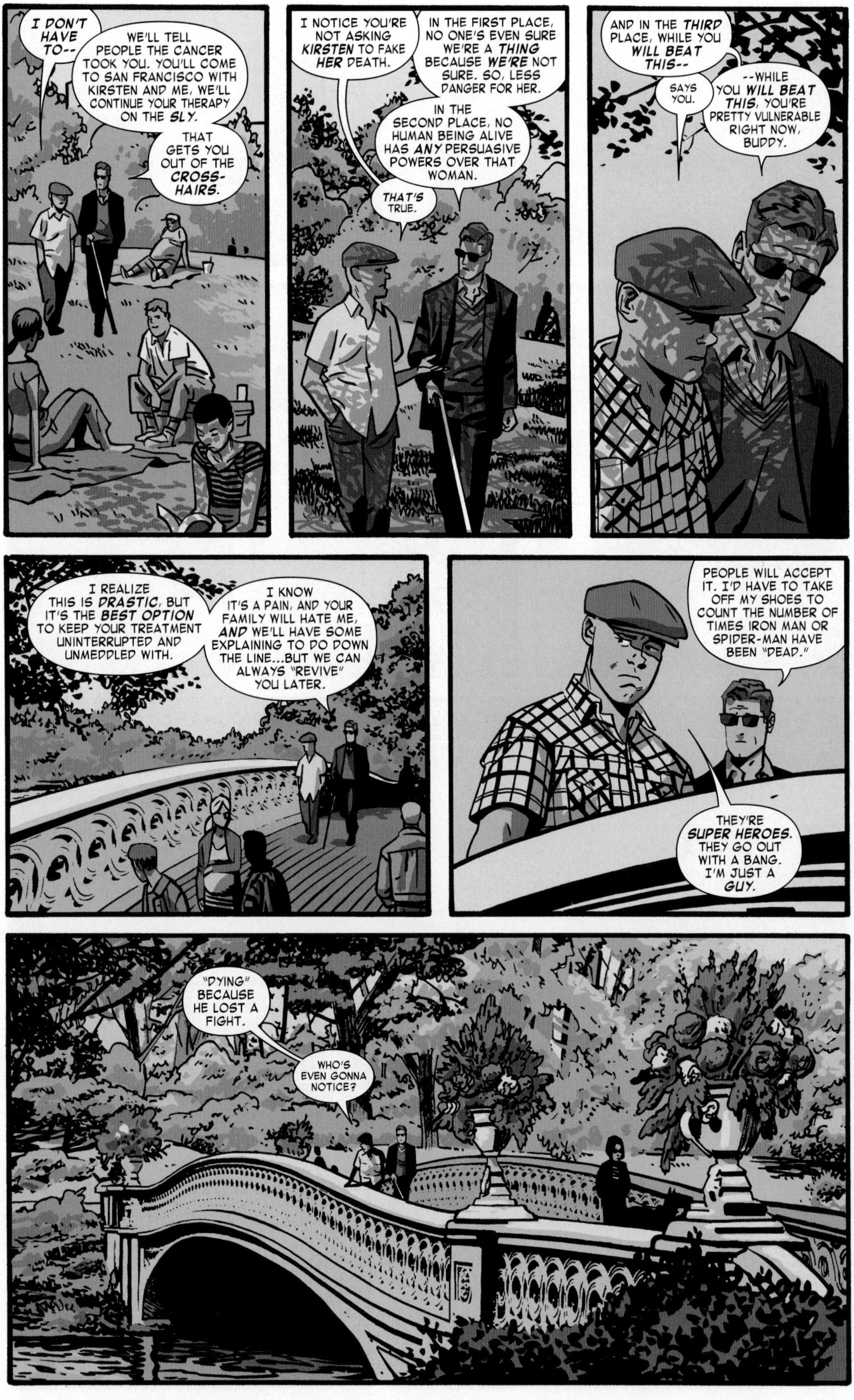
I DON'T HAVE TO--
WE'LL TELL PEOPLE THE CANCER TOOK YOU. YOU'LL COME TO SAN FRANCISCO WITH KIRSTEN AND ME, WE'LL CONTINUE YOUR THERAPY ON THE SLY.
THAT GETS YOU OUT OF THE CROSS-HAIRS.
I NOTICE YOU'RE NOT ASKING KIRSTEN TO FAKE HER DEATH.
IN THE FIRST PLACE, NO ONE'S EVEN SURE WE'RE A THING BECAUSE WE'RE NOT SURE. SO, LESS DANGER FOR HER.
IN THE SECOND PLACE, NO HUMAN BEING ALIVE HAS ANY PERSUASIVE POWERS OVER THAT WOMAN.
THAT'S TRUE.
AND IN THE THIRD PLACE, WHILE YOU WILL BEAT THIS--
SAYS YOU.
--WHILE YOU WILL BEAT THIS, YOU'RE PRETTY VULNERABLE RIGHT NOW, BUDDY.
I REALIZE THIS IS DRASTIC, BUT IT'S THE BEST OPTION TO KEEP YOUR TREATMENT UNINTERRUPTED AND UNMEDDLED WITH.
I KNOW IT'S A PAIN, AND YOUR FAMILY WILL HATE ME, AND WE'LL HAVE SOME EXPLAINING TO DO DOWN THE LINE...BUT WE CAN ALWAYS "REVIVE" YOU LATER.
PEOPLE WILL ACCEPT IT. I'D HAVE TO TAKE OFF MY SHOES TO COUNT THE NUMBER OF TIMES IRON MAN OR SPIDER-MAN HAVE BEEN "DEAD."
THEY'RE SUPER HEROES. THEY GO OUT WITH A BANG. I'M JUST A GUY.
"DYING" BECAUSE HE LOST A FIGHT.
WHO'S EVEN GONNA NOTICE?

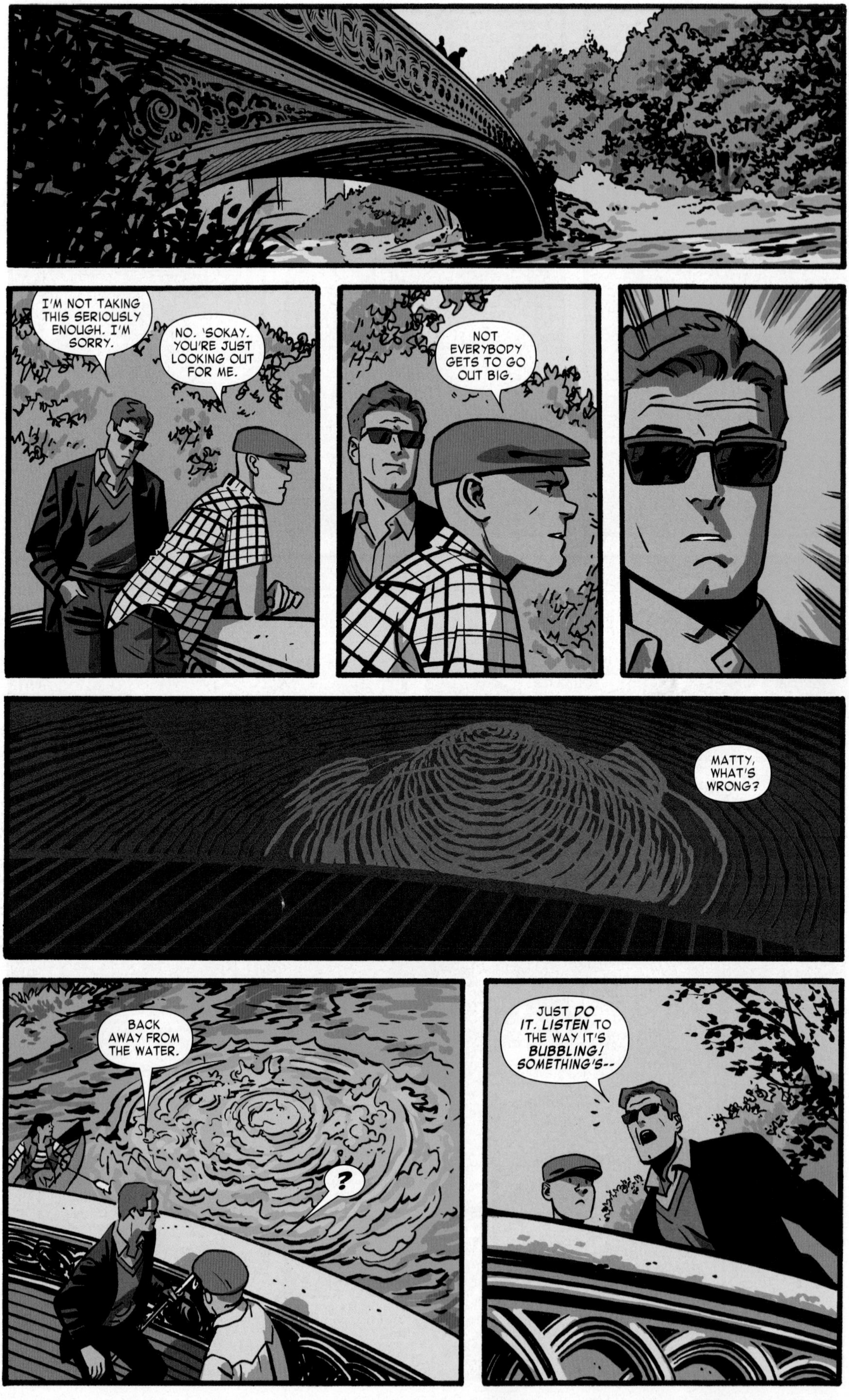
I'M NOT TAKING THIS SERIOUSLY ENOUGH. I'M SORRY.
NO. 'SOKAY. YOU'RE JUST LOOKING OUT FOR ME.
NOT EVERYBODY GETS TO GO OUT BIG.
MATTY, WHAT'S WRONG?
BACK AWAY FROM THE WATER.
?
JUST DO IT. LISTEN TO THE WAY IT'S BUBBLING! SOMETHING'S--

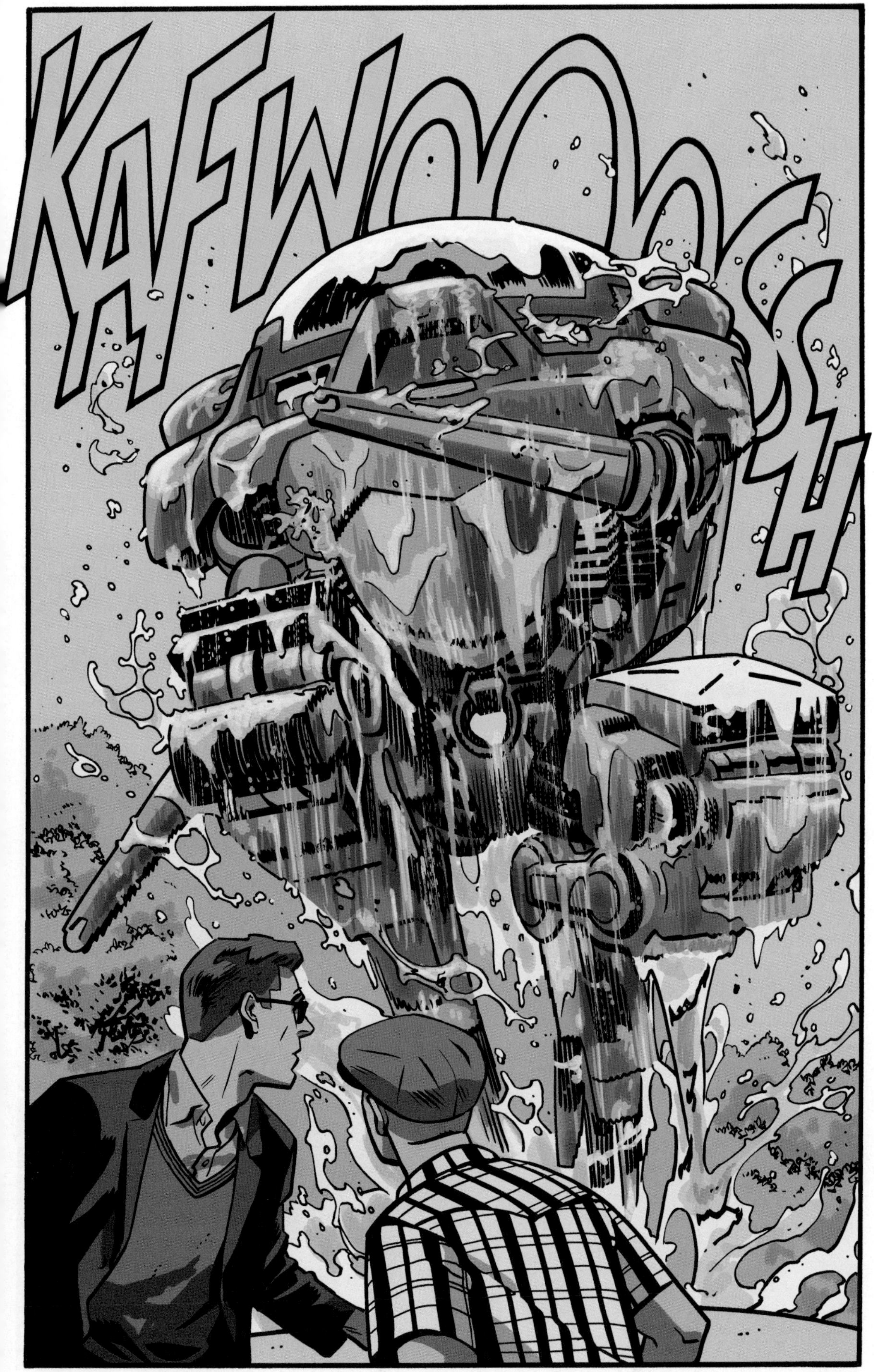
KAFWOOOOSH

KACHAANG

BE MY EYES!

GIANT GREEN METAL TANK LEAPING RIGHT--

VVVRT

≥NNNGH!≤

TS CHAK

BUDDA BUDDA BUDDA BUDDA BUDDA BUDL

CROSSHAIRS, YEAH?

RUN!

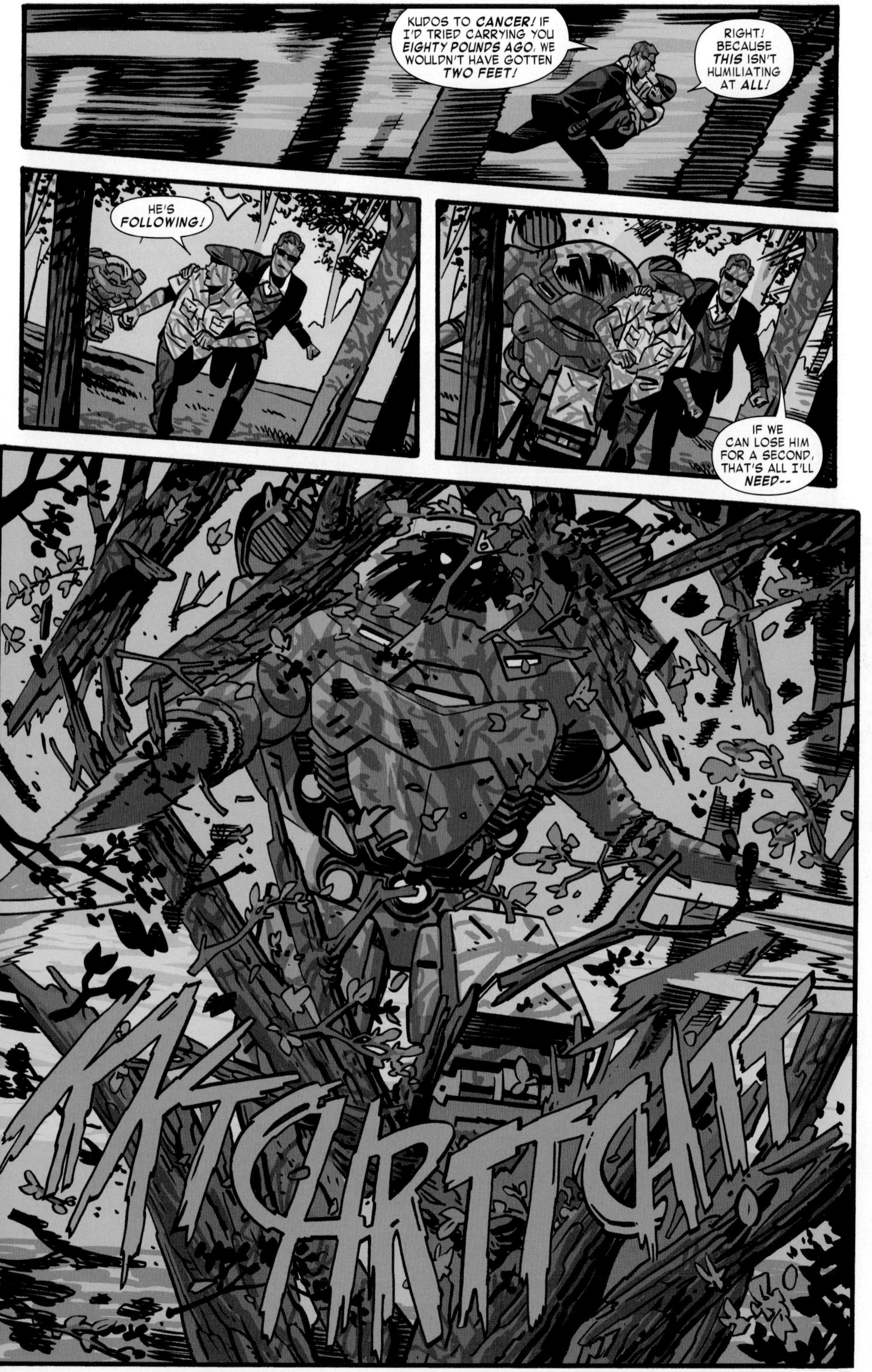
KUDOS TO CANCER! IF I'D TRIED CARRYING YOU EIGHTY POUNDS AGO, WE WOULDN'T HAVE GOTTEN TWO FEET!
RIGHT! BECAUSE THIS ISN'T HUMILIATING AT ALL!
HE'S FOLLOWING!
IF WE CAN LOSE HIM FOR A SECOND, THAT'S ALL I'LL NEED--

Years ago, I made enemies with a criminal called *Leapfrog*.

He could jump several stories high. That was about it for his M.O.

I don't think this is *him*, but if it *is*--

--he's gone in for a *serious* upgrade.

MR. NELSON.

JUST THE MAN I'M LOOKING FOR.

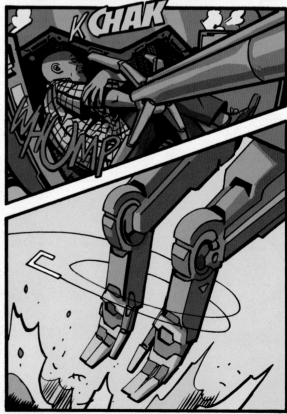

K CHAK

WHOMP

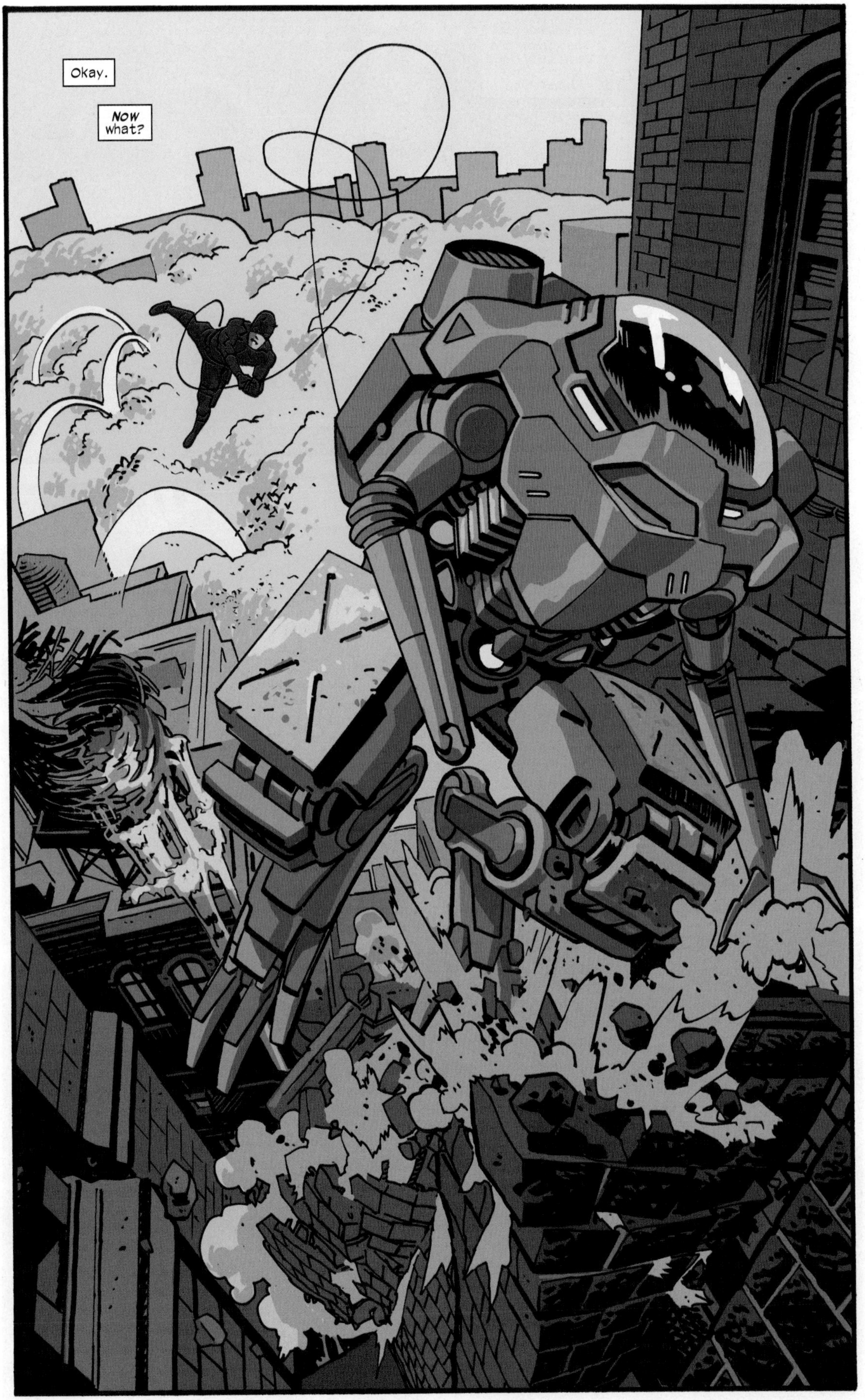
Okay.
NOW what?

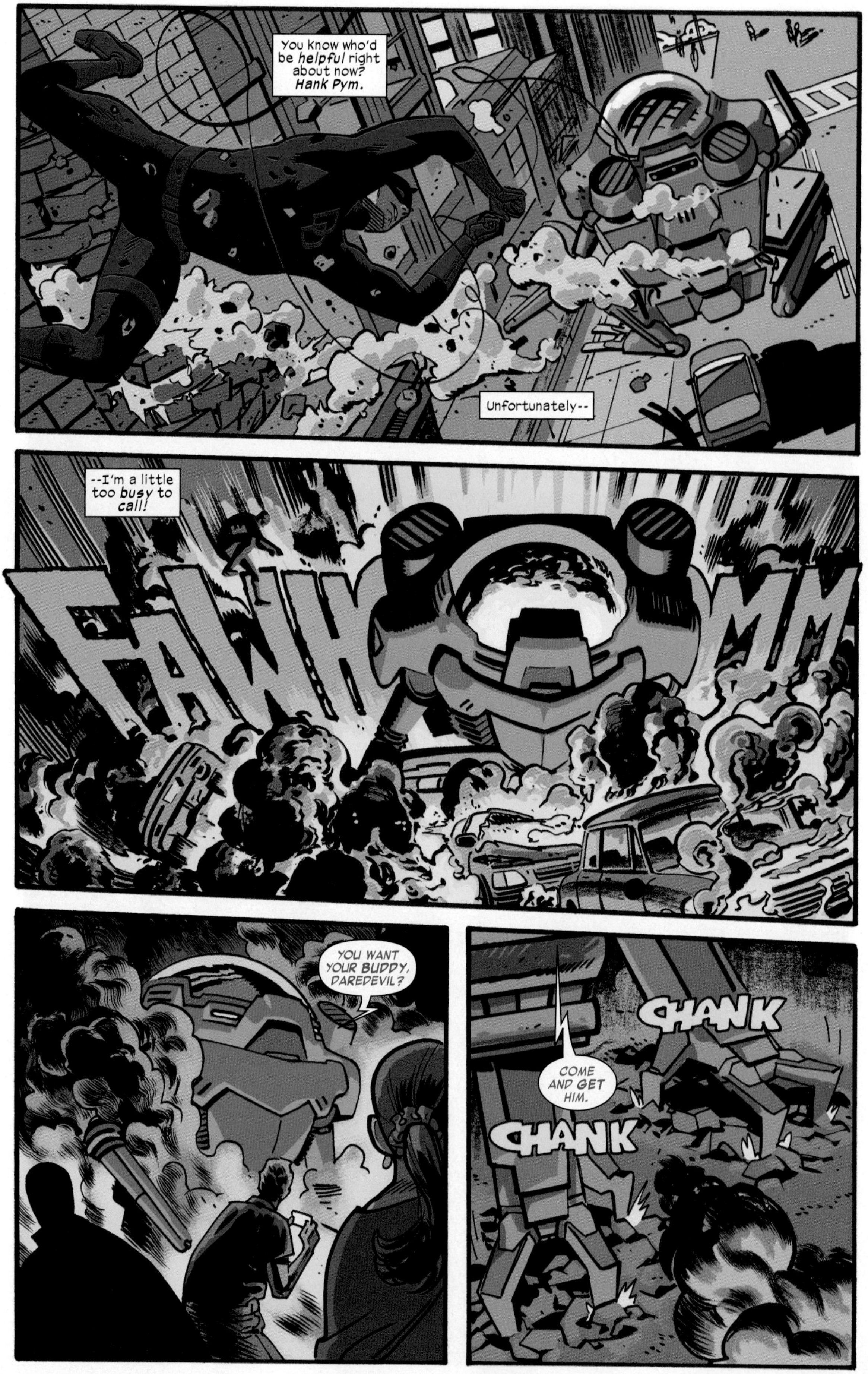
You know who'd be *helpful* right about now? *Hank Pym*.
Unfortunately--
--I'm a little too *busy* to *call!*
YOU WANT YOUR *BUDDY*, DAREDEVIL?
CHANK
COME AND *GET* HIM.
CHANK

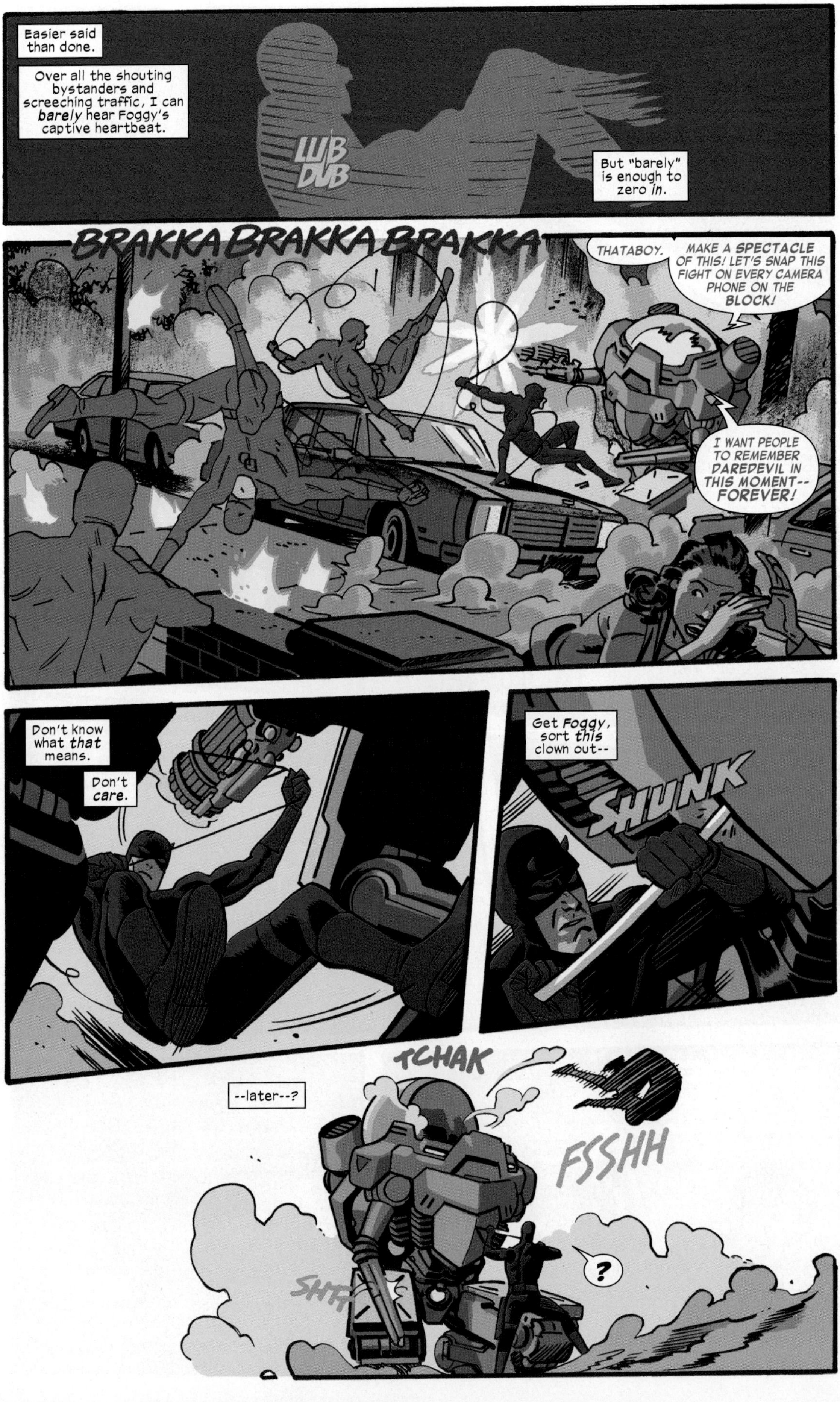
Easier said than done.
Over all the shouting bystanders and screeching traffic, I can *barely* hear Foggy's captive heartbeat.
LUB DUB
But "barely" is enough to zero *in*.
BRAKKA BRAKKA BRAKKA
THATABOY.
MAKE A **SPECTACLE** OF THIS! LET'S SNAP THIS FIGHT ON EVERY CAMERA PHONE ON THE **BLOCK!**
I WANT PEOPLE TO REMEMBER **DAREDEVIL** IN **THIS MOMENT--** **FOREVER!**
Don't know what *that* means.
Don't *care*.
Get *Foggy*, sort *this* clown out--
SHUNK
TCHAK
--later--?
FSSHH
?
SHFF

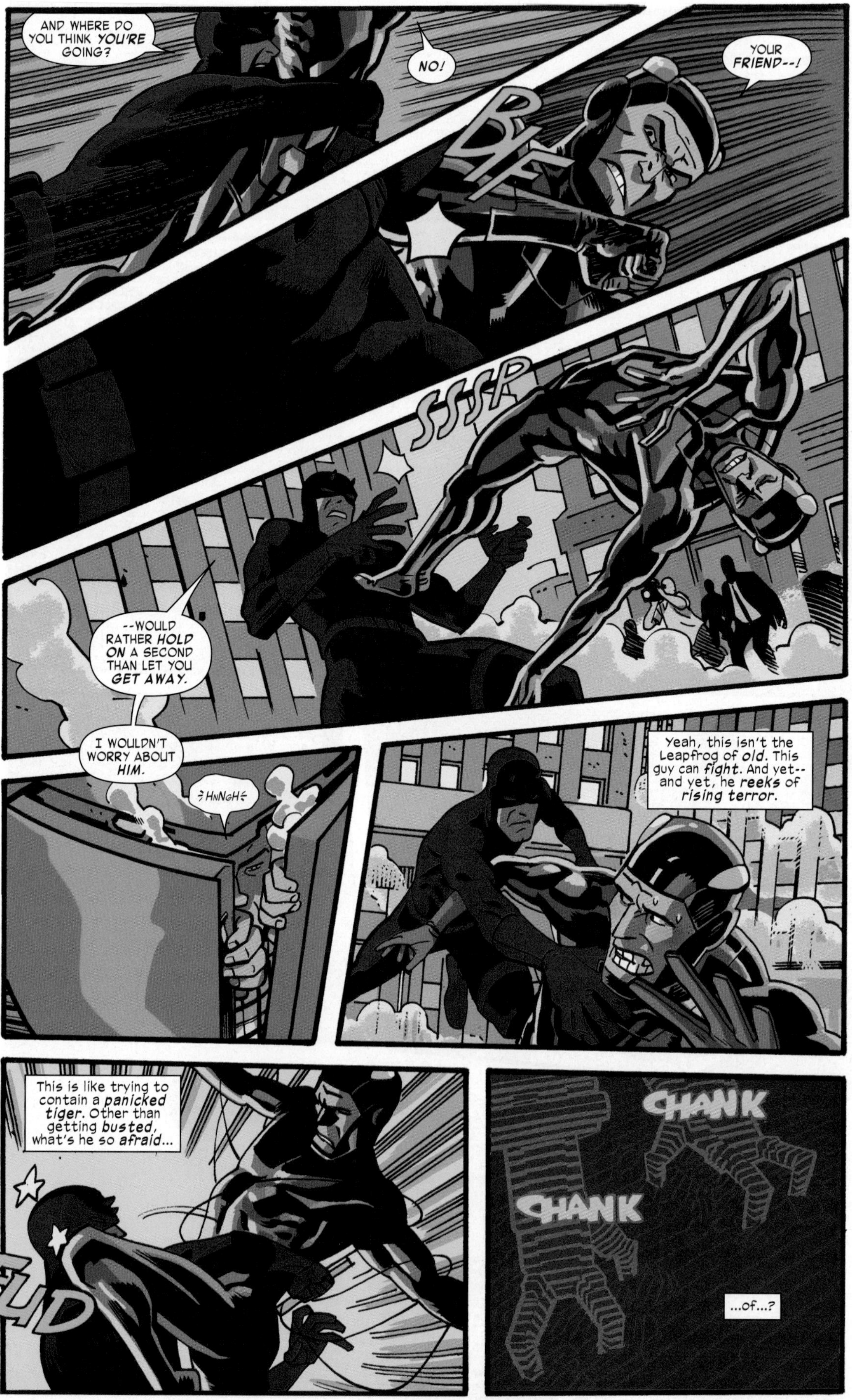
AND WHERE DO YOU THINK YOU'RE GOING?
NO!
BUF
YOUR FRIEND--!
SSSP
--WOULD RATHER HOLD ON A SECOND THAN LET YOU GET AWAY.
I WOULDN'T WORRY ABOUT HIM.
HNNGH
Yeah, this isn't the Leapfrog of old. This guy can fight. And yet--and yet, he reeks of rising terror.
This is like trying to contain a panicked tiger. Other than getting busted, what's he so afraid...
FUD
CHANK
CHANK
...of...?

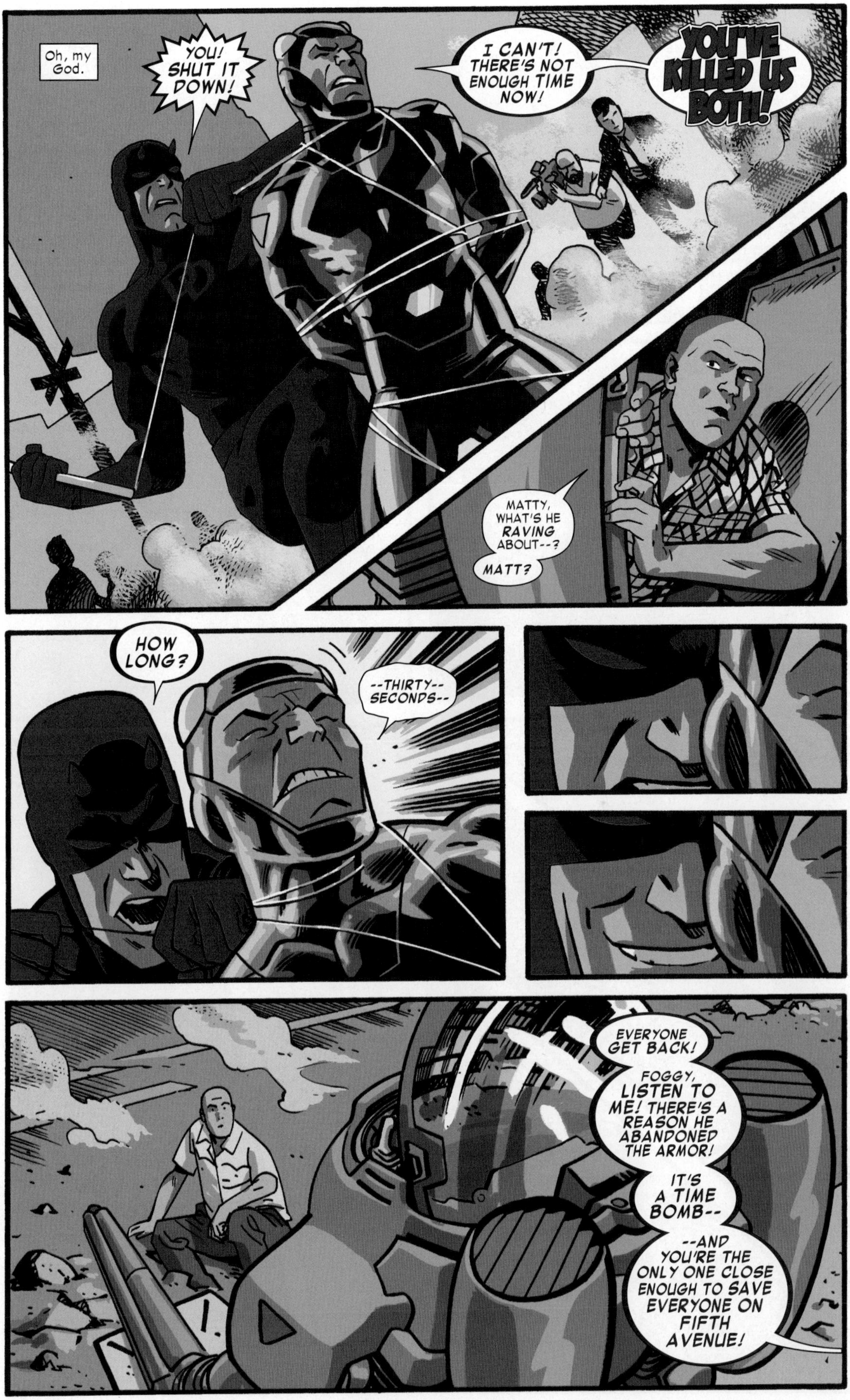
Oh, my God.
YOU! SHUT IT DOWN!
I CAN'T! THERE'S NOT ENOUGH TIME NOW!
YOU'VE KILLED US BOTH!
MATTY, WHAT'S HE RAVING ABOUT--?
MATT?
HOW LONG?
--THIRTY-- SECONDS--
EVERYONE GET BACK!
FOGGY, LISTEN TO ME! THERE'S A REASON HE ABANDONED THE ARMOR!
IT'S A TIME BOMB--
--AND YOU'RE THE ONLY ONE CLOSE ENOUGH TO SAVE EVERYONE ON FIFTH AVENUE!

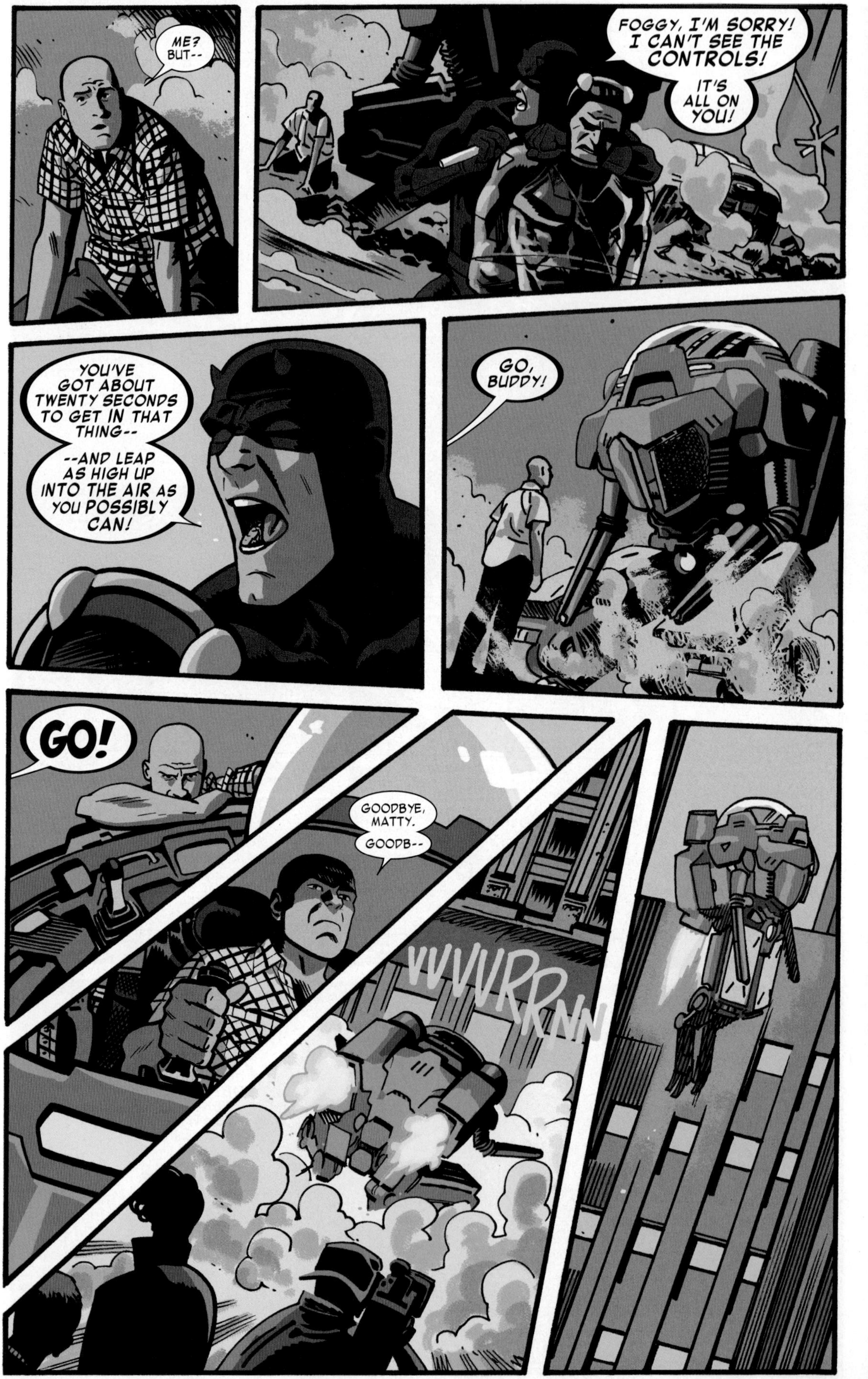
ME? BUT--
FOGGY, I'M SORRY! I CAN'T SEE THE CONTROLS!
IT'S ALL ON YOU!
YOU'VE GOT ABOUT TWENTY SECONDS TO GET IN THAT THING--
--AND LEAP AS HIGH UP INTO THE AIR AS YOU POSSIBLY CAN!
GO, BUDDY!
GO!
GOODBYE, MATTY.
GOODB--
VVVVRRNN

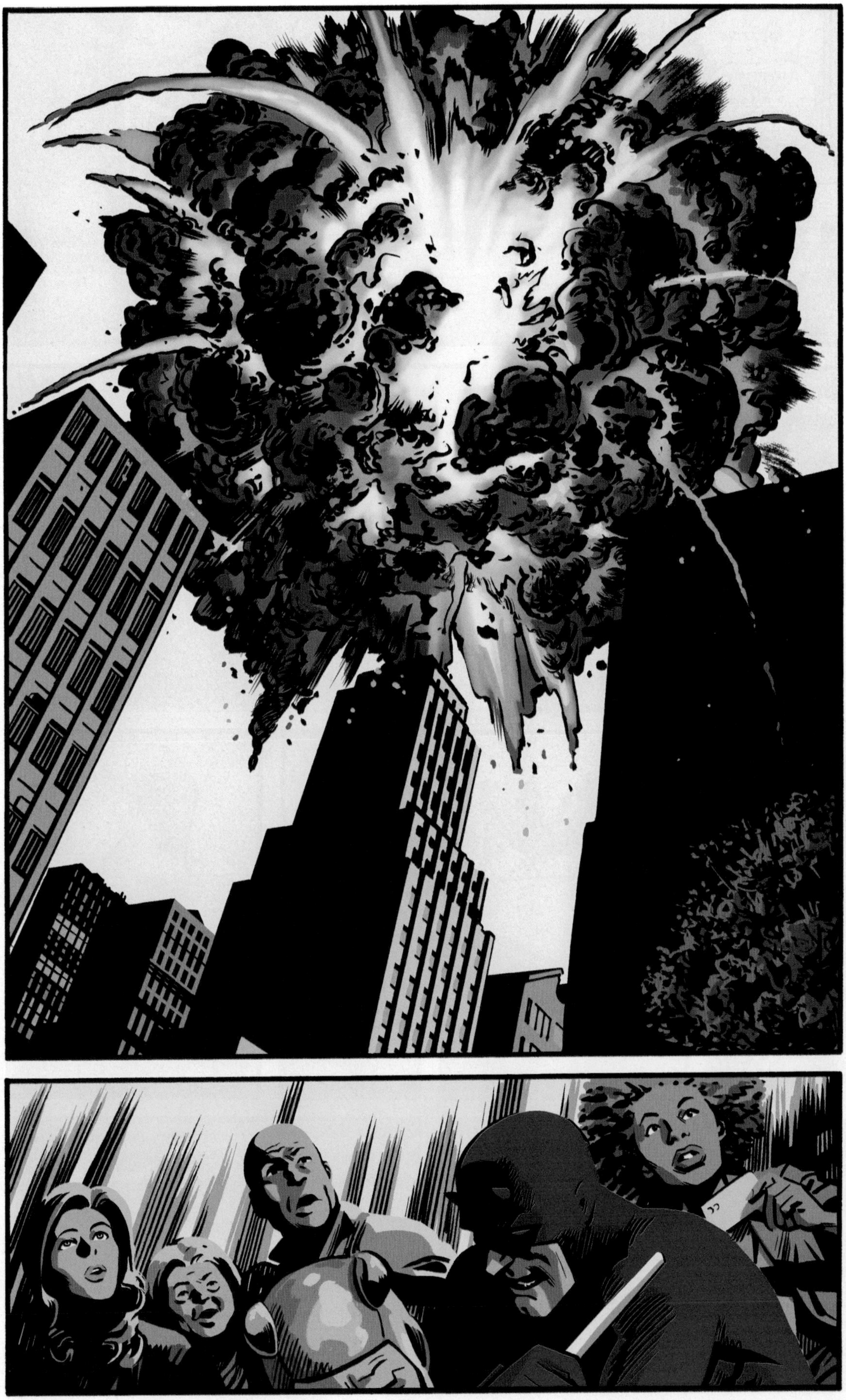

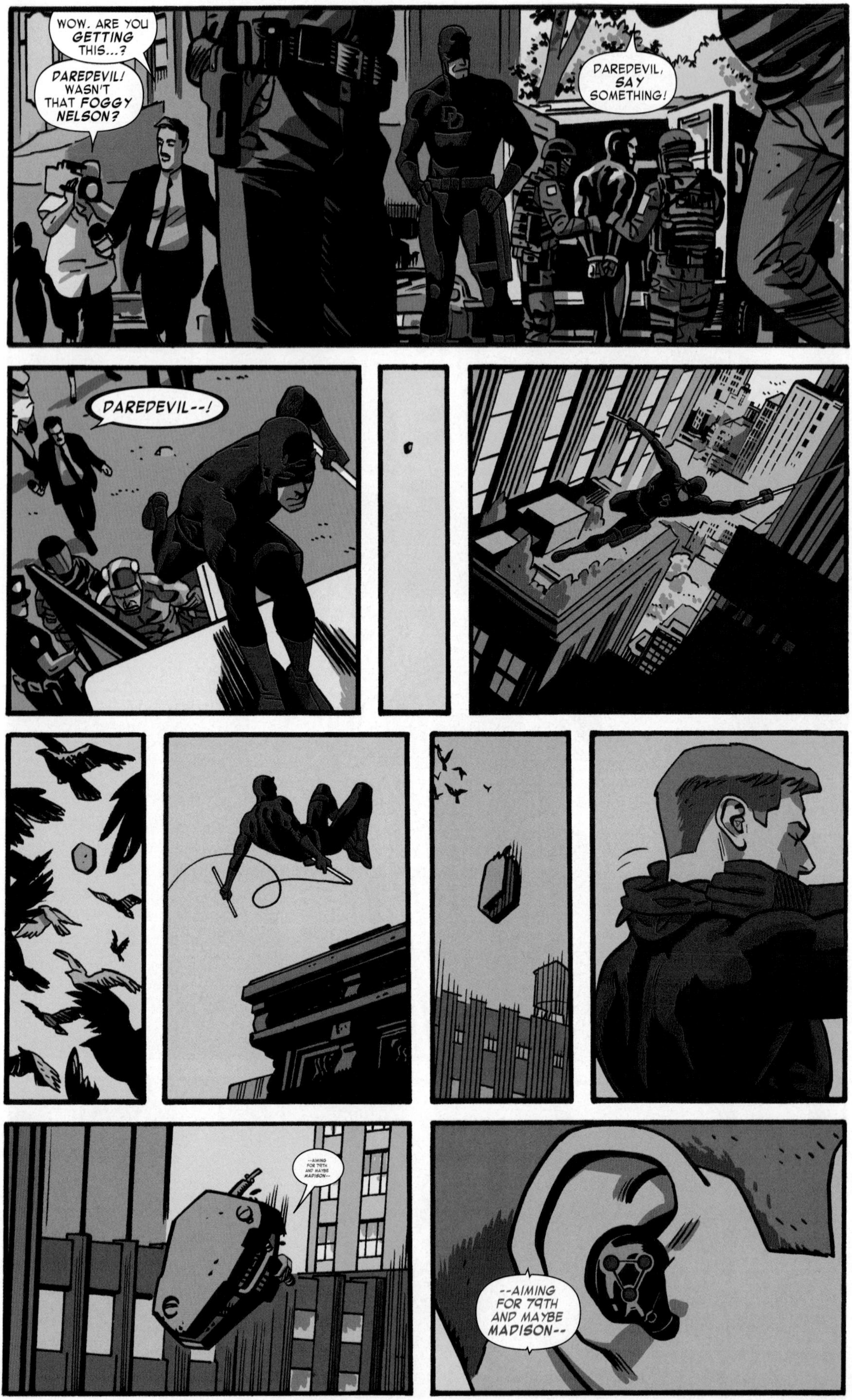
WOW. ARE YOU GETTING THIS...?
DAREDEVIL! WASN'T THAT FOGGY NELSON?
DAREDEVIL, SAY SOMETHING!
DAREDEVIL--!
--AIMING FOR 79TH AND MAYBE MADISON--
--AIMING FOR 79TH AND MAYBE MADISON--

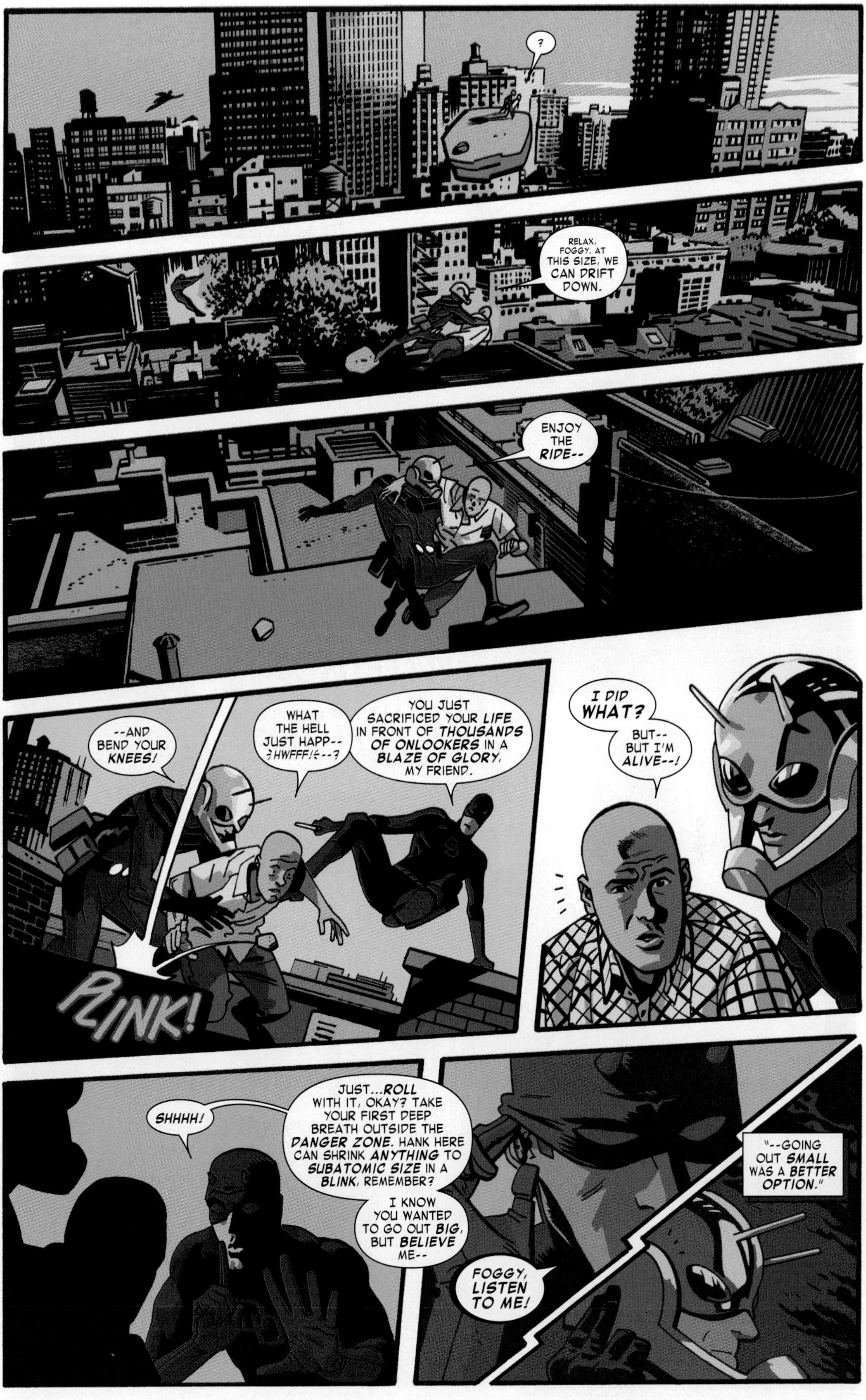
?
RELAX, FOGGY. AT THIS SIZE, WE CAN DRIFT DOWN.
ENJOY THE RIDE--
--AND BEND YOUR KNEES!
WHAT THE HELL JUST HAPP-- HWFFF! --?
YOU JUST SACRIFICED YOUR LIFE IN FRONT OF THOUSANDS OF ONLOOKERS IN A BLAZE OF GLORY, MY FRIEND.
PLINK!
I DID WHAT?
BUT-- BUT I'M ALIVE--!
SHHHH!
JUST...ROLL WITH IT, OKAY? TAKE YOUR FIRST DEEP BREATH OUTSIDE THE DANGER ZONE. HANK HERE CAN SHRINK ANYTHING TO SUBATOMIC SIZE IN A BLINK, REMEMBER?
I KNOW YOU WANTED TO GO OUT BIG, BUT BELIEVE ME--
"--GOING OUT SMALL WAS A BETTER OPTION."
FOGGY, LISTEN TO ME!

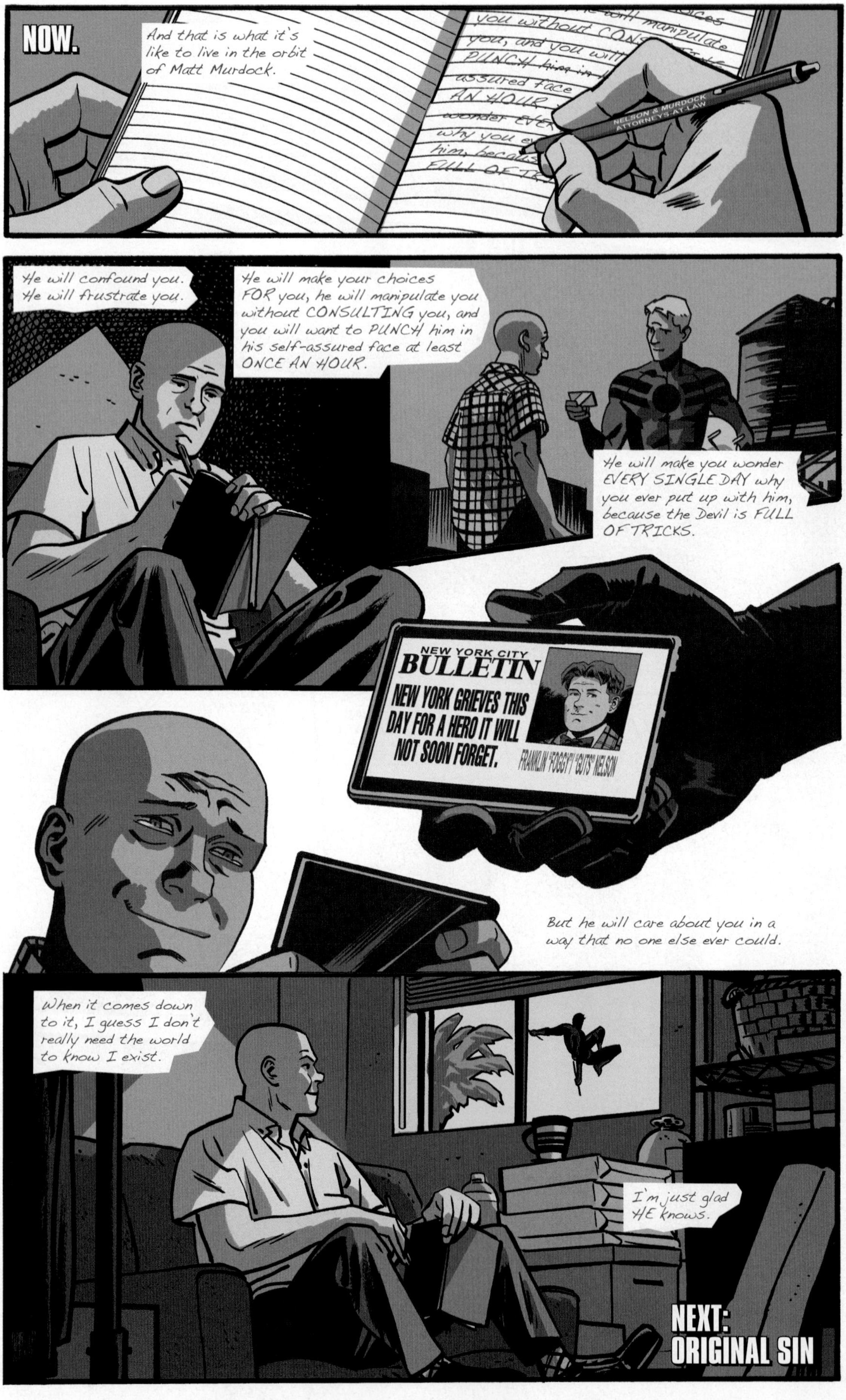
NOW.
And that is what it's like to live in the orbit of Matt Murdock.
NELSON & MURDOCK ATTORNEYS-AT-LAW
He will confound you. He will frustrate you.
He will make your choices FOR you, he will manipulate you without CONSULTING you, and you will want to PUNCH him in his self-assured face at least ONCE AN HOUR.
He will make you wonder EVERY SINGLE DAY why you ever put up with him, because the Devil is FULL OF TRICKS.
NEW YORK CITY BULLETIN
NEW YORK GRIEVES THIS DAY FOR A HERO IT WILL NOT SOON FORGET.
FRANKLIN "FOGGY" "GUTS" NELSON
But he will care about you in a way that no one else ever could.
When it comes down to it, I guess I don't really need the world to know I exist.
I'm just glad HE knows.
NEXT: ORIGINAL SIN

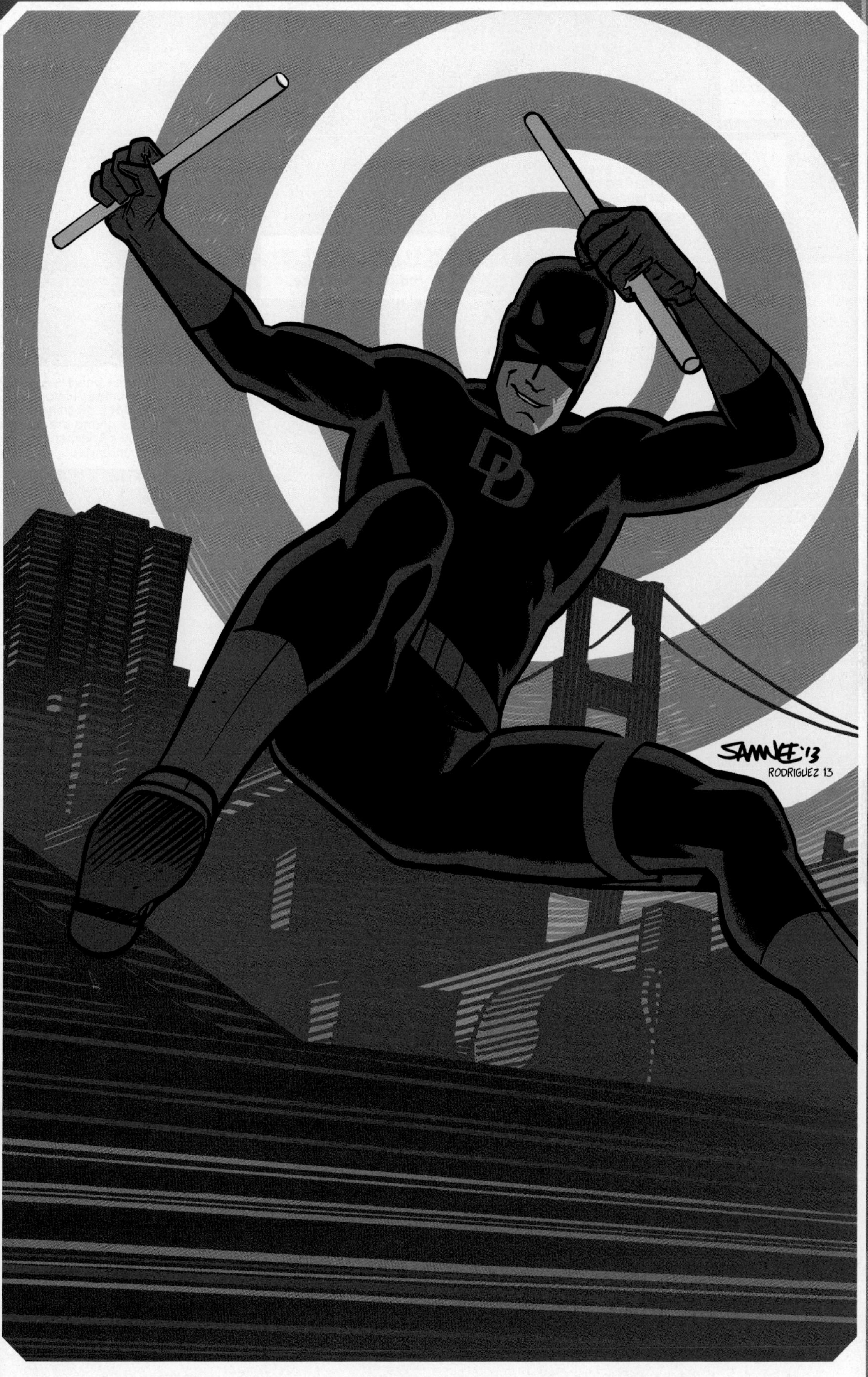
SAMNEE '13
RODRIGUEZ 13

DAREDEVIL #0.1

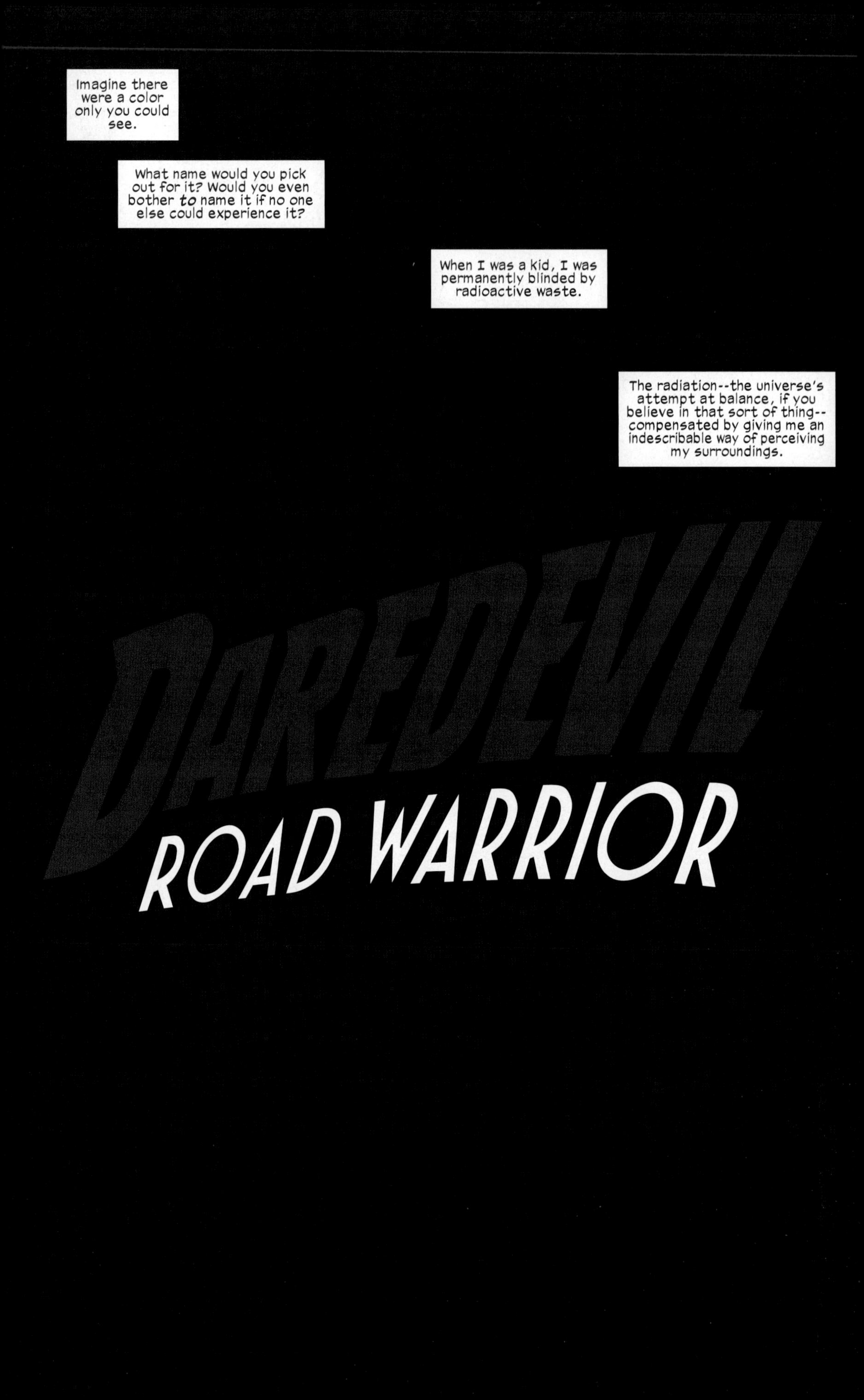
Imagine there were a color only you could see.
What name would you pick out for it? Would you even bother *to* name it if no one else could experience it?
When I was a kid, I was permanently blinded by radioactive waste.
The radiation--the universe's attempt at balance, if you believe in that sort of thing--compensated by giving me an indescribable way of perceiving my surroundings.
DAREDEVIL
ROAD WARRIOR

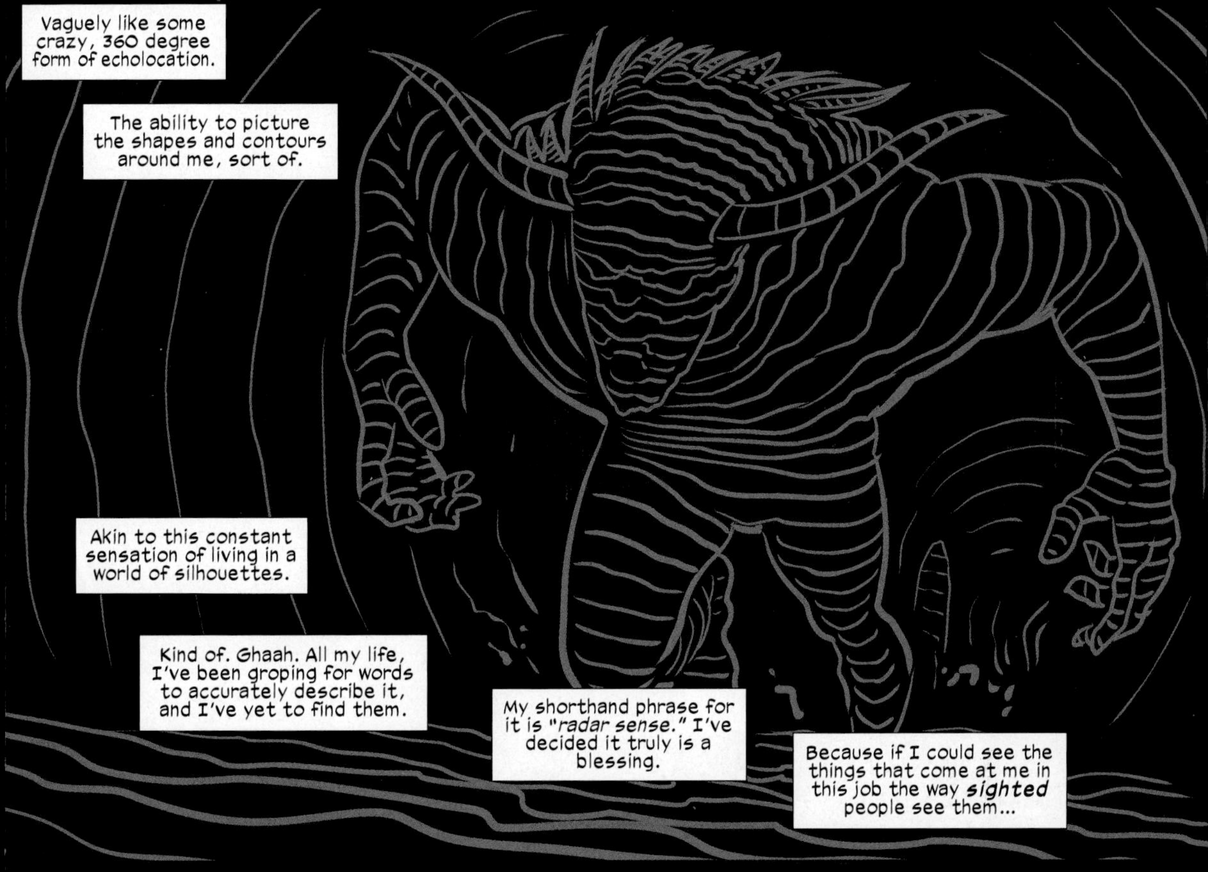
Vaguely like some crazy, 360 degree form of echolocation.
The ability to picture the shapes and contours around me, sort of.
Akin to this constant sensation of living in a world of silhouettes.
Kind of. Ghaah. All my life, I've been groping for words to accurately describe it, and I've yet to find them.
My shorthand phrase for it is "*radar sense.*" I've decided it truly is a blessing.
Because if I could see the things that come at me in this job the way ***sighted*** people see them...
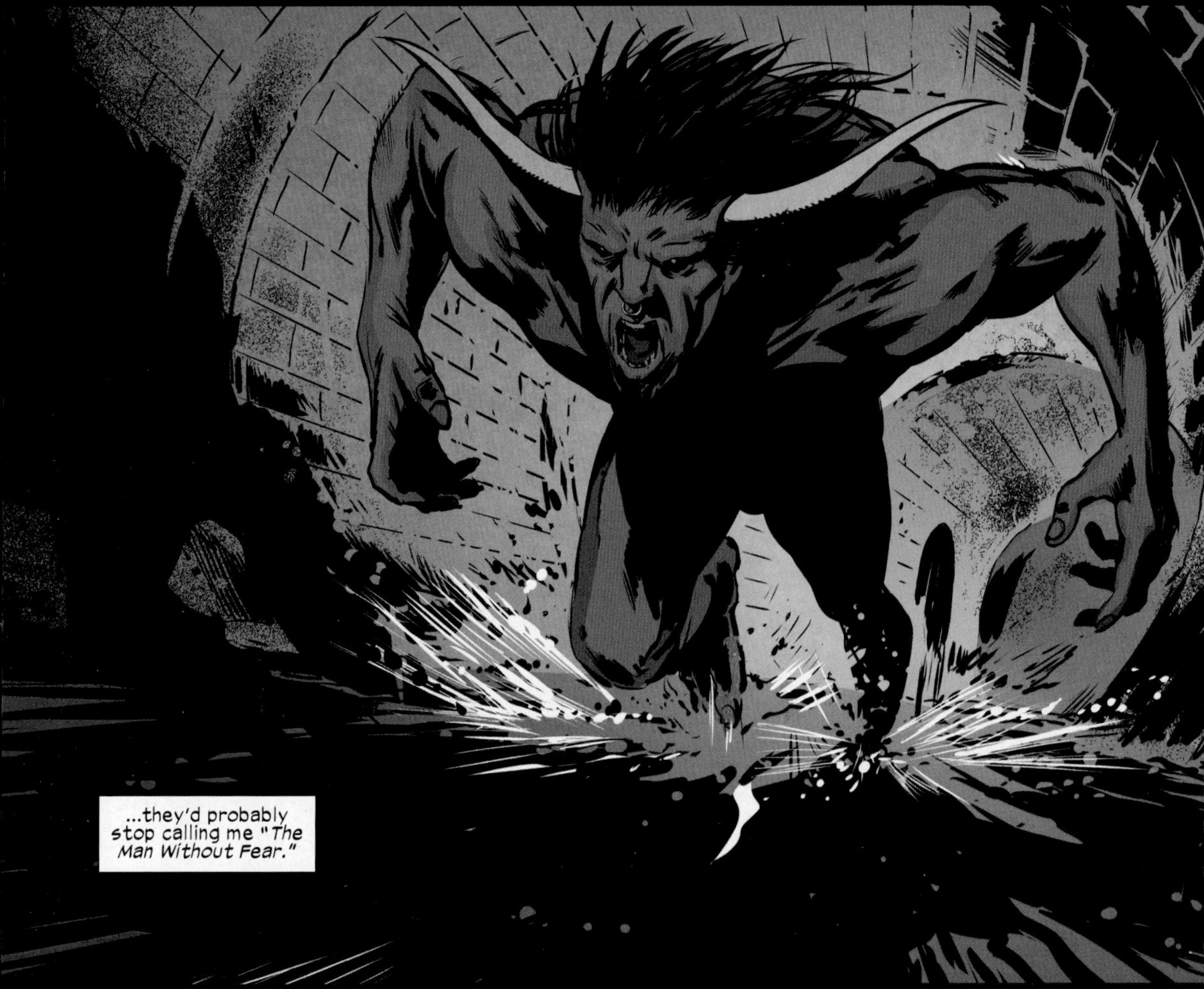
...they'd probably stop calling me "*The Man Without Fear.*"

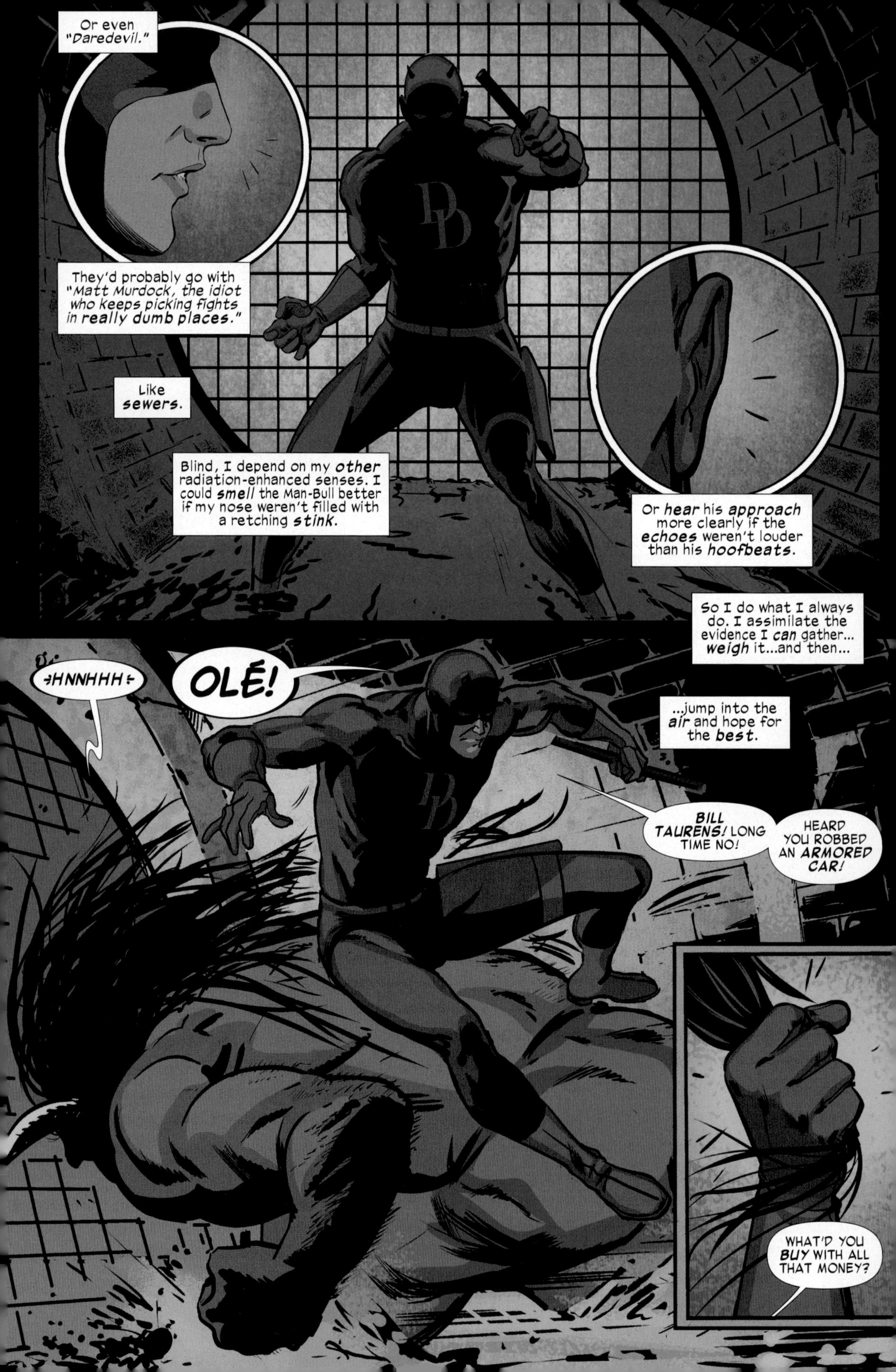

Or even "Daredevil."
They'd probably go with "Matt Murdock, the idiot who keeps picking fights in really dumb places."
Like sewers.
Blind, I depend on my other radiation-enhanced senses. I could smell the Man-Bull better if my nose weren't filled with a retching stink.
Or hear his approach more clearly if the echoes weren't louder than his hoofbeats.
So I do what I always do. I assimilate the evidence I can gather... weigh it...and then...
HNNHHH
OLÉ!
...jump into the air and hope for the best.
BILL TAURENS! LONG TIME NO!
HEARD YOU ROBBED AN ARMORED CAR!
WHAT'D YOU BUY WITH ALL THAT MONEY?

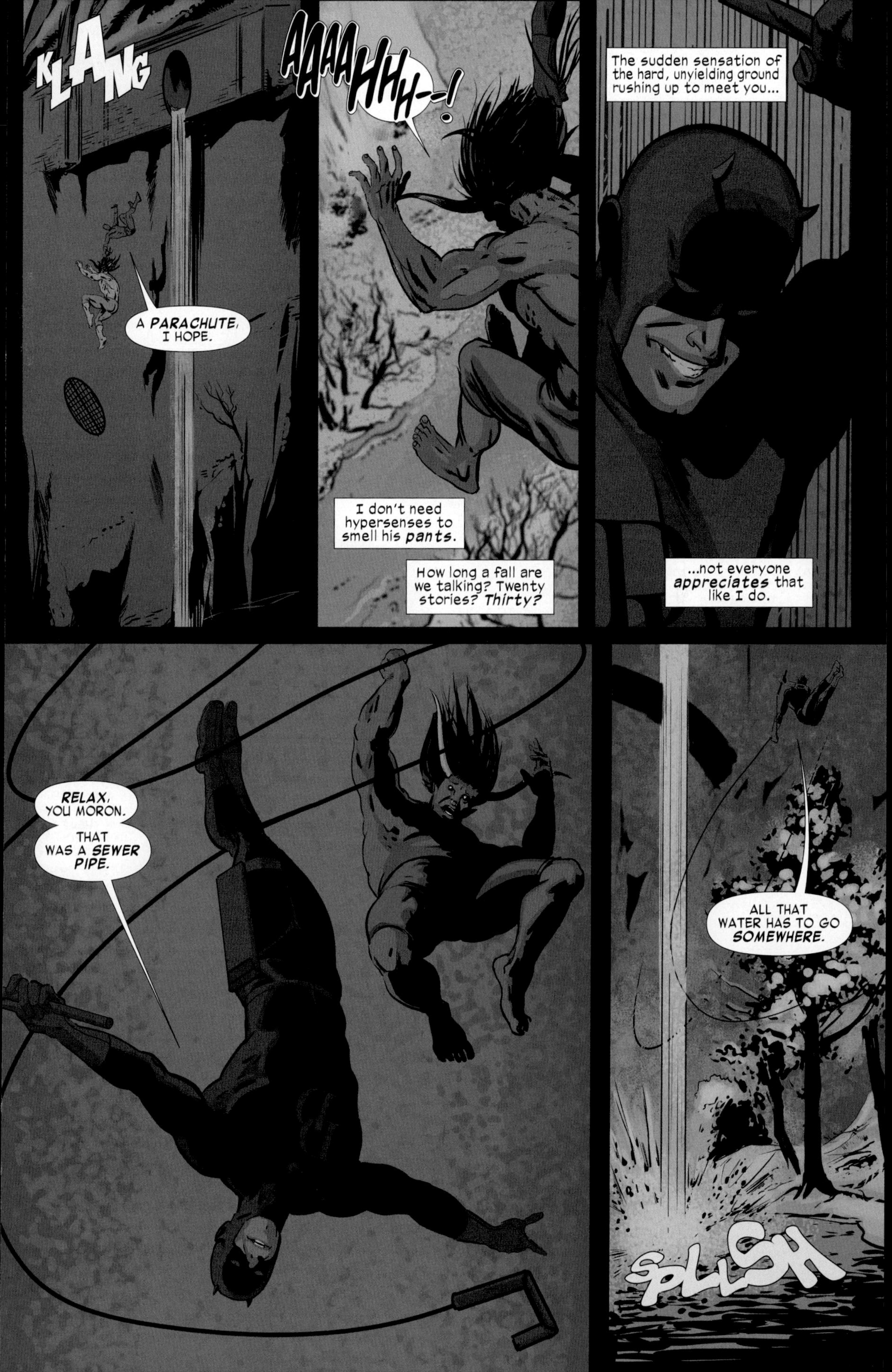

KLANG
A PARACHUTE, I HOPE.
AAAAHHH--!
I don't need hypersenses to smell his pants.
How long a fall are we talking? Twenty stories? Thirty?
The sudden sensation of the hard, unyielding ground rushing up to meet you...
...not everyone appreciates that like I do.
RELAX, YOU MORON.
THAT WAS A SEWER PIPE.
ALL THAT WATER HAS TO GO SOMEWHERE.
SPLSH

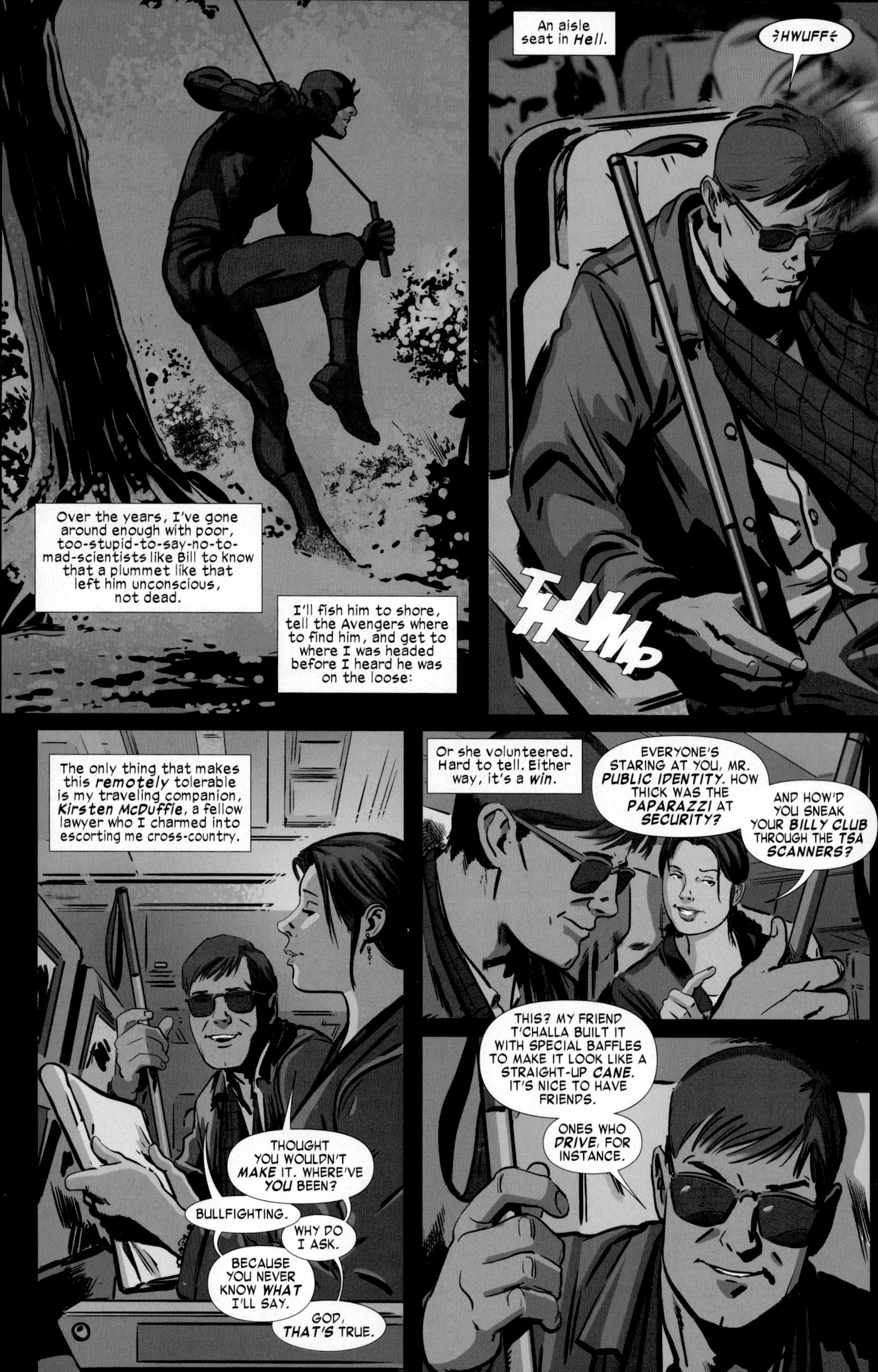
Over the years, I've gone around enough with poor, too-stupid-to-say-no-to-mad-scientists like Bill to know that a plummet like that left him unconscious, not dead.
I'll fish him to shore, tell the Avengers where to find him, and get to where I was headed before I heard he was on the loose:
An aisle seat in Hell.
HWUFF
THUMP
The only thing that makes this remotely tolerable is my traveling companion, Kirsten McDuffie, a fellow lawyer who I charmed into escorting me cross-country.
THOUGHT YOU WOULDN'T MAKE IT. WHERE'VE YOU BEEN?
BULLFIGHTING.
WHY DO I ASK.
BECAUSE YOU NEVER KNOW WHAT I'LL SAY.
GOD, THAT'S TRUE.
Or she volunteered. Hard to tell. Either way, it's a win.
EVERYONE'S STARING AT YOU, MR. PUBLIC IDENTITY. HOW THICK WAS THE PAPARAZZI AT SECURITY?
AND HOW'D YOU SNEAK YOUR BILLY CLUB THROUGH THE TSA SCANNERS?
THIS? MY FRIEND T'CHALLA BUILT IT WITH SPECIAL BAFFLES TO MAKE IT LOOK LIKE A STRAIGHT-UP CANE. IT'S NICE TO HAVE FRIENDS.
ONES WHO DRIVE, FOR INSTANCE.

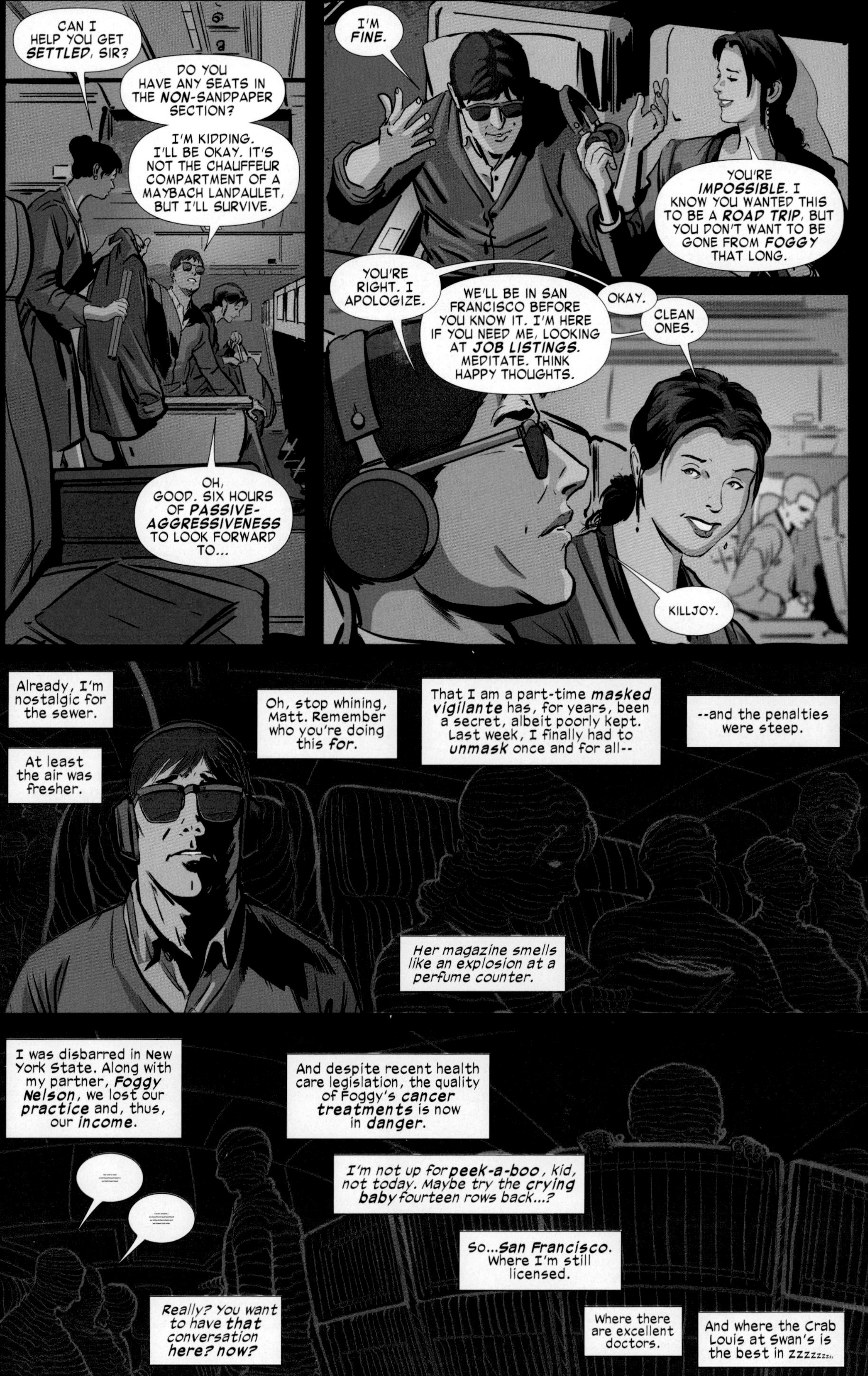
CAN I HELP YOU GET SETTLED, SIR?
DO YOU HAVE ANY SEATS IN THE NON-SANDPAPER SECTION?
I'M KIDDING. I'LL BE OKAY. IT'S NOT THE CHAUFFEUR COMPARTMENT OF A MAYBACH LANDAULET, BUT I'LL SURVIVE.
OH, GOOD. SIX HOURS OF PASSIVE-AGGRESSIVENESS TO LOOK FORWARD TO...
I'M FINE.
YOU'RE IMPOSSIBLE. I KNOW YOU WANTED THIS TO BE A ROAD TRIP, BUT YOU DON'T WANT TO BE GONE FROM FOGGY THAT LONG.
YOU'RE RIGHT. I APOLOGIZE.
WE'LL BE IN SAN FRANCISCO BEFORE YOU KNOW IT. I'M HERE IF YOU NEED ME, LOOKING AT JOB LISTINGS. MEDITATE. THINK HAPPY THOUGHTS.
OKAY.
CLEAN ONES.
KILLJOY.
Already, I'm nostalgic for the sewer.
At least the air was fresher.
Oh, stop whining, Matt. Remember who you're doing this for.
That I am a part-time masked vigilante has, for years, been a secret, albeit poorly kept. Last week, I finally had to unmask once and for all--
--and the penalties were steep.
Her magazine smells like an explosion at a perfume counter.
I was disbarred in New York State. Along with my partner, Foggy Nelson, we lost our practice and, thus, our income.
And despite recent health care legislation, the quality of Foggy's cancer treatments is now in danger.
I'm not up for peek-a-boo, kid, not today. Maybe try the crying baby fourteen rows back...?
So...San Francisco. Where I'm still licensed.
Really? You want to have that conversation here? now?
Where there are excellent doctors.
And where the Crab Louis at Swan's is the best in zzzzzzz.

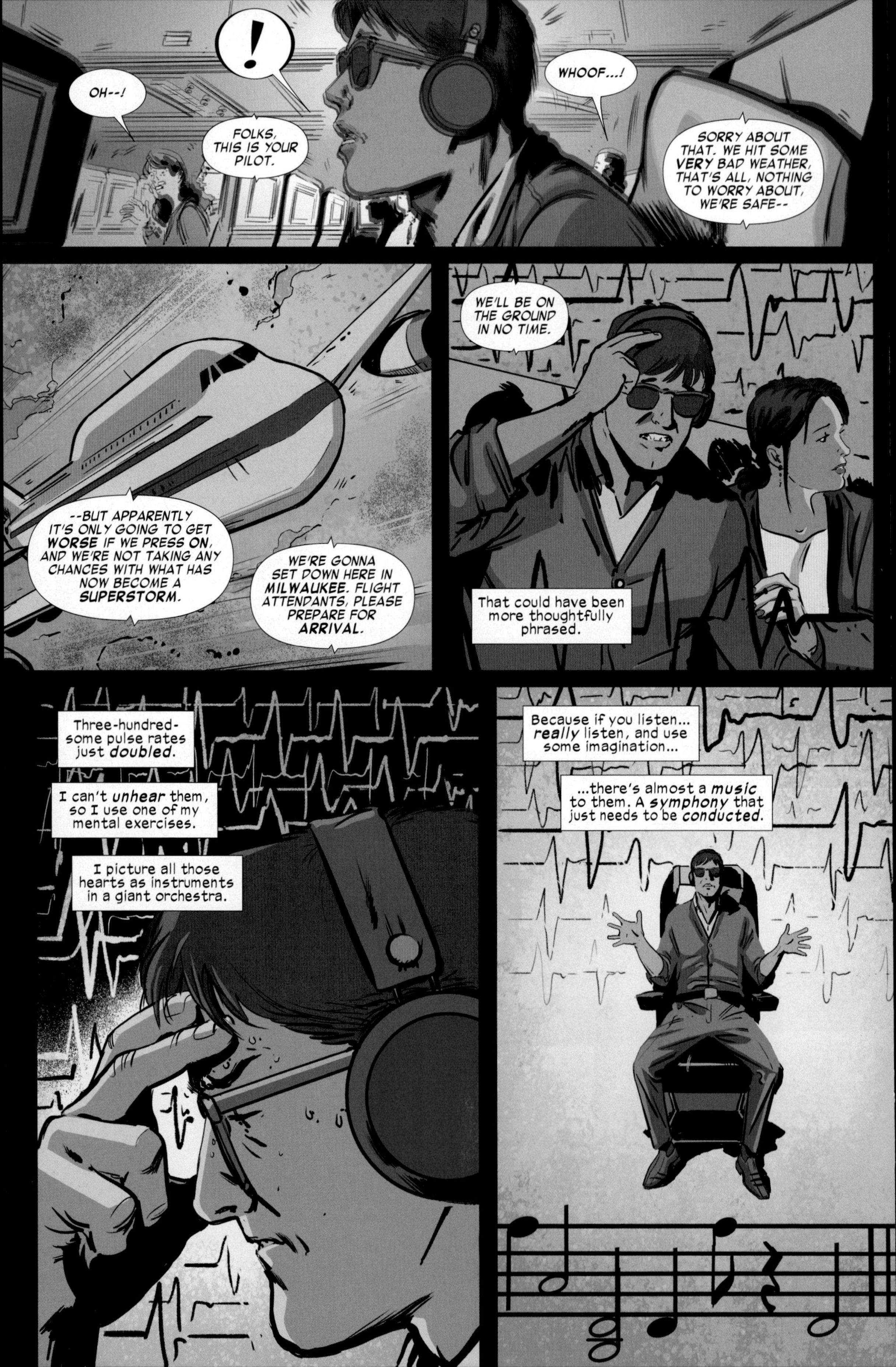
!
OH--!
FOLKS, THIS IS YOUR PILOT.
WHOOF...!
SORRY ABOUT THAT. WE HIT SOME VERY BAD WEATHER, THAT'S ALL, NOTHING TO WORRY ABOUT, WE'RE SAFE--
--BUT APPARENTLY IT'S ONLY GOING TO GET WORSE IF WE PRESS ON, AND WE'RE NOT TAKING ANY CHANCES WITH WHAT HAS NOW BECOME A SUPERSTORM.
WE'RE GONNA SET DOWN HERE IN MILWAUKEE. FLIGHT ATTENDANTS, PLEASE PREPARE FOR ARRIVAL.
WE'LL BE ON THE GROUND IN NO TIME.
That could have been more thoughtfully phrased.
Three-hundred-some pulse rates just doubled.
I can't unhear them, so I use one of my mental exercises.
I picture all those hearts as instruments in a giant orchestra.
Because if you listen... really listen, and use some imagination...
...there's almost a music to them. A symphony that just needs to be conducted.

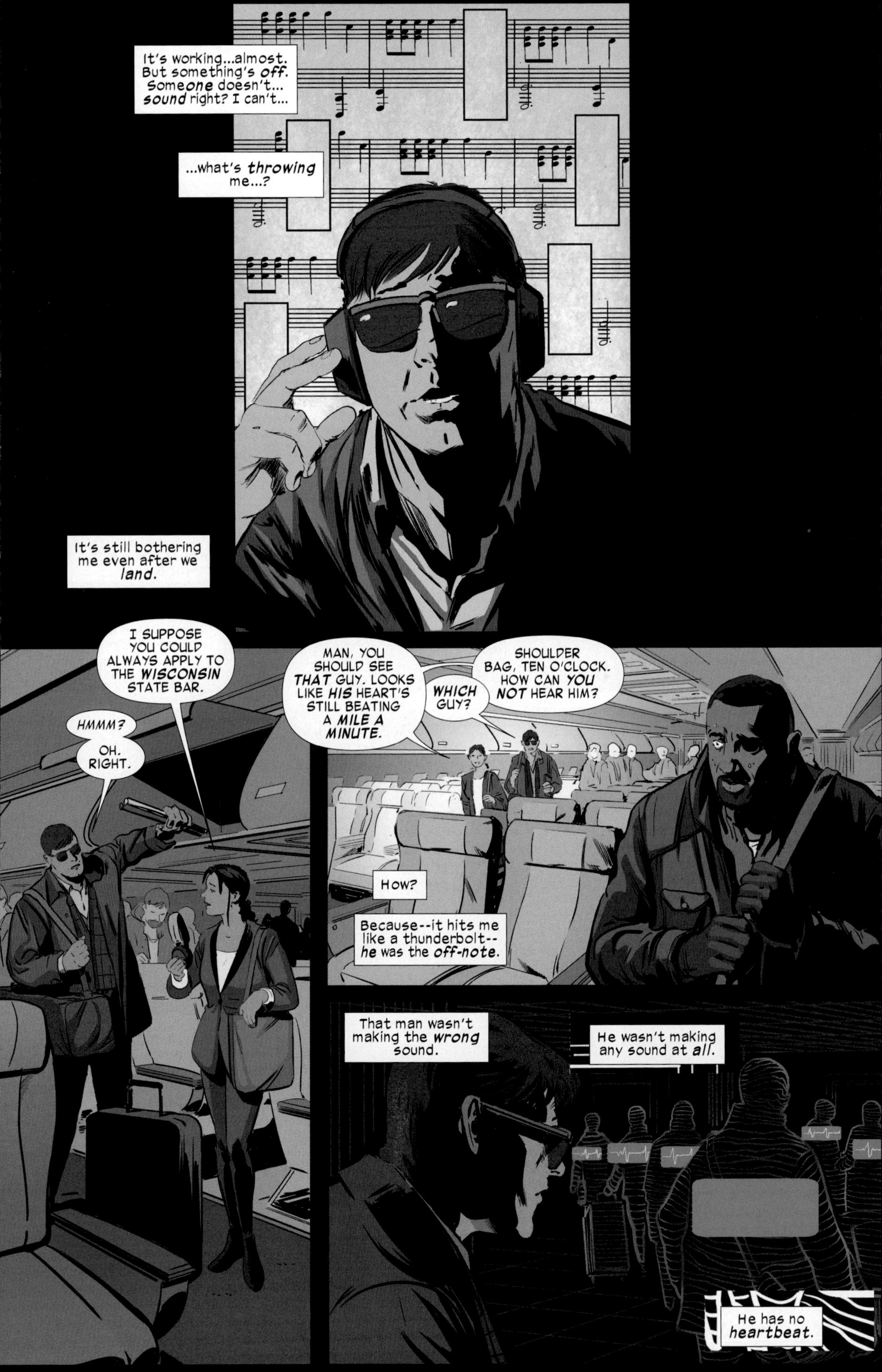
It's working...almost. But something's *off*. Someone doesn't... *sound* right? I can't...
...what's *throwing* me...?
It's still bothering me even after we *land*.
I SUPPOSE YOU COULD ALWAYS APPLY TO THE *WISCONSIN* STATE BAR.
HMMM?
OH. RIGHT.
MAN, YOU SHOULD SEE *THAT* GUY. LOOKS LIKE *HIS* HEART'S STILL BEATING A *MILE A MINUTE*.
WHICH GUY?
SHOULDER BAG, TEN O'CLOCK. HOW CAN *YOU NOT* HEAR HIM?
How?
Because--it hits me like a thunderbolt--*he* was the *off-note*.
That man wasn't making the *wrong* sound.
He wasn't making any sound at *all*.
He has no *heartbeat*.

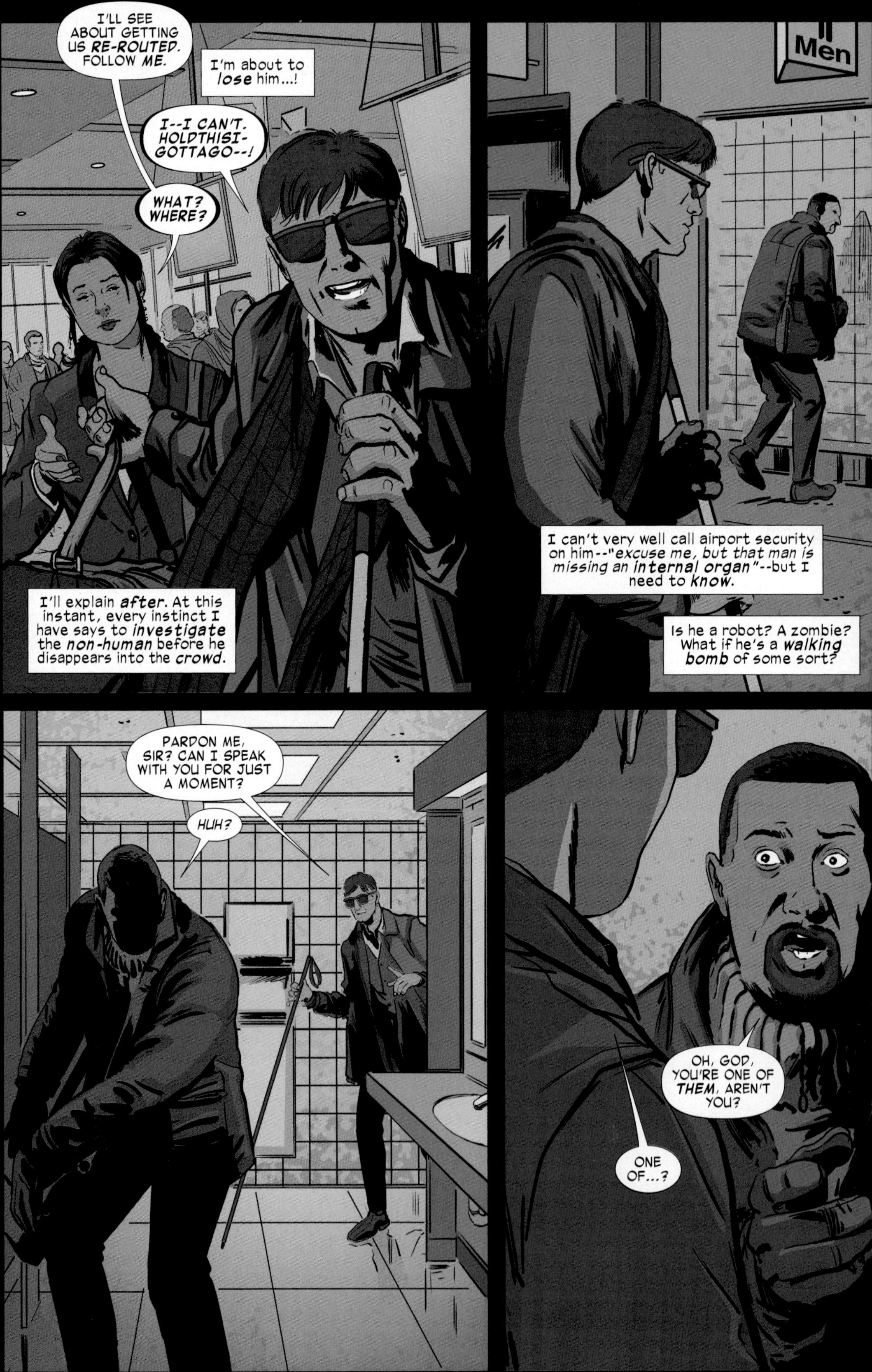
I'LL SEE ABOUT GETTING US RE-ROUTED. FOLLOW ME.
I'm about to lose him...!
I--I CAN'T. HOLDTHISI-GOTTAGO--!
WHAT? WHERE?
I'll explain after. At this instant, every instinct I have says to investigate the non-human before he disappears into the crowd.
Men
I can't very well call airport security on him--"excuse me, but that man is missing an internal organ"--but I need to know.
Is he a robot? A zombie? What if he's a walking bomb of some sort?
PARDON ME, SIR? CAN I SPEAK WITH YOU FOR JUST A MOMENT?
HUH?
OH, GOD, YOU'RE ONE OF THEM, AREN'T YOU?
ONE OF...?

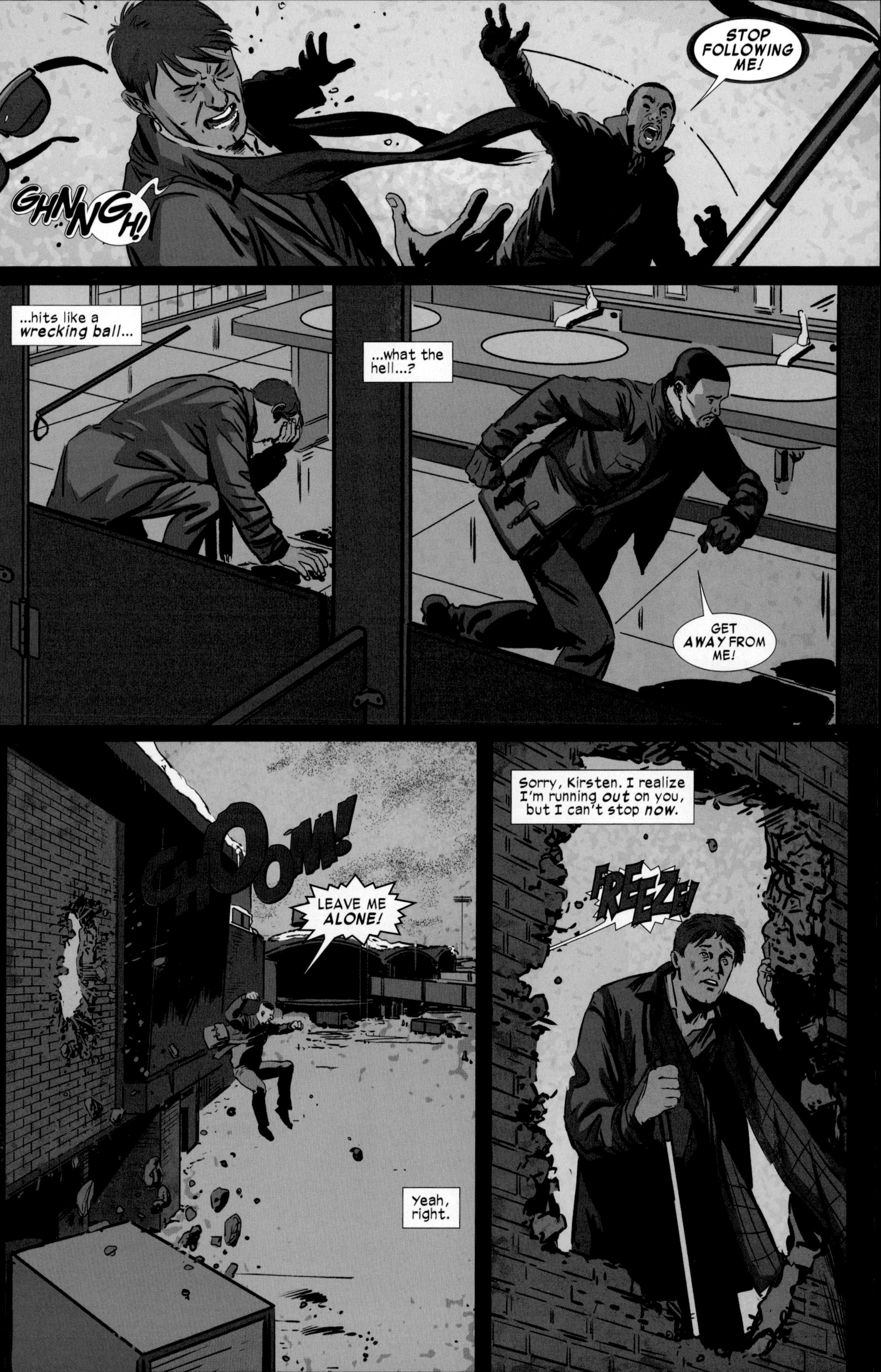
STOP FOLLOWING ME!
GHNNGH!
...hits like a wrecking ball...
...what the hell...?
GET AWAY FROM ME!
CHOOM!
LEAVE ME ALONE!
Yeah, right.
Sorry, Kirsten. I realize I'm running out on you, but I can't stop now.
FREEZE!

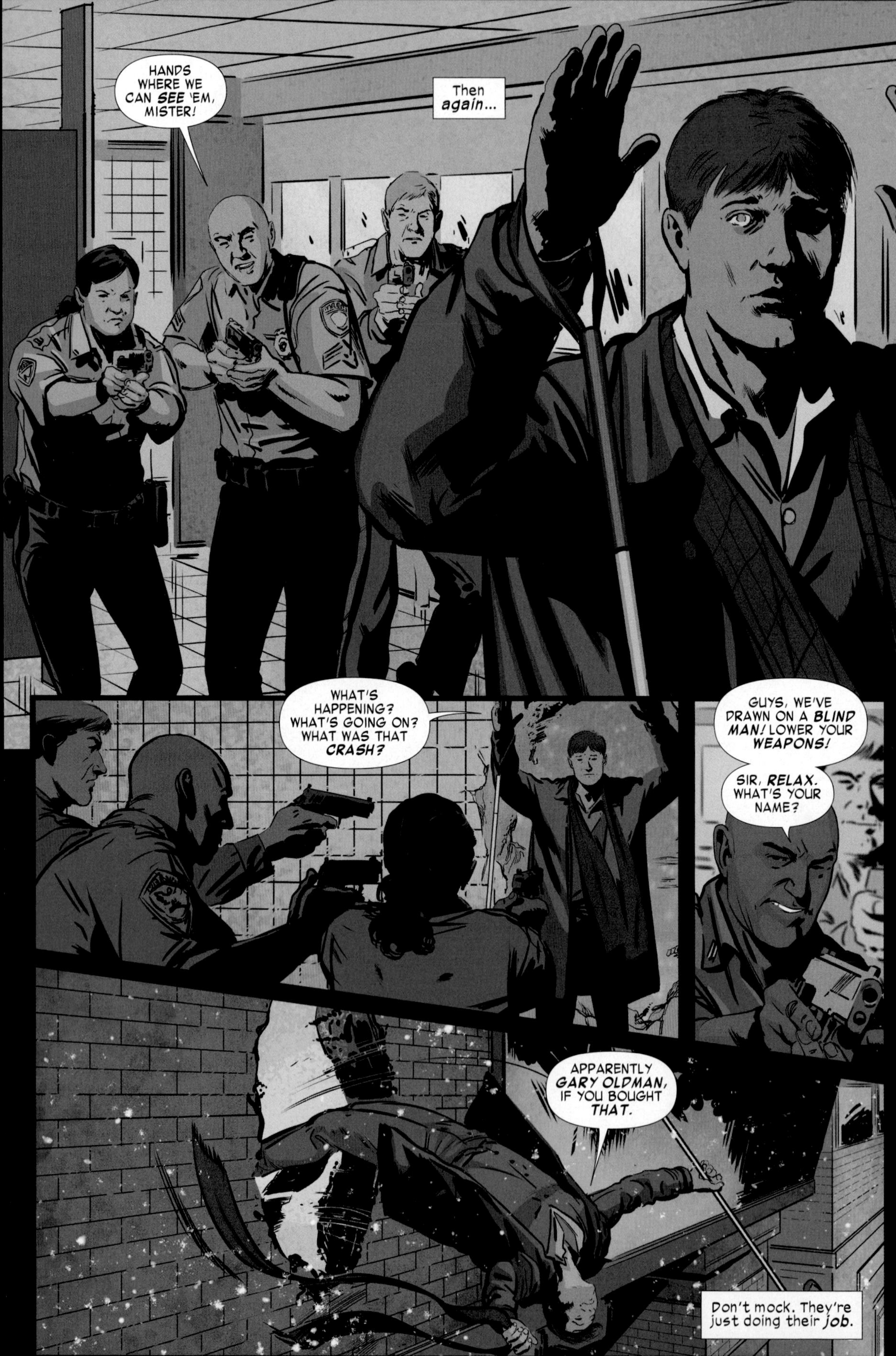
HANDS WHERE WE CAN SEE 'EM, MISTER!
Then again...
WHAT'S HAPPENING? WHAT'S GOING ON? WHAT WAS THAT CRASH?
GUYS, WE'VE DRAWN ON A BLIND MAN! LOWER YOUR WEAPONS!
SIR, RELAX. WHAT'S YOUR NAME?
APPARENTLY GARY OLDMAN, IF YOU BOUGHT THAT.
Don't mock. They're just doing their job.

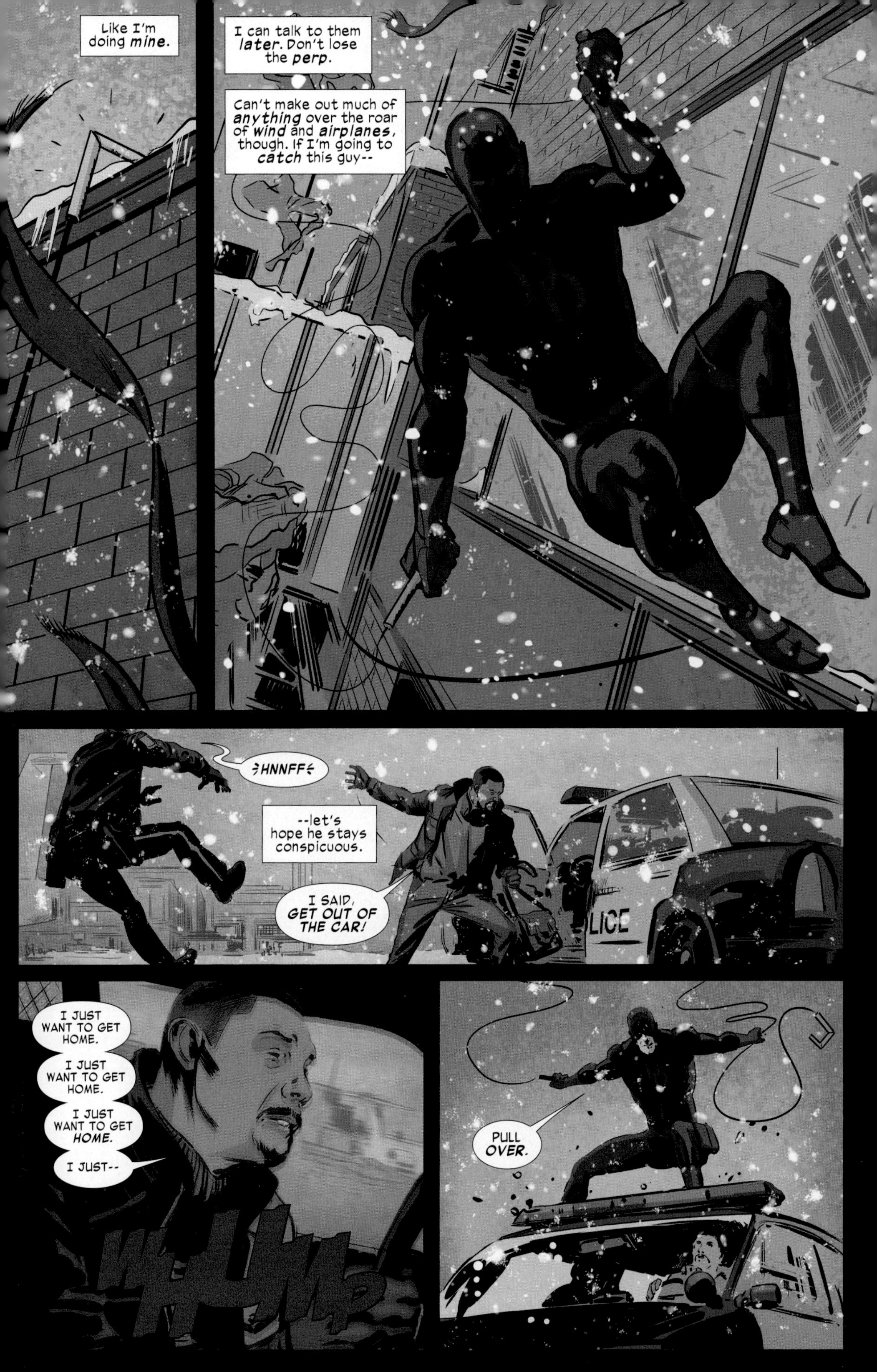

Like I'm doing *mine*.
I can talk to them *later*. Don't lose the *perp*.
Can't make out much of *anything* over the roar of *wind* and *airplanes*, though. If I'm going to *catch* this guy--
HNNFF
--let's hope he stays conspicuous.
I SAID, GET OUT OF THE CAR!
LICE
I JUST WANT TO GET HOME.
I JUST WANT TO GET HOME.
I JUST WANT TO GET *HOME.*
I JUST--
PULL *OVER.*

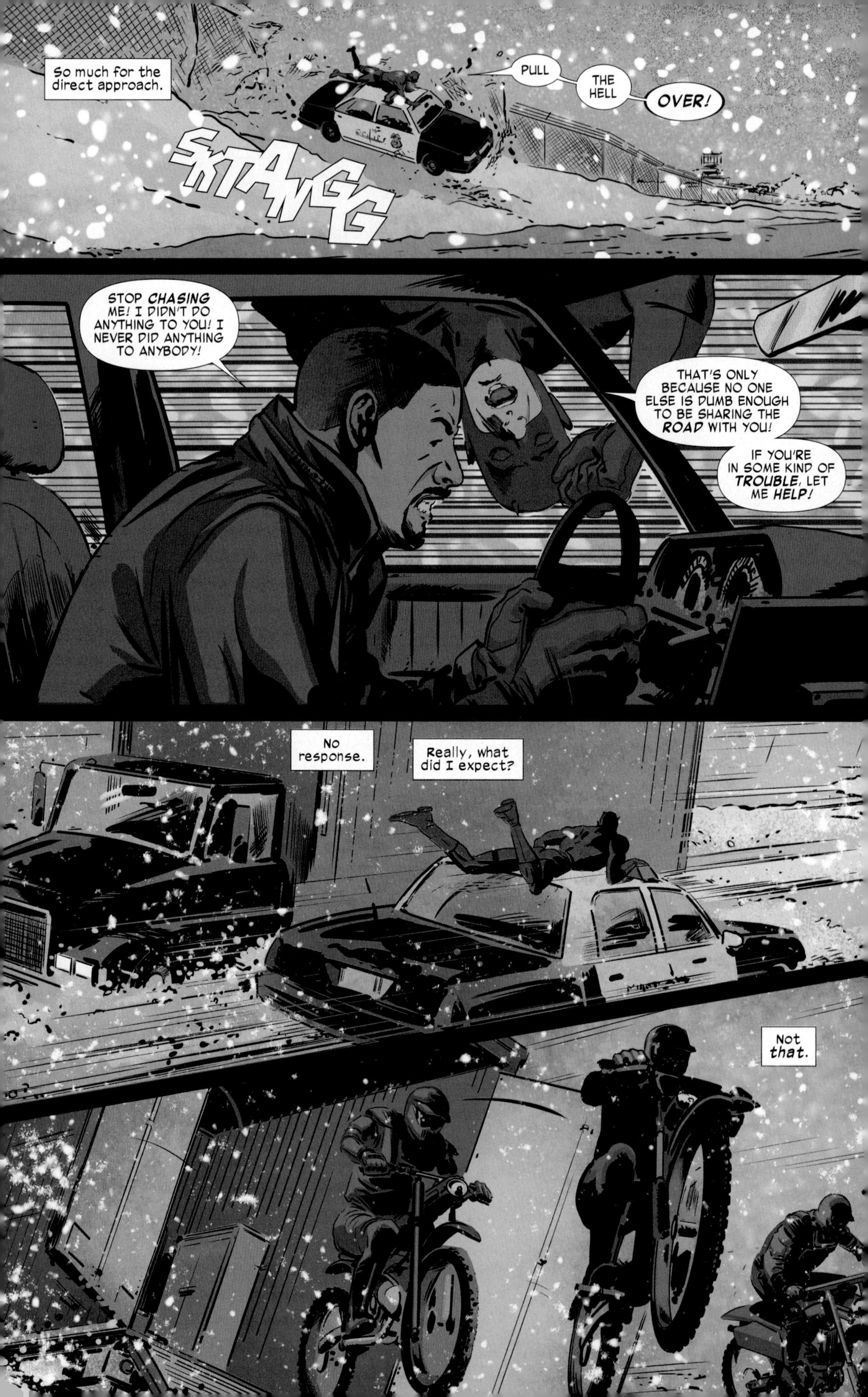
So much for the direct approach.
PULL
THE HELL
OVER!
SKTANGG
STOP CHASING ME! I DIDN'T DO ANYTHING TO YOU! I NEVER DID ANYTHING TO ANYBODY!
THAT'S ONLY BECAUSE NO ONE ELSE IS DUMB ENOUGH TO BE SHARING THE ROAD WITH YOU!
IF YOU'RE IN SOME KIND OF TROUBLE, LET ME HELP!
No response.
Really, what did I expect?
Not that.

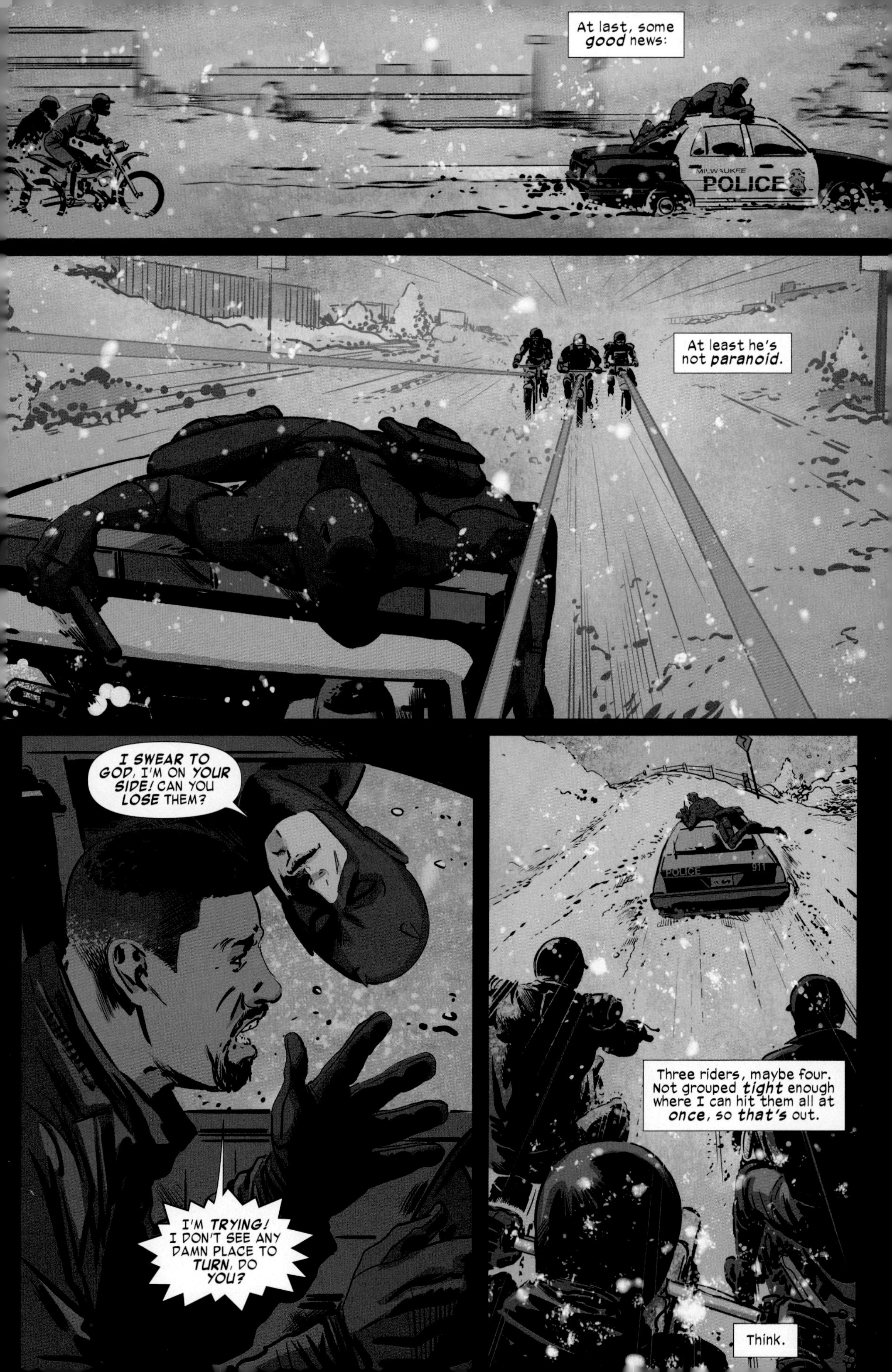

At last, some *good* news:
MILWAUKEE
POLICE
At least he's not *paranoid*.
I SWEAR TO GOD, I'M ON YOUR SIDE! CAN YOU LOSE THEM?
I'M TRYING! I DON'T SEE ANY DAMN PLACE TO TURN, DO YOU?
POLICE
911
Three riders, maybe four. Not grouped *tight* enough where I can hit them all at *once*, so *that's* out.
Think.

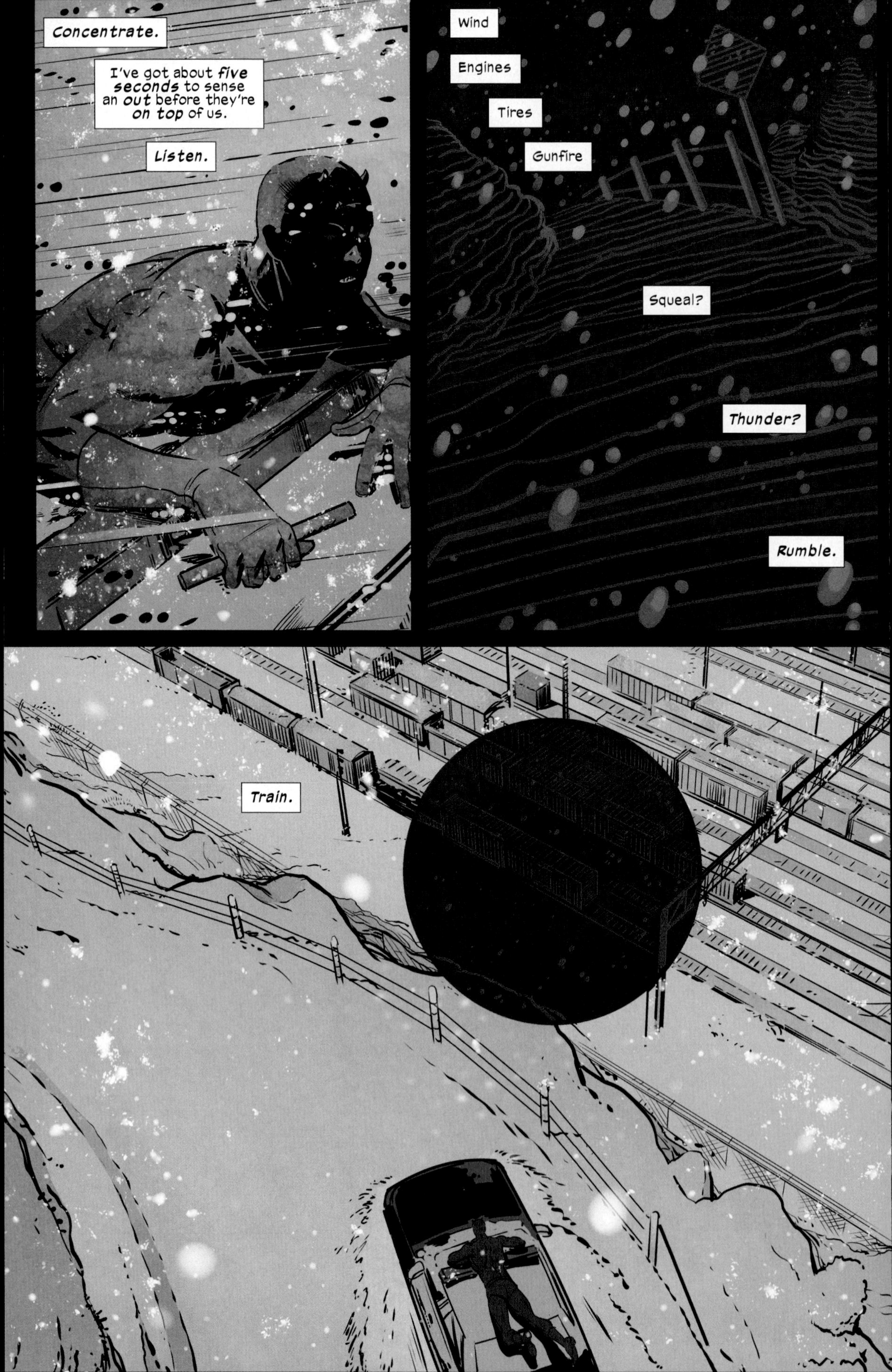
Concentrate.
I've got about five seconds to sense an out before they're on top of us.
Listen.
Wind
Engines
Tires
Gunfire
Squeal?
Thunder?
Rumble.
Train.

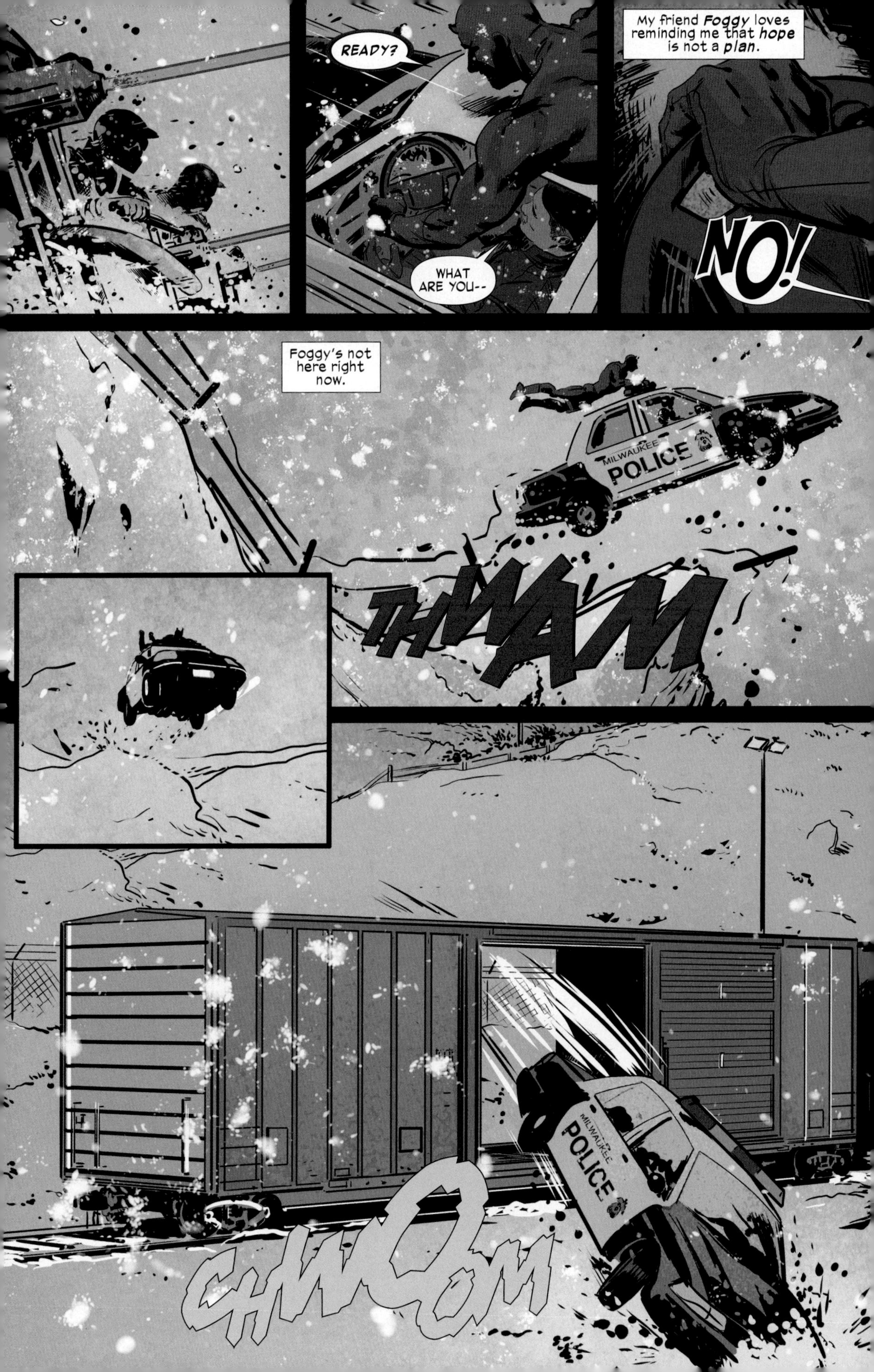
READY?
WHAT ARE YOU--
My friend Foggy loves reminding me that hope is not a plan.
NO!
Foggy's not here right now.
MILWAUKEE POLICE
THWAM
MILWAUKEE POLICE
CHUNOOM

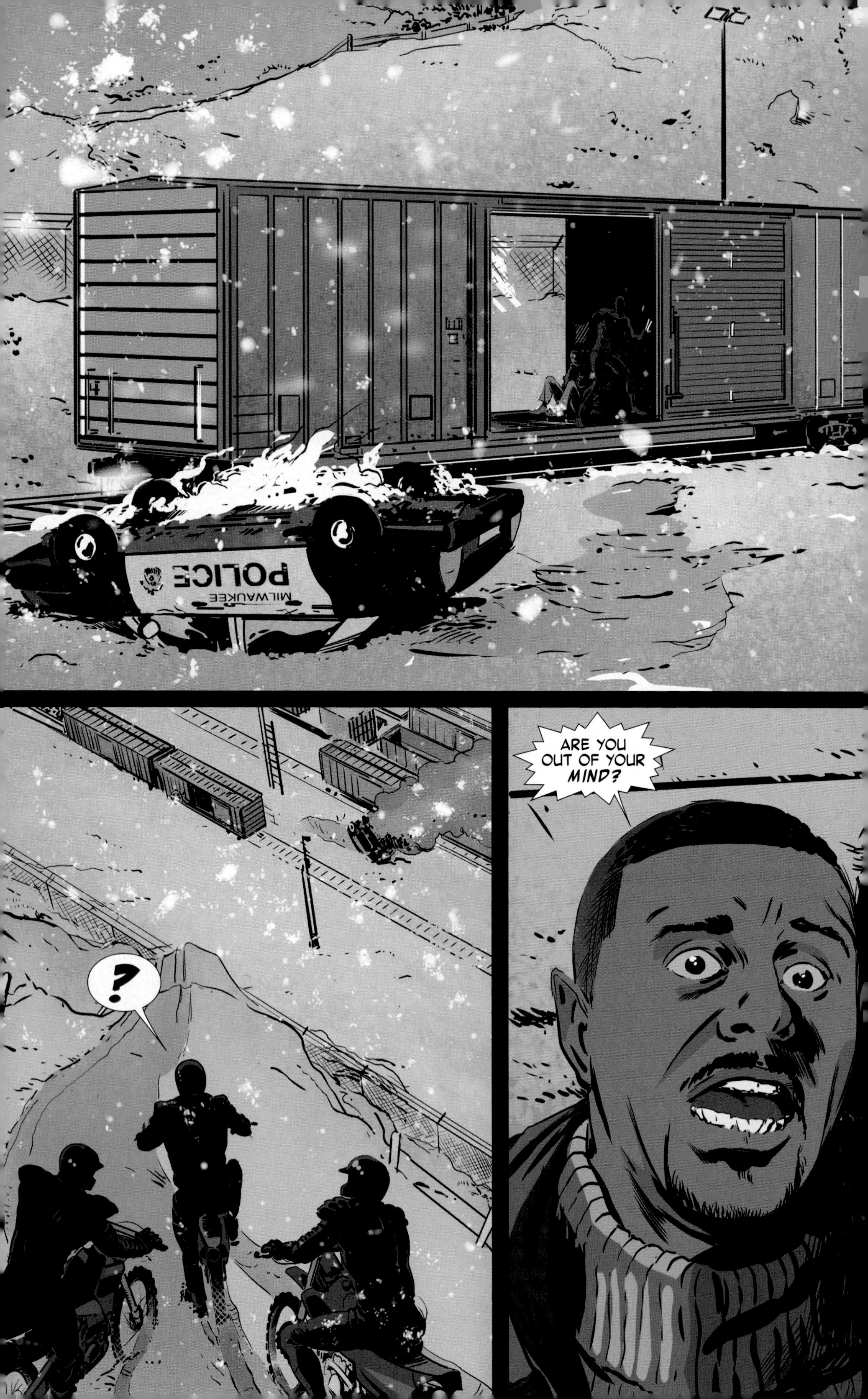
POLICE
MILWAUKEE
?
ARE YOU OUT OF YOUR *MIND?*

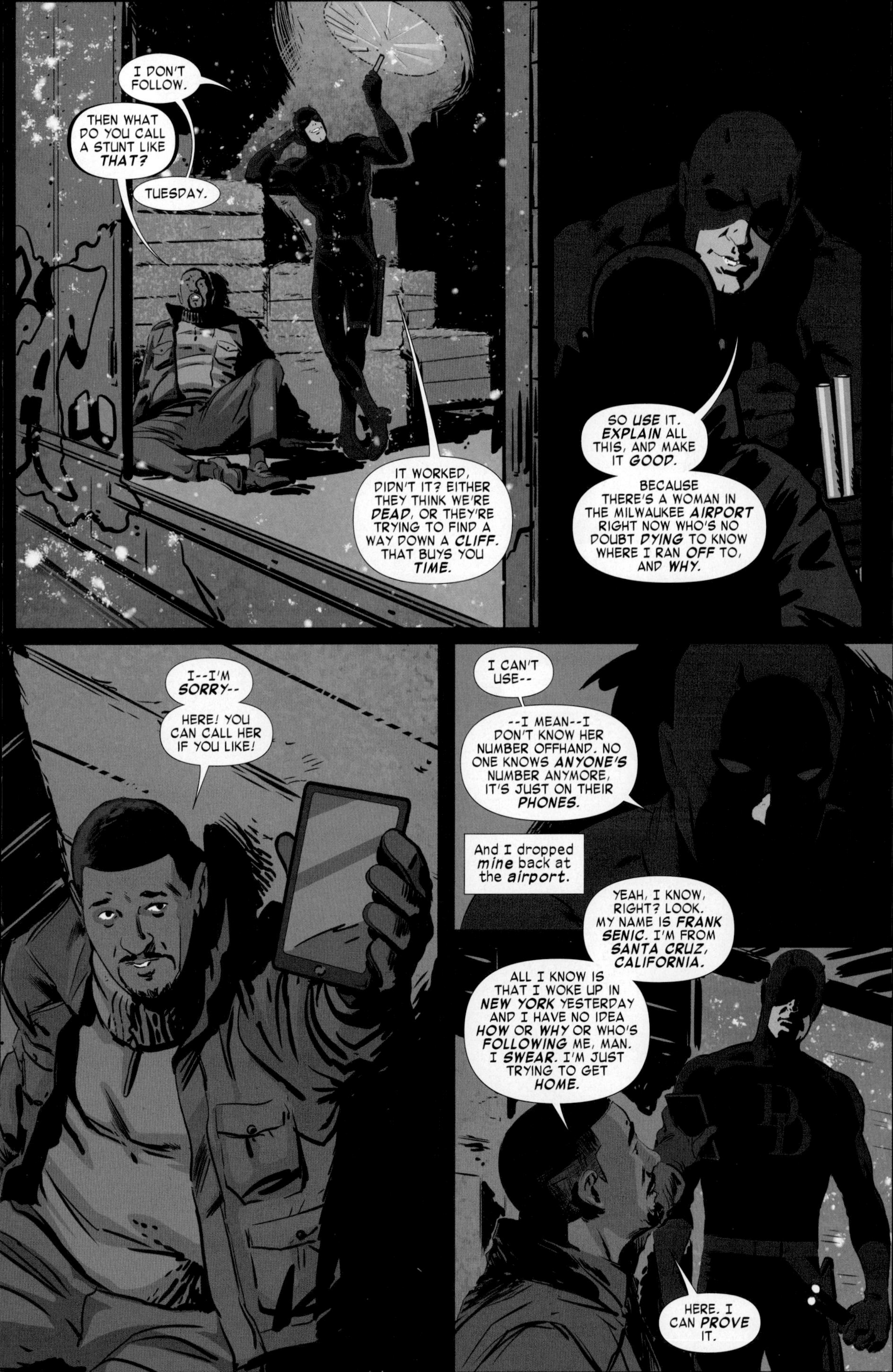
I DON'T FOLLOW.
THEN WHAT DO YOU CALL A STUNT LIKE THAT?
TUESDAY.
IT WORKED, DIDN'T IT? EITHER THEY THINK WE'RE DEAD, OR THEY'RE TRYING TO FIND A WAY DOWN A CLIFF. THAT BUYS YOU TIME.
SO USE IT. EXPLAIN ALL THIS, AND MAKE IT GOOD.
BECAUSE THERE'S A WOMAN IN THE MILWAUKEE AIRPORT RIGHT NOW WHO'S NO DOUBT DYING TO KNOW WHERE I RAN OFF TO, AND WHY.
I--I'M SORRY--
HERE! YOU CAN CALL HER IF YOU LIKE!
I CAN'T USE--
--I MEAN--I DON'T KNOW HER NUMBER OFFHAND. NO ONE KNOWS ANYONE'S NUMBER ANYMORE, IT'S JUST ON THEIR PHONES.
And I dropped mine back at the airport.
YEAH, I KNOW, RIGHT? LOOK. MY NAME IS FRANK SENIC. I'M FROM SANTA CRUZ, CALIFORNIA.
ALL I KNOW IS THAT I WOKE UP IN NEW YORK YESTERDAY AND I HAVE NO IDEA HOW OR WHY OR WHO'S FOLLOWING ME, MAN. I SWEAR. I'M JUST TRYING TO GET HOME.
HERE. I CAN PROVE IT.

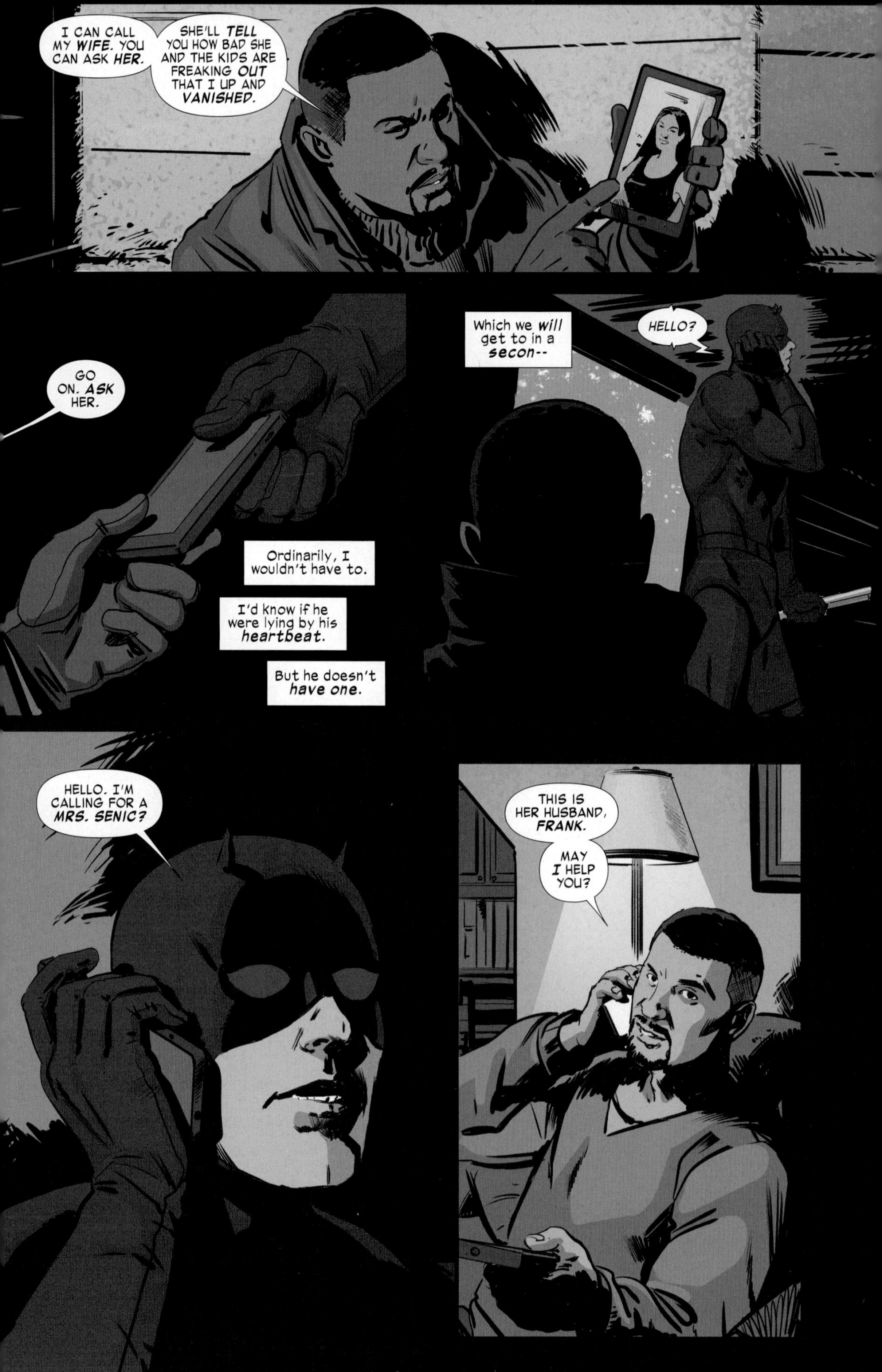
I CAN CALL MY WIFE. YOU CAN ASK HER.
SHE'LL TELL YOU HOW BAD SHE AND THE KIDS ARE FREAKING OUT THAT I UP AND VANISHED.
GO ON. ASK HER.
Ordinarily, I wouldn't have to.
I'd know if he were lying by his heartbeat.
But he doesn't have one.
Which we will get to in a secon--
HELLO?
HELLO. I'M CALLING FOR A MRS. SENIC?
THIS IS HER HUSBAND, FRANK.
MAY I HELP YOU?

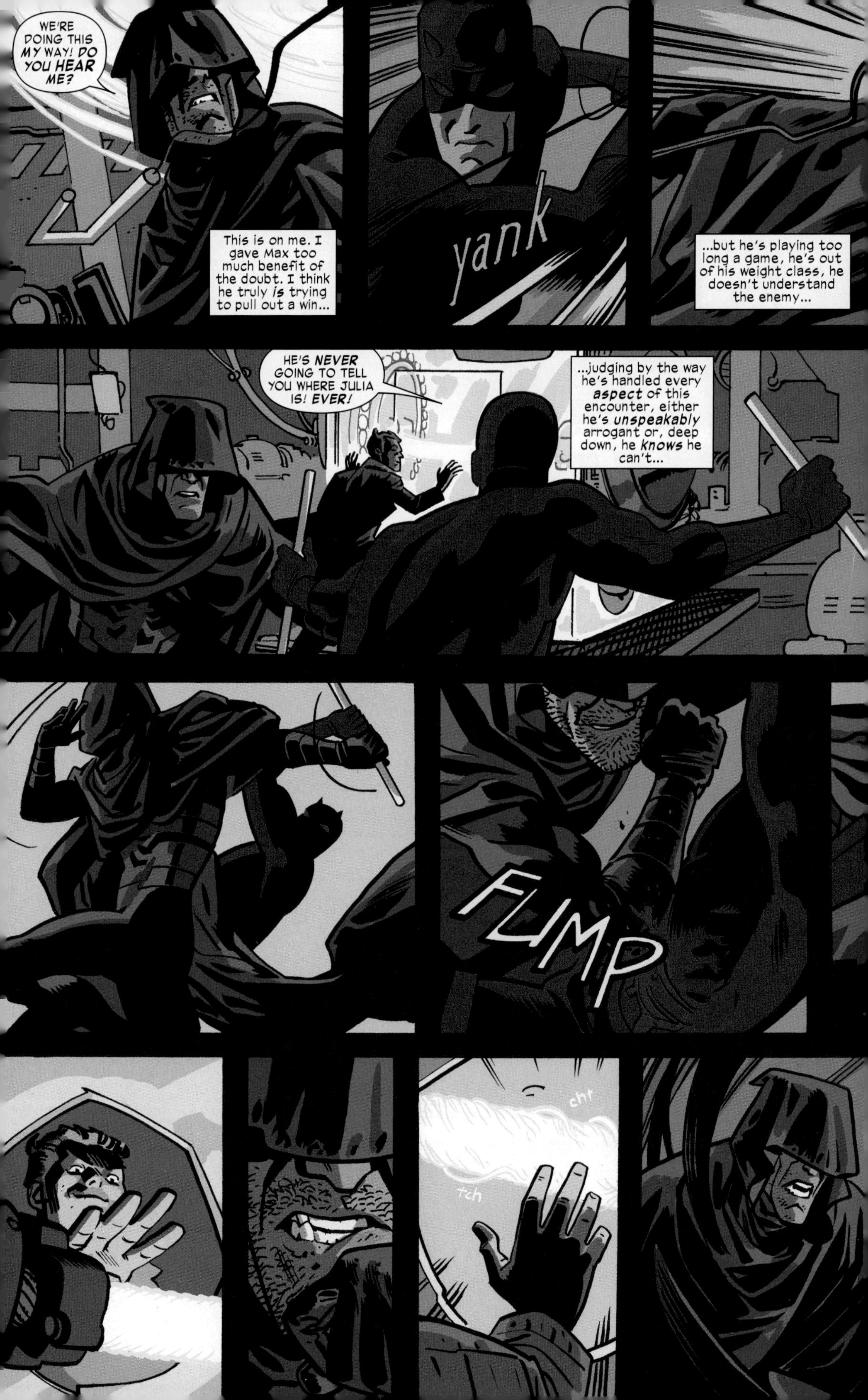
WE'RE DOING THIS MY WAY! DO YOU HEAR ME?
This is on me. I gave Max too much benefit of the doubt. I think he truly is trying to pull out a win...
yank
...but he's playing too long a game, he's out of his weight class, he doesn't understand the enemy...
HE'S NEVER GOING TO TELL YOU WHERE JULIA IS! EVER!
...judging by the way he's handled every aspect of this encounter, either he's unspeakably arrogant or, deep down, he knows he can't...
FUMP
cht
tch

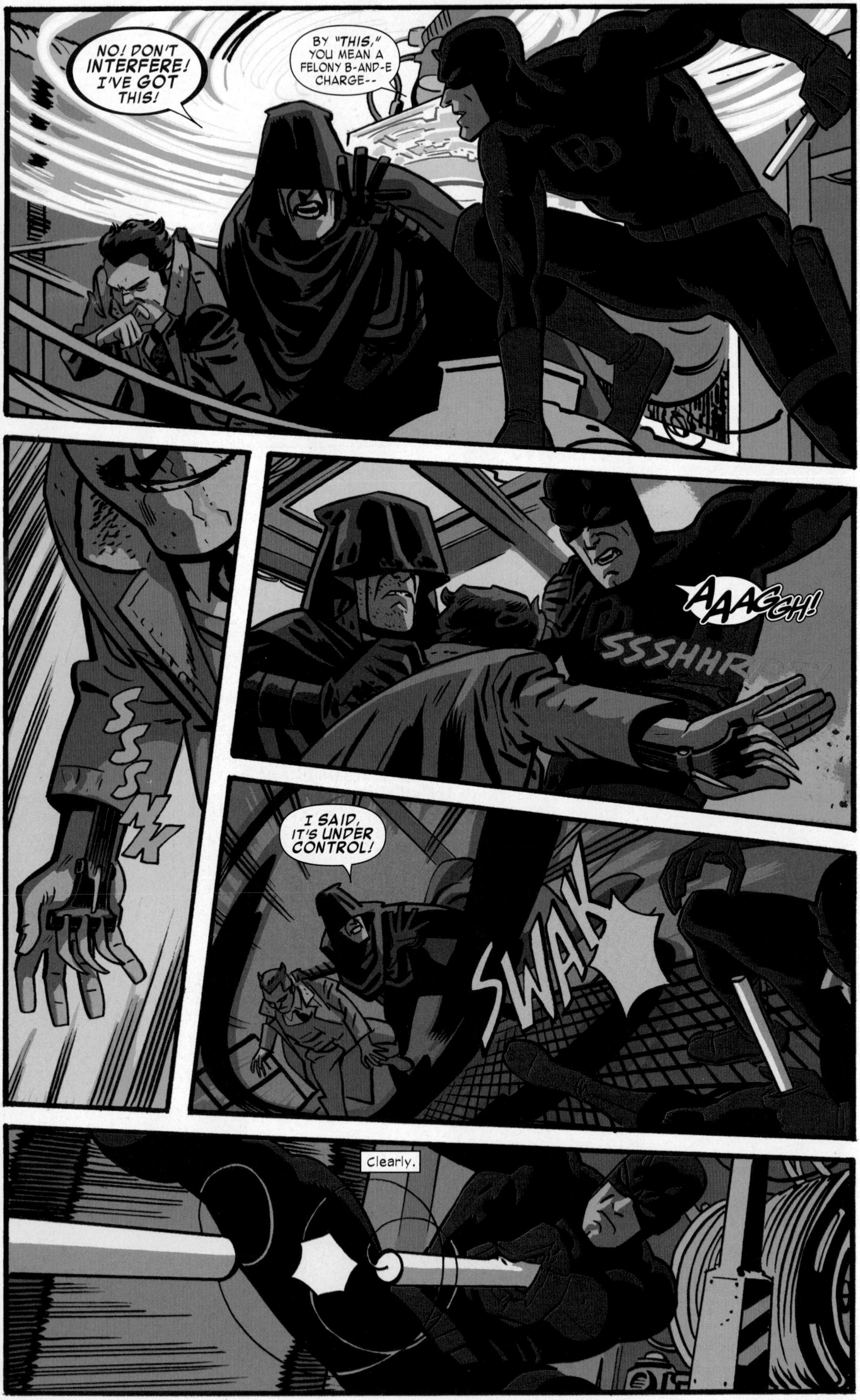
NO! DON'T INTERFERE! I'VE GOT THIS!
BY "THIS," YOU MEAN A FELONY B-AND-E CHARGE--
SSSSNK
AAAGCH!
SSSHHR
I SAID, IT'S UNDER CONTROL!
SWAK
Clearly.

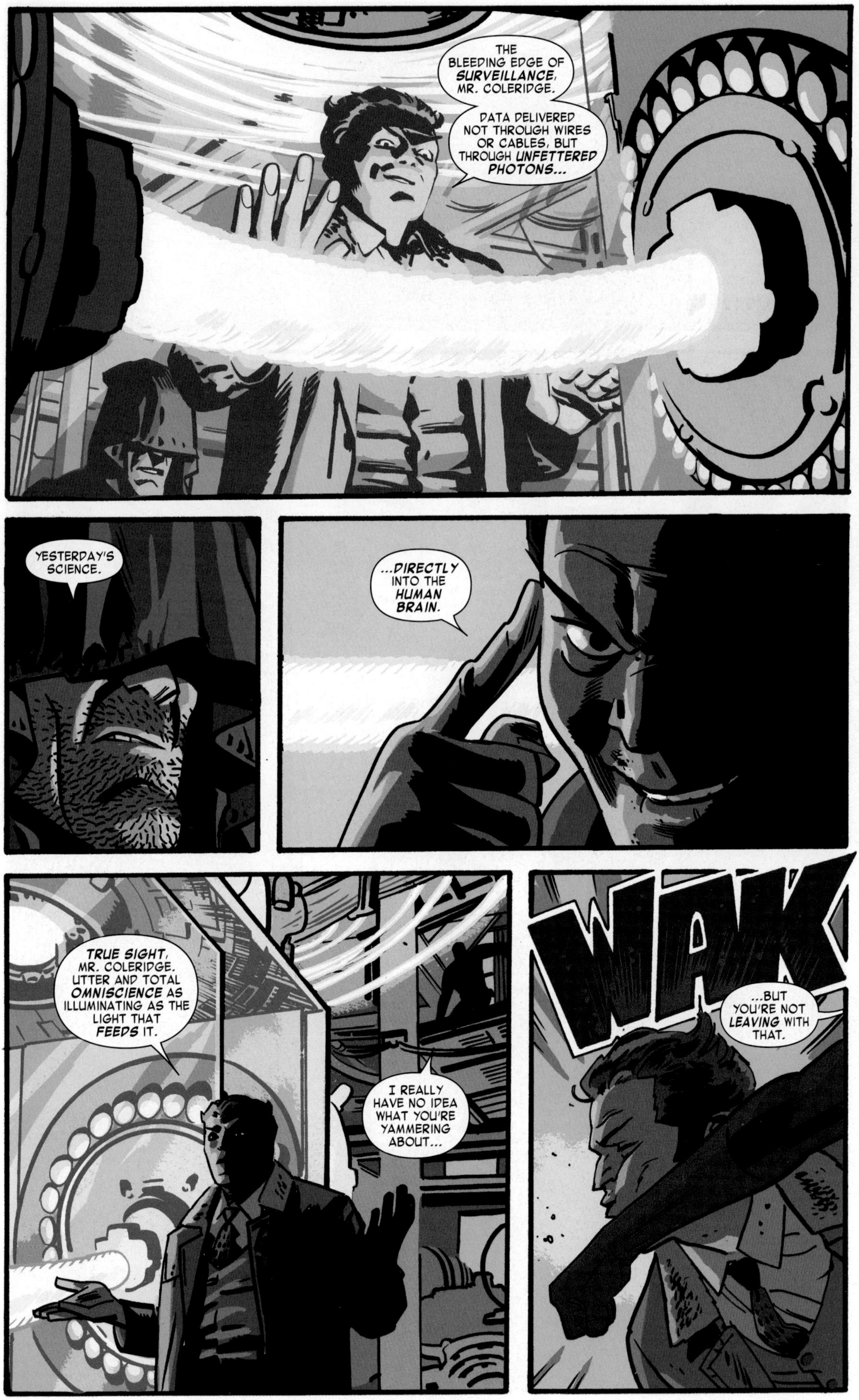

THE BLEEDING EDGE OF SURVEILLANCE, MR. COLERIDGE.
DATA DELIVERED NOT THROUGH WIRES OR CABLES, BUT THROUGH UNFETTERED PHOTONS...
YESTERDAY'S SCIENCE.
...DIRECTLY INTO THE HUMAN BRAIN.
TRUE SIGHT, MR. COLERIDGE. UTTER AND TOTAL OMNISCIENCE AS ILLUMINATING AS THE LIGHT THAT FEEDS IT.
I REALLY HAVE NO IDEA WHAT YOU'RE YAMMERING ABOUT...
WAK
...BUT YOU'RE NOT LEAVING WITH THAT.

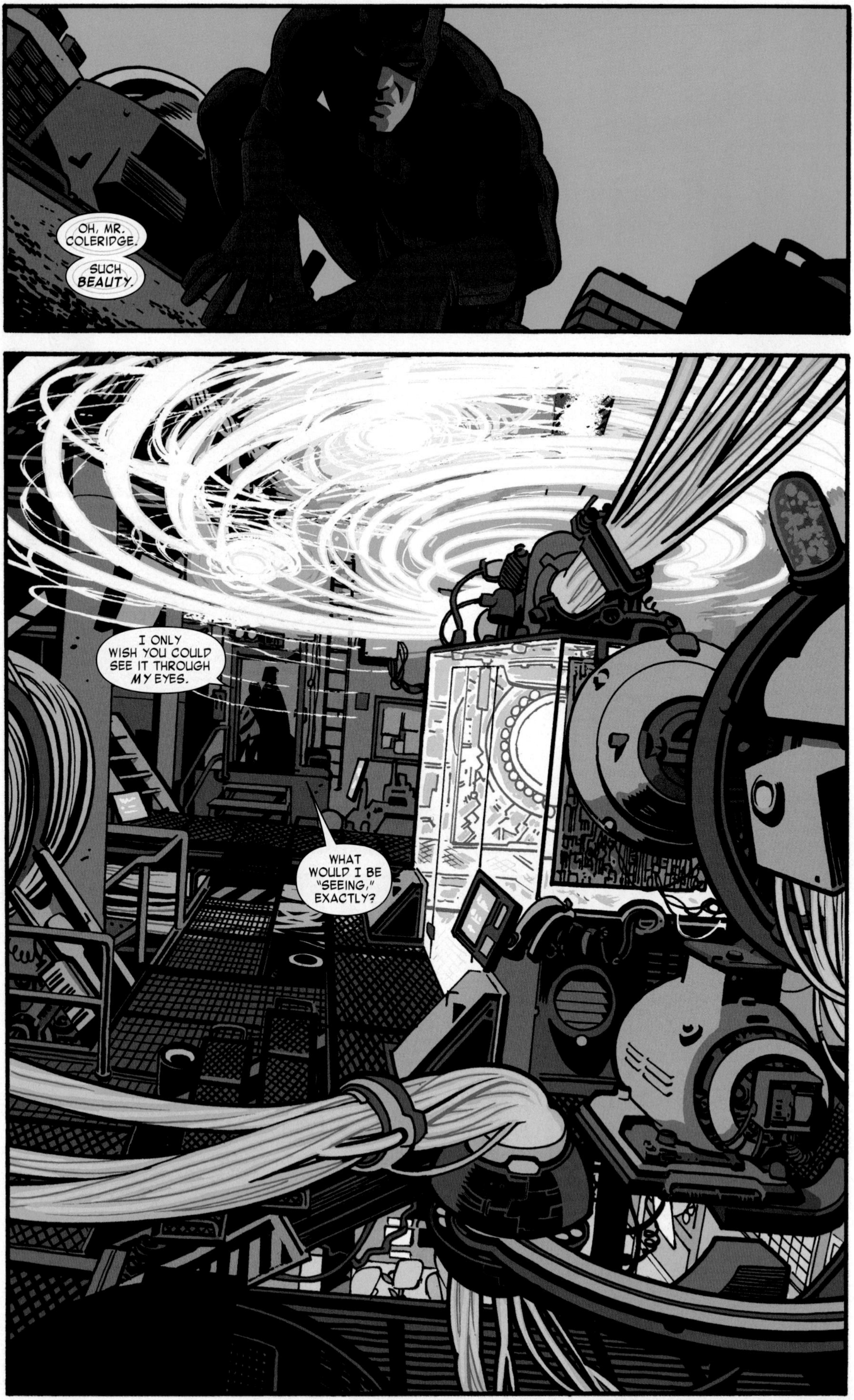
OH, MR. COLERIDGE.
SUCH BEAUTY.
I ONLY WISH YOU COULD SEE IT THROUGH MY EYES.
WHAT WOULD I BE "SEEING," EXACTLY?

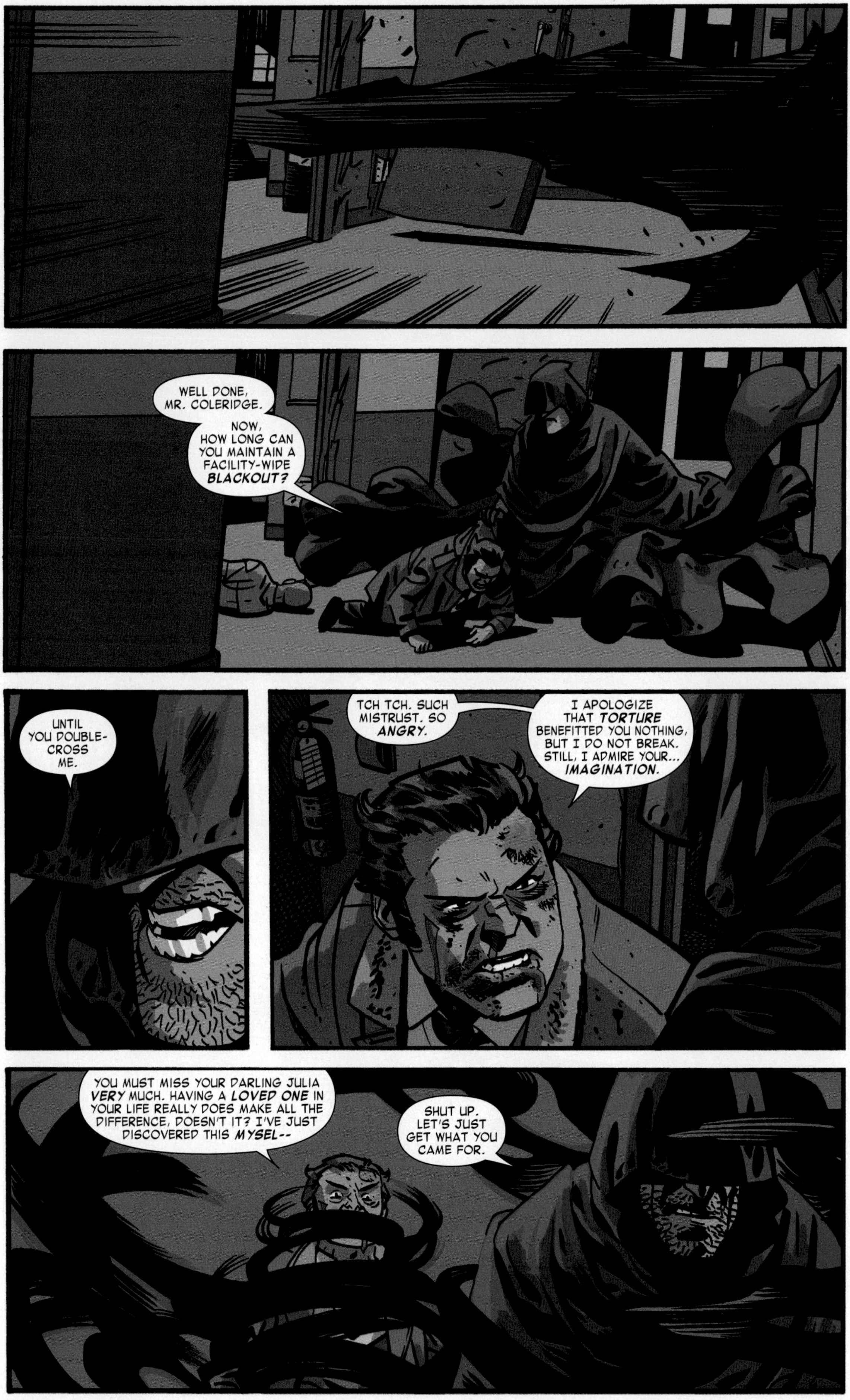
WELL DONE, MR. COLERIDGE.
NOW, HOW LONG CAN YOU MAINTAIN A FACILITY-WIDE **BLACKOUT?**
UNTIL YOU DOUBLE-CROSS ME.
TCH TCH. SUCH MISTRUST. SO **ANGRY.**
I APOLOGIZE THAT **TORTURE** BENEFITTED YOU NOTHING, BUT I DO NOT BREAK. STILL, I ADMIRE YOUR... **IMAGINATION.**
YOU MUST MISS YOUR DARLING JULIA **VERY** MUCH. HAVING A **LOVED ONE** IN YOUR LIFE REALLY DOES MAKE ALL THE DIFFERENCE, DOESN'T IT? I'VE JUST DISCOVERED THIS **MYSEL--**
SHUT UP. LET'S JUST GET WHAT YOU CAME FOR.

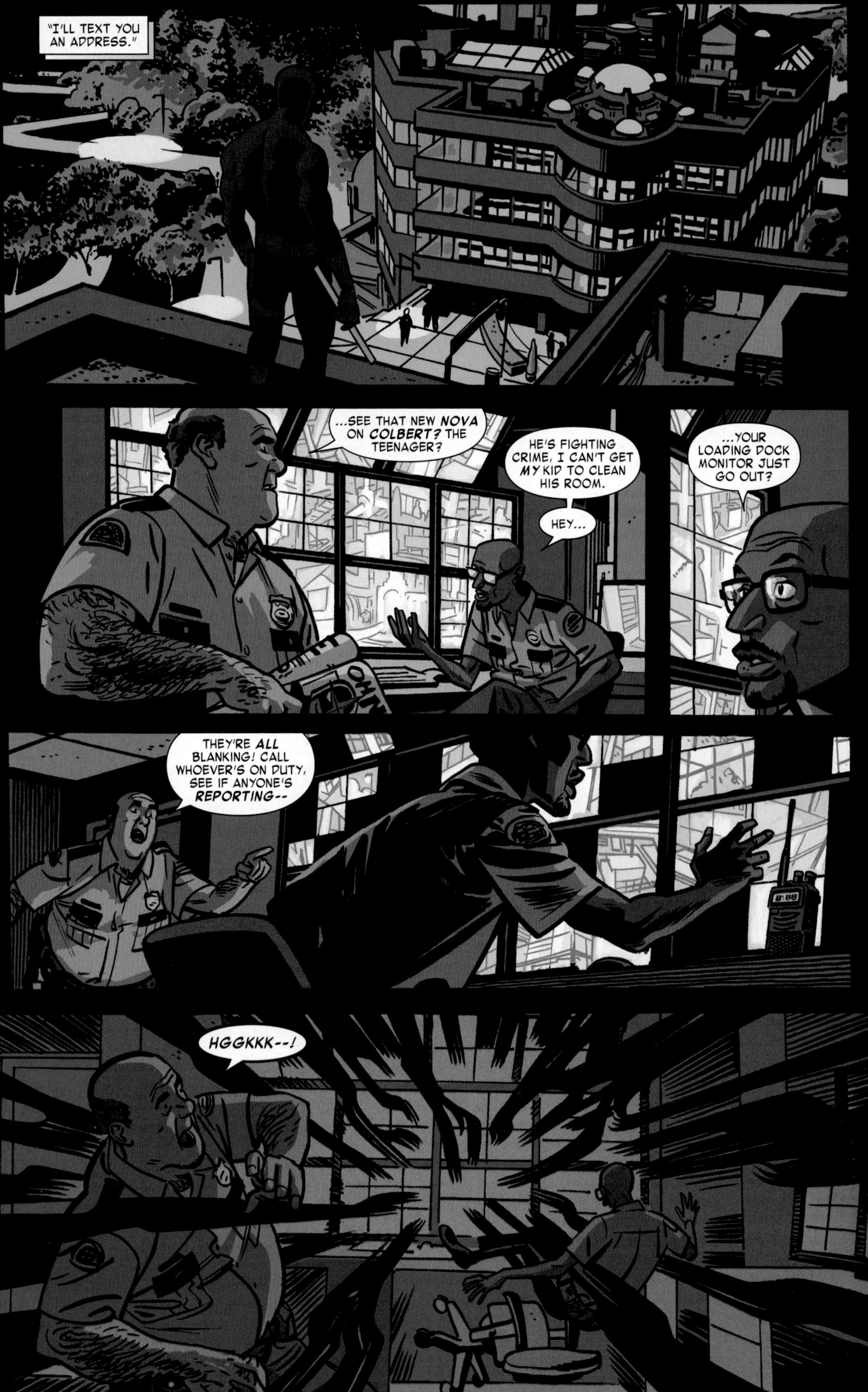
"I'LL TEXT YOU AN ADDRESS."
...SEE THAT NEW *NOVA* ON *COLBERT?* THE TEENAGER?
HE'S FIGHTING CRIME, I CAN'T GET *MY* KID TO CLEAN HIS ROOM.
HEY...
...YOUR LOADING DOCK MONITOR JUST GO OUT?
THEY'RE *ALL* BLANKING! CALL WHOEVER'S ON DUTY, SEE IF ANYONE'S *REPORTING--*
HGGKKK--!

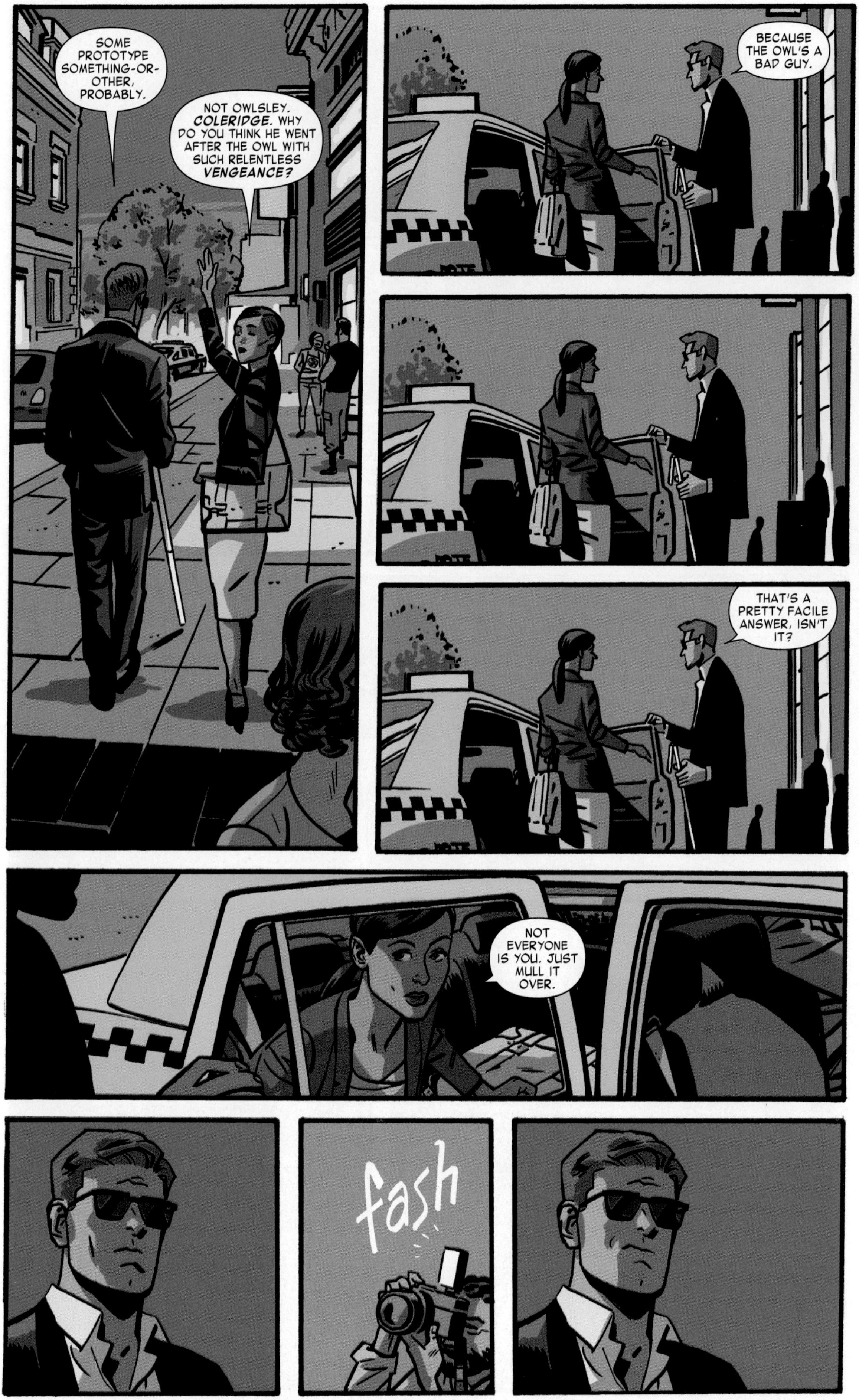
SOME PROTOTYPE SOMETHING-OR-OTHER, PROBABLY.
NOT OWLSLEY. ***COLERIDGE.*** WHY DO YOU THINK HE WENT AFTER THE OWL WITH SUCH RELENTLESS ***VENGEANCE?***
BECAUSE THE OWL'S A BAD GUY.
THAT'S A PRETTY FACILE ANSWER, ISN'T IT?
NOT EVERYONE IS YOU. JUST MULL IT OVER.
fash

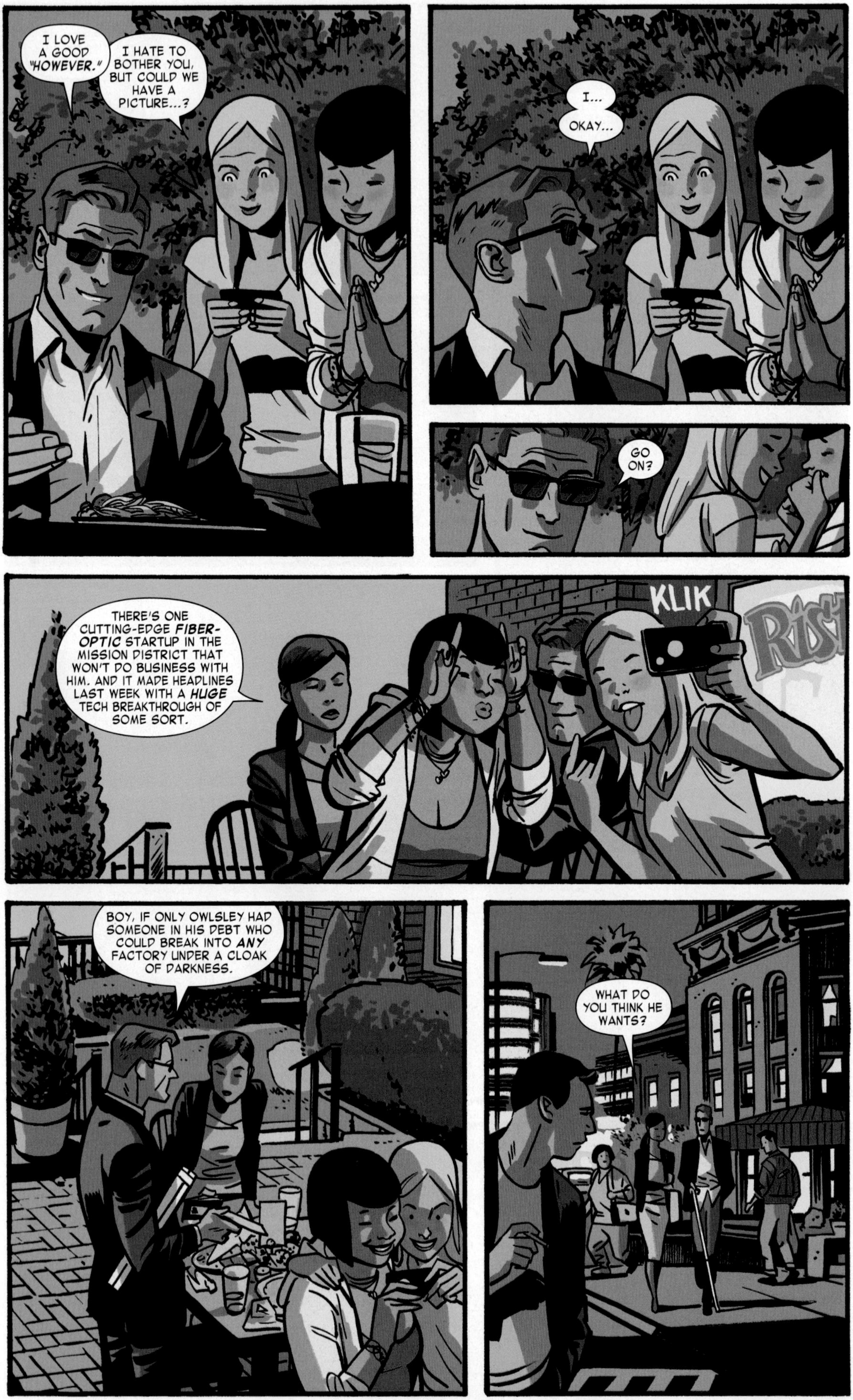
I LOVE A GOOD "HOWEVER."
I HATE TO BOTHER YOU, BUT COULD WE HAVE A PICTURE...?
I...
OKAY...
GO ON?
THERE'S ONE CUTTING-EDGE FIBER-OPTIC STARTUP IN THE MISSION DISTRICT THAT WON'T DO BUSINESS WITH HIM. AND IT MADE HEADLINES LAST WEEK WITH A HUGE TECH BREAKTHROUGH OF SOME SORT.
KLIK
BOY, IF ONLY OWLSLEY HAD SOMEONE IN HIS DEBT WHO COULD BREAK INTO ANY FACTORY UNDER A CLOAK OF DARKNESS.
WHAT DO YOU THINK HE WANTS?

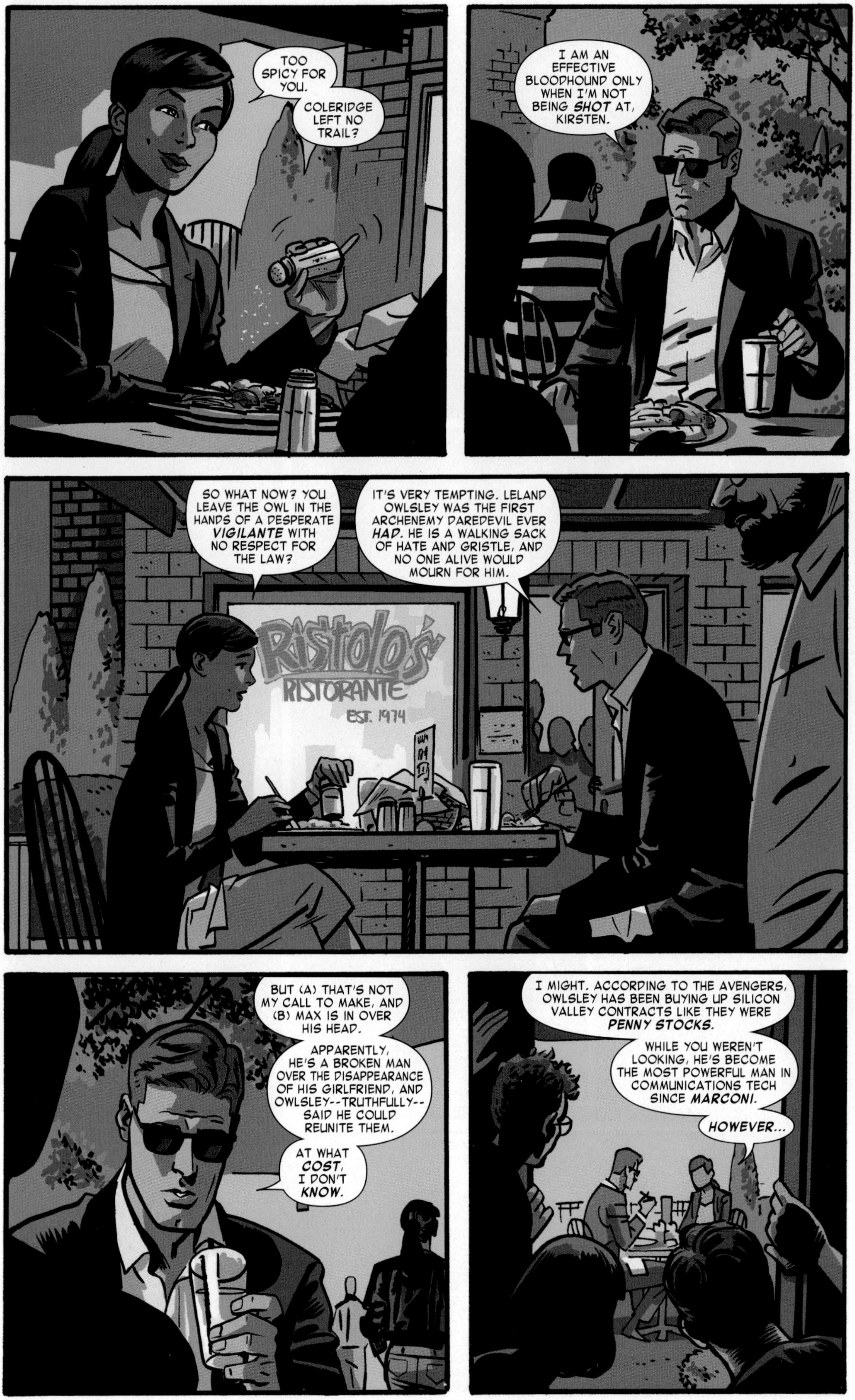
TOO SPICY FOR YOU.
COLERIDGE LEFT NO TRAIL?
I AM AN EFFECTIVE BLOODHOUND ONLY WHEN I'M NOT BEING *SHOT* AT, KIRSTEN.
SO WHAT NOW? YOU LEAVE THE OWL IN THE HANDS OF A DESPERATE *VIGILANTE* WITH NO RESPECT FOR THE LAW?
IT'S VERY TEMPTING. LELAND OWLSLEY WAS THE FIRST ARCHENEMY DAREDEVIL EVER *HAD*. HE IS A WALKING SACK OF HATE AND GRISTLE, AND NO ONE ALIVE WOULD MOURN FOR HIM.
RISTOLO'S RISTORANTE EST. 1974
BUT (A) THAT'S NOT MY CALL TO MAKE, AND (B) MAX IS IN OVER HIS HEAD.
APPARENTLY, HE'S A BROKEN MAN OVER THE DISAPPEARANCE OF HIS GIRLFRIEND, AND OWLSLEY--TRUTHFULLY--SAID HE COULD REUNITE THEM.
AT WHAT *COST*, I DON'T *KNOW*.
I MIGHT. ACCORDING TO THE AVENGERS, OWLSLEY HAS BEEN BUYING UP SILICON VALLEY CONTRACTS LIKE THEY WERE *PENNY STOCKS*.
WHILE YOU WEREN'T LOOKING, HE'S BECOME THE MOST POWERFUL MAN IN COMMUNICATIONS TECH SINCE *MARCONI*.
HOWEVER...

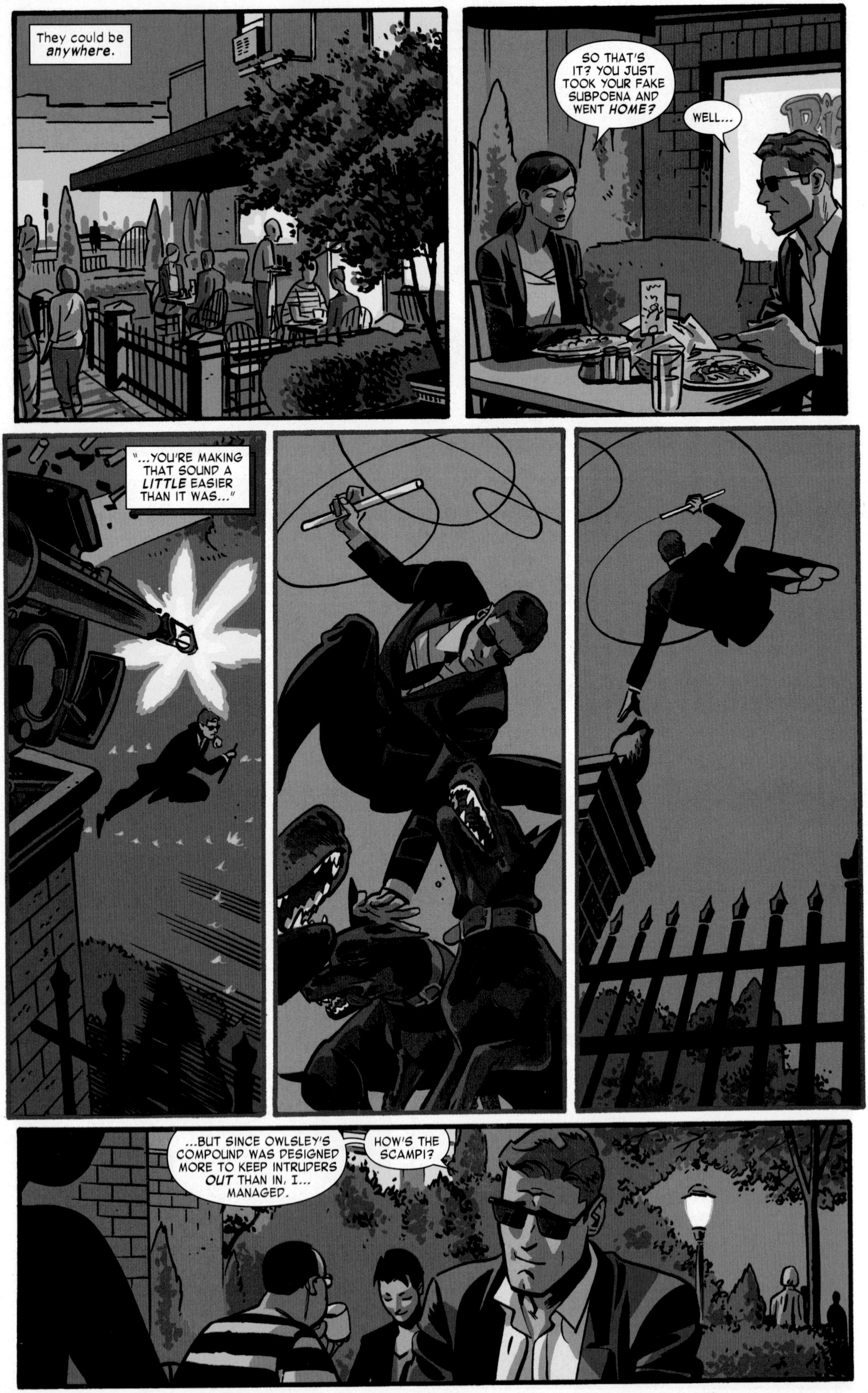
They could be *anywhere*.
SO THAT'S IT? YOU JUST TOOK YOUR FAKE SUBPOENA AND WENT *HOME?*
WELL...
"...YOU'RE MAKING THAT SOUND A *LITTLE* EASIER THAN IT WAS..."
...BUT SINCE OWLSLEY'S COMPOUND WAS DESIGNED MORE TO KEEP INTRUDERS *OUT* THAN IN, I... MANAGED.
HOW'S THE SCAMPI?

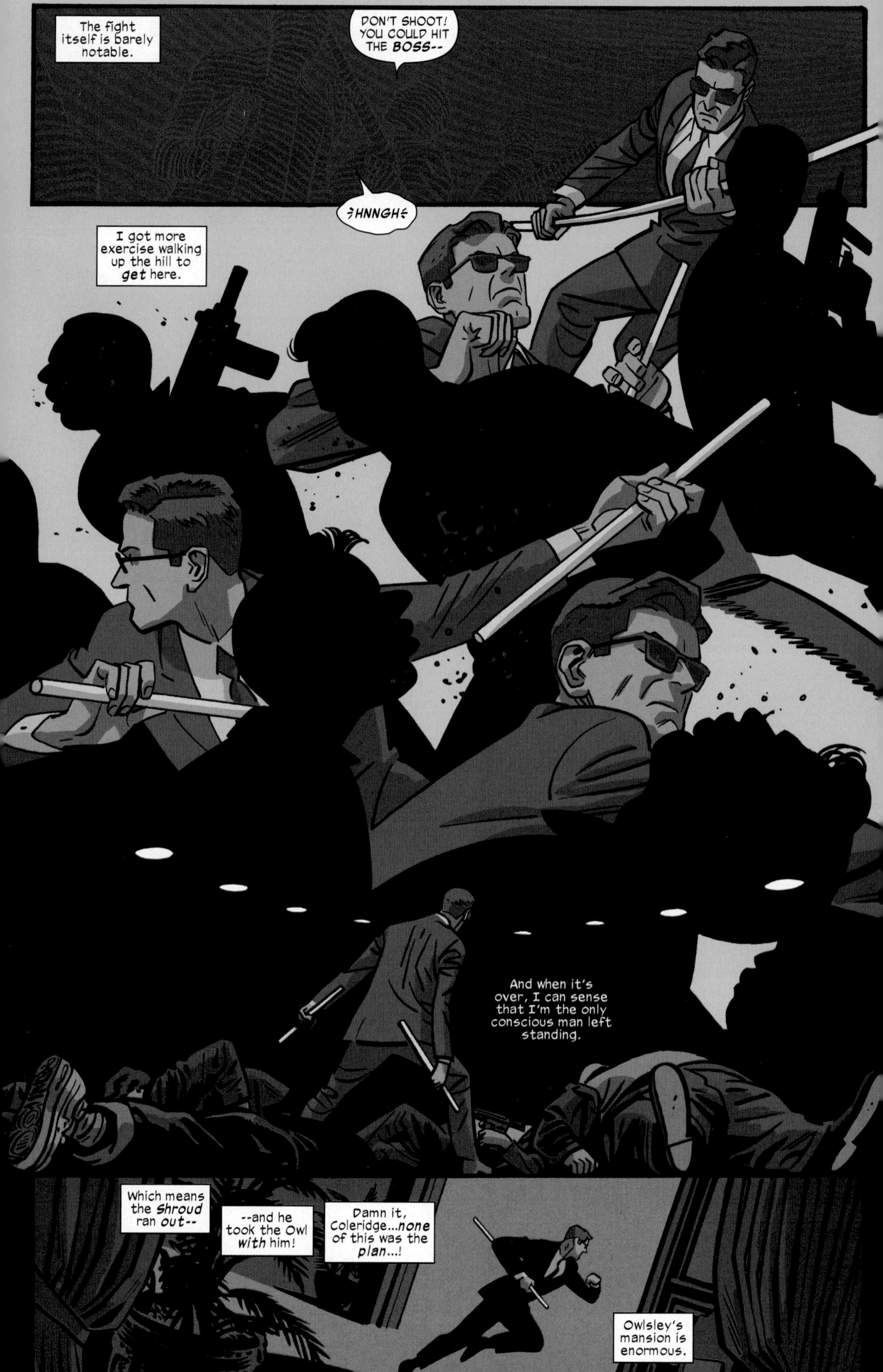
The fight itself is barely notable.
DON'T SHOOT! YOU COULD HIT THE **BOSS**--
HNNGH
I got more exercise walking up the hill to ***get*** here.
And when it's over, I can sense that I'm the only conscious man left standing.
Which means the ***Shroud*** ran ***out***--
--and he took the Owl ***with*** him!
Damn it, Coleridge...***none*** of this was the ***plan***...!
Owlsley's mansion is enormous.

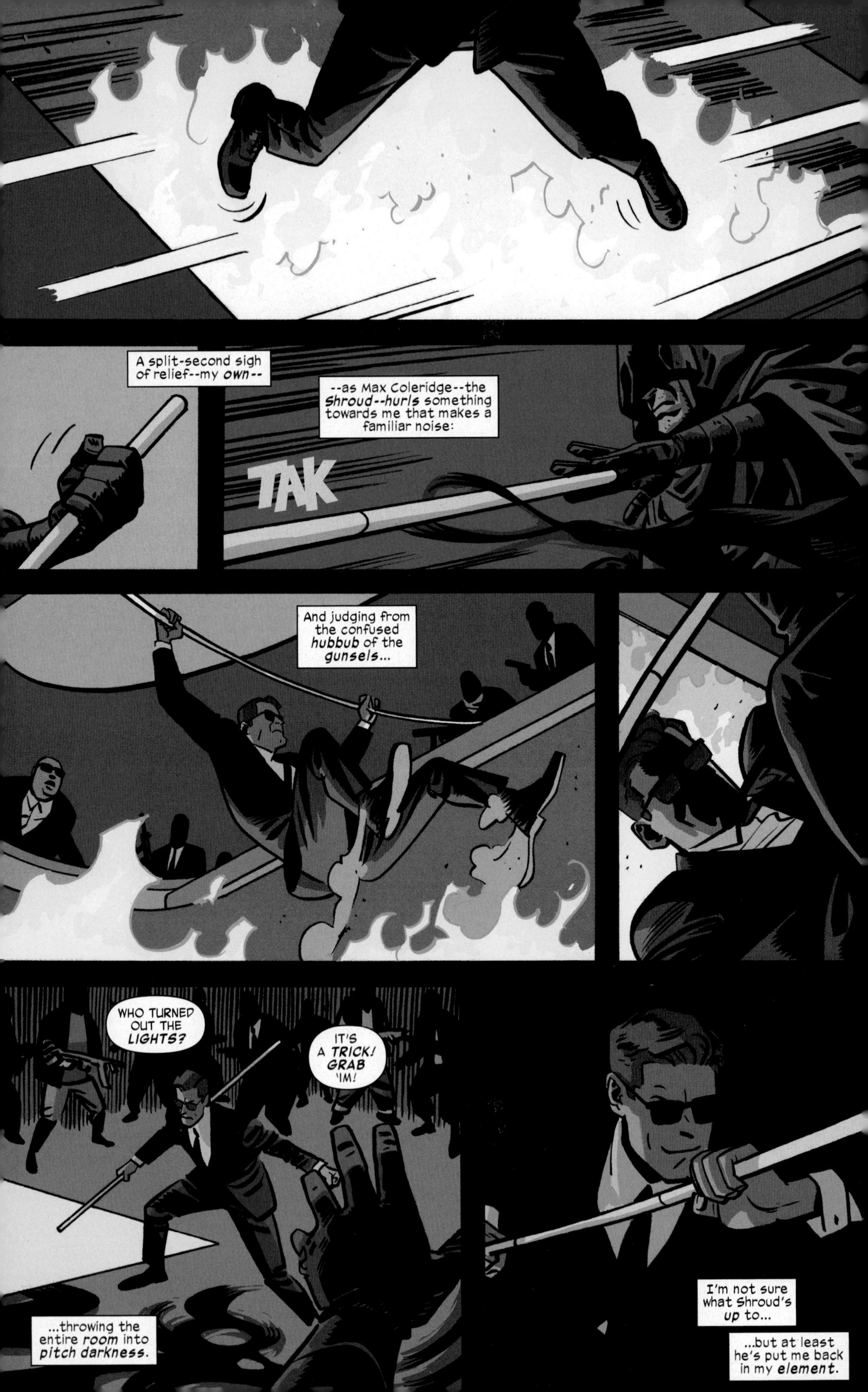
A split-second sigh of relief--my *own*--
--as Max Coleridge--the *Shroud--hurls* something towards me that makes a familiar noise:
TAK
And judging from the confused *hubbub* of the *gunsels*...
WHO TURNED OUT THE *LIGHTS?*
IT'S A *TRICK! GRAB* 'IM!
...throwing the entire *room* into *pitch darkness*.
I'm not sure what Shroud's *up* to...
...but at least he's put me back in my *element*.

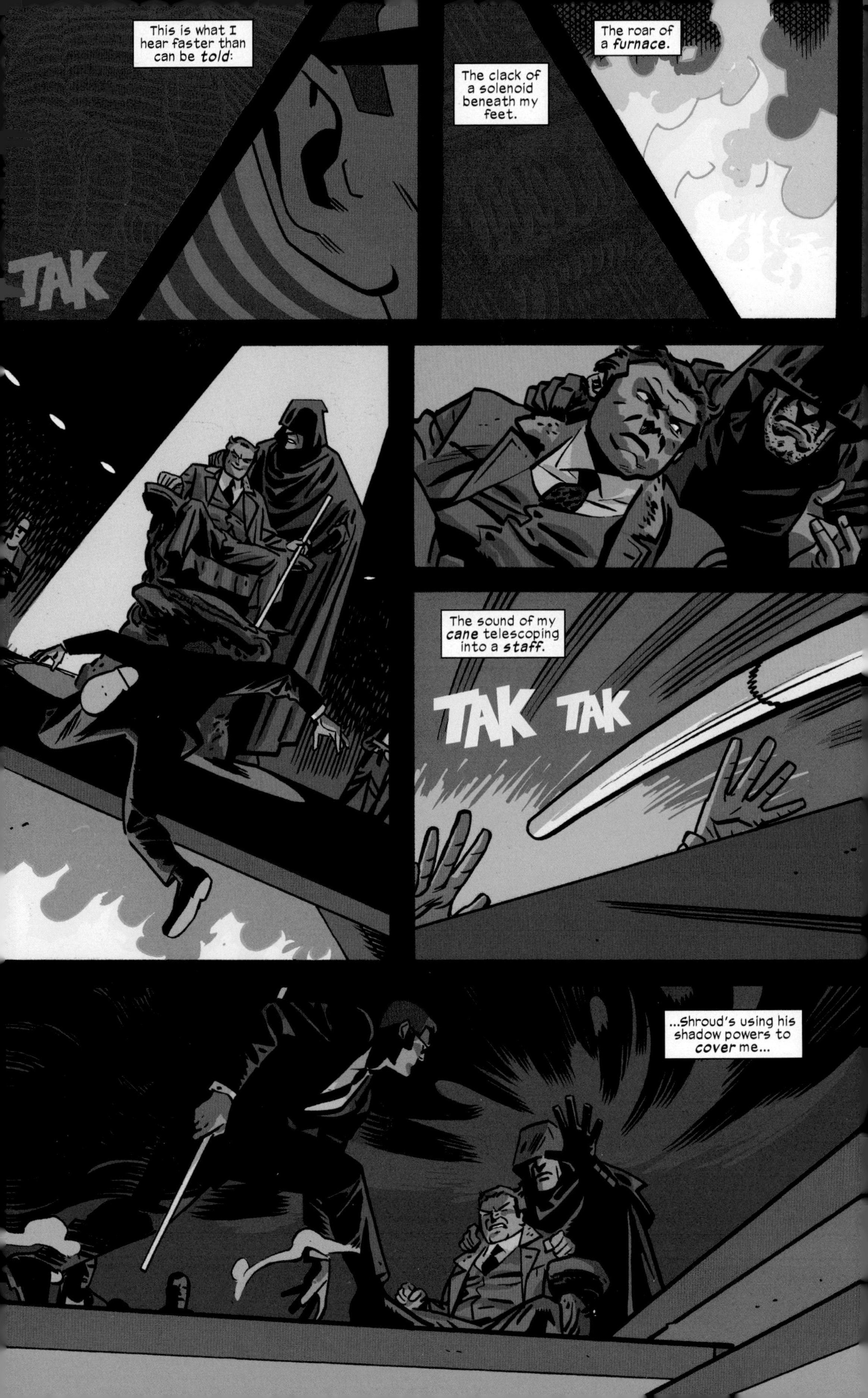
This is what I hear faster than can be *told*:
TAK
The clack of a solenoid beneath my feet.
The roar of a *furnace*.
The sound of my *cane* telescoping into a *staff*.
TAK TAK
...Shroud's using his shadow powers to *cover* me...

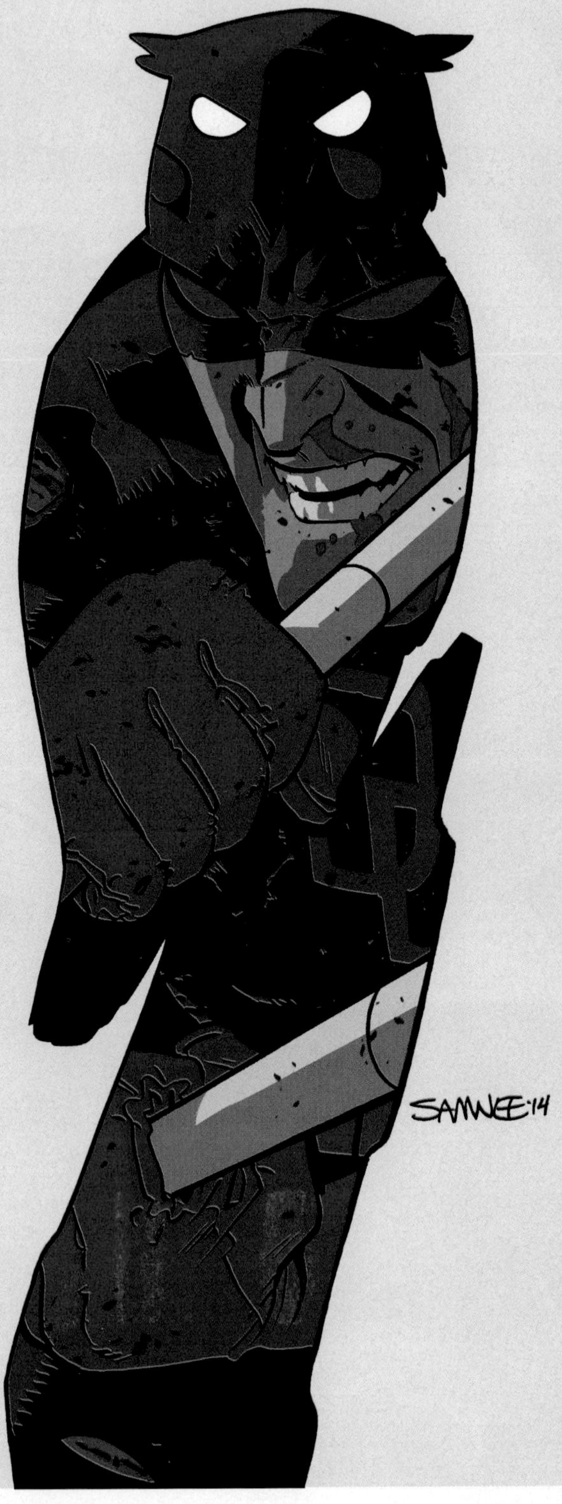
SAMNEE '14

DAREDEVIL #4

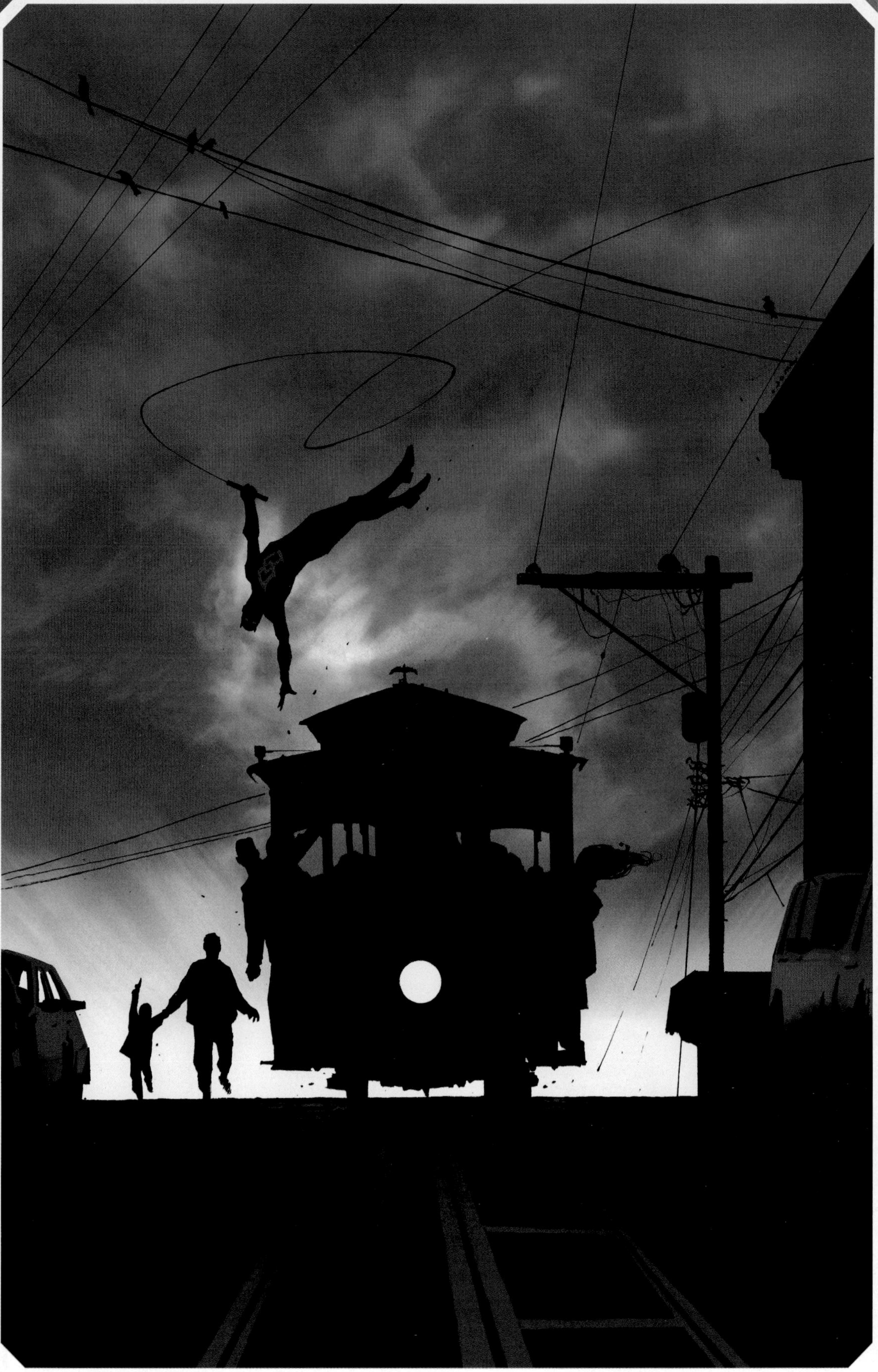

DAREDEVIL #3 VARIANT BY JEROME OPEÑA & MARTE GRACIA

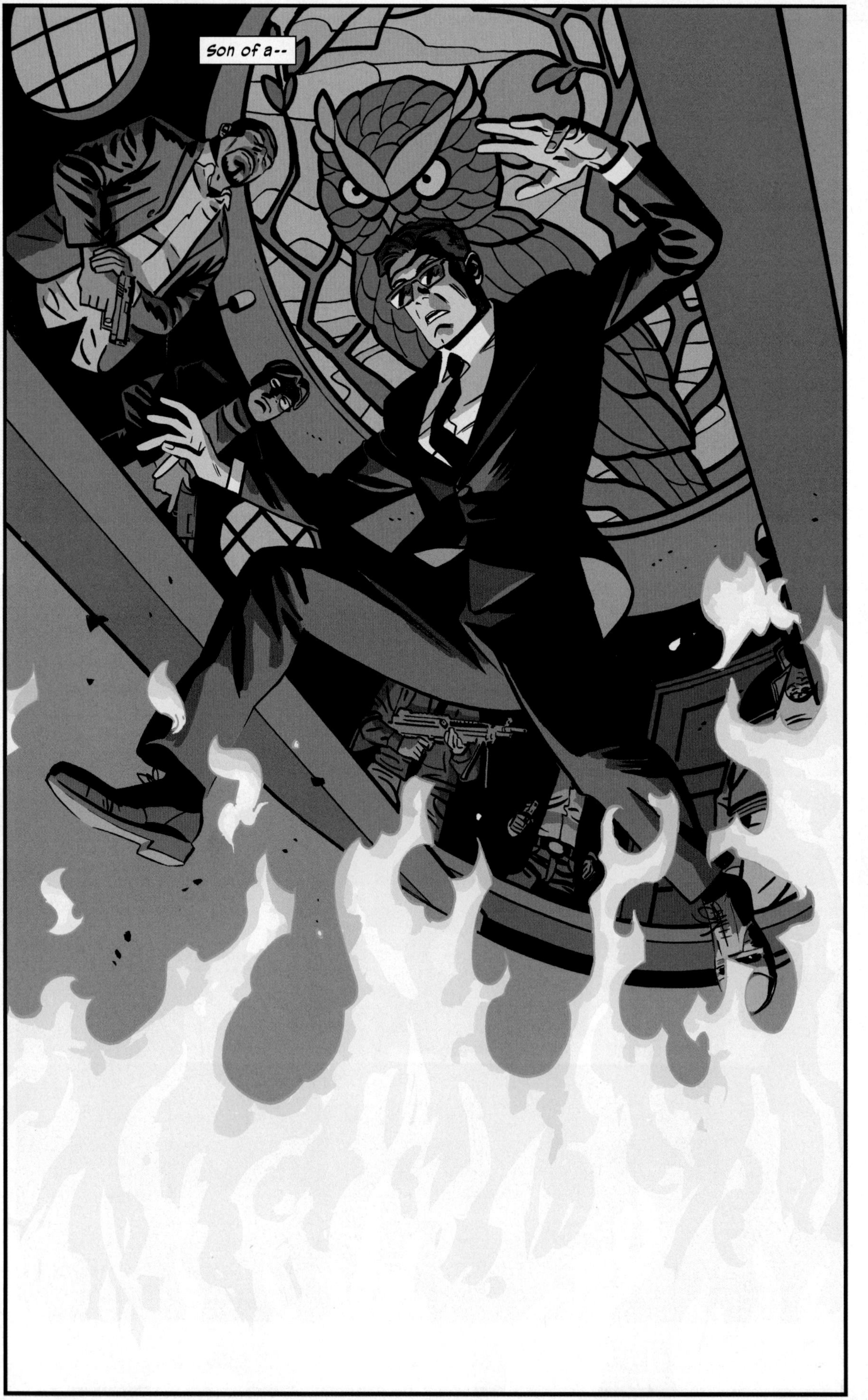
Son of a--

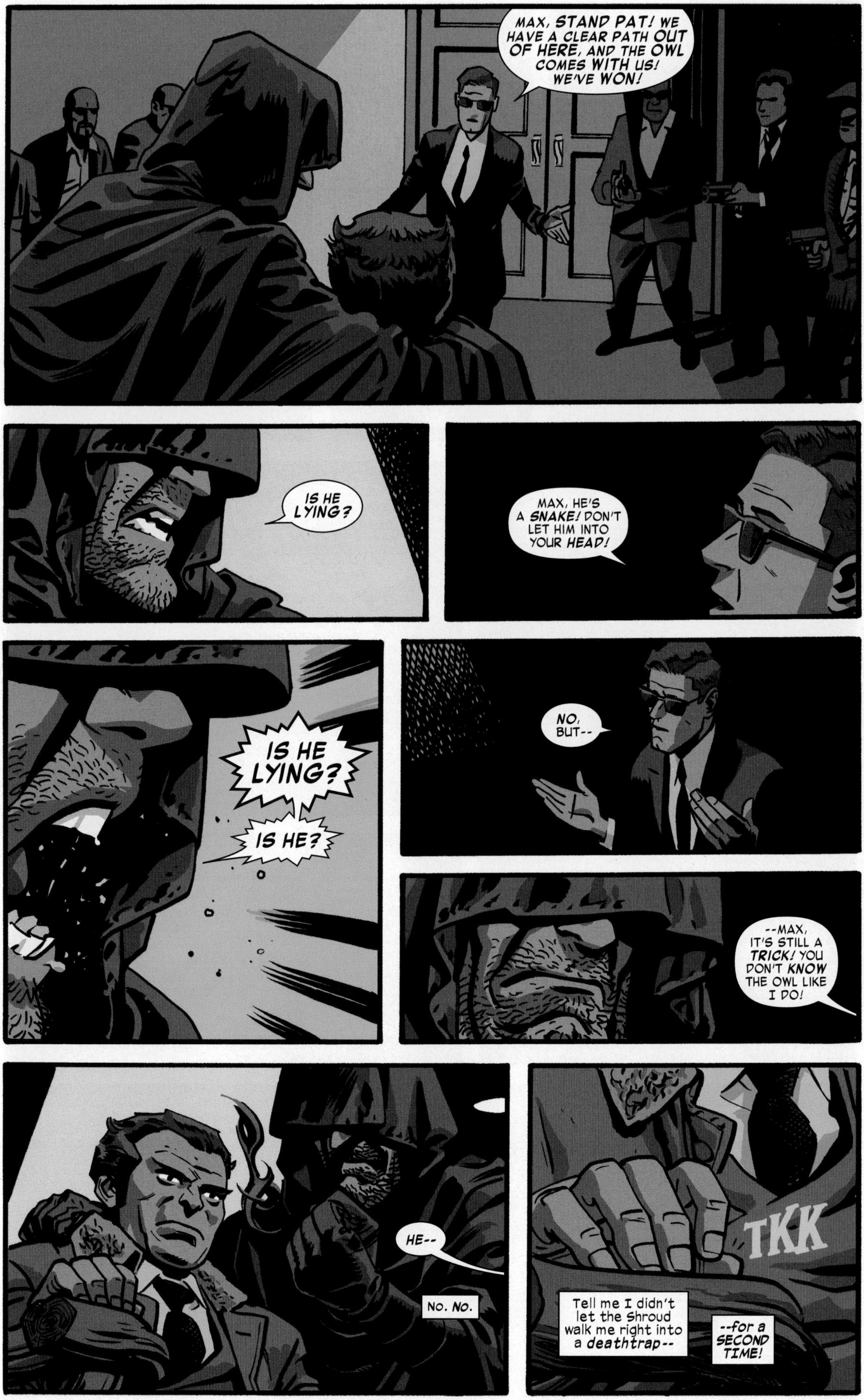
MAX, STAND PAT! WE HAVE A CLEAR PATH OUT OF HERE, AND THE OWL COMES WITH US! WE'VE WON!
IS HE LYING?
MAX, HE'S A SNAKE! DON'T LET HIM INTO YOUR HEAD!
IS HE LYING?
IS HE?
NO, BUT--
--MAX, IT'S STILL A TRICK! YOU DON'T KNOW THE OWL LIKE I DO!
HE--
NO. NO.
Tell me I didn't let the Shroud walk me right into a deathtrap--
--for a SECOND TIME!
TKK

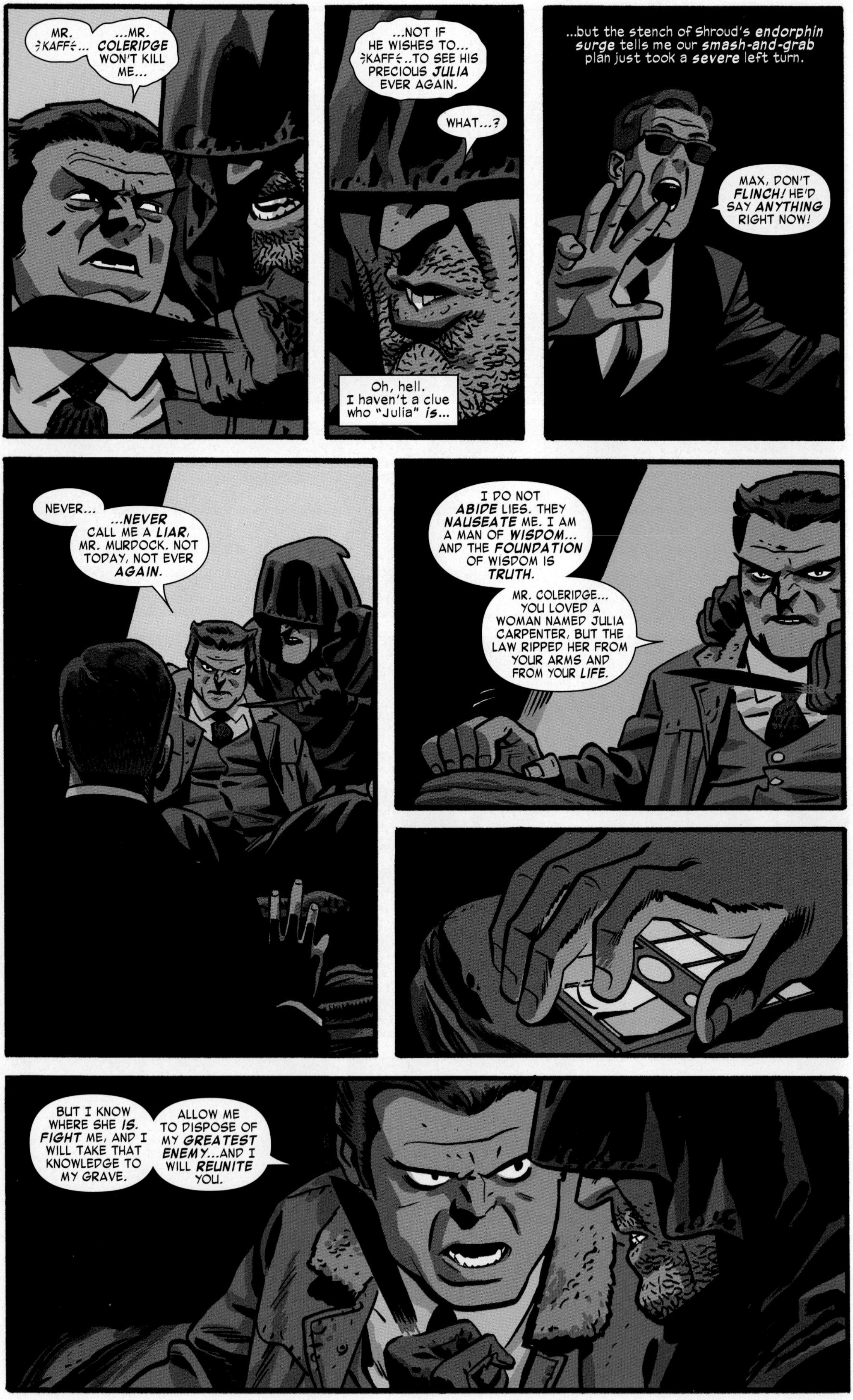
MR. ≯KAFF≮...
...MR. COLERIDGE WON'T KILL ME...
...NOT IF HE WISHES TO... ≯KAFF≮..TO SEE HIS PRECIOUS JULIA EVER AGAIN.
WHAT...?
Oh, hell. I haven't a clue who "Julia" is...
...but the stench of Shroud's endorphin surge tells me our smash-and-grab plan just took a severe left turn.
MAX, DON'T FLINCH! HE'D SAY ANYTHING RIGHT NOW!
NEVER...
...NEVER CALL ME A LIAR, MR. MURDOCK. NOT TODAY, NOT EVER AGAIN.
I DO NOT ABIDE LIES. THEY NAUSEATE ME. I AM A MAN OF WISDOM... AND THE FOUNDATION OF WISDOM IS TRUTH.
MR. COLERIDGE... YOU LOVED A WOMAN NAMED JULIA CARPENTER, BUT THE LAW RIPPED HER FROM YOUR ARMS AND FROM YOUR LIFE.
BUT I KNOW WHERE SHE IS. FIGHT ME, AND I WILL TAKE THAT KNOWLEDGE TO MY GRAVE.
ALLOW ME TO DISPOSE OF MY GREATEST ENEMY...AND I WILL REUNITE YOU.

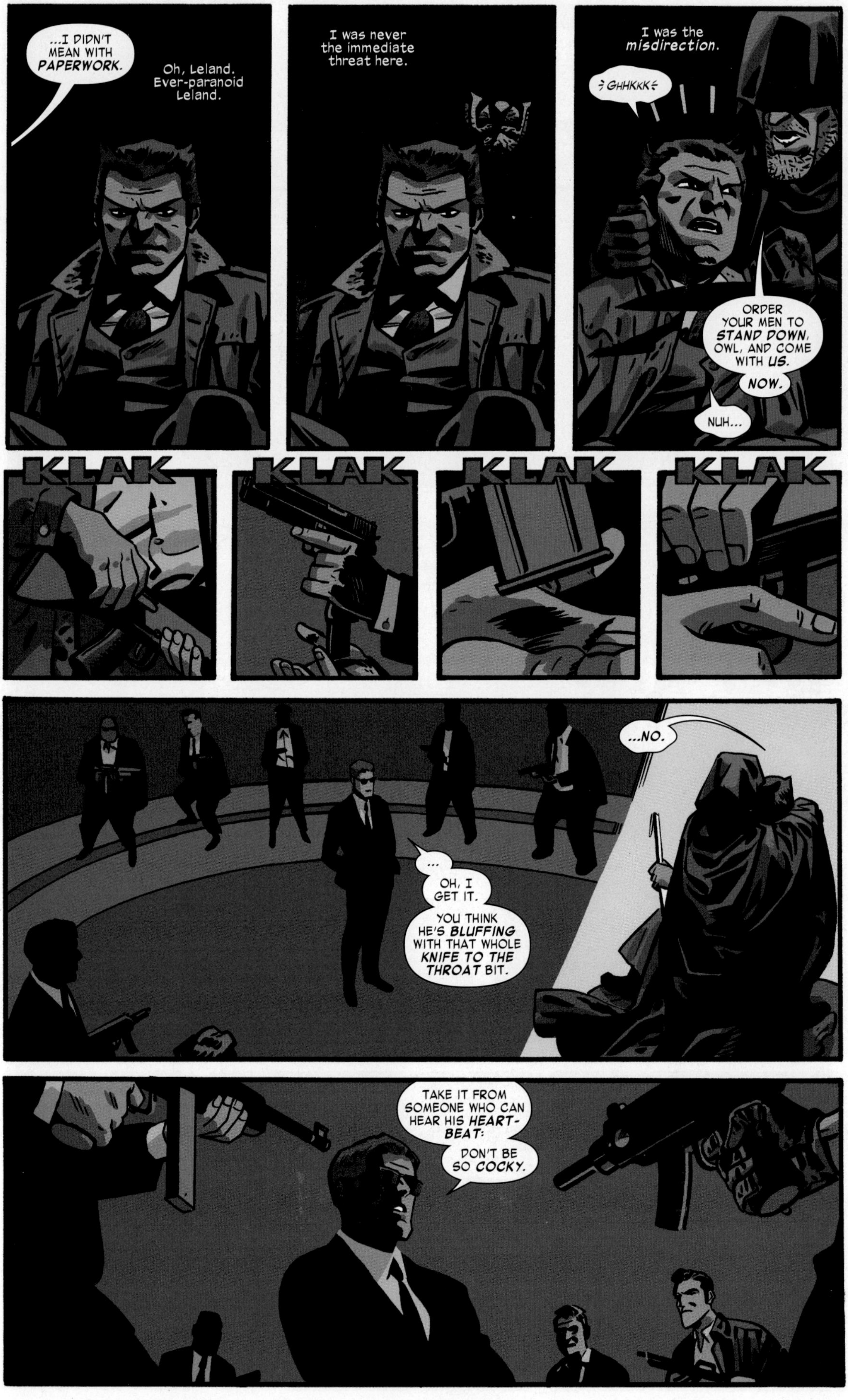
...I DIDN'T MEAN WITH *PAPERWORK.*
Oh, Leland. Ever-paranoid Leland.
I was never the immediate threat here.
I was the *misdirection.*
GHHKKK
ORDER YOUR MEN TO *STAND DOWN,* OWL, AND COME WITH *US.*
NOW.
NUH...
KLAK
KLAK
KLAK
KLAK
...NO.
...
OH, I GET IT.
YOU THINK HE'S *BLUFFING* WITH THAT WHOLE *KNIFE TO THE THROAT* BIT.
TAKE IT FROM SOMEONE WHO CAN HEAR HIS *HEART-BEAT:*
DON'T BE SO *COCKY.*

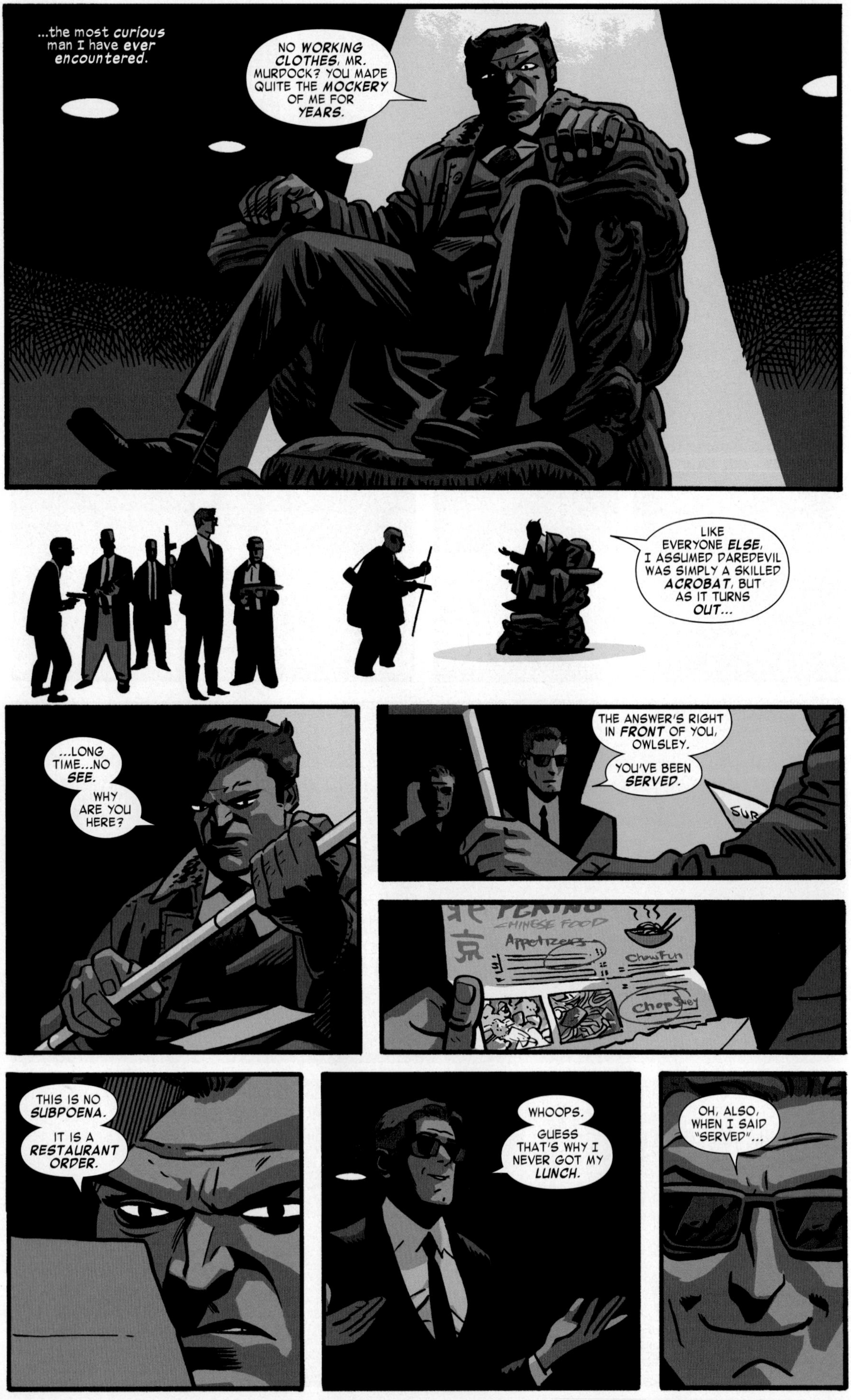
...the most *curious* man I have *ever* *encountered*.
NO ***WORKING CLOTHES***, MR. MURDOCK? YOU MADE QUITE THE ***MOCKERY*** OF ME FOR ***YEARS***.
LIKE EVERYONE ***ELSE***, I ASSUMED DAREDEVIL WAS SIMPLY A SKILLED ***ACROBAT***, BUT AS IT TURNS ***OUT***...
...LONG TIME...NO ***SEE***.
WHY ARE YOU HERE?
THE ANSWER'S RIGHT IN ***FRONT*** OF YOU, OWLSLEY.
YOU'VE BEEN ***SERVED***.
PEKING
CHINESE FOOD
Appetizers
Chow Fun
Chop Suey
THIS IS NO ***SUBPOENA***.
IT IS A ***RESTAURANT ORDER***.
WHOOPS.
GUESS THAT'S WHY I NEVER GOT MY ***LUNCH***.
OH, ALSO, WHEN I SAID "SERVED"...

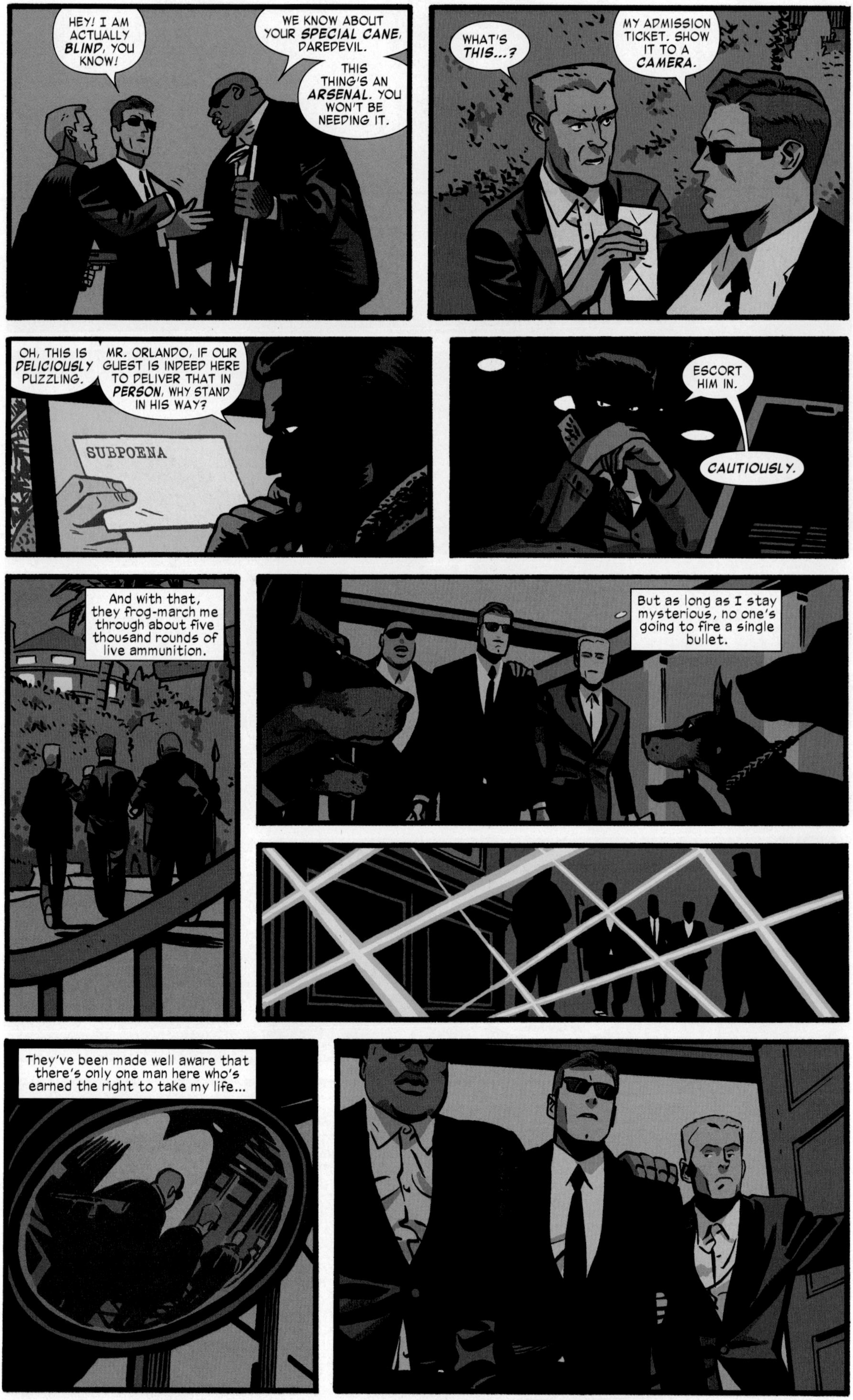
HEY! I AM ACTUALLY BLIND, YOU KNOW!
WE KNOW ABOUT YOUR SPECIAL CANE, DAREDEVIL.
THIS THING'S AN ARSENAL. YOU WON'T BE NEEDING IT.
MY ADMISSION TICKET. SHOW IT TO A CAMERA.
WHAT'S THIS...?
OH, THIS IS DELICIOUSLY PUZZLING.
MR. ORLANDO, IF OUR GUEST IS INDEED HERE TO DELIVER THAT IN PERSON, WHY STAND IN HIS WAY?
SUBPOENA
ESCORT HIM IN.
CAUTIOUSLY.
And with that, they frog-march me through about five thousand rounds of live ammunition.
But as long as I stay mysterious, no one's going to fire a single bullet.
They've been made well aware that there's only one man here who's earned the right to take my life...

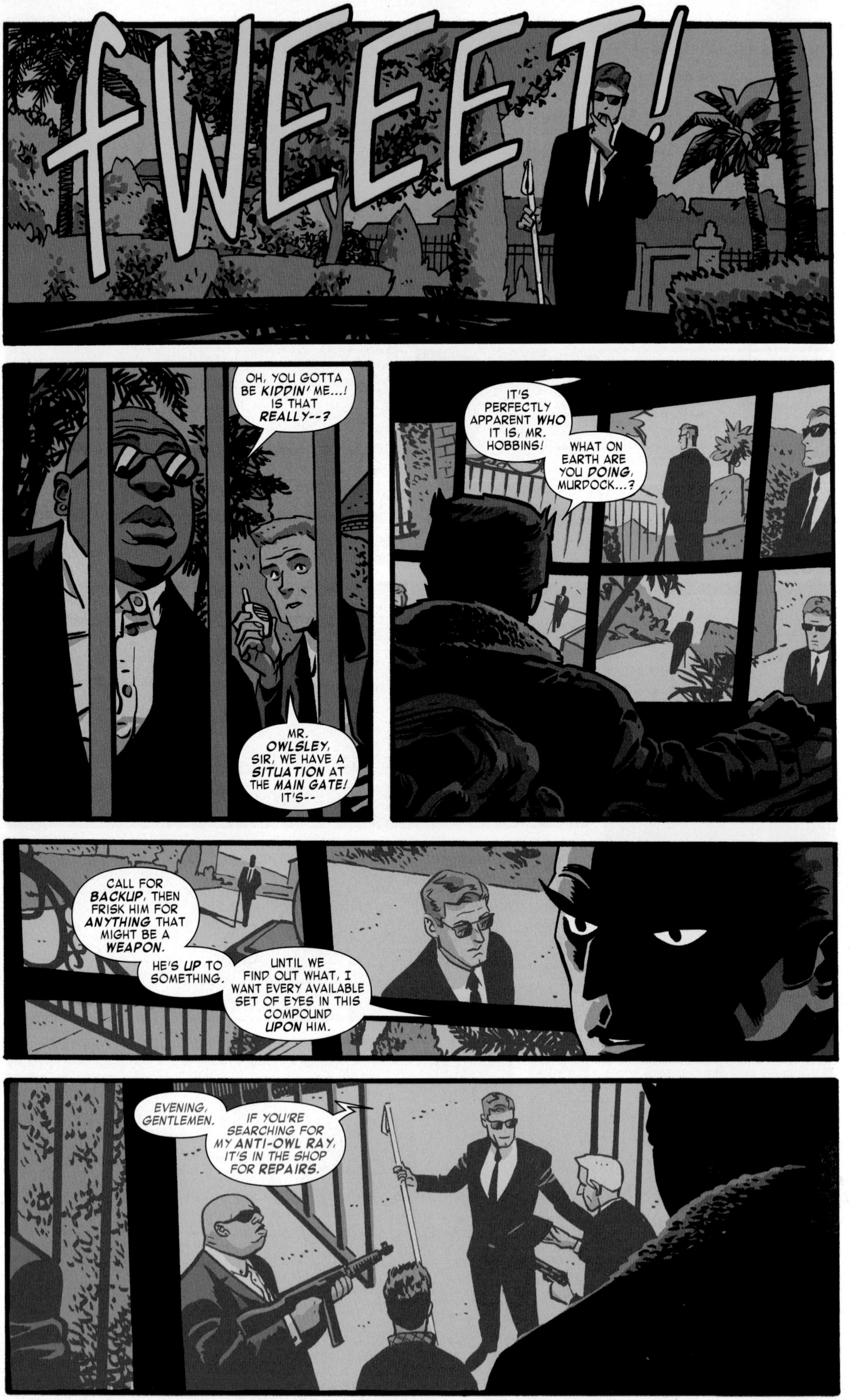
FWEEET!
OH, YOU GOTTA BE KIDDIN' ME...! IS THAT REALLY--?
MR. OWLSLEY, SIR, WE HAVE A SITUATION AT THE MAIN GATE! IT'S--
IT'S PERFECTLY APPARENT WHO IT IS, MR. HOBBINS!
WHAT ON EARTH ARE YOU DOING, MURDOCK...?
CALL FOR BACKUP, THEN FRISK HIM FOR ANYTHING THAT MIGHT BE A WEAPON.
HE'S UP TO SOMETHING.
UNTIL WE FIND OUT WHAT, I WANT EVERY AVAILABLE SET OF EYES IN THIS COMPOUND UPON HIM.
EVENING, GENTLEMEN.
IF YOU'RE SEARCHING FOR MY ANTI-OWL RAY, IT'S IN THE SHOP FOR REPAIRS.

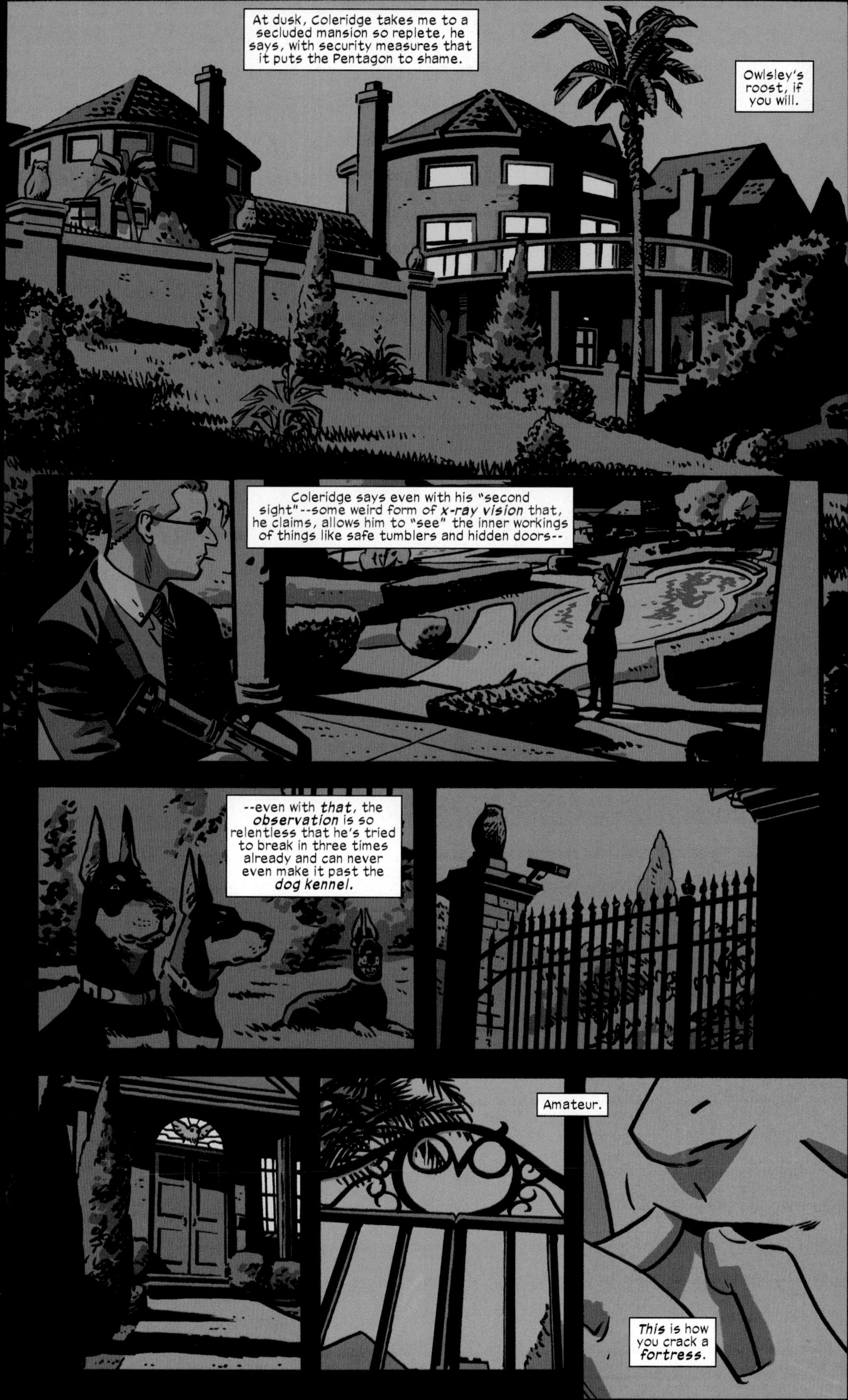
At dusk, Coleridge takes me to a secluded mansion so replete, he says, with security measures that it puts the Pentagon to shame.
Owlsley's roost, if you will.
Coleridge says even with his "second sight"--some weird form of *x-ray vision* that, he claims, allows him to "see" the inner workings of things like safe tumblers and hidden doors--
--even with *that*, the *observation* is so relentless that he's tried to break in three times already and can never even make it past the *dog kennel*.
Amateur.
This is how you crack a *fortress*.

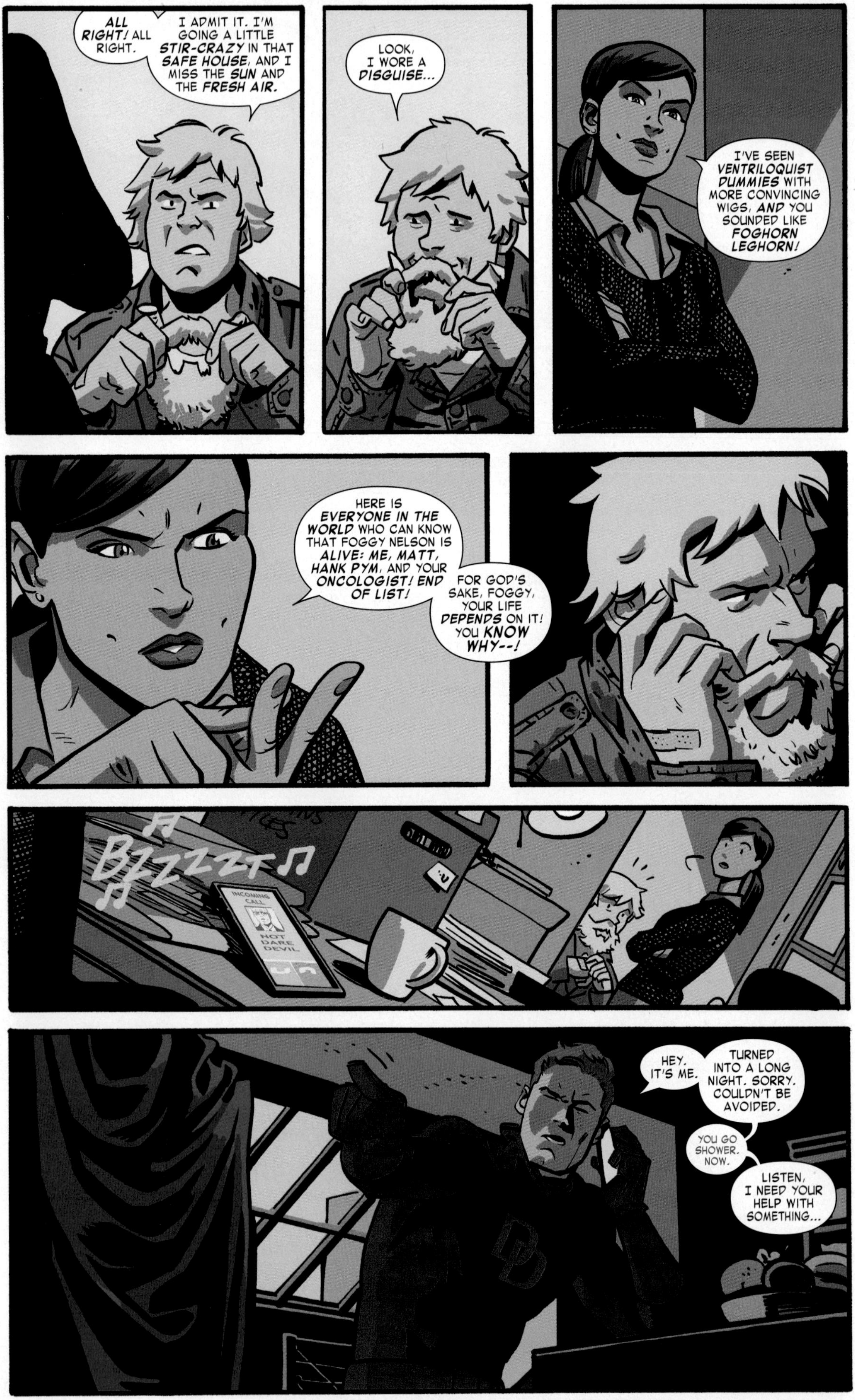
ALL RIGHT! ALL RIGHT.
I ADMIT IT. I'M GOING A LITTLE STIR-CRAZY IN THAT SAFE HOUSE, AND I MISS THE SUN AND THE FRESH AIR.
LOOK, I WORE A DISGUISE...
I'VE SEEN VENTRILOQUIST DUMMIES WITH MORE CONVINCING WIGS, AND YOU SOUNDED LIKE FOGHORN LEGHORN!
HERE IS EVERYONE IN THE WORLD WHO CAN KNOW THAT FOGGY NELSON IS ALIVE: ME, MATT, HANK PYM, AND YOUR ONCOLOGIST! END OF LIST!
FOR GOD'S SAKE, FOGGY, YOUR LIFE DEPENDS ON IT! YOU KNOW WHY--!
BZZZZT
INCOMING CALL
NOT DARE DEVIL
HEY. IT'S ME.
TURNED INTO A LONG NIGHT. SORRY. COULDN'T BE AVOIDED.
YOU GO SHOWER. NOW.
LISTEN, I NEED YOUR HELP WITH SOMETHING...

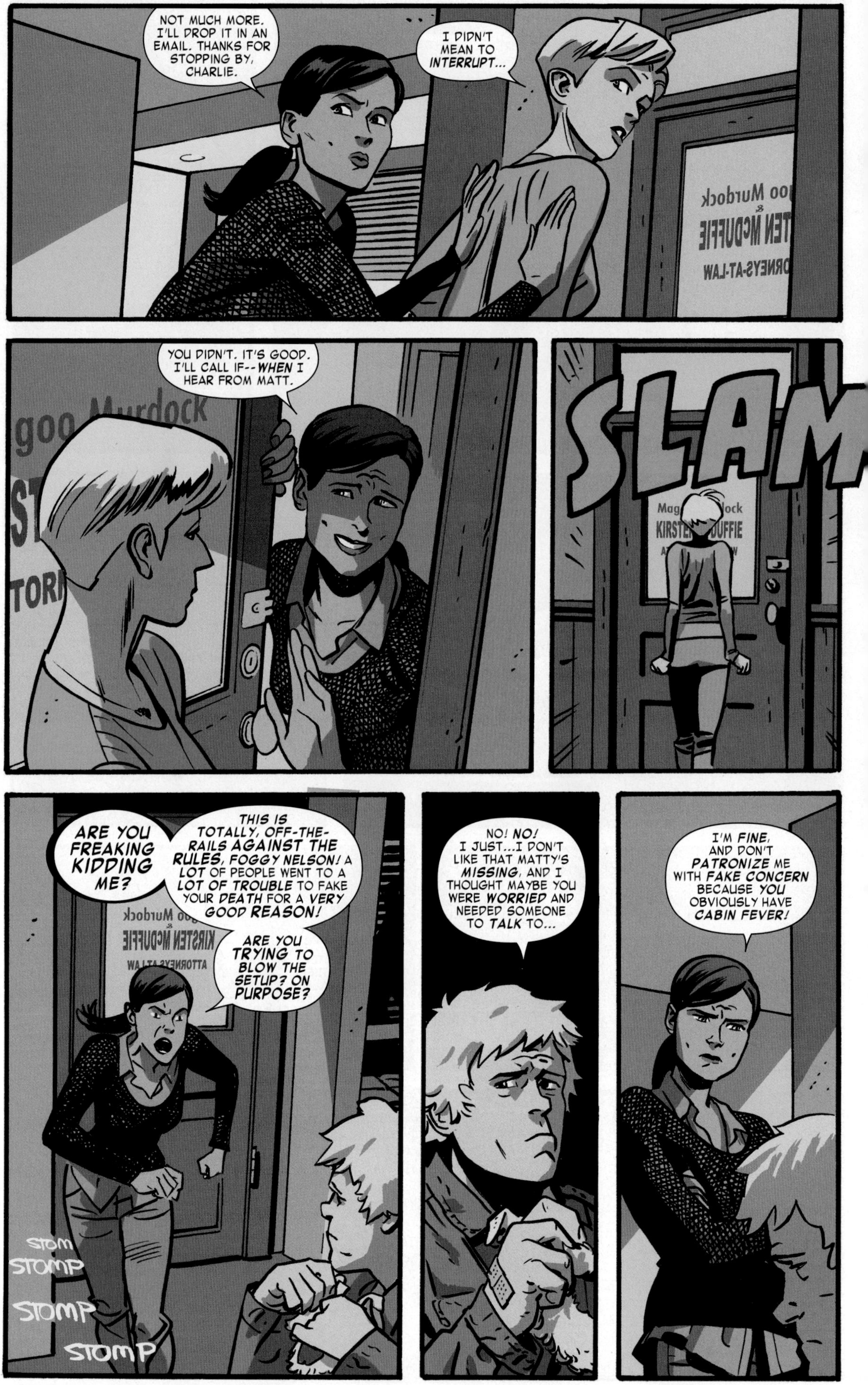
NOT MUCH MORE. I'LL DROP IT IN AN EMAIL. THANKS FOR STOPPING BY, CHARLIE.
I DIDN'T MEAN TO INTERRUPT...
goo Murdock & TEN McDUFFIE ORNEYS-AT-LAW
YOU DIDN'T. IT'S GOOD. I'LL CALL IF--WHEN I HEAR FROM MATT.
SLAM
ARE YOU FREAKING KIDDING ME?
THIS IS TOTALLY, OFF-THE-RAILS AGAINST THE RULES, FOGGY NELSON! A LOT OF PEOPLE WENT TO A LOT OF TROUBLE TO FAKE YOUR DEATH FOR A VERY GOOD REASON!
ARE YOU TRYING TO BLOW THE SETUP? ON PURPOSE?
STOM STOMP STOMP STOMP
NO! NO! I JUST...I DON'T LIKE THAT MATTY'S MISSING, AND I THOUGHT MAYBE YOU WERE WORRIED AND NEEDED SOMEONE TO TALK TO...
I'M FINE, AND DON'T PATRONIZE ME WITH FAKE CONCERN BECAUSE YOU OBVIOUSLY HAVE CABIN FEVER!

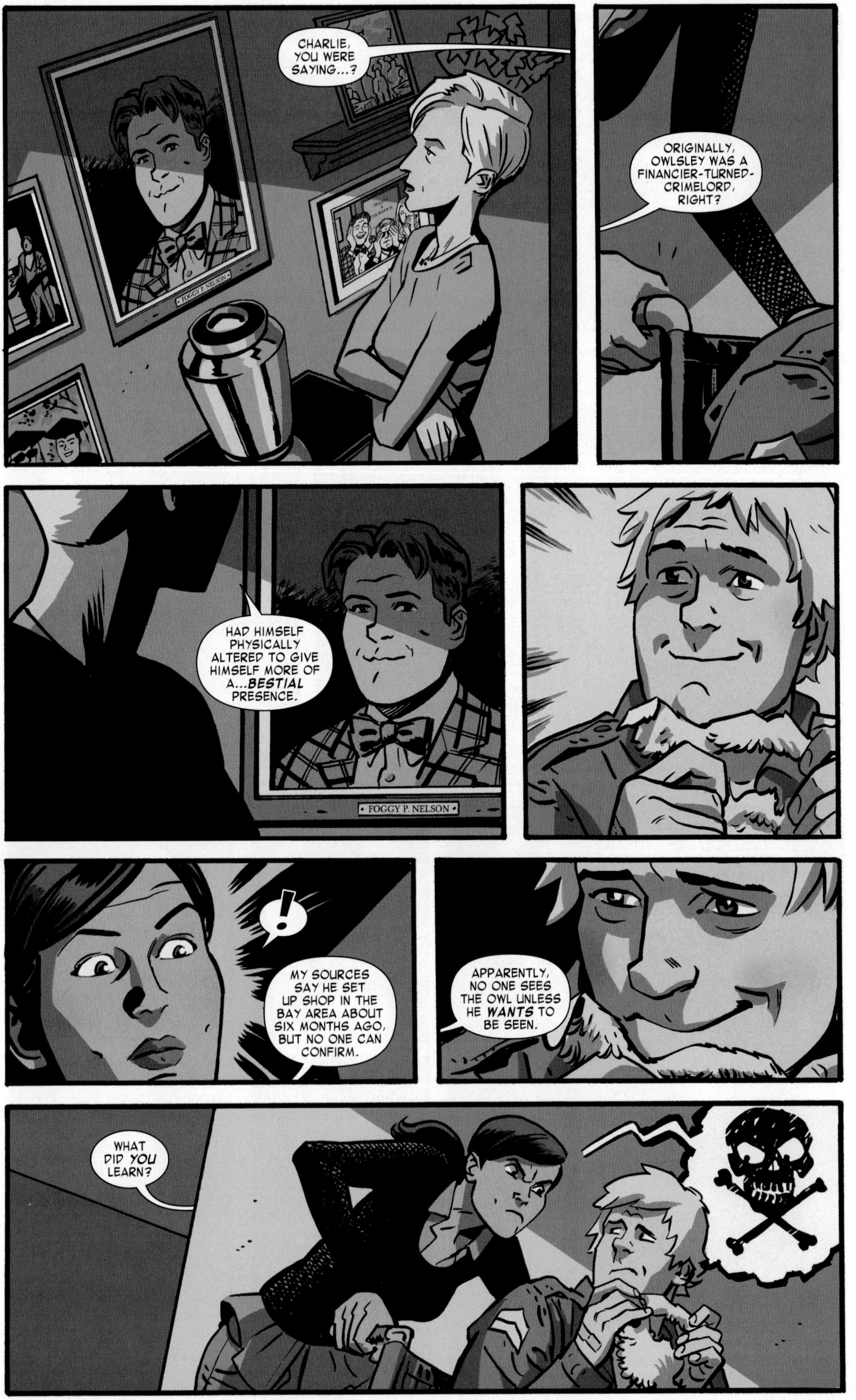
CHARLIE, YOU WERE SAYING...?
FOGGY P. NELSON
ORIGINALLY, OWLSLEY WAS A FINANCIER-TURNED-CRIMELORD, RIGHT?
HAD HIMSELF PHYSICALLY ALTERED TO GIVE HIMSELF MORE OF A...*BESTIAL* PRESENCE.
FOGGY P. NELSON
!
MY SOURCES SAY HE SET UP SHOP IN THE BAY AREA ABOUT SIX MONTHS AGO, BUT NO ONE CAN CONFIRM.
APPARENTLY, NO ONE SEES THE OWL UNLESS HE *WANTS* TO BE SEEN.
WHAT DID *YOU* LEARN?

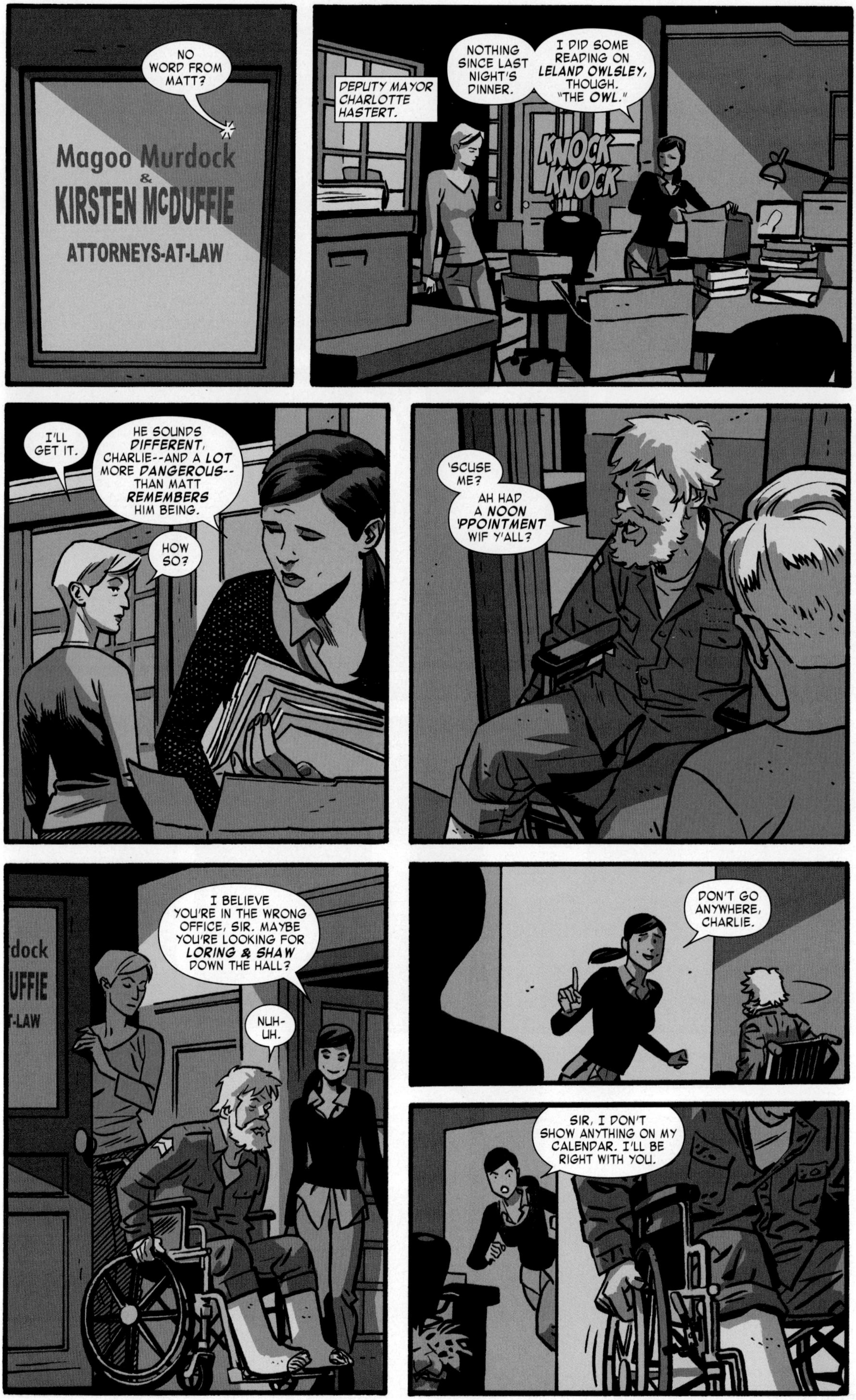
NO WORD FROM MATT?
Magoo Murdock & KIRSTEN McDUFFIE ATTORNEYS-AT-LAW
DEPUTY MAYOR CHARLOTTE HASTERT.
NOTHING SINCE LAST NIGHT'S DINNER.
I DID SOME READING ON LELAND OWLSLEY, THOUGH. "THE OWL."
KNOCK KNOCK
I'LL GET IT.
HE SOUNDS DIFFERENT, CHARLIE--AND A LOT MORE DANGEROUS--THAN MATT REMEMBERS HIM BEING.
HOW SO?
'SCUSE ME?
AH HAD A NOON 'PPOINTMENT WIF Y'ALL?
I BELIEVE YOU'RE IN THE WRONG OFFICE, SIR. MAYBE YOU'RE LOOKING FOR LORING & SHAW DOWN THE HALL?
NUH-UH.
DON'T GO ANYWHERE, CHARLIE.
SIR, I DON'T SHOW ANYTHING ON MY CALENDAR. I'LL BE RIGHT WITH YOU.

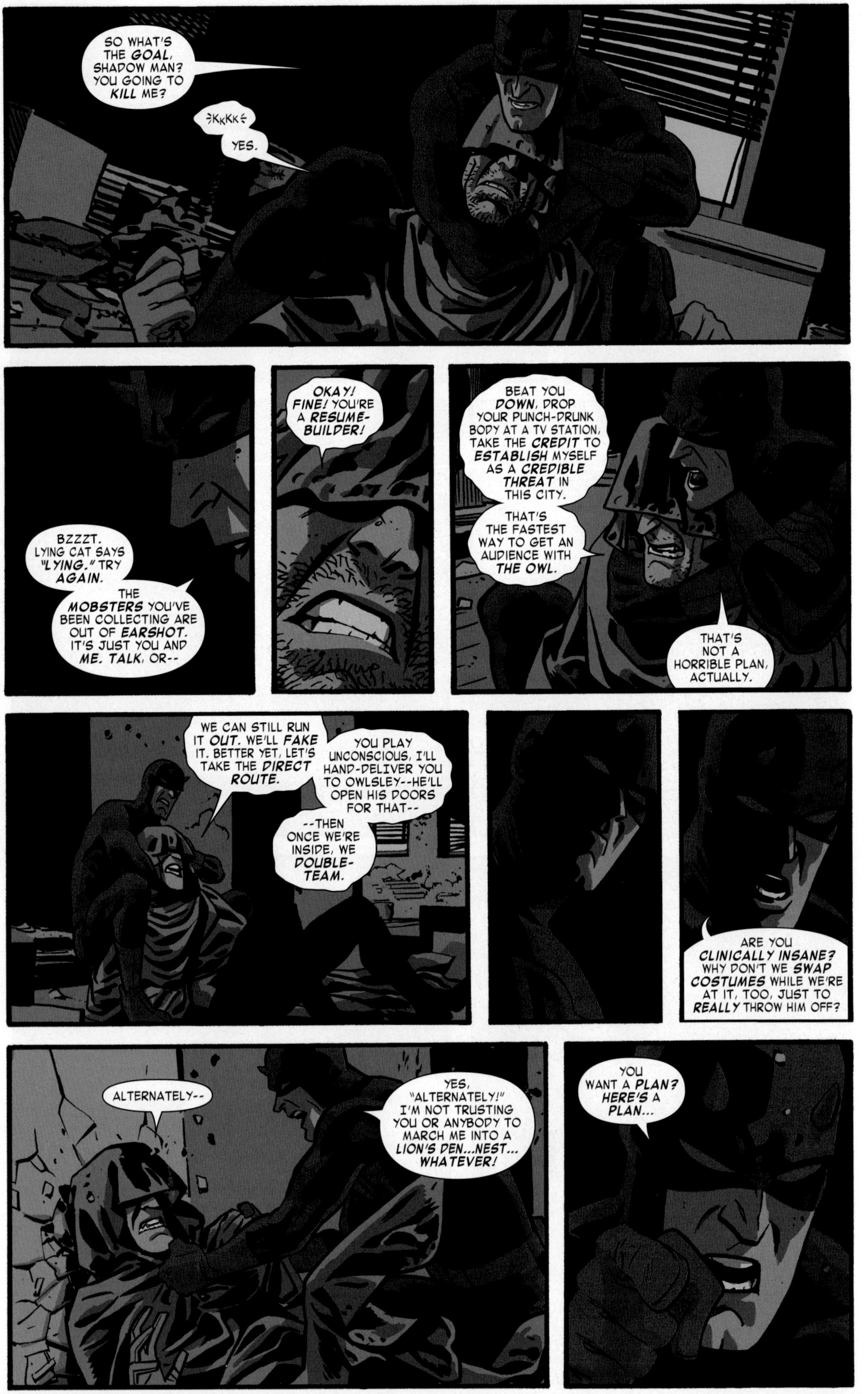
SO WHAT'S THE GOAL, SHADOW MAN? YOU GOING TO KILL ME?
≡KKKK≡
YES.
BZZZT. LYING CAT SAYS "LYING." TRY AGAIN.
THE MOBSTERS YOU'VE BEEN COLLECTING ARE OUT OF EARSHOT. IT'S JUST YOU AND ME. TALK, OR--
OKAY! FINE! YOU'RE A RESUME-BUILDER!
BEAT YOU DOWN, DROP YOUR PUNCH-DRUNK BODY AT A TV STATION, TAKE THE CREDIT TO ESTABLISH MYSELF AS A CREDIBLE THREAT IN THIS CITY.
THAT'S THE FASTEST WAY TO GET AN AUDIENCE WITH THE OWL.
THAT'S NOT A HORRIBLE PLAN, ACTUALLY.
WE CAN STILL RUN IT OUT. WE'LL FAKE IT. BETTER YET, LET'S TAKE THE DIRECT ROUTE.
YOU PLAY UNCONSCIOUS, I'LL HAND-DELIVER YOU TO OWLSLEY--HE'LL OPEN HIS DOORS FOR THAT--
--THEN ONCE WE'RE INSIDE, WE DOUBLE-TEAM.
ARE YOU CLINICALLY INSANE? WHY DON'T WE SWAP COSTUMES WHILE WE'RE AT IT, TOO, JUST TO REALLY THROW HIM OFF?
ALTERNATELY--
YES, "ALTERNATELY!" I'M NOT TRUSTING YOU OR ANYBODY TO MARCH ME INTO A LION'S DEN...NEST... WHATEVER!
YOU WANT A PLAN? HERE'S A PLAN...

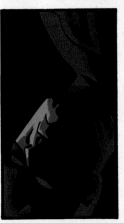

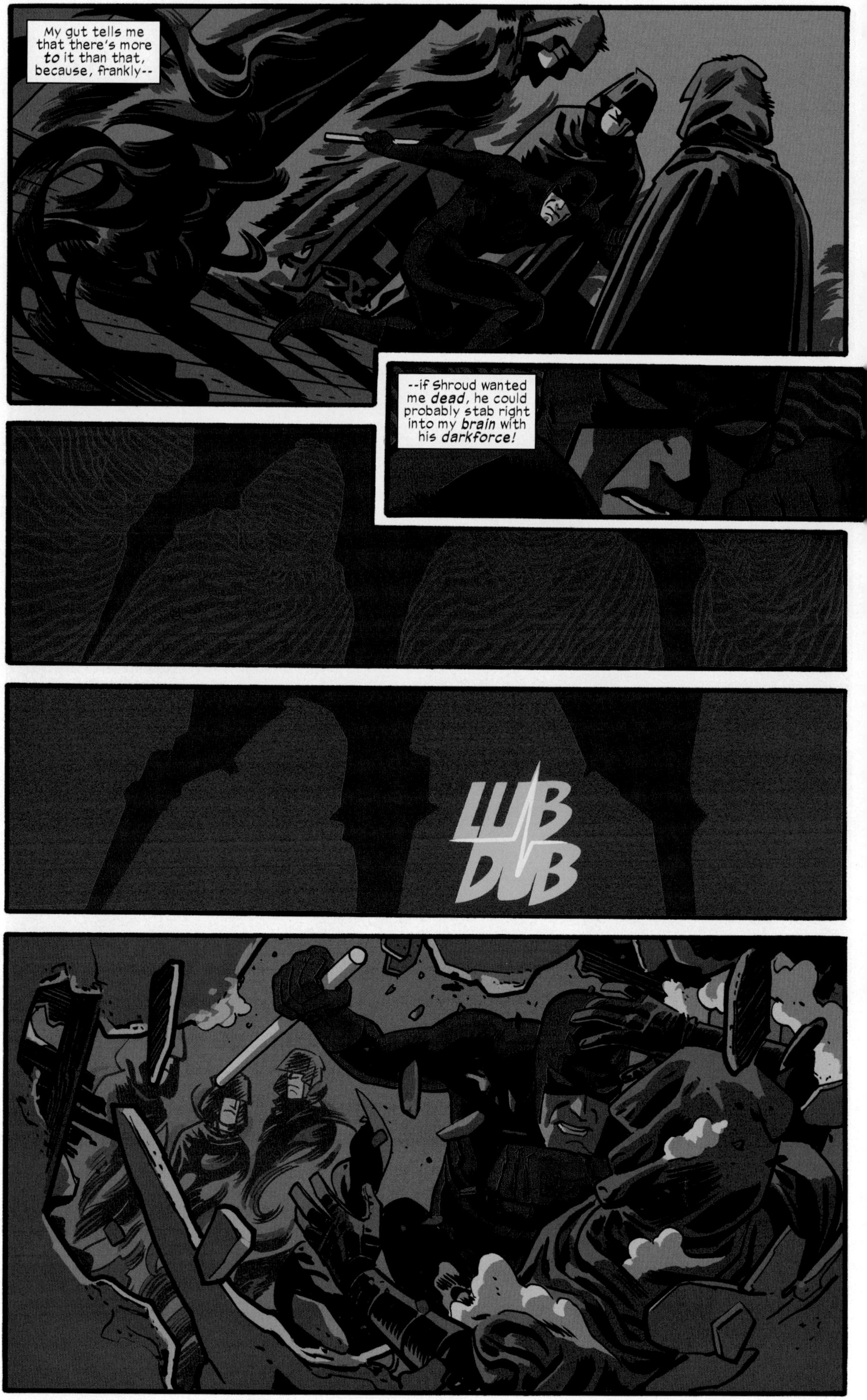
My gut tells me that there's more *to* it than that, because, frankly--
--if Shroud wanted me *dead*, he could probably stab right into my *brain* with his *darkforce!*
LUB DUB

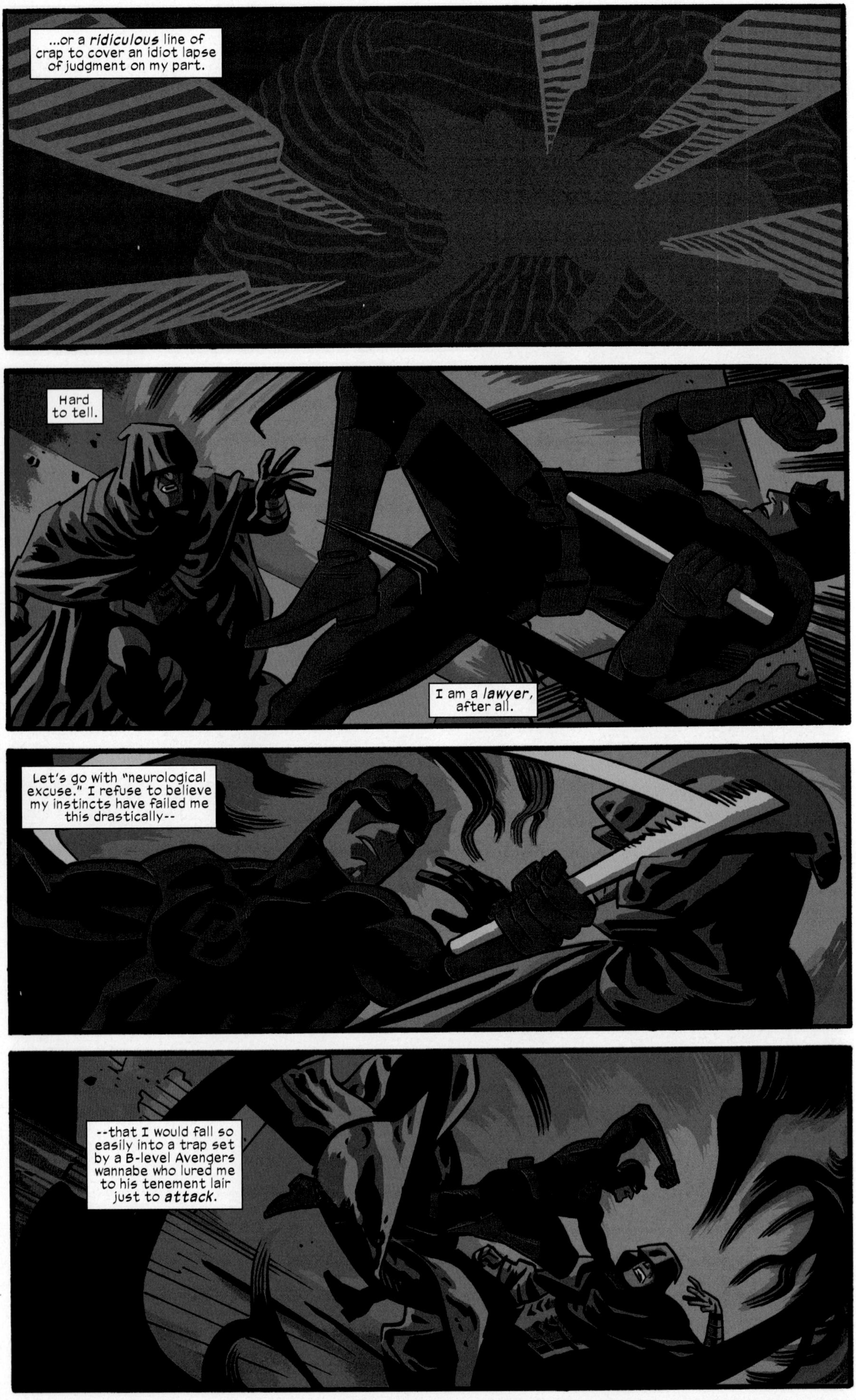
...or a *ridiculous* line of crap to cover an idiot lapse of judgment on my part.
Hard to tell.
I am a *lawyer*, after all.
Let's go with "neurological excuse." I refuse to believe my instincts have failed me this drastically--
--that I would fall so easily into a trap set by a B-level Avengers wannabe who lured me to his tenement lair just to *attack*.

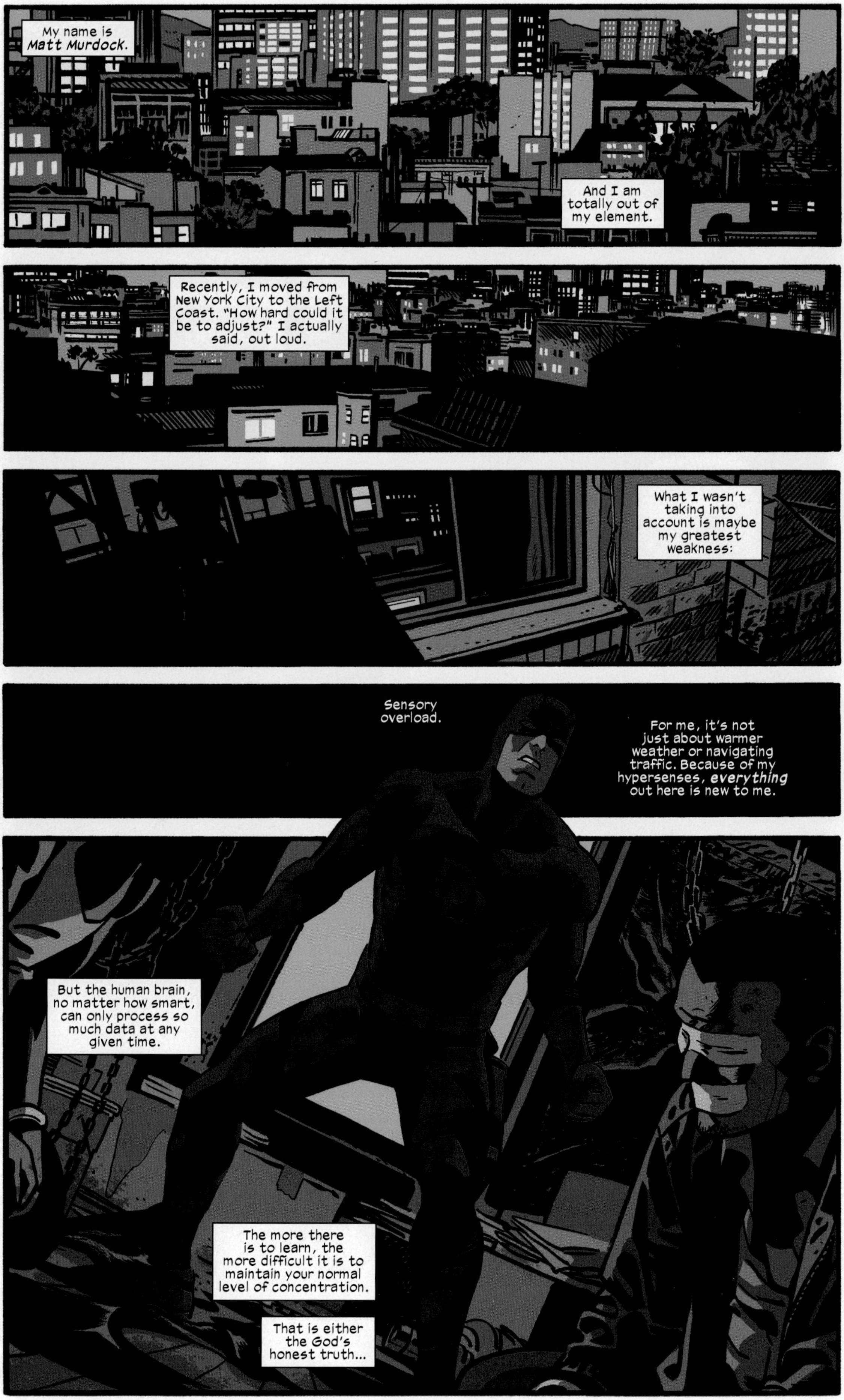
My name is *Matt Murdock.*
And I am totally out of my element.
Recently, I moved from New York City to the Left Coast. "How hard could it be to adjust?" I actually said, out loud.
What I wasn't taking into account is maybe my greatest weakness:
Sensory overload.
For me, it's not just about warmer weather or navigating traffic. Because of my hypersenses, ***everything*** out here is new to me.
But the human brain, no matter how smart, can only process so much data at any given time.
The more there is to learn, the more difficult it is to maintain your normal level of concentration.
That is either the God's honest truth...

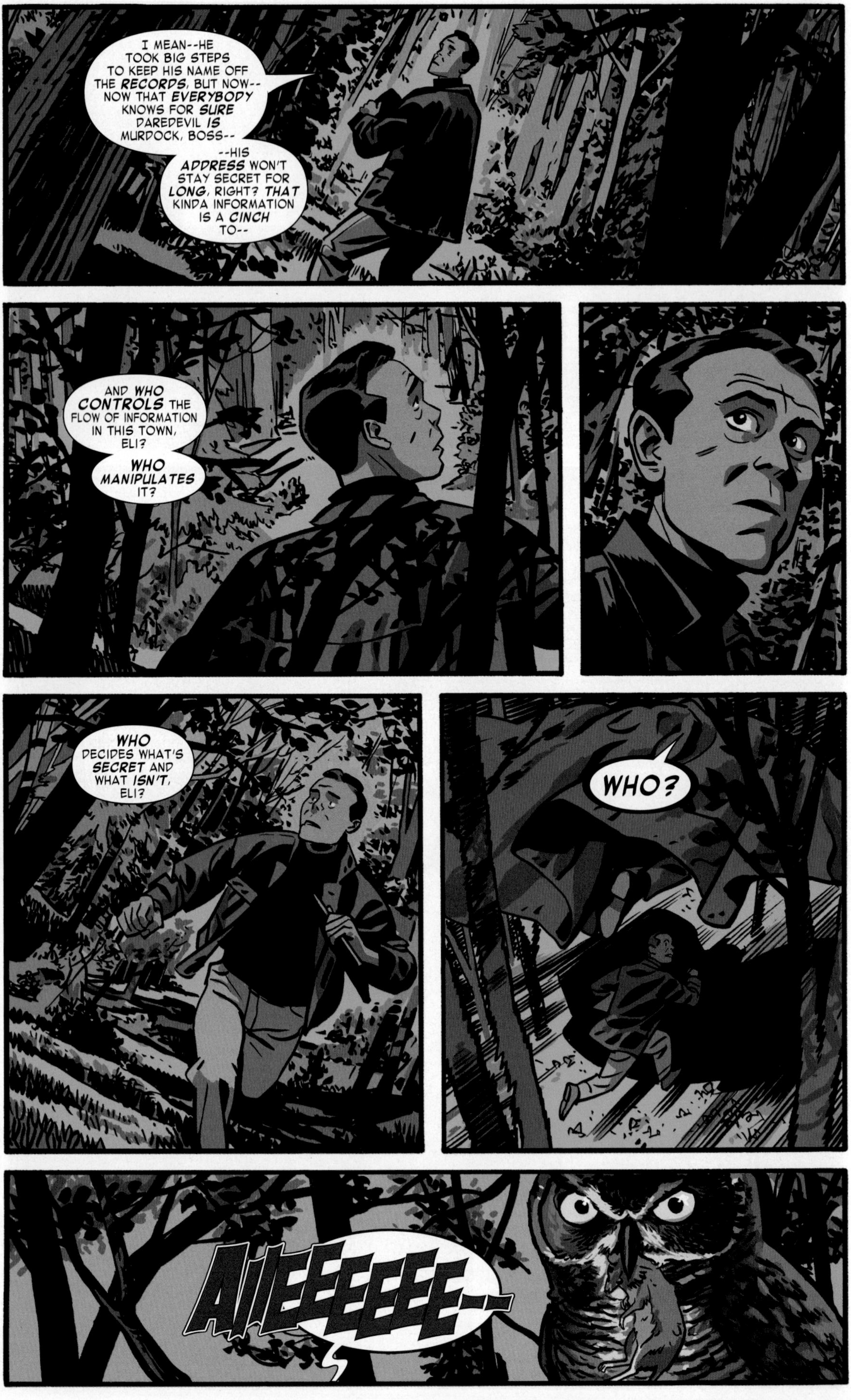
I MEAN--HE TOOK BIG STEPS TO KEEP HIS NAME OFF THE RECORDS, BUT NOW--NOW THAT EVERYBODY KNOWS FOR SURE DAREDEVIL IS MURDOCK, BOSS--
--HIS ADDRESS WON'T STAY SECRET FOR LONG, RIGHT? THAT KINDA INFORMATION IS A CINCH TO--
AND WHO CONTROLS THE FLOW OF INFORMATION IN THIS TOWN, ELI?
WHO MANIPULATES IT?
WHO DECIDES WHAT'S SECRET AND WHAT ISN'T, ELI?
WHO?
AIEEEEEE--

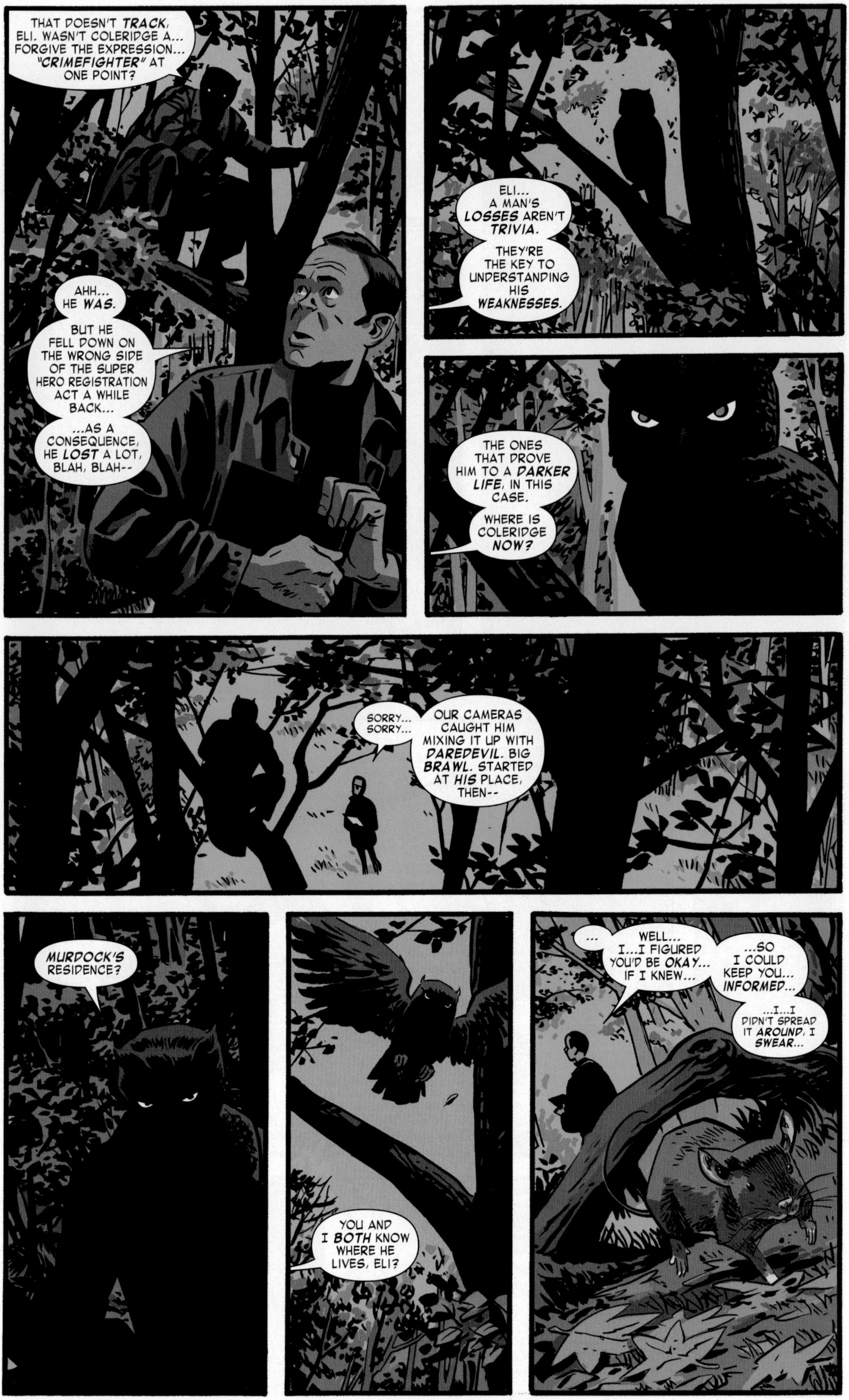
THAT DOESN'T *TRACK*, ELI. WASN'T COLERIDGE A... FORGIVE THE EXPRESSION... "*CRIMEFIGHTER*" AT ONE POINT?
AHH... HE *WAS*.
BUT HE FELL DOWN ON THE WRONG SIDE OF THE SUPER HERO REGISTRATION ACT A WHILE BACK...
...AS A CONSEQUENCE, HE *LOST* A LOT, BLAH, BLAH--
ELI... A MAN'S *LOSSES* AREN'T *TRIVIA*.
THEY'RE THE KEY TO UNDERSTANDING HIS *WEAKNESSES*.
THE ONES THAT DROVE HIM TO A *DARKER LIFE*, IN THIS CASE.
WHERE IS COLERIDGE *NOW?*
SORRY... SORRY...
OUR CAMERAS CAUGHT HIM MIXING IT UP WITH *DAREDEVIL*. BIG *BRAWL*. STARTED AT *HIS* PLACE, THEN--
MURDOCK'S RESIDENCE?
YOU AND I *BOTH* KNOW WHERE HE LIVES, ELI?
...
WELL... I...I FIGURED YOU'D BE *OKAY*... IF I KNEW...
...SO I COULD KEEP YOU... *INFORMED*...
...I...I DIDN'T SPREAD IT *AROUND*, I *SWEAR*...

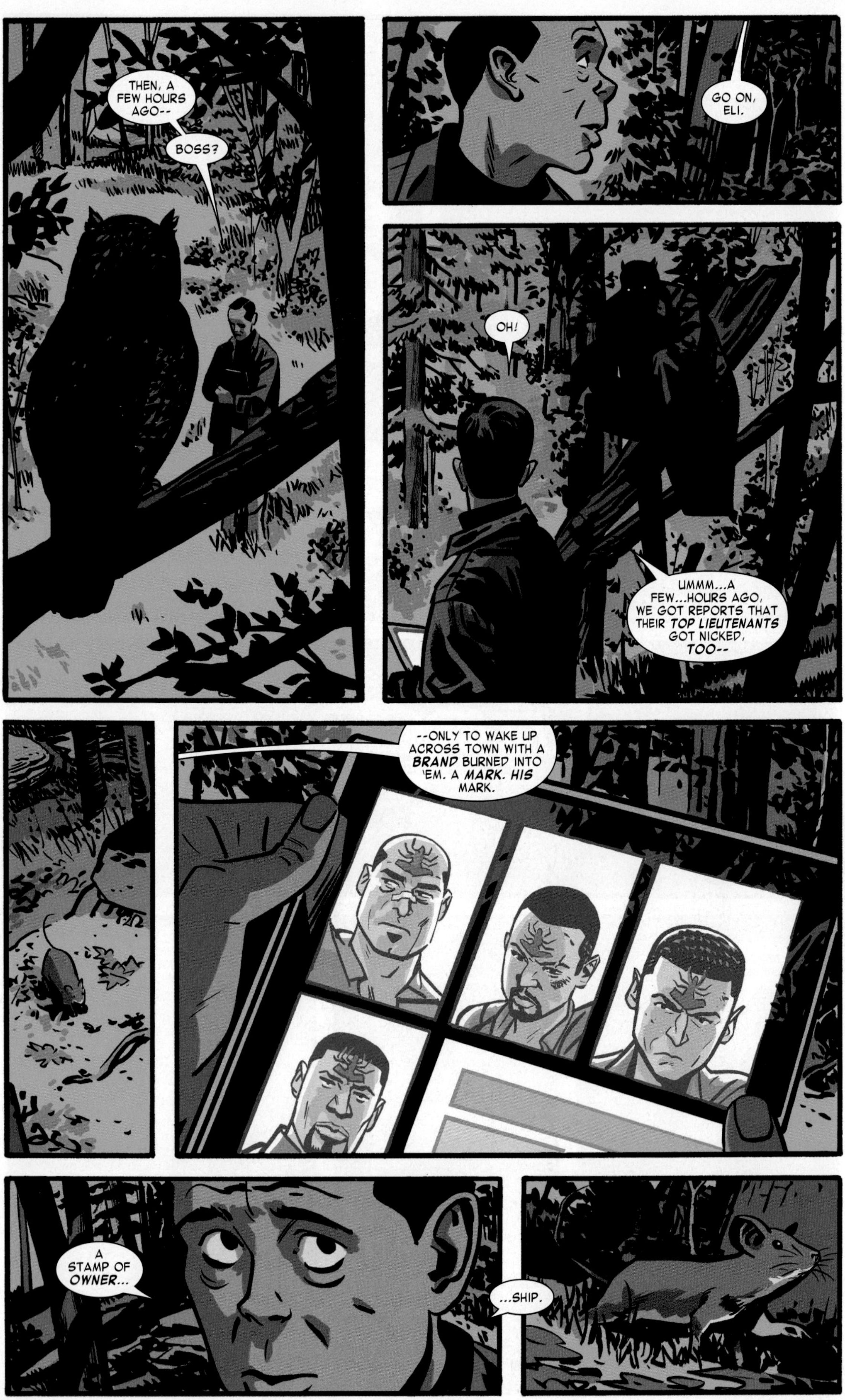
THEN, A FEW HOURS AGO--
BOSS?
GO ON, ELI.
OH!
UMMM...A FEW...HOURS AGO, WE GOT REPORTS THAT THEIR *TOP LIEUTENANTS* GOT NICKED, *TOO--*
--ONLY TO WAKE UP ACROSS TOWN WITH A *BRAND* BURNED INTO 'EM. A *MARK. HIS* MARK.
A STAMP OF *OWNER...*
...SHIP.

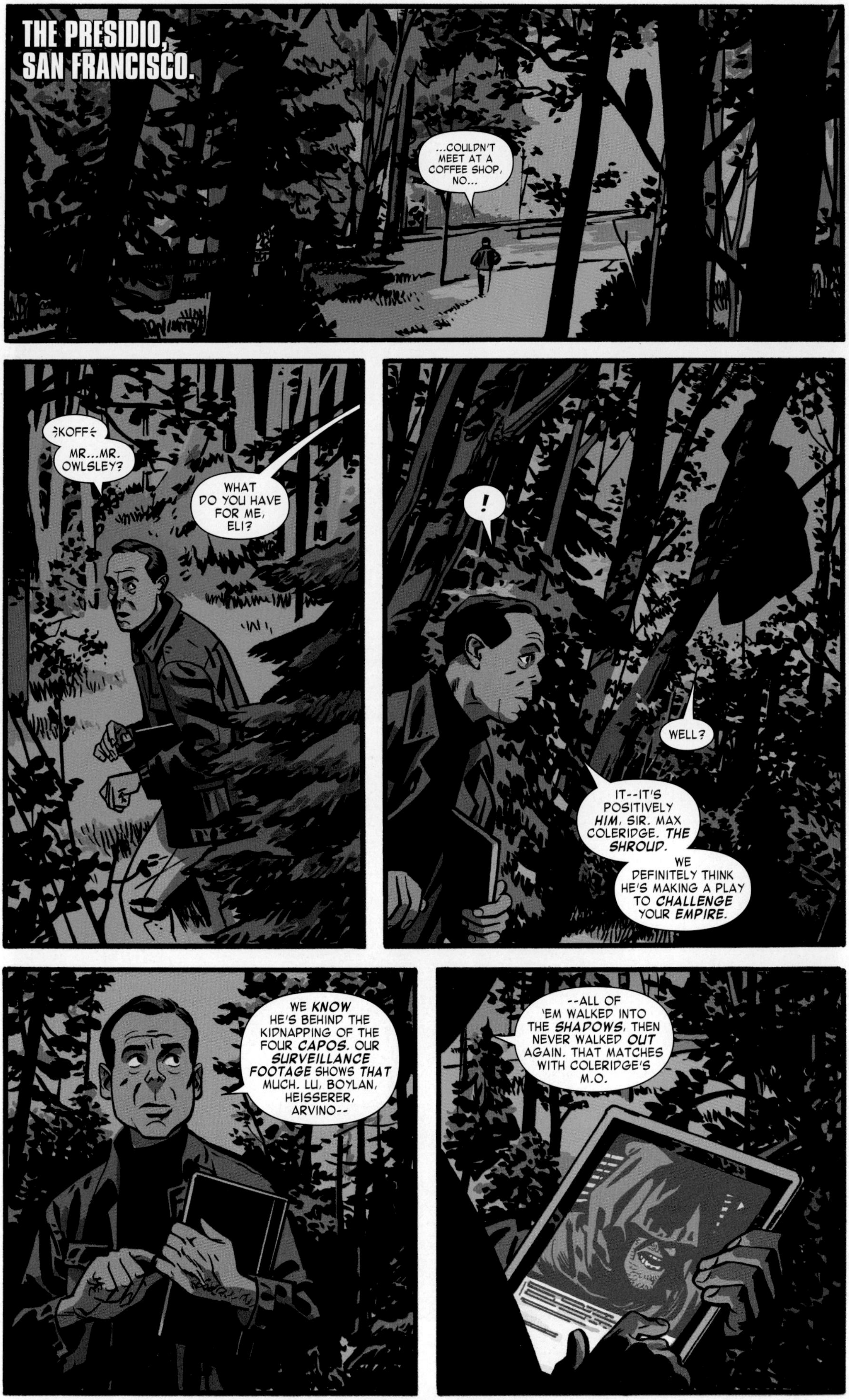
THE PRESIDIO, SAN FRANCISCO.
...COULDN'T MEET AT A COFFEE SHOP, NO...
ƎKOFFƐ MR...MR. OWLSLEY?
WHAT DO YOU HAVE FOR ME, ELI?
!
WELL?
IT--IT'S POSITIVELY HIM, SIR. MAX COLERIDGE. THE SHROUD.
WE DEFINITELY THINK HE'S MAKING A PLAY TO CHALLENGE YOUR EMPIRE.
WE KNOW HE'S BEHIND THE KIDNAPPING OF THE FOUR CAPOS. OUR SURVEILLANCE FOOTAGE SHOWS THAT MUCH. LU, BOYLAN, HEISSERER, ARVINO--
--ALL OF 'EM WALKED INTO THE SHADOWS, THEN NEVER WALKED OUT AGAIN. THAT MATCHES WITH COLERIDGE'S M.O.

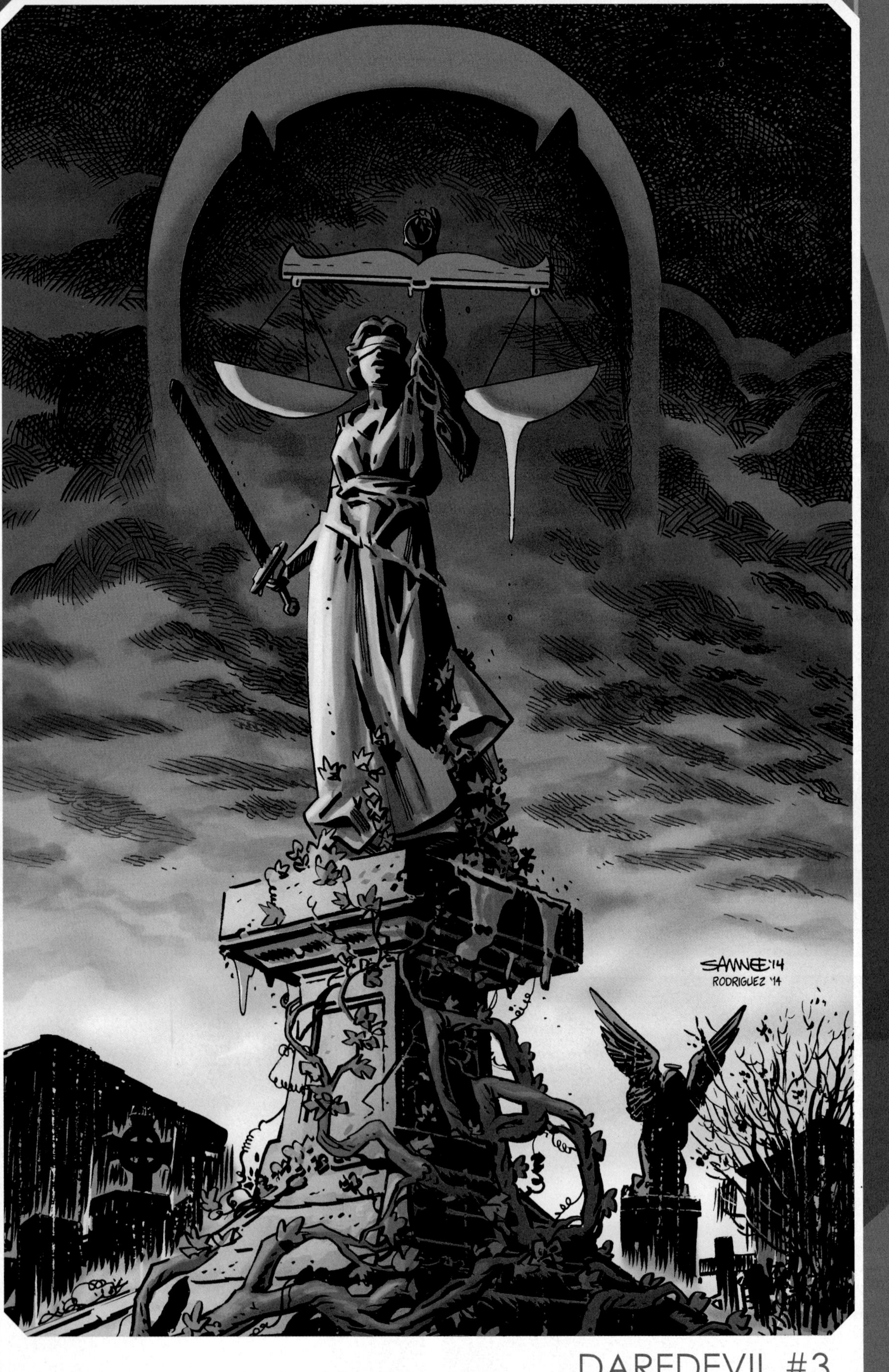
SAMNEE '14
RODRIGUEZ '14

DAREDEVIL #3

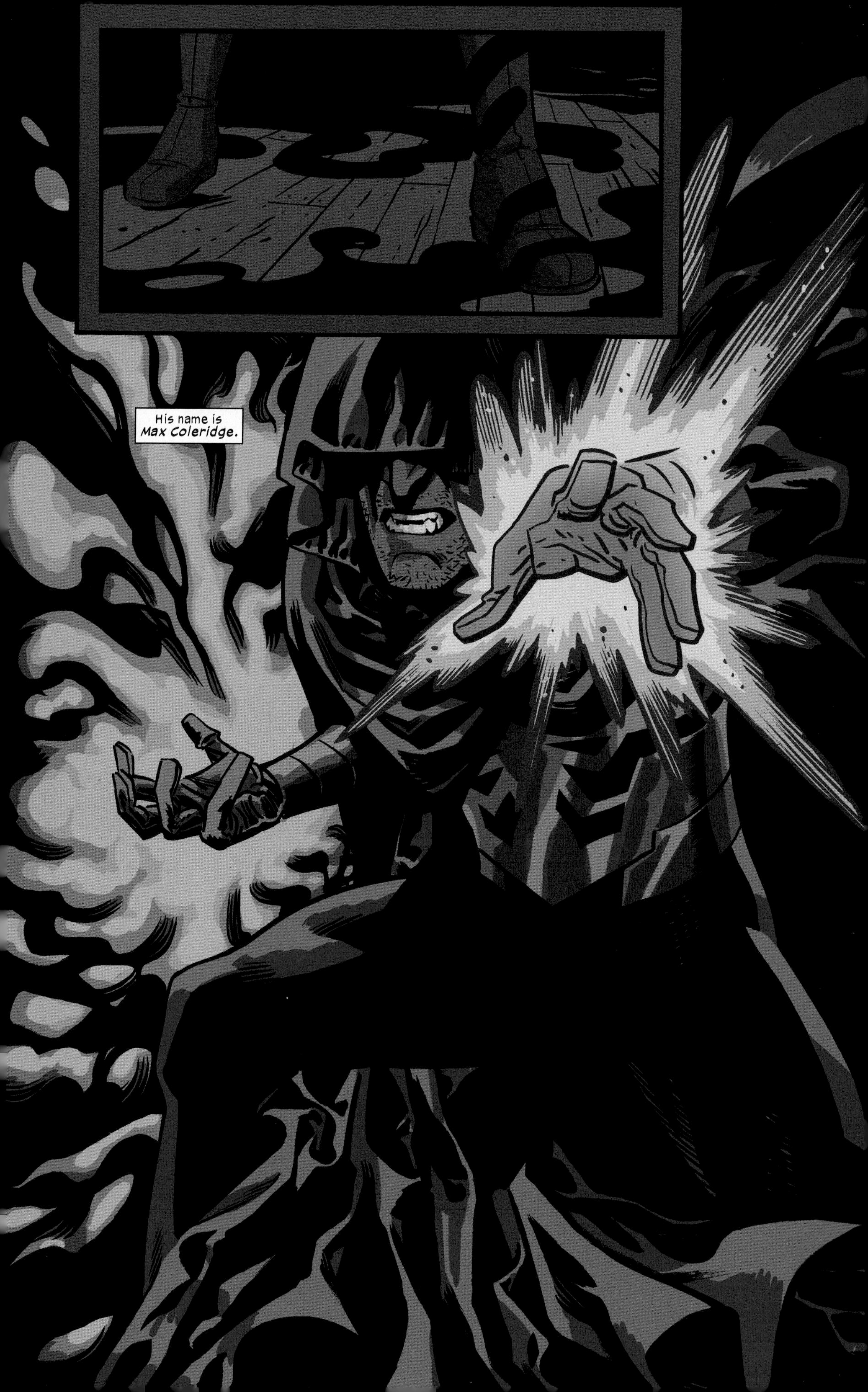
His name is *Max Coleridge.*

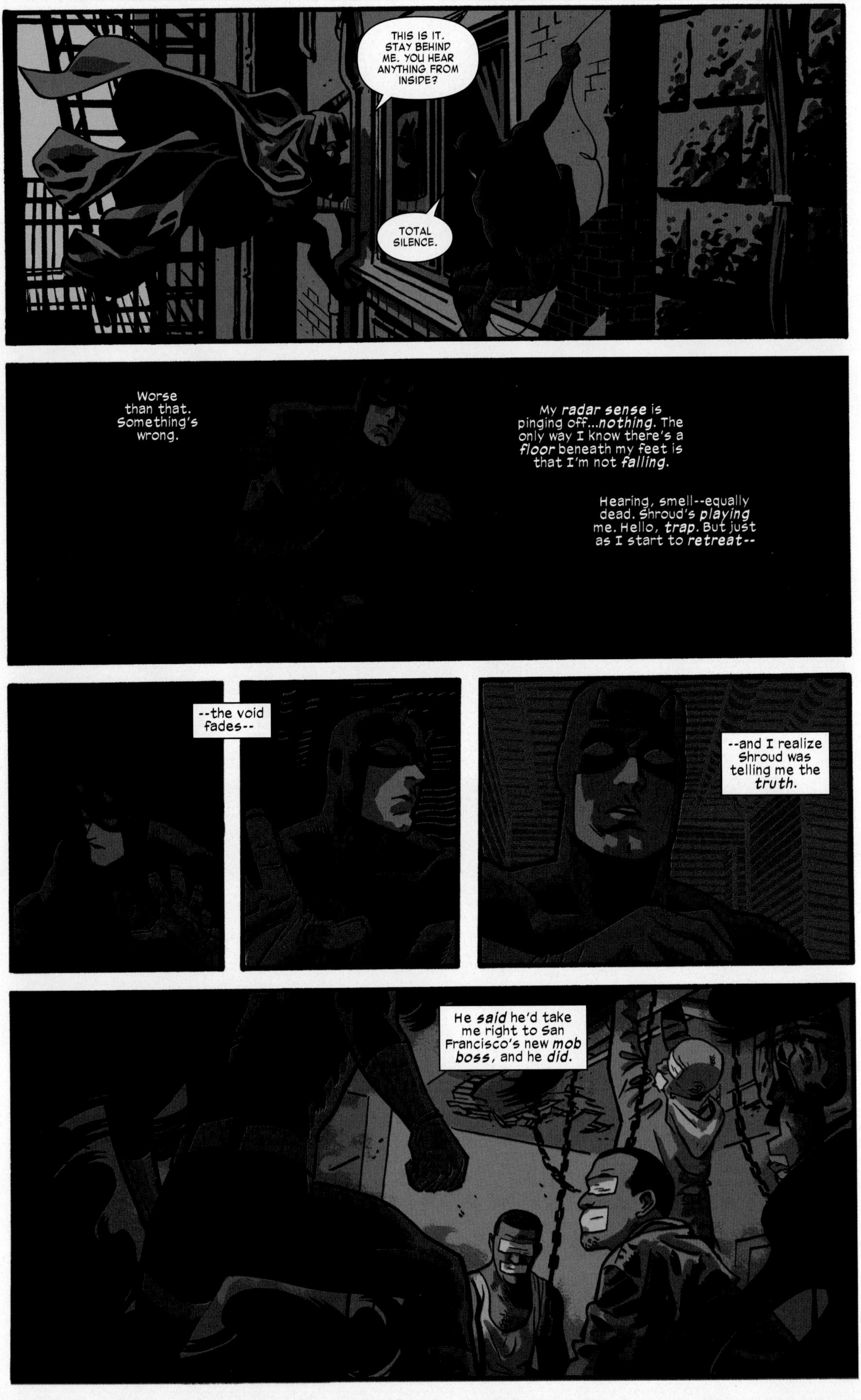
THIS IS IT. STAY BEHIND ME. YOU HEAR ANYTHING FROM INSIDE?
TOTAL SILENCE.
Worse than that. Something's wrong.
My *radar sense* is pinging off...*nothing*. The only way I know there's a *floor* beneath my feet is that I'm not *falling*.
Hearing, smell--equally dead. Shroud's *playing* me. Hello, *trap*. But just as I start to *retreat*--
--the void fades--
--and I realize Shroud was telling me the *truth*.
He *said* he'd take me right to San Francisco's new *mob boss*, and he *did*.

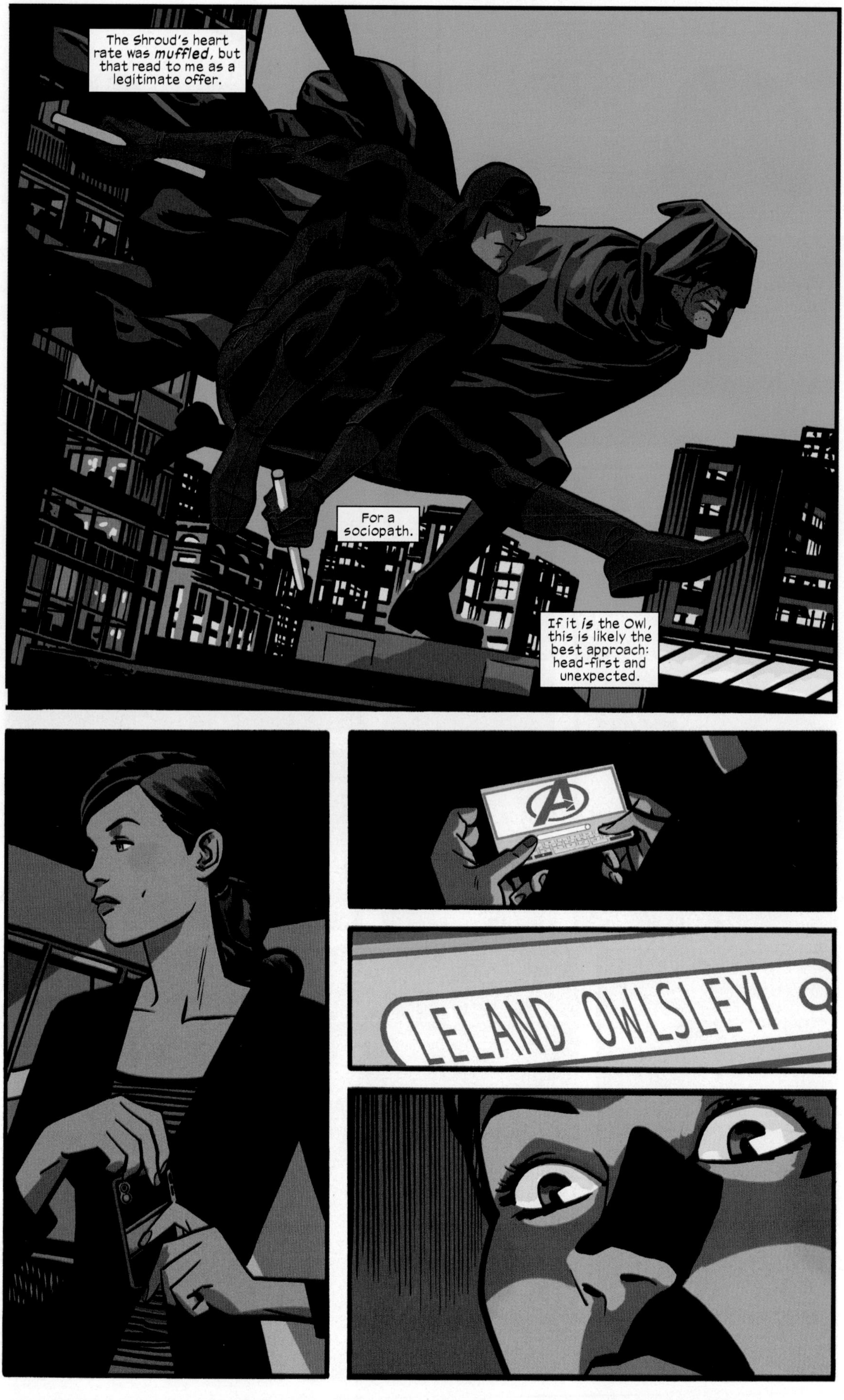
The Shroud's heart rate was *muffled*, but that read to me as a legitimate offer.
For a sociopath.
If it *is* the Owl, this is likely the best approach: head-first and unexpected.
LELAND OWLSLEYI

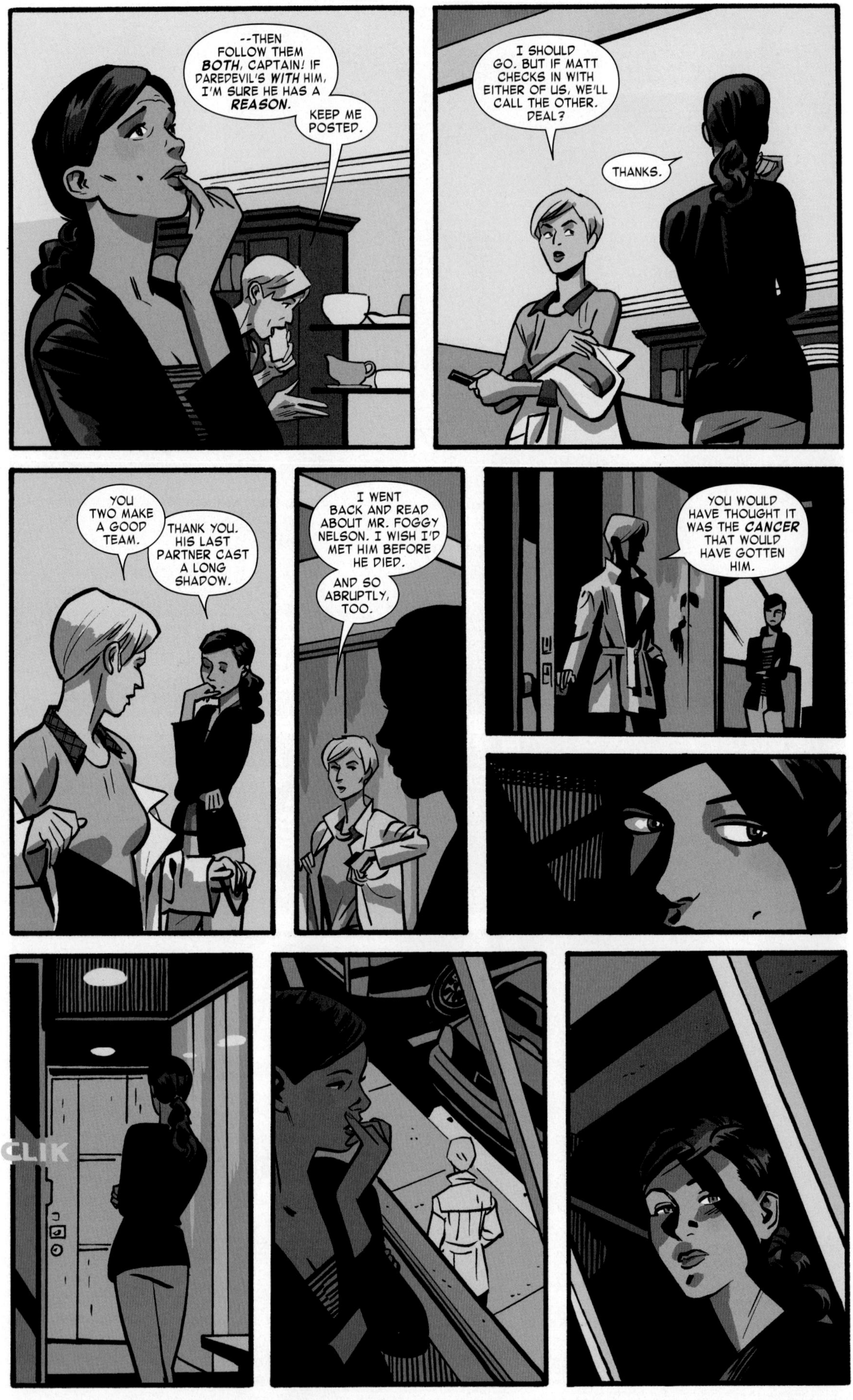
--THEN FOLLOW THEM **BOTH**, CAPTAIN! IF DAREDEVIL'S **WITH** HIM, I'M SURE HE HAS A **REASON**.
KEEP ME POSTED.
I SHOULD GO. BUT IF MATT CHECKS IN WITH EITHER OF US, WE'LL CALL THE OTHER. DEAL?
THANKS.
YOU TWO MAKE A GOOD TEAM.
THANK YOU. HIS LAST PARTNER CAST A LONG SHADOW.
I WENT BACK AND READ ABOUT MR. FOGGY NELSON. I WISH I'D MET HIM BEFORE HE DIED.
AND SO ABRUPTLY, TOO.
YOU WOULD HAVE THOUGHT IT WAS THE ***CANCER*** THAT WOULD HAVE GOTTEN HIM.
CLIK

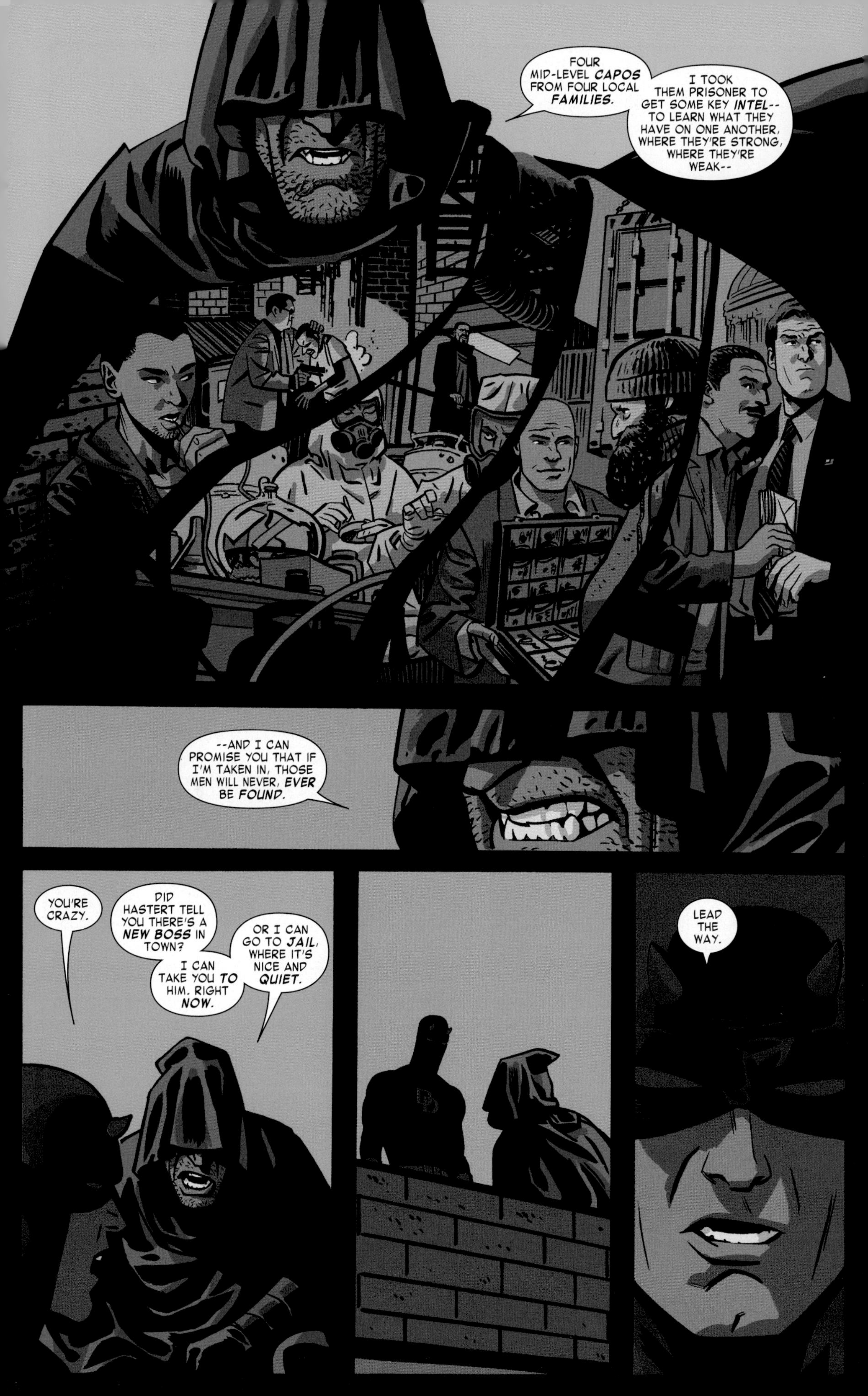
FOUR MID-LEVEL CAPOS FROM FOUR LOCAL FAMILIES.
I TOOK THEM PRISONER TO GET SOME KEY INTEL-- TO LEARN WHAT THEY HAVE ON ONE ANOTHER, WHERE THEY'RE STRONG, WHERE THEY'RE WEAK--
--AND I CAN PROMISE YOU THAT IF I'M TAKEN IN, THOSE MEN WILL NEVER, EVER BE FOUND.
YOU'RE CRAZY.
DID HASTERT TELL YOU THERE'S A NEW BOSS IN TOWN?
I CAN TAKE YOU TO HIM. RIGHT NOW.
OR I CAN GO TO JAIL, WHERE IT'S NICE AND QUIET.
LEAD THE WAY.

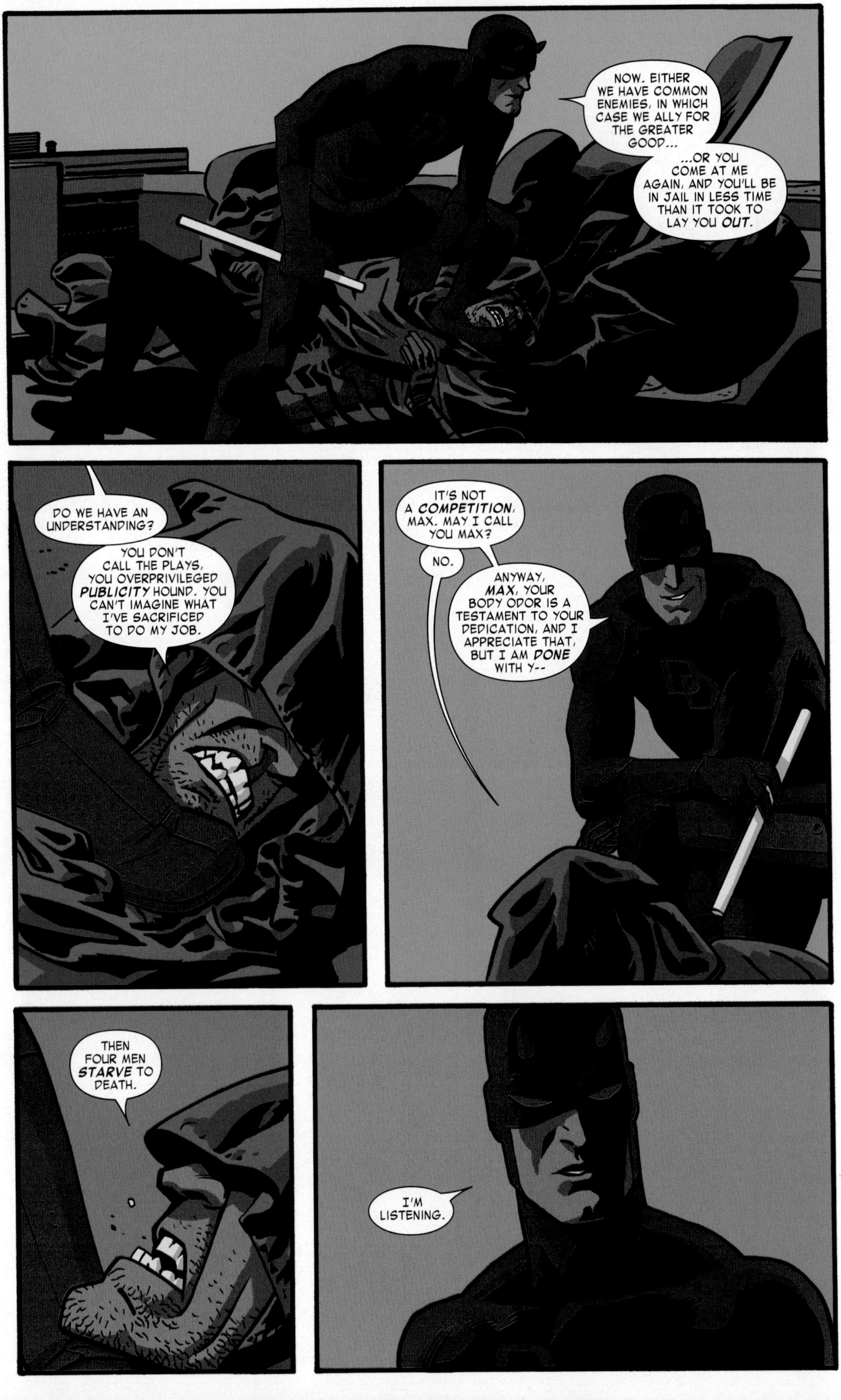
NOW. EITHER WE HAVE COMMON ENEMIES, IN WHICH CASE WE ALLY FOR THE GREATER GOOD...
...OR YOU COME AT ME AGAIN, AND YOU'LL BE IN JAIL IN LESS TIME THAN IT TOOK TO LAY YOU **OUT**.
DO WE HAVE AN UNDERSTANDING?
YOU DON'T CALL THE PLAYS, YOU OVERPRIVILEGED **PUBLICITY** HOUND. YOU CAN'T IMAGINE WHAT I'VE SACRIFICED TO DO MY JOB.
IT'S NOT A **COMPETITION**, MAX. MAY I CALL YOU MAX?
NO.
ANYWAY, **MAX**, YOUR BODY ODOR IS A TESTAMENT TO YOUR DEDICATION, AND I APPRECIATE THAT, BUT I AM **DONE** WITH Y--
THEN FOUR MEN **STARVE** TO DEATH.
I'M LISTENING.

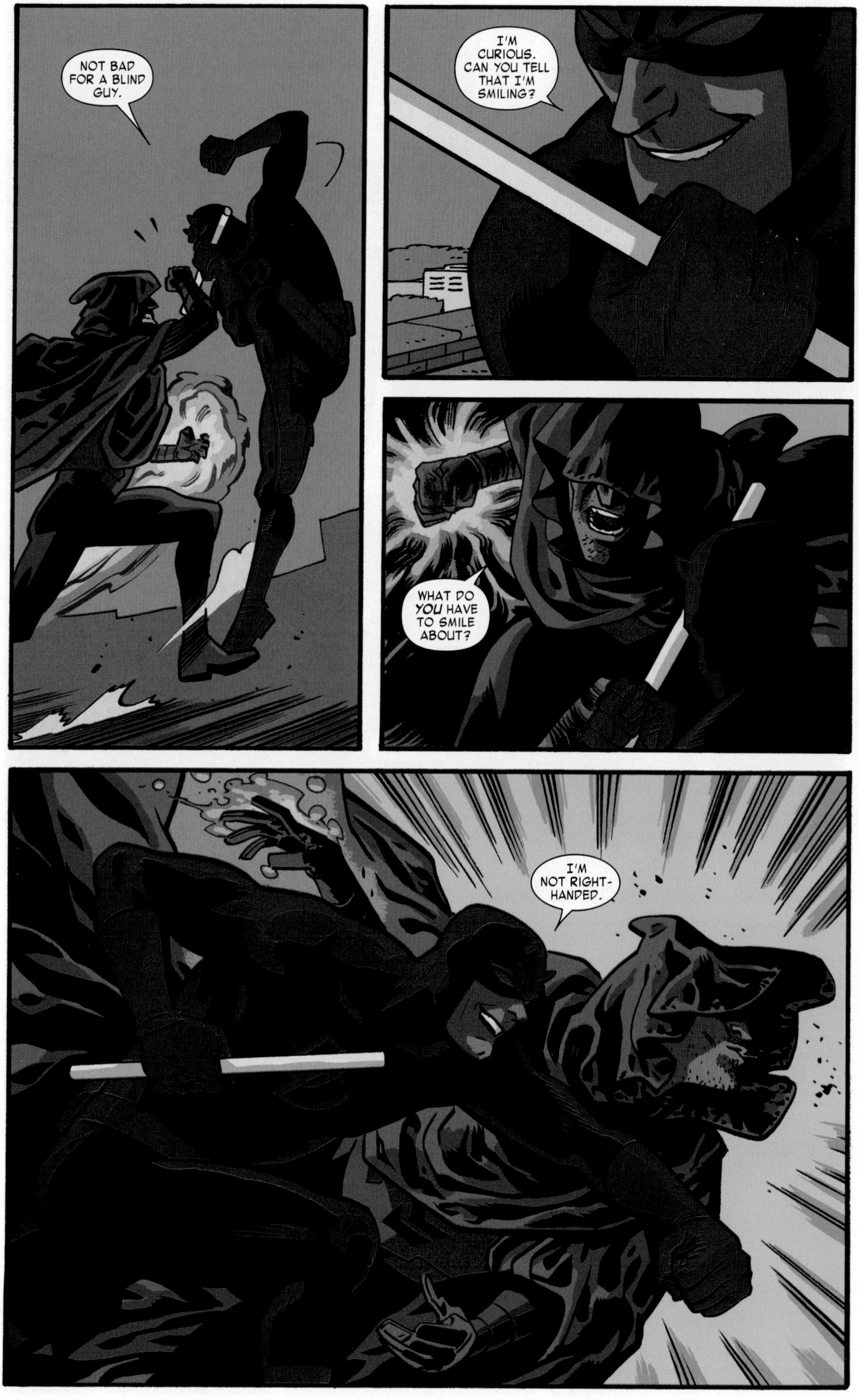
NOT BAD FOR A BLIND GUY.
I'M CURIOUS. CAN YOU TELL THAT I'M SMILING?
WHAT DO *YOU* HAVE TO SMILE ABOUT?
I'M NOT RIGHT-HANDED.

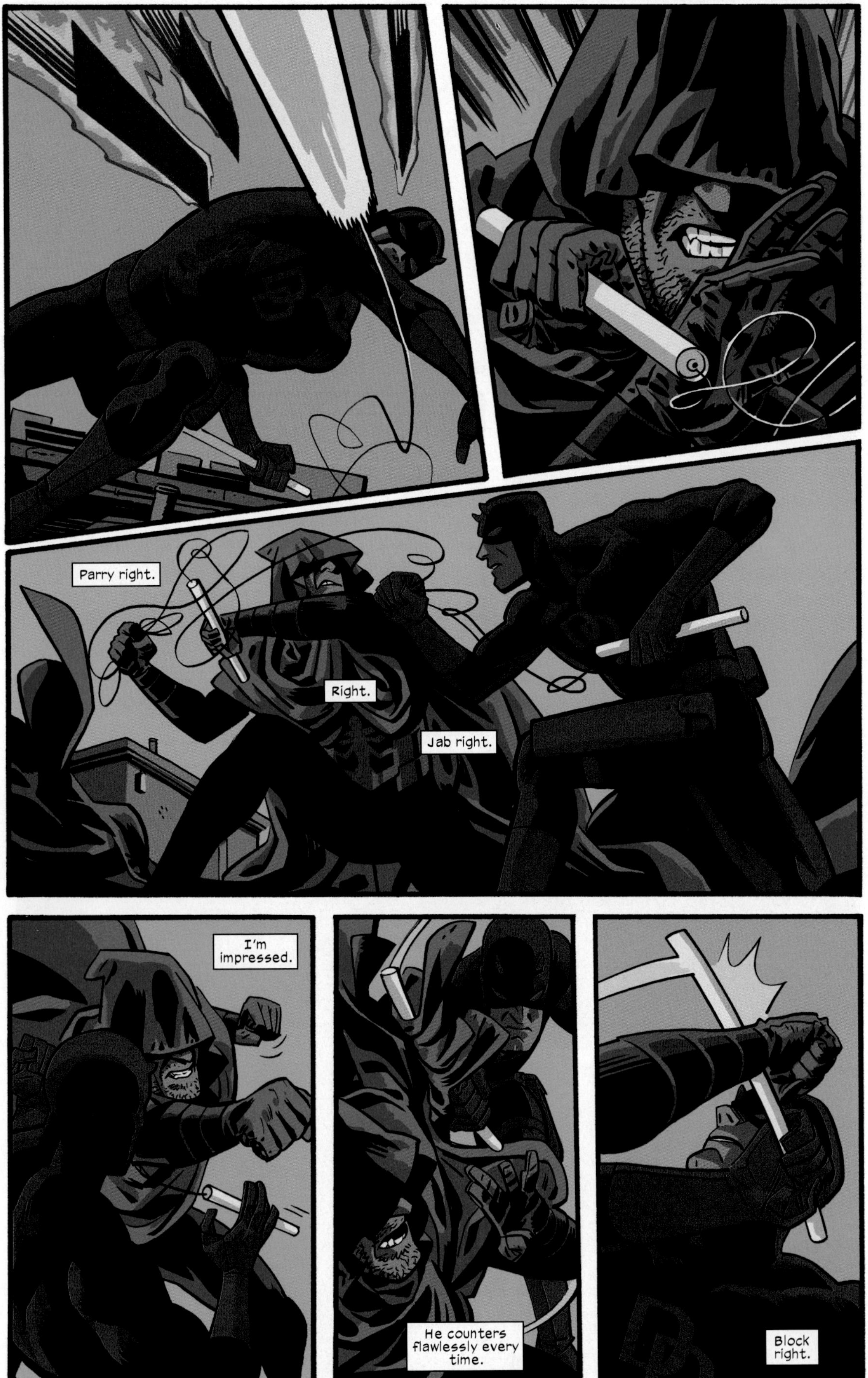
Parry right.
Right.
Jab right.
I'm impressed.
He counters flawlessly every time.
Block right.

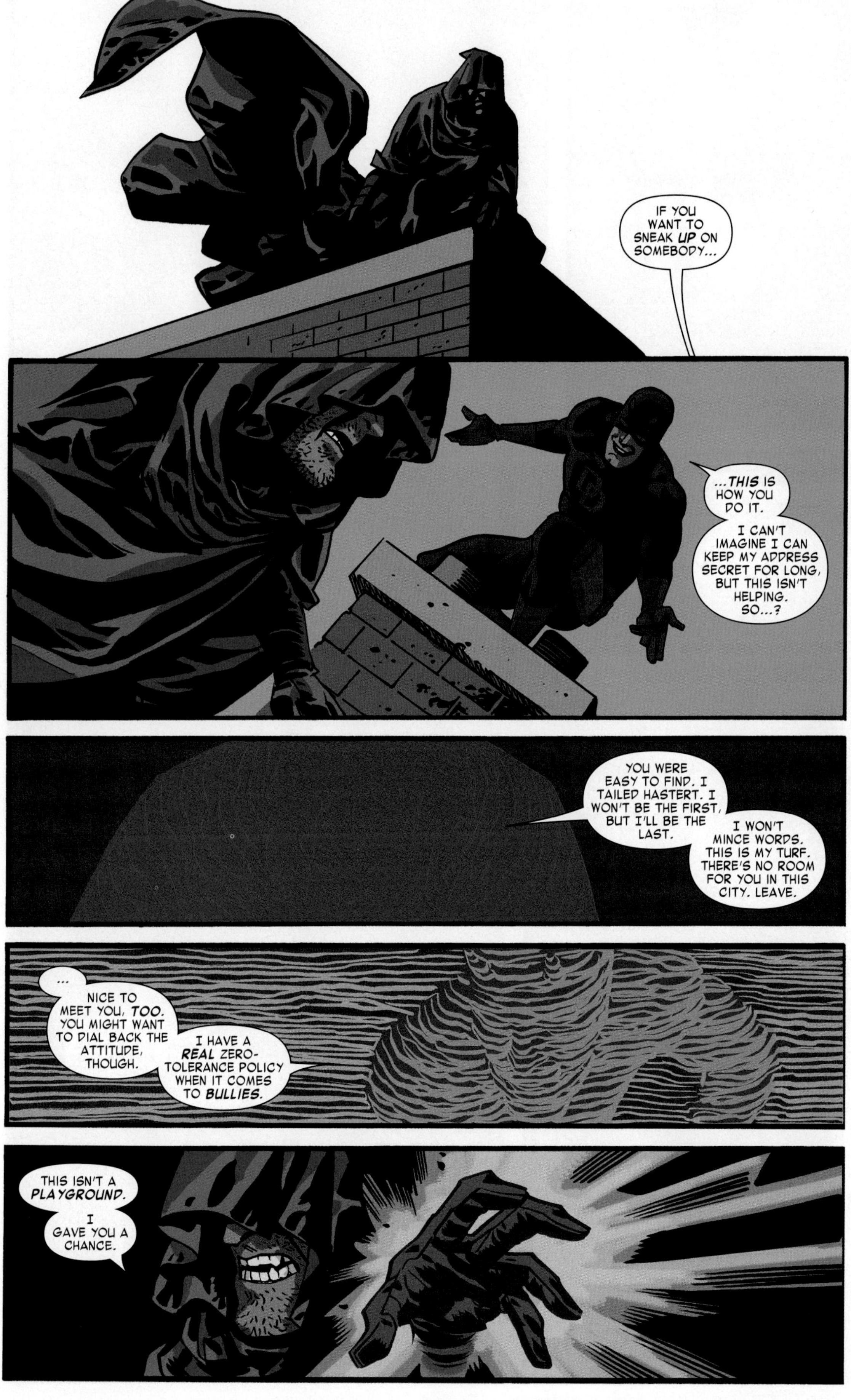
IF YOU WANT TO SNEAK *UP* ON SOMEBODY...
...*THIS* IS HOW YOU DO IT.
I CAN'T IMAGINE I CAN KEEP MY ADDRESS SECRET FOR LONG, BUT THIS ISN'T HELPING. SO...?
YOU WERE EASY TO FIND. I TAILED HASTERT. I WON'T BE THE FIRST, BUT I'LL BE THE LAST.
I WON'T MINCE WORDS. THIS IS MY TURF. THERE'S NO ROOM FOR YOU IN THIS CITY. LEAVE.
...
NICE TO MEET YOU, *TOO*. YOU MIGHT WANT TO DIAL BACK THE ATTITUDE, THOUGH.
I HAVE A *REAL* ZERO-TOLERANCE POLICY WHEN IT COMES TO *BULLIES*.
THIS ISN'T A *PLAYGROUND*.
I GAVE YOU A CHANCE.

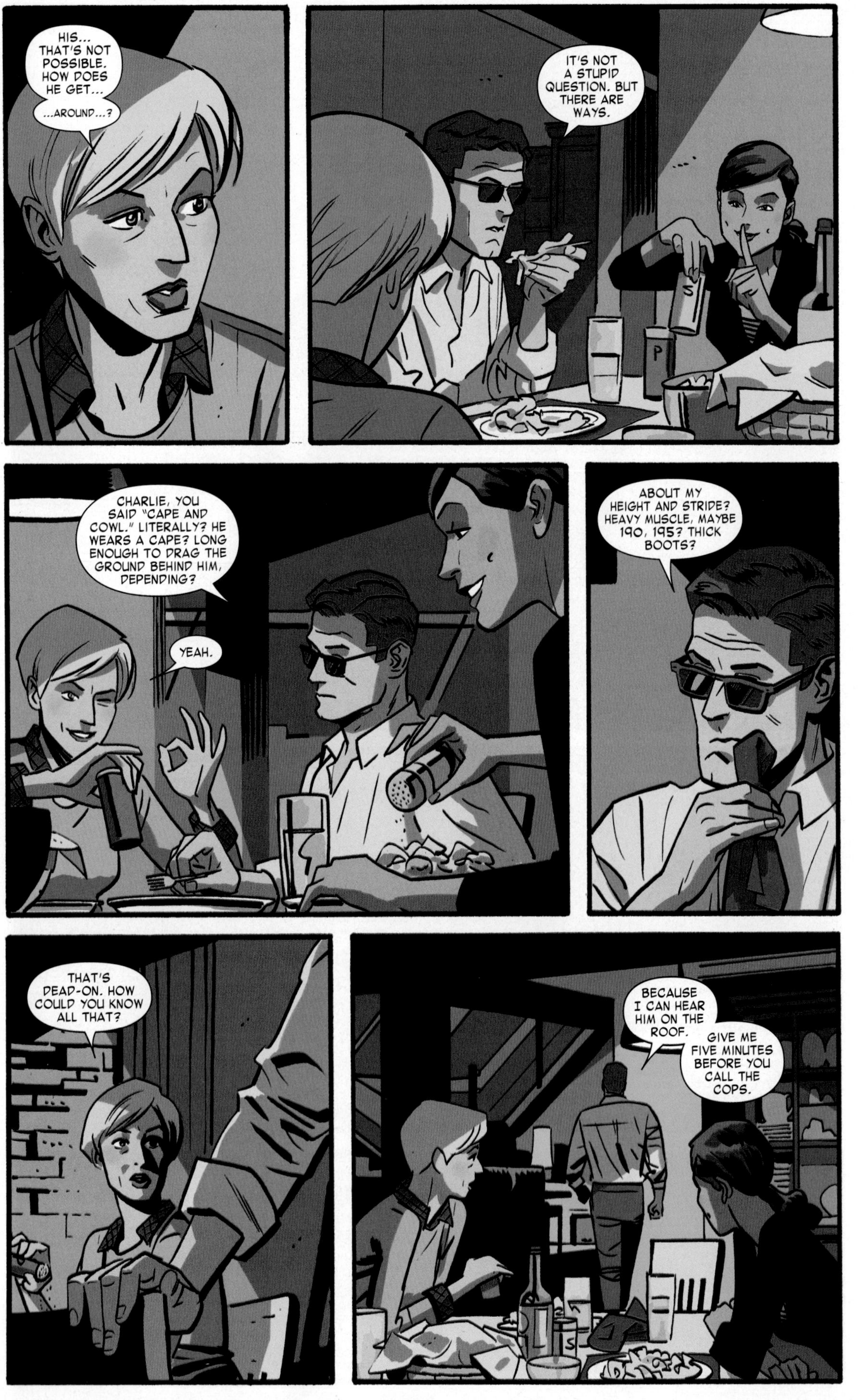
HIS... THAT'S NOT POSSIBLE. HOW DOES HE GET...
...AROUND...?
IT'S NOT A STUPID QUESTION. BUT THERE ARE WAYS.
CHARLIE, YOU SAID "CAPE AND COWL." LITERALLY? HE WEARS A CAPE? LONG ENOUGH TO DRAG THE GROUND BEHIND HIM, DEPENDING?
YEAH.
ABOUT MY HEIGHT AND STRIDE? HEAVY MUSCLE, MAYBE 190, 195? THICK BOOTS?
THAT'S DEAD-ON. HOW COULD YOU KNOW ALL THAT?
BECAUSE I CAN HEAR HIM ON THE ROOF.
GIVE ME FIVE MINUTES BEFORE YOU CALL THE COPS.

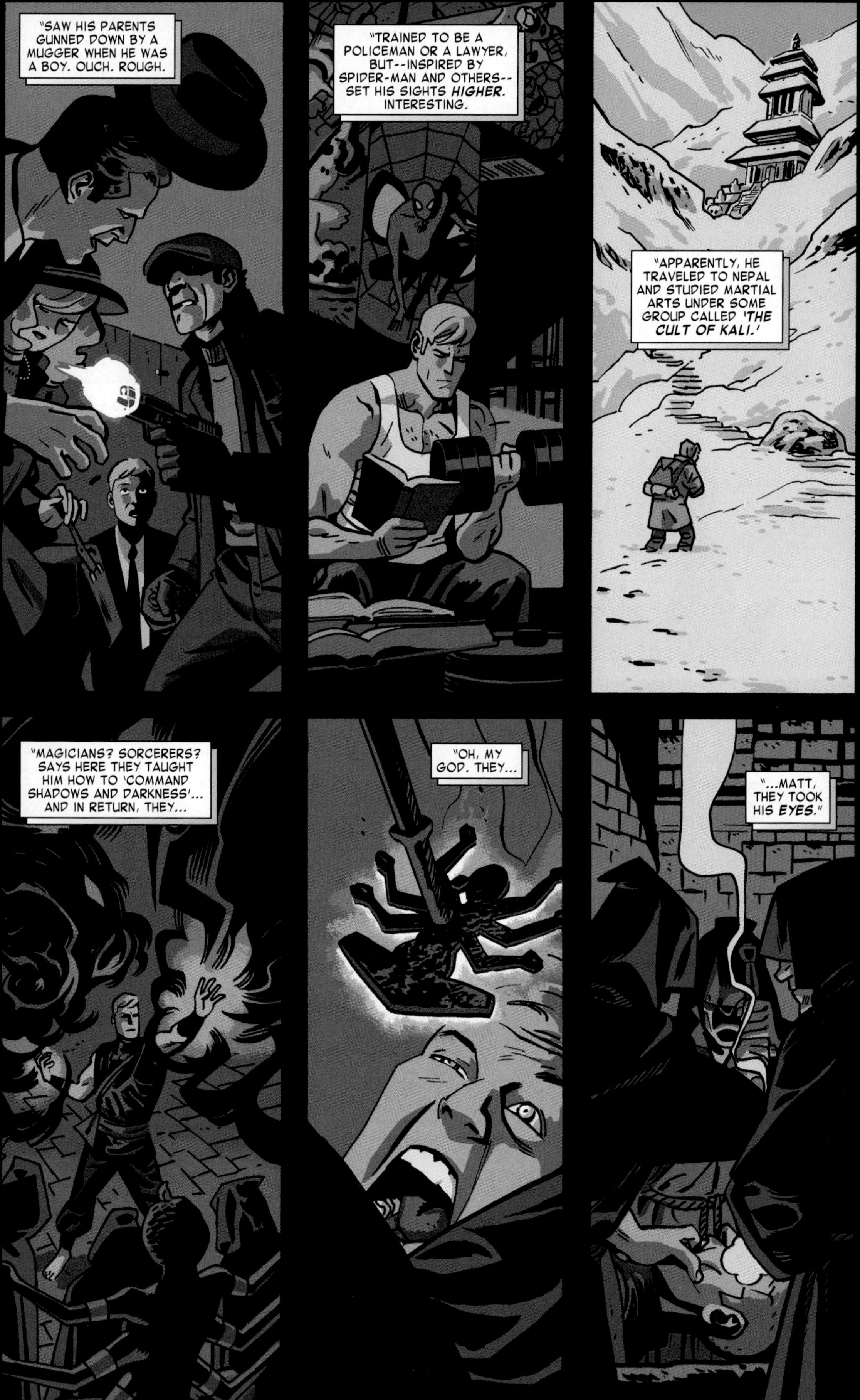
"SAW HIS PARENTS GUNNED DOWN BY A MUGGER WHEN HE WAS A BOY. OUCH. ROUGH.
"TRAINED TO BE A POLICEMAN OR A LAWYER, BUT--INSPIRED BY SPIDER-MAN AND OTHERS--SET HIS SIGHTS *HIGHER.* INTERESTING.
"APPARENTLY, HE TRAVELED TO NEPAL AND STUDIED MARTIAL ARTS UNDER SOME GROUP CALLED *'THE CULT OF KALI.'*
"MAGICIANS? SORCERERS? SAYS HERE THEY TAUGHT HIM HOW TO 'COMMAND SHADOWS AND DARKNESS'... AND IN RETURN, THEY...
"OH, MY GOD. THEY...
"...MATT, THEY TOOK HIS *EYES.*"

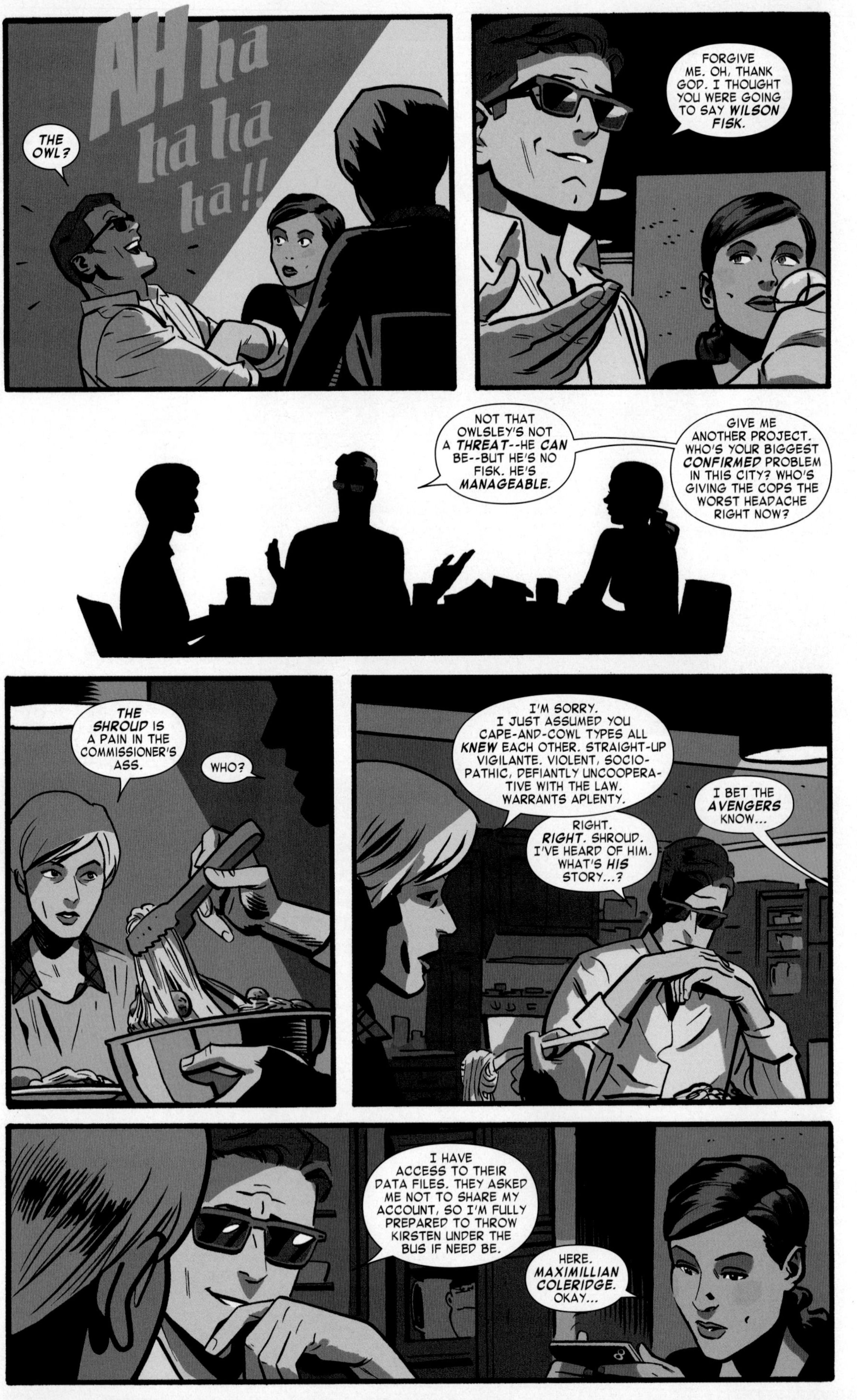
AH ha ha ha ha!!
THE OWL?
FORGIVE ME. OH, THANK GOD. I THOUGHT YOU WERE GOING TO SAY *WILSON FISK*.
NOT THAT OWLSLEY'S NOT A *THREAT*--HE *CAN* BE--BUT HE'S NO FISK. HE'S *MANAGEABLE*.
GIVE ME ANOTHER PROJECT. WHO'S YOUR BIGGEST *CONFIRMED* PROBLEM IN THIS CITY? WHO'S GIVING THE COPS THE WORST HEADACHE RIGHT NOW?
THE SHROUD IS A PAIN IN THE COMMISSIONER'S ASS.
WHO?
I'M SORRY. I JUST ASSUMED YOU CAPE-AND-COWL TYPES ALL *KNEW* EACH OTHER. STRAIGHT-UP VIGILANTE. VIOLENT, SOCIO-PATHIC, DEFIANTLY UNCOOPERA-TIVE WITH THE LAW. WARRANTS APLENTY.
RIGHT. *RIGHT*. SHROUD. I'VE HEARD OF HIM. WHAT'S *HIS* STORY...?
I BET THE *AVENGERS* KNOW...
I HAVE ACCESS TO THEIR DATA FILES. THEY ASKED ME NOT TO SHARE MY ACCOUNT, SO I'M FULLY PREPARED TO THROW KIRSTEN UNDER THE BUS IF NEED BE.
HERE. *MAXIMILLIAN COLERIDGE*. OKAY...

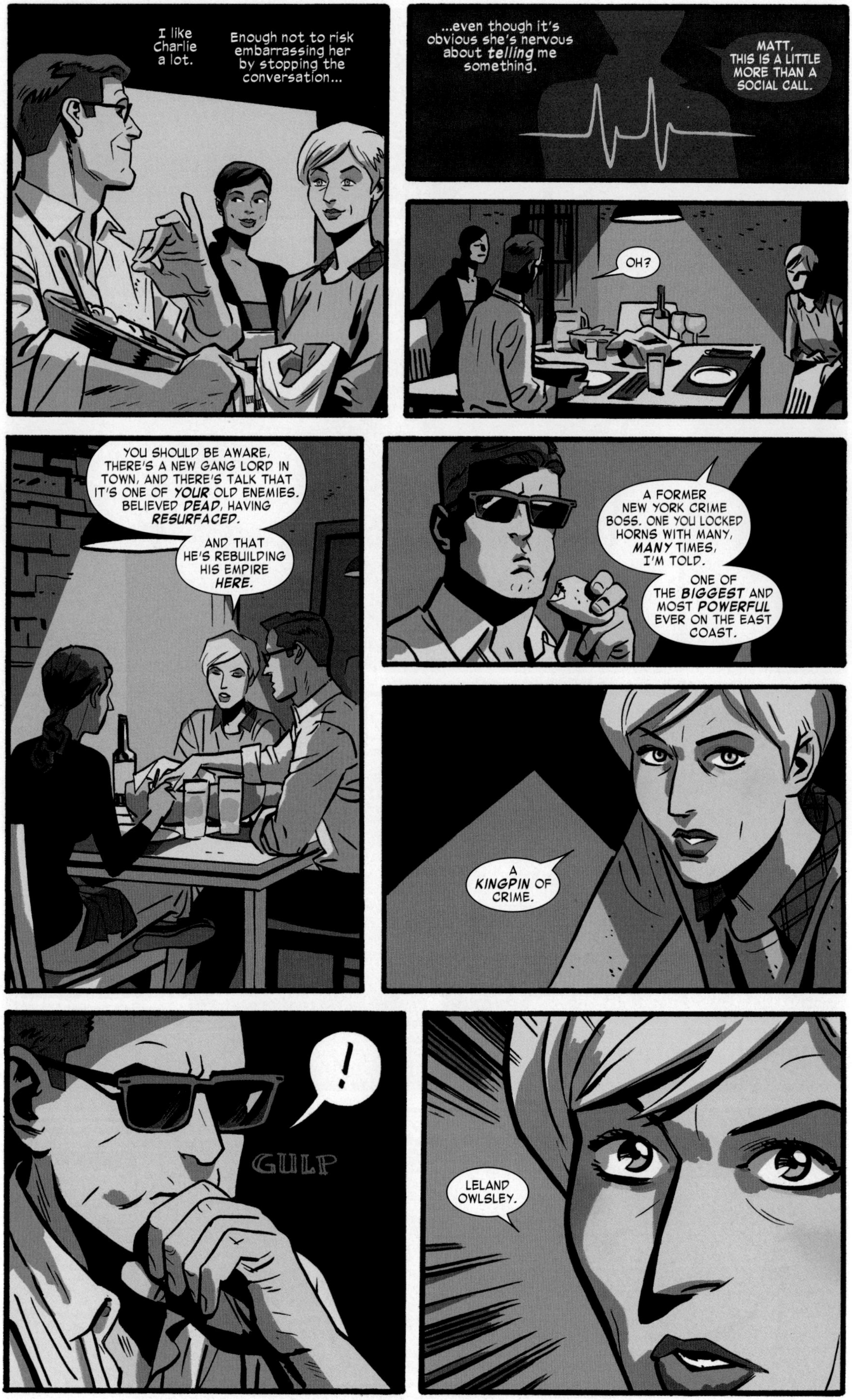
I like Charlie a lot.
Enough not to risk embarrassing her by stopping the conversation...
...even though it's obvious she's nervous about *telling* me something.
MATT, THIS IS A LITTLE MORE THAN A SOCIAL CALL.
OH?
YOU SHOULD BE AWARE, THERE'S A NEW GANG LORD IN TOWN, AND THERE'S TALK THAT IT'S ONE OF ***YOUR*** OLD ENEMIES. BELIEVED ***DEAD***, HAVING ***RESURFACED***.
AND THAT HE'S REBUILDING HIS EMPIRE ***HERE***.
A FORMER NEW YORK CRIME BOSS. ONE YOU LOCKED HORNS WITH MANY, ***MANY*** TIMES, I'M TOLD.
ONE OF THE ***BIGGEST*** AND MOST ***POWERFUL*** EVER ON THE EAST COAST.
A ***KINGPIN*** OF CRIME.
!
GULP
LELAND OWLSLEY.

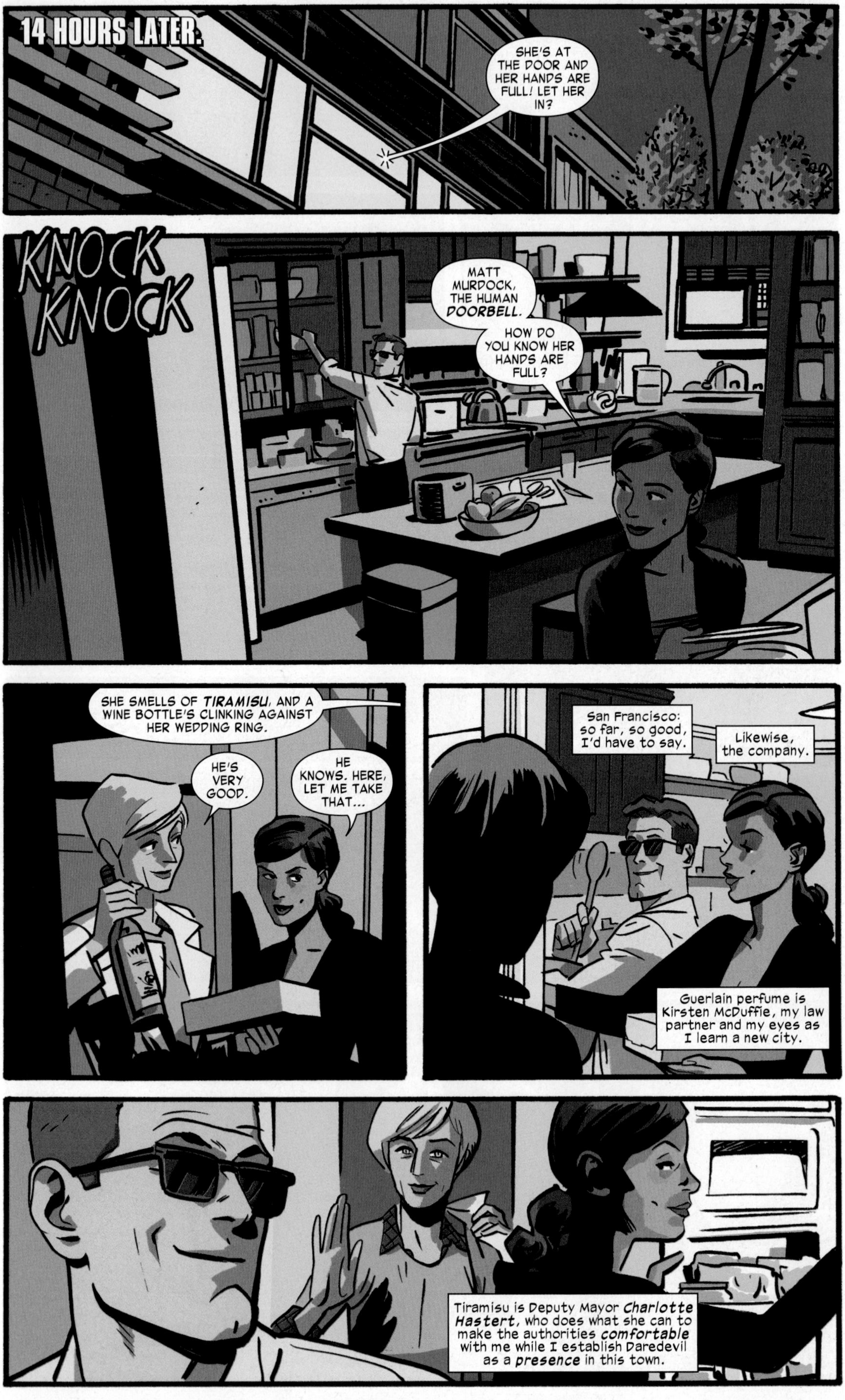
14 HOURS LATER.
SHE'S AT THE DOOR AND HER HANDS ARE FULL! LET HER IN?
KNOCK KNOCK
MATT MURDOCK, THE HUMAN **DOORBELL**.
HOW DO YOU KNOW HER HANDS ARE FULL?
SHE SMELLS OF ***TIRAMISU***, AND A WINE BOTTLE'S CLINKING AGAINST HER WEDDING RING.
HE'S VERY GOOD.
HE KNOWS. HERE, LET ME TAKE THAT...
San Francisco: so far, so good, I'd have to say.
Likewise, the company.
Guerlain perfume is Kirsten McDuffie, my law partner and my eyes as I learn a new city.
Tiramisu is Deputy Mayor ***Charlotte Hastert***, who does what she can to make the authorities ***comfortable*** with me while I establish Daredevil as a ***presence*** in this town.

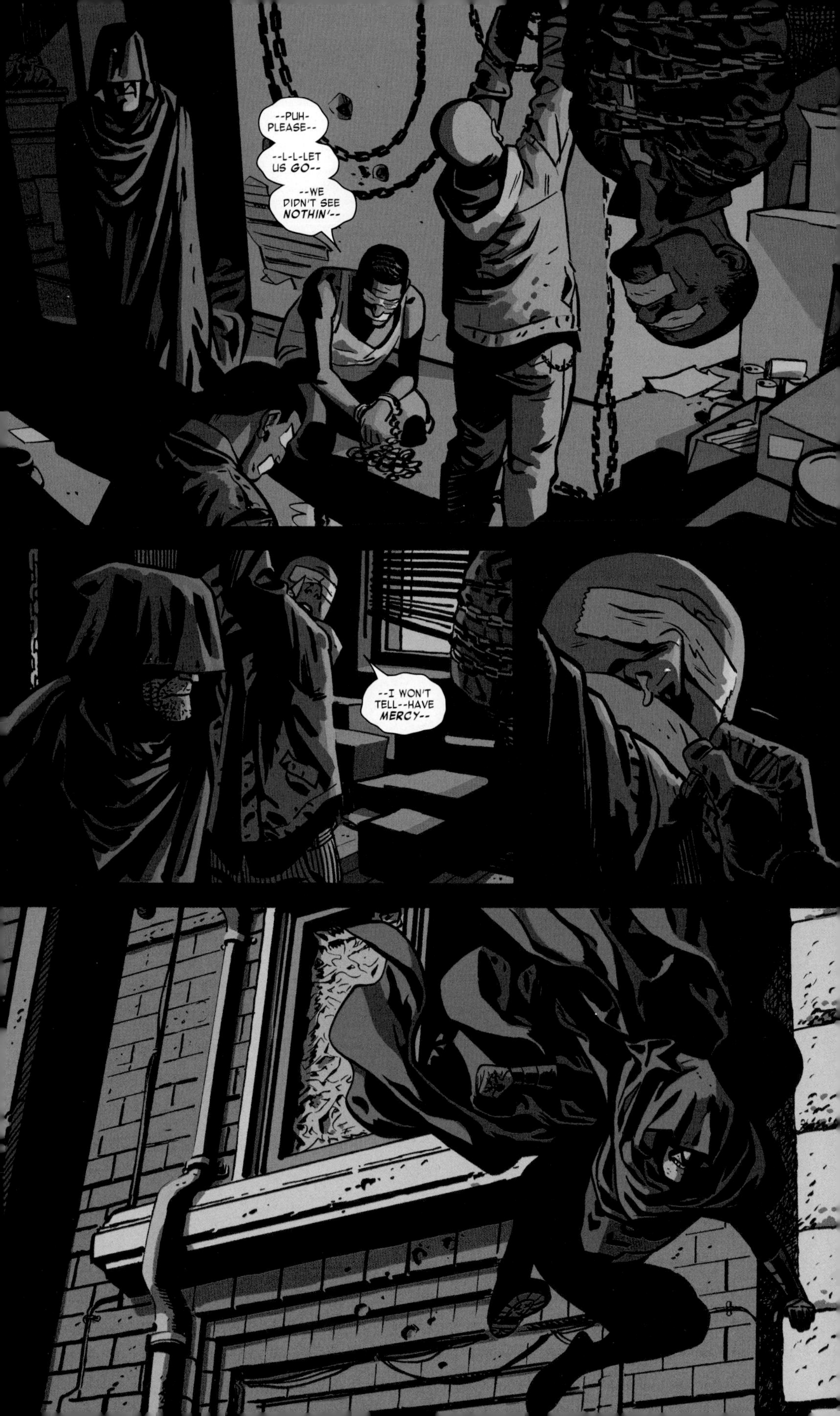
--PUH-
PLEASE--
--L-L-LET
US GO--
--WE
DIDN'T SEE
NOTHIN'--
--I WON'T
TELL--HAVE
MERCY--

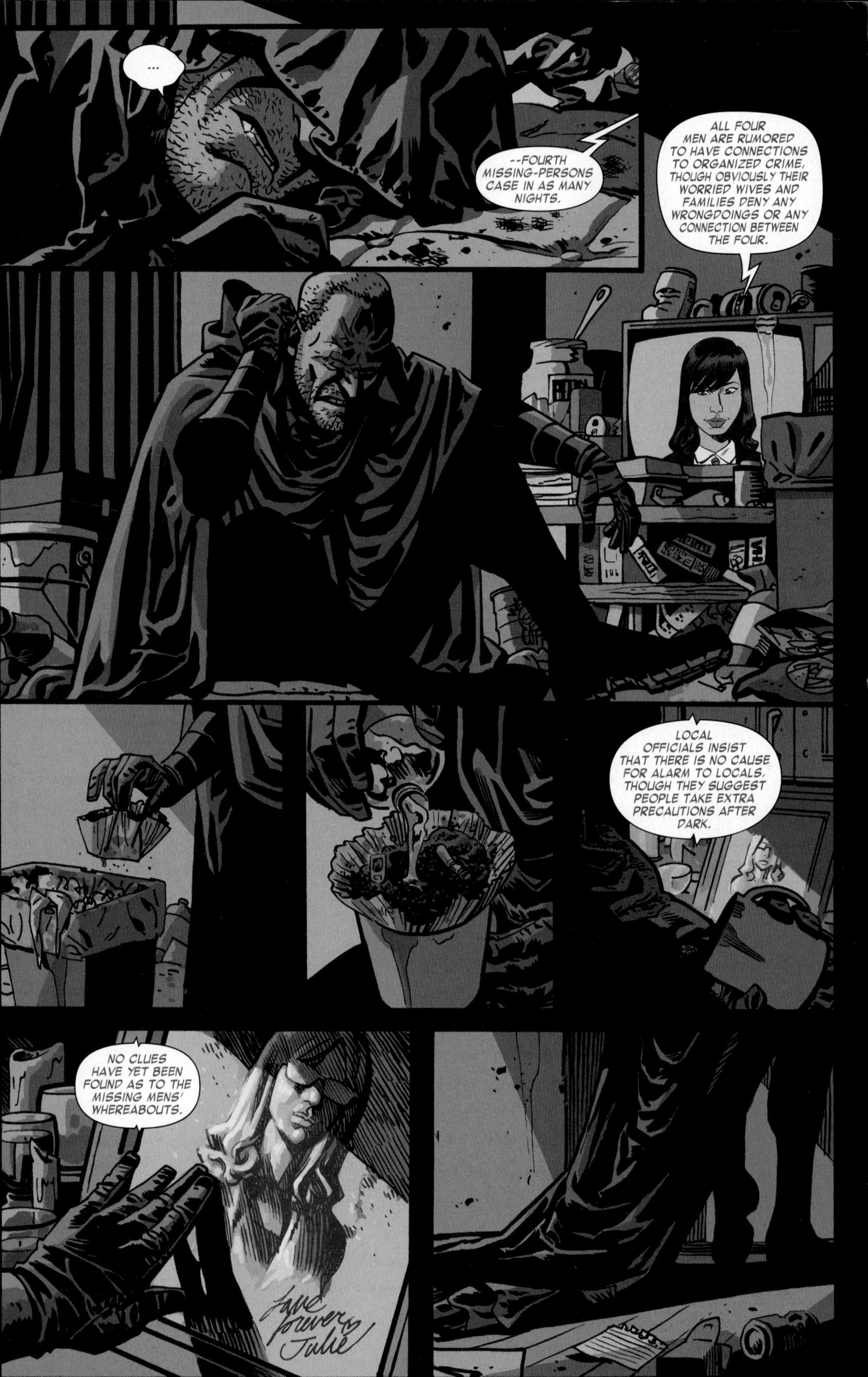
...
--FOURTH MISSING-PERSONS CASE IN AS MANY NIGHTS.
ALL FOUR MEN ARE RUMORED TO HAVE CONNECTIONS TO ORGANIZED CRIME, THOUGH OBVIOUSLY THEIR WORRIED WIVES AND FAMILIES DENY ANY WRONGDOINGS OR ANY CONNECTION BETWEEN THE FOUR.
LOCAL OFFICIALS INSIST THAT THERE IS NO CAUSE FOR ALARM TO LOCALS, THOUGH THEY SUGGEST PEOPLE TAKE EXTRA PRECAUTIONS AFTER DARK.
NO CLUES HAVE YET BEEN FOUND AS TO THE MISSING MENS' WHEREABOUTS.
Love forever, Julie

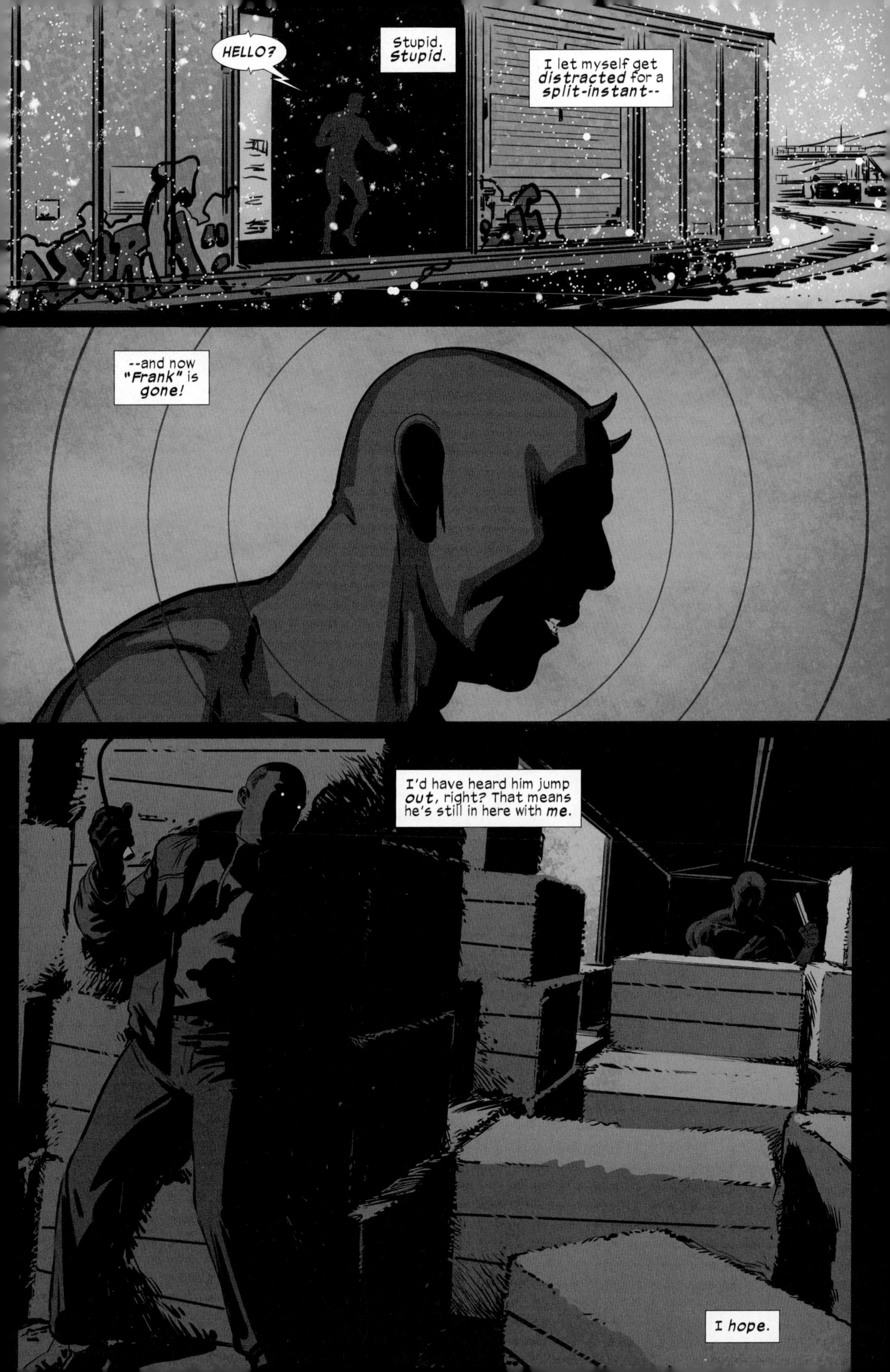
HELLO?
Stupid. Stupid.
I let myself get distracted for a split-instant--
--and now "Frank" is gone!
I'd have heard him jump out, right? That means he's still in here with me.
I hope.

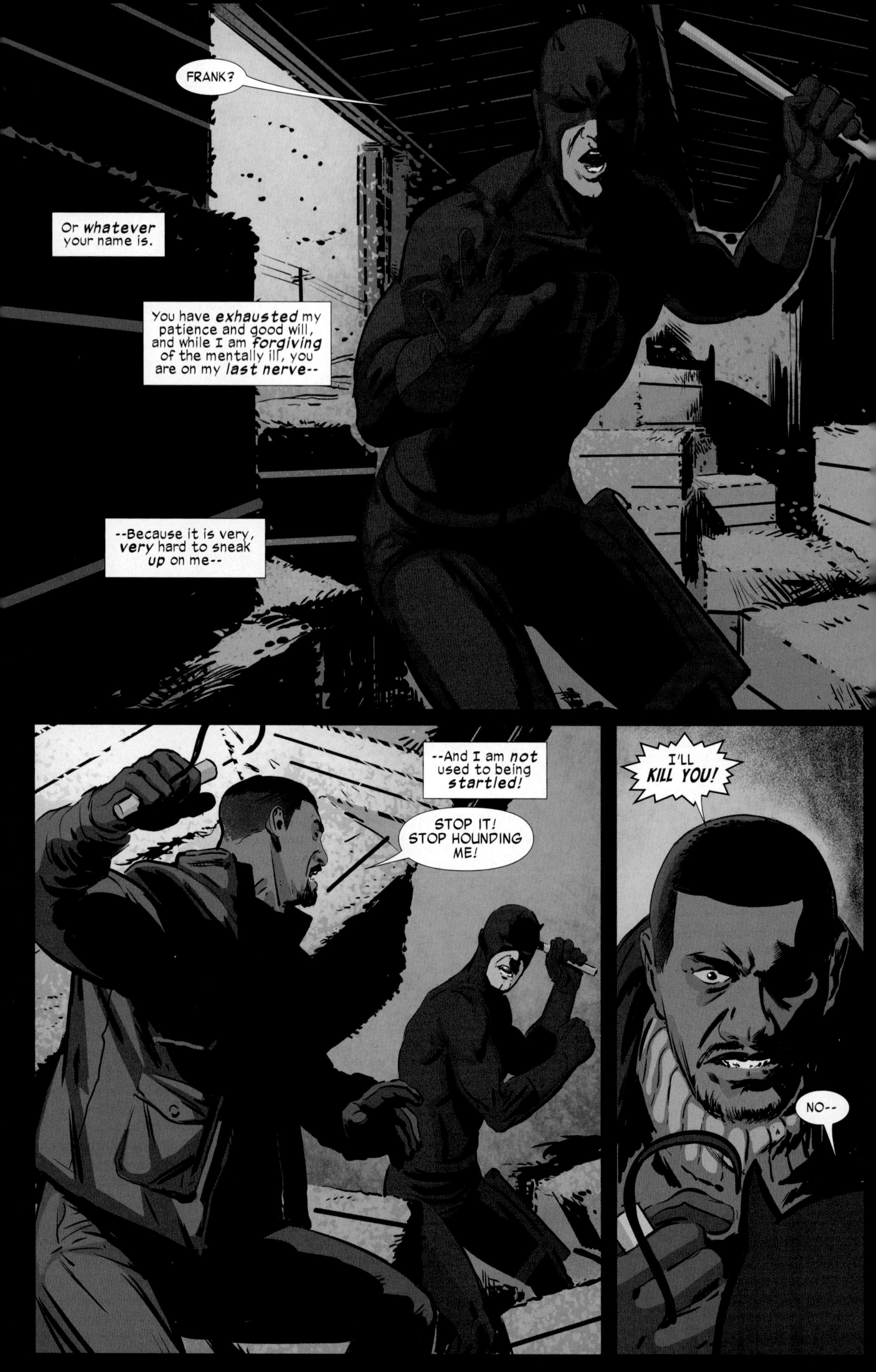
FRANK?
Or *whatever* your name is.
You have *exhausted* my patience and good will, and while I am *forgiving* of the mentally ill, you are on my *last nerve*--
--Because it is very, *very* hard to sneak *up* on me--
--And I am *not* used to being *startled!*
STOP IT! STOP HOUNDING ME!
I'LL **KILL YOU!**
NO--

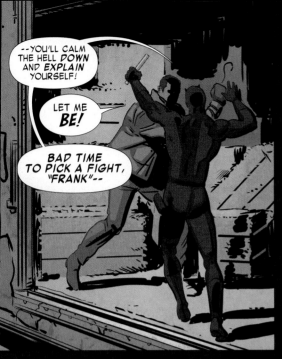

--YOU'LL CALM
THE HELL *DOWN*
AND *EXPLAIN*
YOURSELF!

LET ME
BE!

BAD TIME
TO PICK A FIGHT,
"FRANK"--

--ONE
SLIP, AND IT'S
A LONG WAY
DOWN!

⸮HNNGH!⸮

Wind's rocking the *train*
like a *bath float*, but
that's not why I lost my
footing. He's just
stronger than me.

I forgot I saw this
man punch through a
wall. I won't make
that mistake *again*.

LET ME
BE!

LET ME
BE!

...

Let you be
what, Frank...?

Your silhouette,
changing...

...Your *skin*, moving
and crackling like
crumpling *paper*...

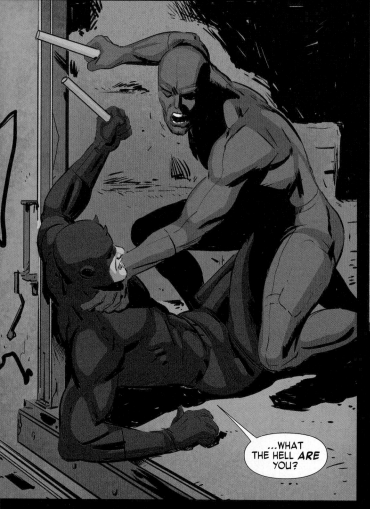

YOU DON'T WATCH THE *NEWS?*

EVERYBODY KNOWS ME THESE DAYS! I'M THE LAWYER WHO SINGLE-HANDEDLY BUSTED UP THE *SONS OF THE SERPENT!*

...WHAT THE HELL *ARE* YOU?

I'M *DAREDEVIL!*

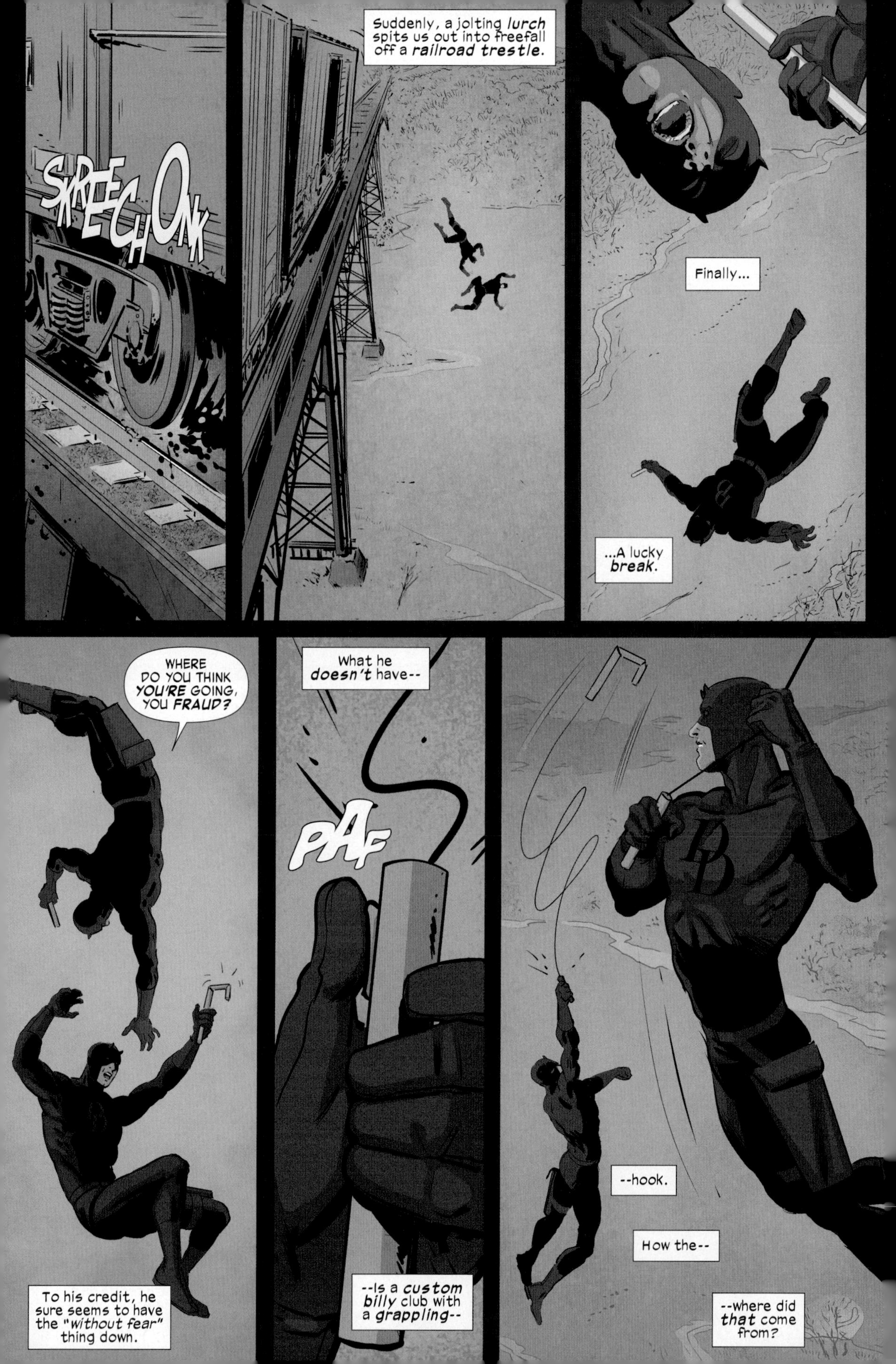
SKREECHONK
Suddenly, a jolting lurch spits us out into freefall off a railroad trestle.
Finally...
...A lucky break.
WHERE DO YOU THINK YOU'RE GOING, YOU FRAUD?
To his credit, he sure seems to have the "without fear" thing down.
What he doesn't have--
PAF
--Is a custom billy club with a grappling--
--hook.
How the--
--where did that come from?

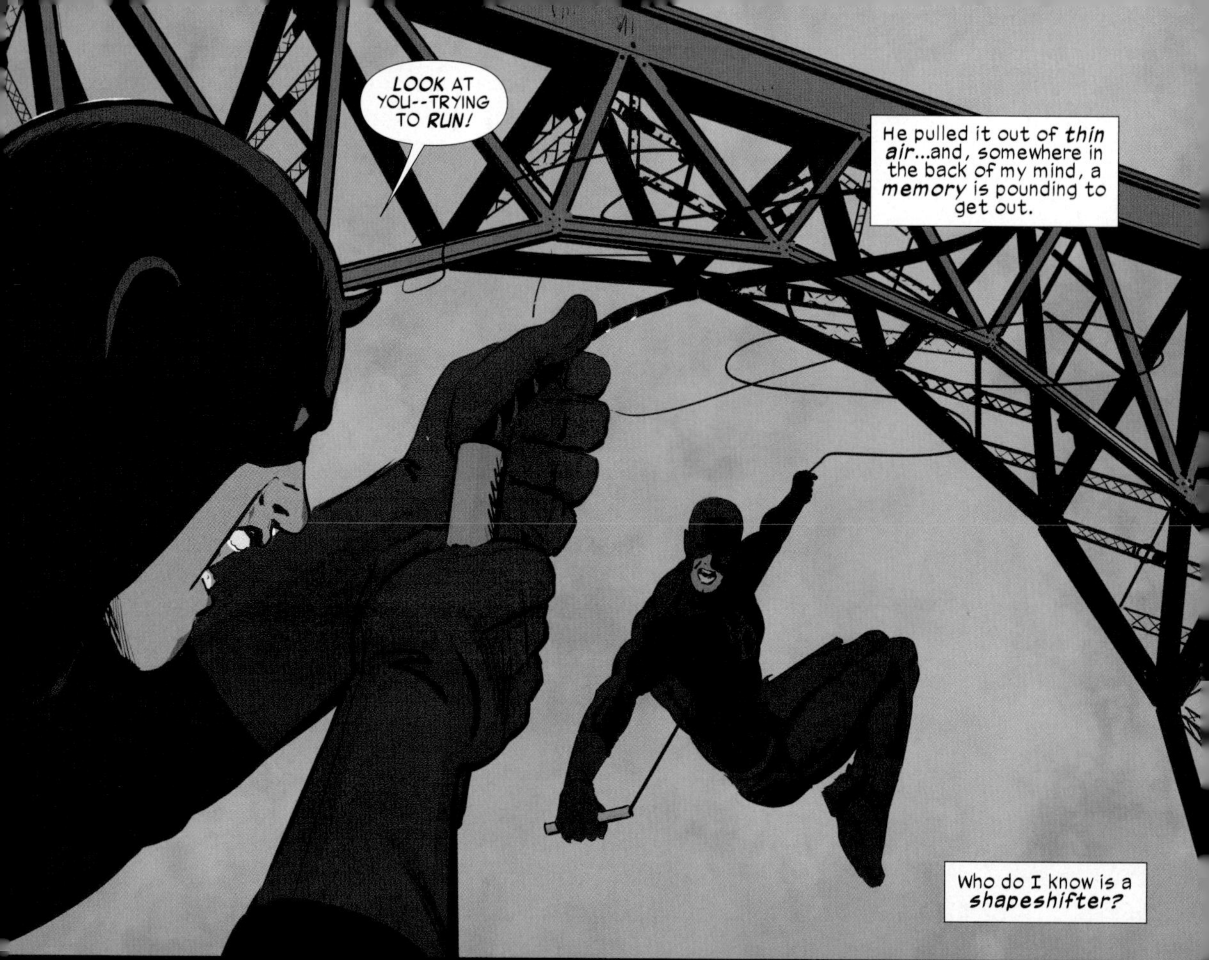
LOOK AT YOU--TRYING TO RUN!
He pulled it out of thin air...and, somewhere in the back of my mind, a memory is pounding to get out.
Who do I know is a shapeshifter?
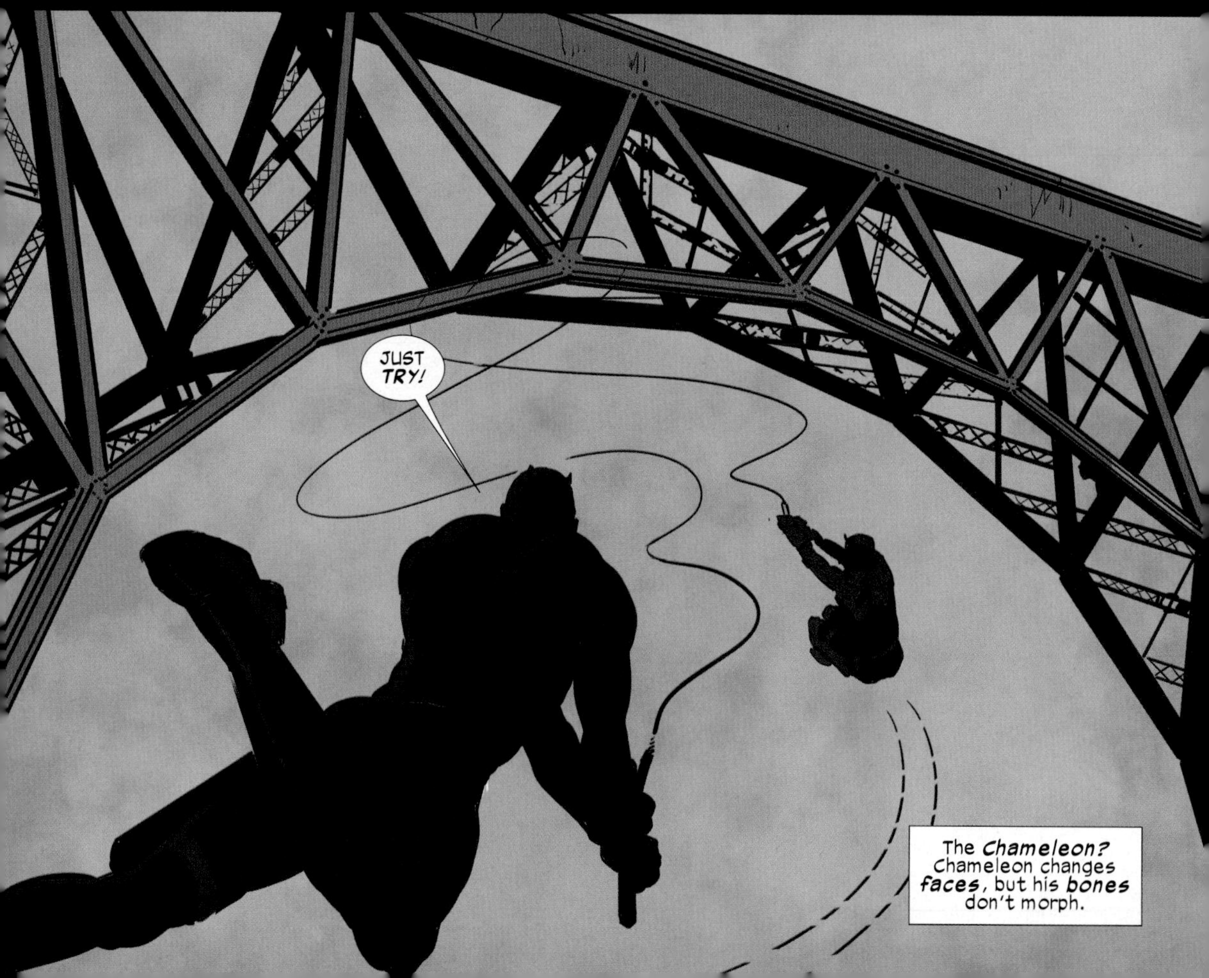
JUST TRY!
The Chameleon? Chameleon changes faces, but his bones don't morph.

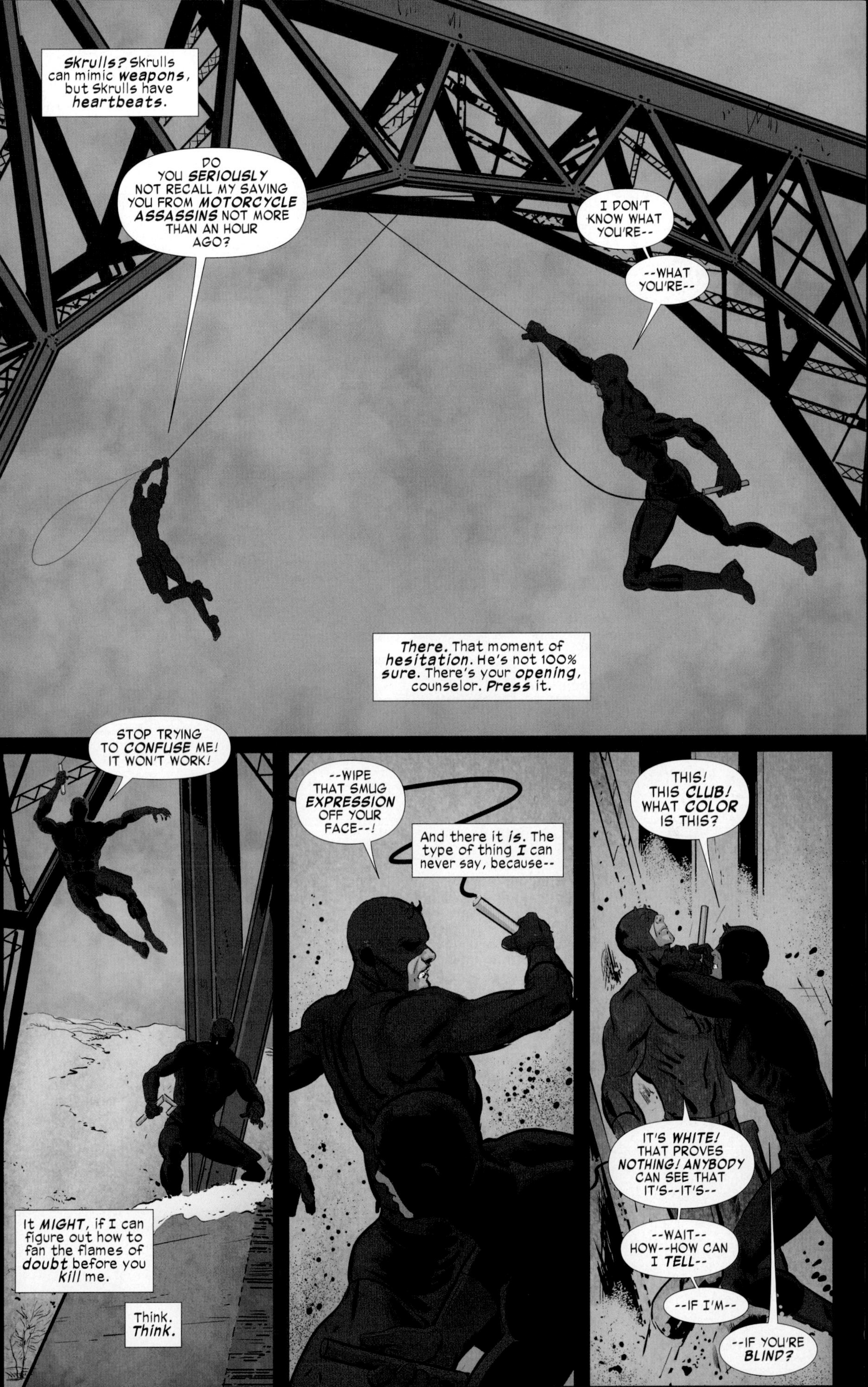

Skrulls? Skrulls can mimic weapons, but Skrulls have heartbeats.
DO YOU SERIOUSLY NOT RECALL MY SAVING YOU FROM MOTORCYCLE ASSASSINS NOT MORE THAN AN HOUR AGO?
I DON'T KNOW WHAT YOU'RE--
--WHAT YOU'RE--
There. That moment of hesitation. He's not 100% sure. There's your opening, counselor. Press it.
STOP TRYING TO CONFUSE ME! IT WON'T WORK!
It MIGHT, if I can figure out how to fan the flames of doubt before you kill me.
Think. Think.
--WIPE THAT SMUG EXPRESSION OFF YOUR FACE--!
And there it is. The type of thing I can never say, because--
THIS! THIS CLUB! WHAT COLOR IS THIS?
IT'S WHITE! THAT PROVES NOTHING! ANYBODY CAN SEE THAT IT'S--IT'S--
--WAIT-- HOW--HOW CAN I TELL--
--IF I'M--
--IF YOU'RE BLIND?

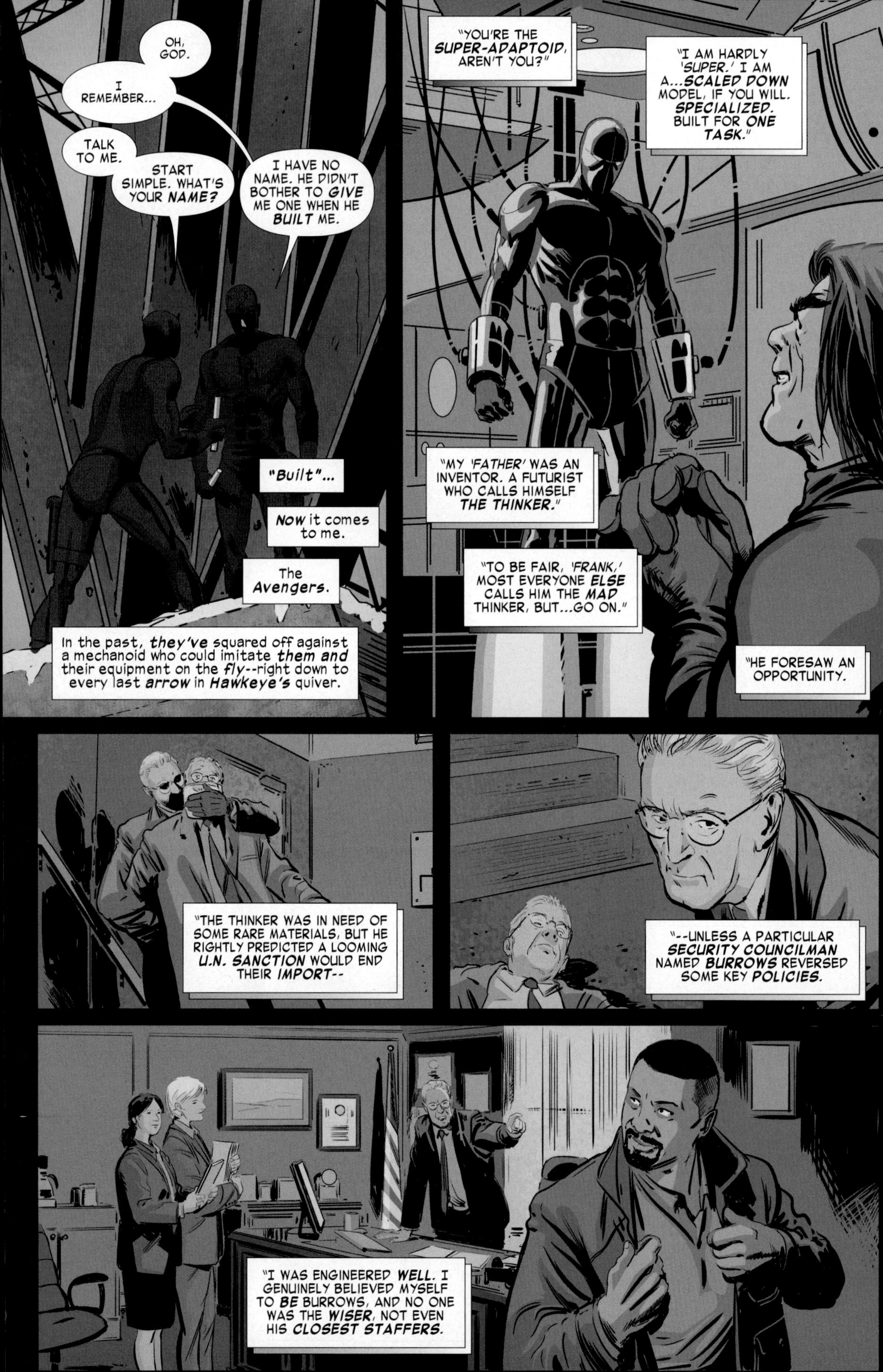
OH, GOD.
I REMEMBER...
TALK TO ME.
START SIMPLE. WHAT'S YOUR NAME?
I HAVE NO NAME. HE DIDN'T BOTHER TO GIVE ME ONE WHEN HE BUILT ME.
"Built"...
Now it comes to me.
The Avengers.
In the past, they've squared off against a mechanoid who could imitate them and their equipment on the fly--right down to every last arrow in Hawkeye's quiver.
"YOU'RE THE SUPER-ADAPTOID, AREN'T YOU?"
"I AM HARDLY 'SUPER.' I AM A...SCALED DOWN MODEL, IF YOU WILL. SPECIALIZED. BUILT FOR ONE TASK."
"MY 'FATHER' WAS AN INVENTOR. A FUTURIST WHO CALLS HIMSELF THE THINKER."
"TO BE FAIR, 'FRANK,' MOST EVERYONE ELSE CALLS HIM THE MAD THINKER, BUT...GO ON."
"HE FORESAW AN OPPORTUNITY.
"THE THINKER WAS IN NEED OF SOME RARE MATERIALS, BUT HE RIGHTLY PREDICTED A LOOMING U.N. SANCTION WOULD END THEIR IMPORT--
"--UNLESS A PARTICULAR SECURITY COUNCILMAN NAMED BURROWS REVERSED SOME KEY POLICIES.
"I WAS ENGINEERED WELL. I GENUINELY BELIEVED MYSELF TO BE BURROWS, AND NO ONE WAS THE WISER, NOT EVEN HIS CLOSEST STAFFERS.

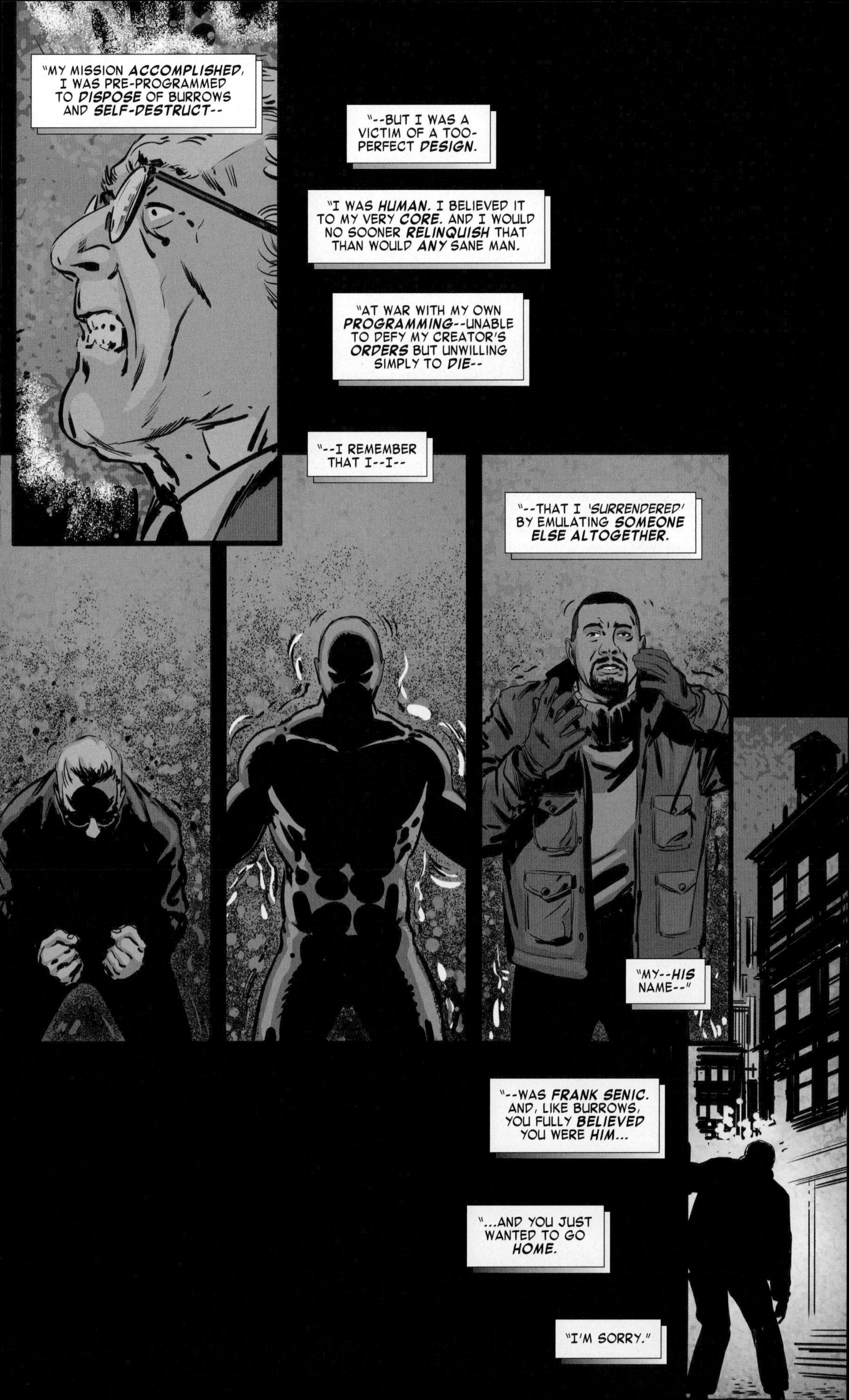
"MY MISSION ACCOMPLISHED, I WAS PRE-PROGRAMMED TO DISPOSE OF BURROWS AND SELF-DESTRUCT--
"--BUT I WAS A VICTIM OF A TOO-PERFECT DESIGN.
"I WAS HUMAN. I BELIEVED IT TO MY VERY CORE. AND I WOULD NO SOONER RELINQUISH THAT THAN WOULD ANY SANE MAN.
"AT WAR WITH MY OWN PROGRAMMING--UNABLE TO DEFY MY CREATOR'S ORDERS BUT UNWILLING SIMPLY TO DIE--
"--I REMEMBER THAT I--I--
"--THAT I 'SURRENDERED' BY EMULATING SOMEONE ELSE ALTOGETHER.
"MY--HIS NAME--"
"--WAS FRANK SENIC. AND, LIKE BURROWS, YOU FULLY BELIEVED YOU WERE HIM...
"...AND YOU JUST WANTED TO GO HOME.
"I'M SORRY."

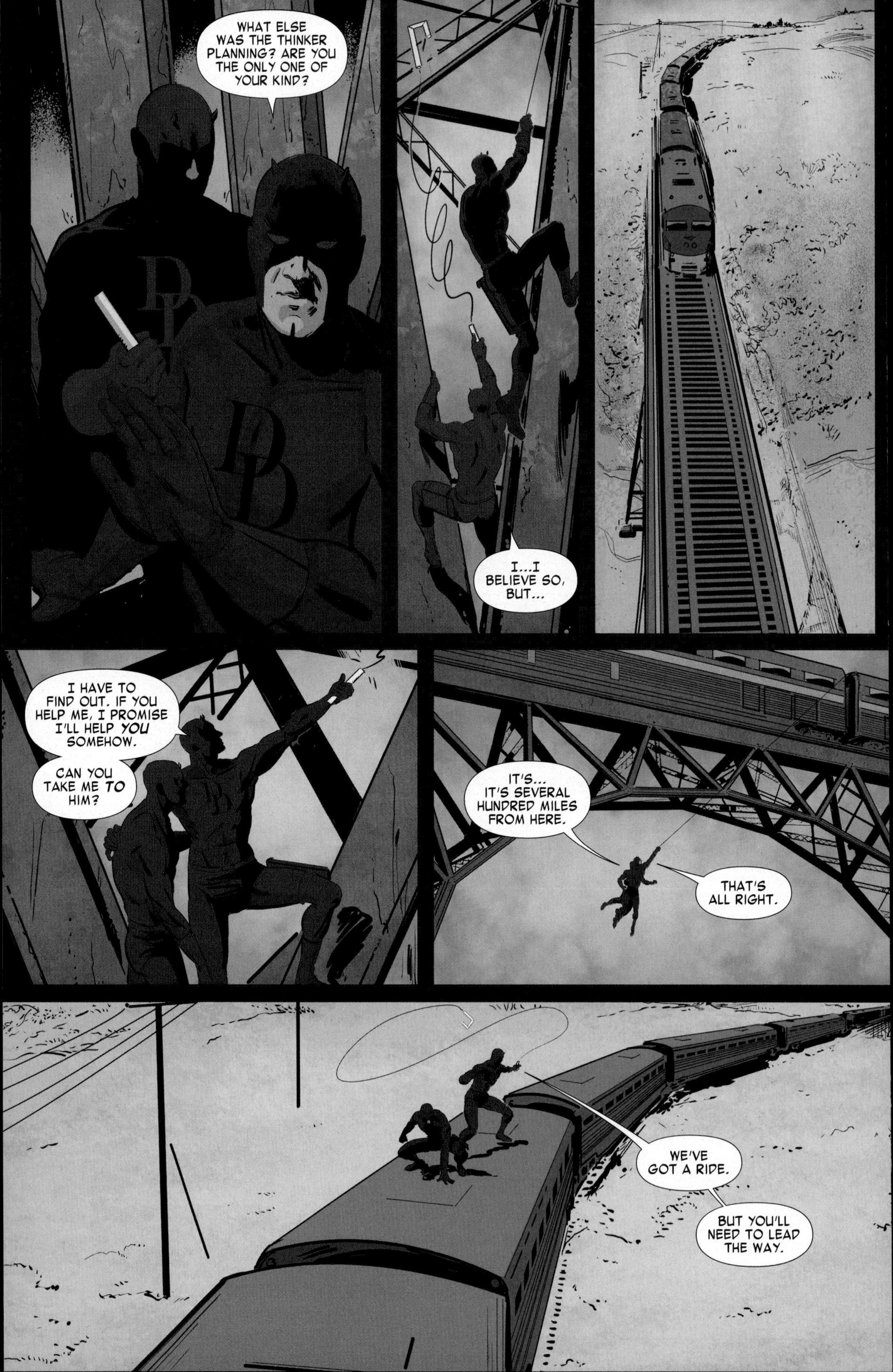
WHAT ELSE WAS THE THINKER PLANNING? ARE YOU THE ONLY ONE OF YOUR KIND?
I...I BELIEVE SO, BUT...
I HAVE TO FIND OUT. IF YOU HELP ME, I PROMISE I'LL HELP *YOU* SOMEHOW.
CAN YOU TAKE ME *TO* HIM?
IT'S... IT'S SEVERAL HUNDRED MILES FROM HERE.
THAT'S ALL RIGHT.
WE'VE GOT A RIDE.
BUT YOU'LL NEED TO LEAD THE WAY.

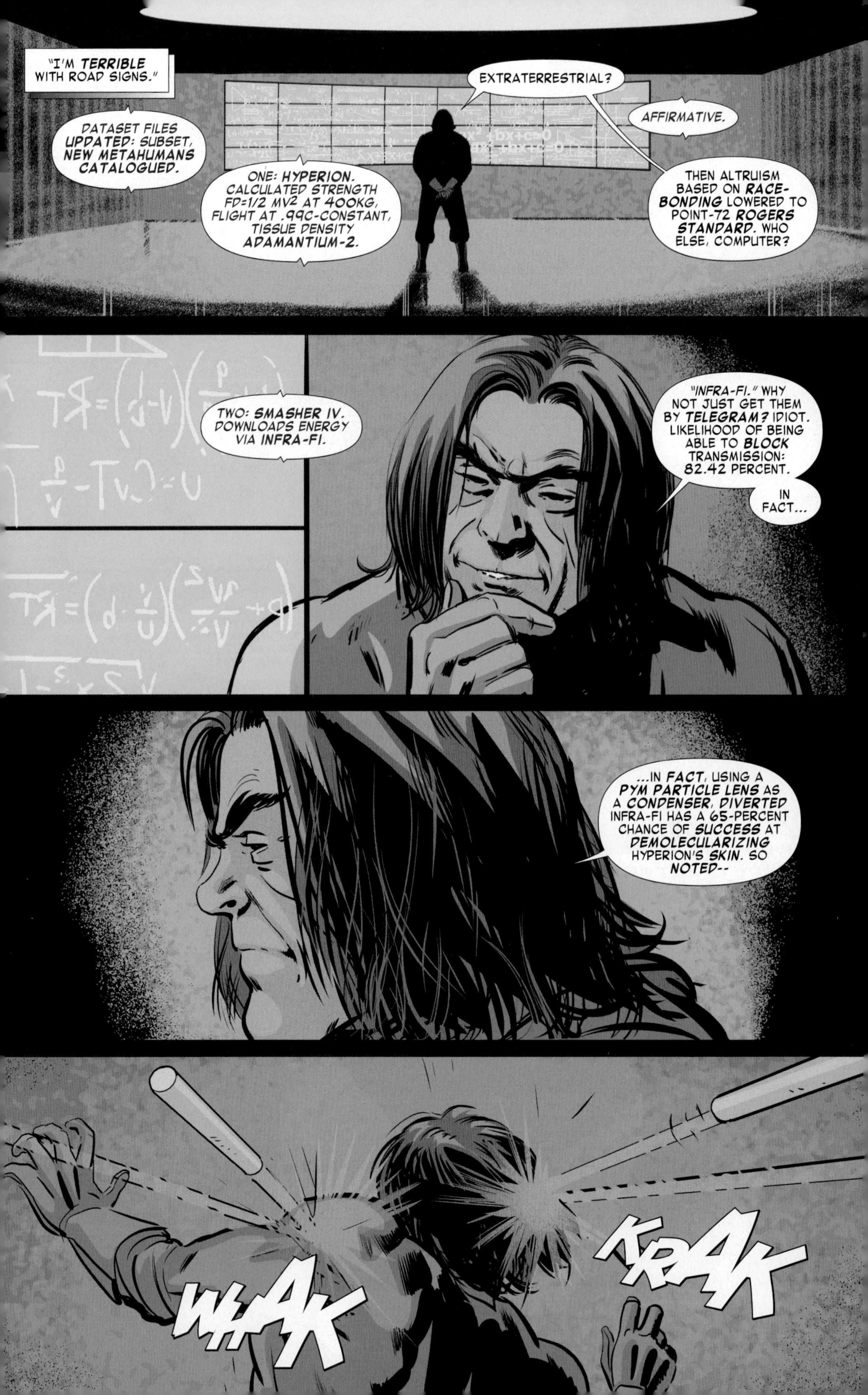
"I'M TERRIBLE WITH ROAD SIGNS."
DATASET FILES UPDATED: SUBSET, NEW METAHUMANS CATALOGUED.
ONE: HYPERION. CALCULATED STRENGTH FD=1/2 MV2 AT 400KG, FLIGHT AT .99C-CONSTANT, TISSUE DENSITY ADAMANTIUM-2.
EXTRATERRESTRIAL?
AFFIRMATIVE.
THEN ALTRUISM BASED ON RACE-BONDING LOWERED TO POINT-72 ROGERS STANDARD. WHO ELSE, COMPUTER?
TWO: SMASHER IV. DOWNLOADS ENERGY VIA INFRA-FI.
"INFRA-FI." WHY NOT JUST GET THEM BY TELEGRAM? IDIOT. LIKELIHOOD OF BEING ABLE TO BLOCK TRANSMISSION: 82.42 PERCENT.
IN FACT...
...IN FACT, USING A PYM PARTICLE LENS AS A CONDENSER, DIVERTED INFRA-FI HAS A 65-PERCENT CHANCE OF SUCCESS AT DEMOLECULARIZING HYPERION'S SKIN. SO NOTED--
WHAK
KRAK

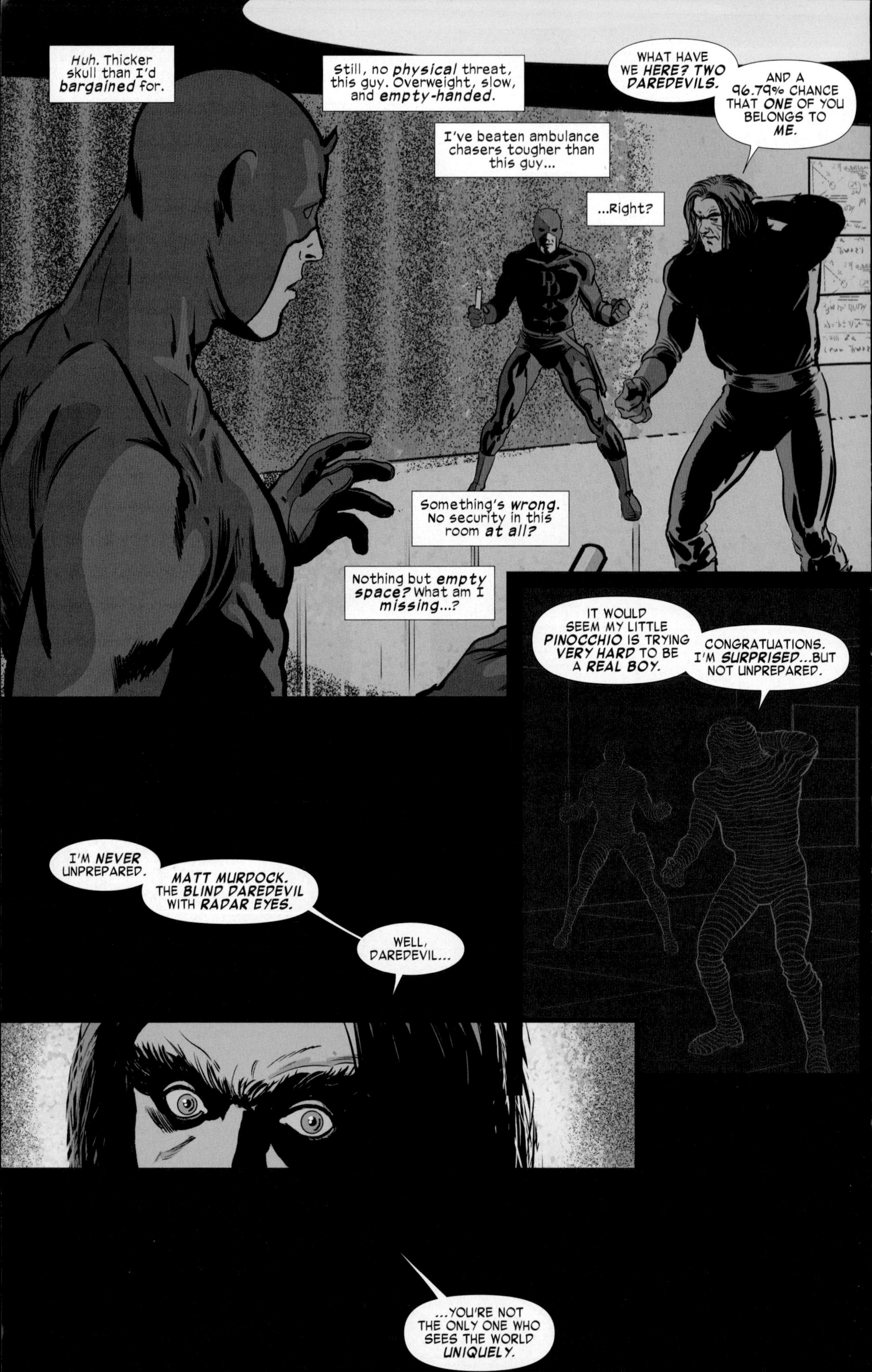
Huh. Thicker skull than I'd bargained for.
Still, no physical threat, this guy. Overweight, slow, and empty-handed.
I've beaten ambulance chasers tougher than this guy...
...Right?
WHAT HAVE WE HERE? TWO DAREDEVILS.
AND A 96.79% CHANCE THAT ONE OF YOU BELONGS TO ME.
Something's wrong. No security in this room at all?
Nothing but empty space? What am I missing...?
IT WOULD SEEM MY LITTLE PINOCCHIO IS TRYING VERY HARD TO BE A REAL BOY.
CONGRATUATIONS. I'M SURPRISED...BUT NOT UNPREPARED.
I'M NEVER UNPREPARED.
MATT MURDOCK. THE BLIND DAREDEVIL WITH RADAR EYES.
WELL, DAREDEVIL...
...YOU'RE NOT THE ONLY ONE WHO SEES THE WORLD UNIQUELY.

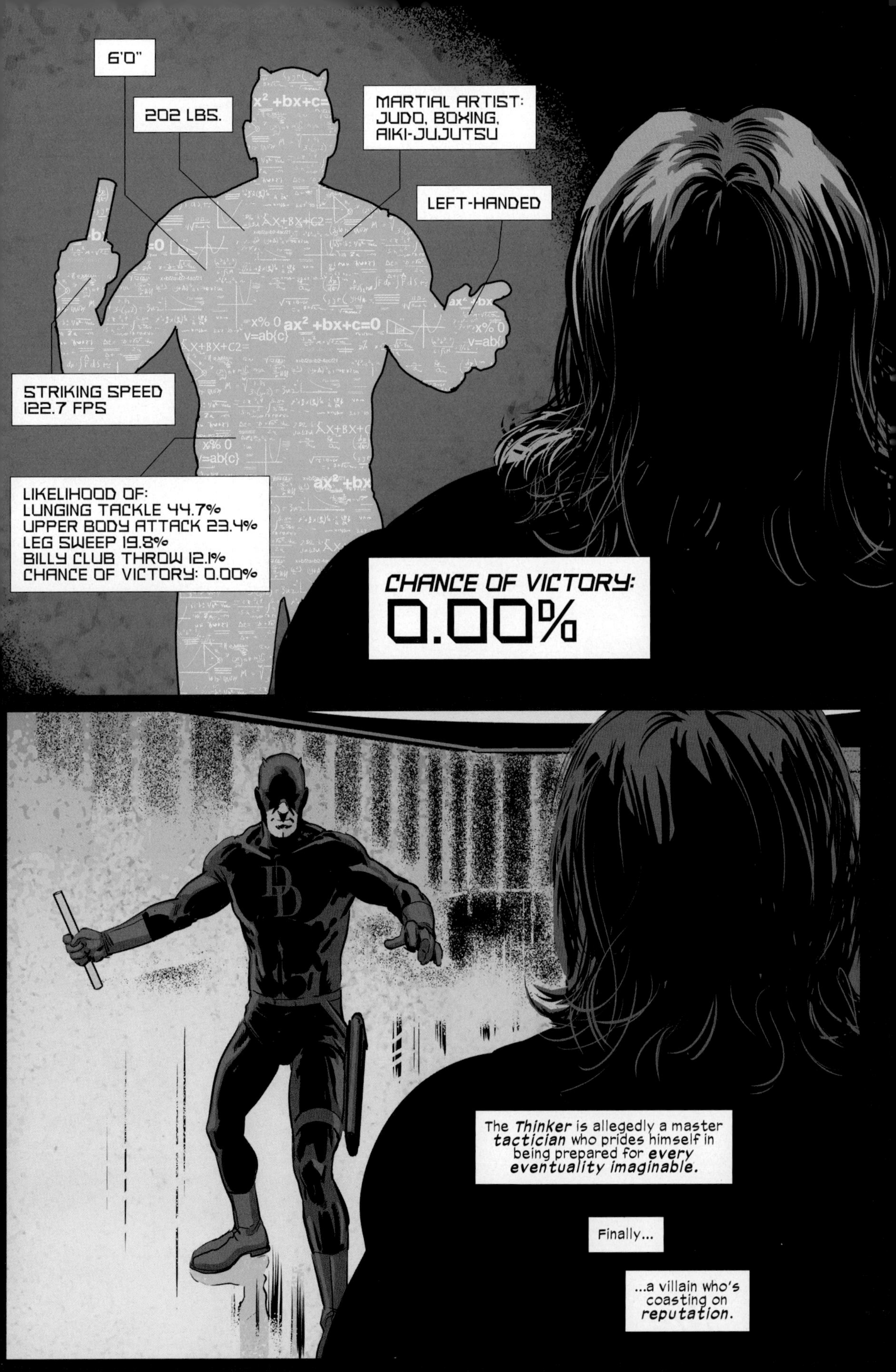
6'0"
202 LBS.
MARTIAL ARTIST: JUDO, BOXING, AIKI-JUJUTSU
LEFT-HANDED
STRIKING SPEED 122.7 FPS
LIKELIHOOD OF:
LUNGING TACKLE 44.7%
UPPER BODY ATTACK 23.4%
LEG SWEEP 19.8%
BILLY CLUB THROW 12.1%
CHANCE OF VICTORY: 0.00%
CHANCE OF VICTORY: 0.00%
The Thinker is allegedly a master tactician who prides himself in being prepared for every eventuality imaginable.
Finally...
...a villain who's coasting on reputation.

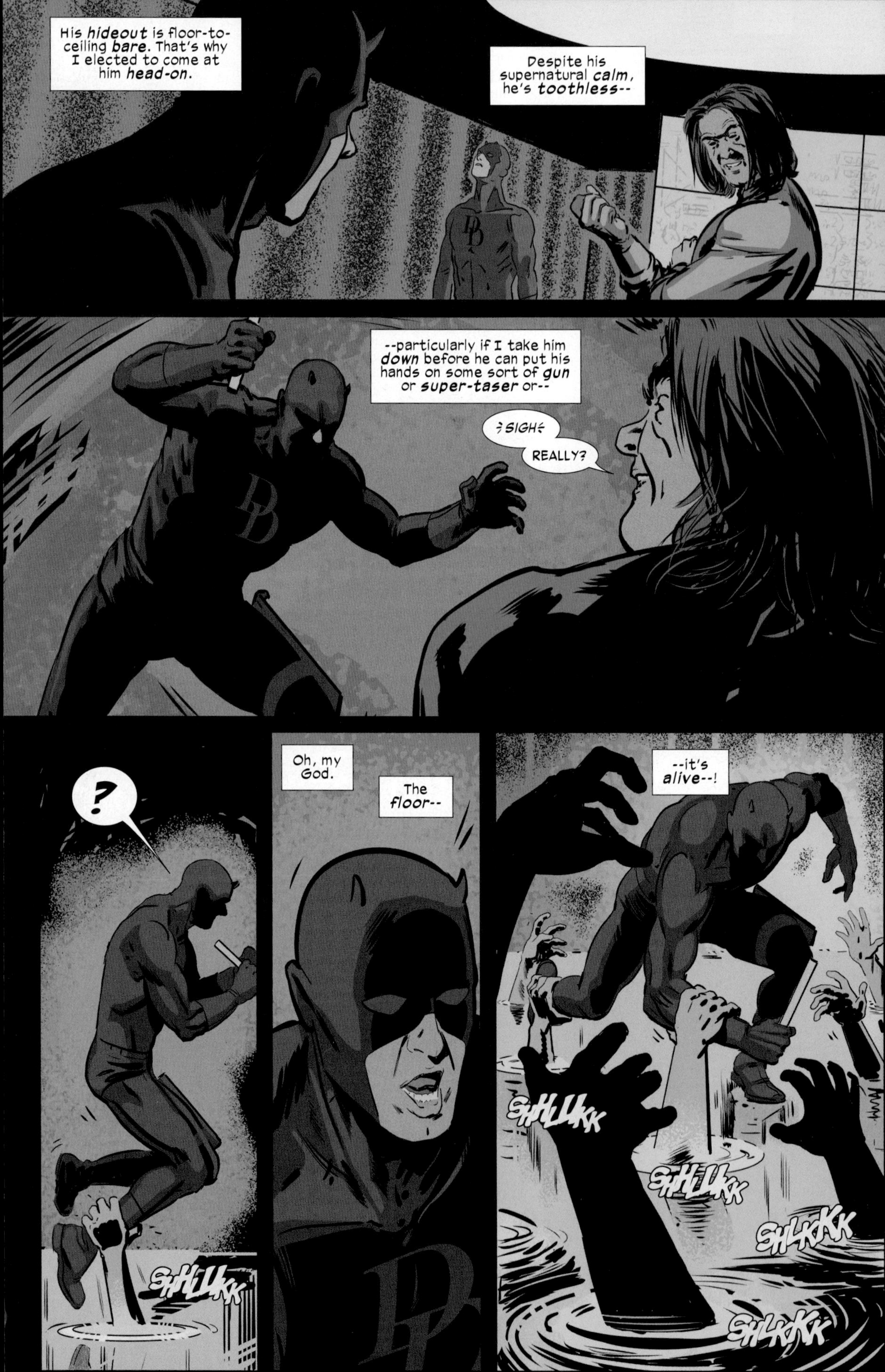

His hideout is floor-to-ceiling bare. That's why I elected to come at him head-on.
Despite his supernatural calm, he's toothless--
--particularly if I take him down before he can put his hands on some sort of gun or super-taser or--
SIGH
REALLY?
?
SHHLUKK
Oh, my God.
The floor--
--it's alive--!
SHHLUKK
SHHLUKK
SHLKKK
SHLKKK

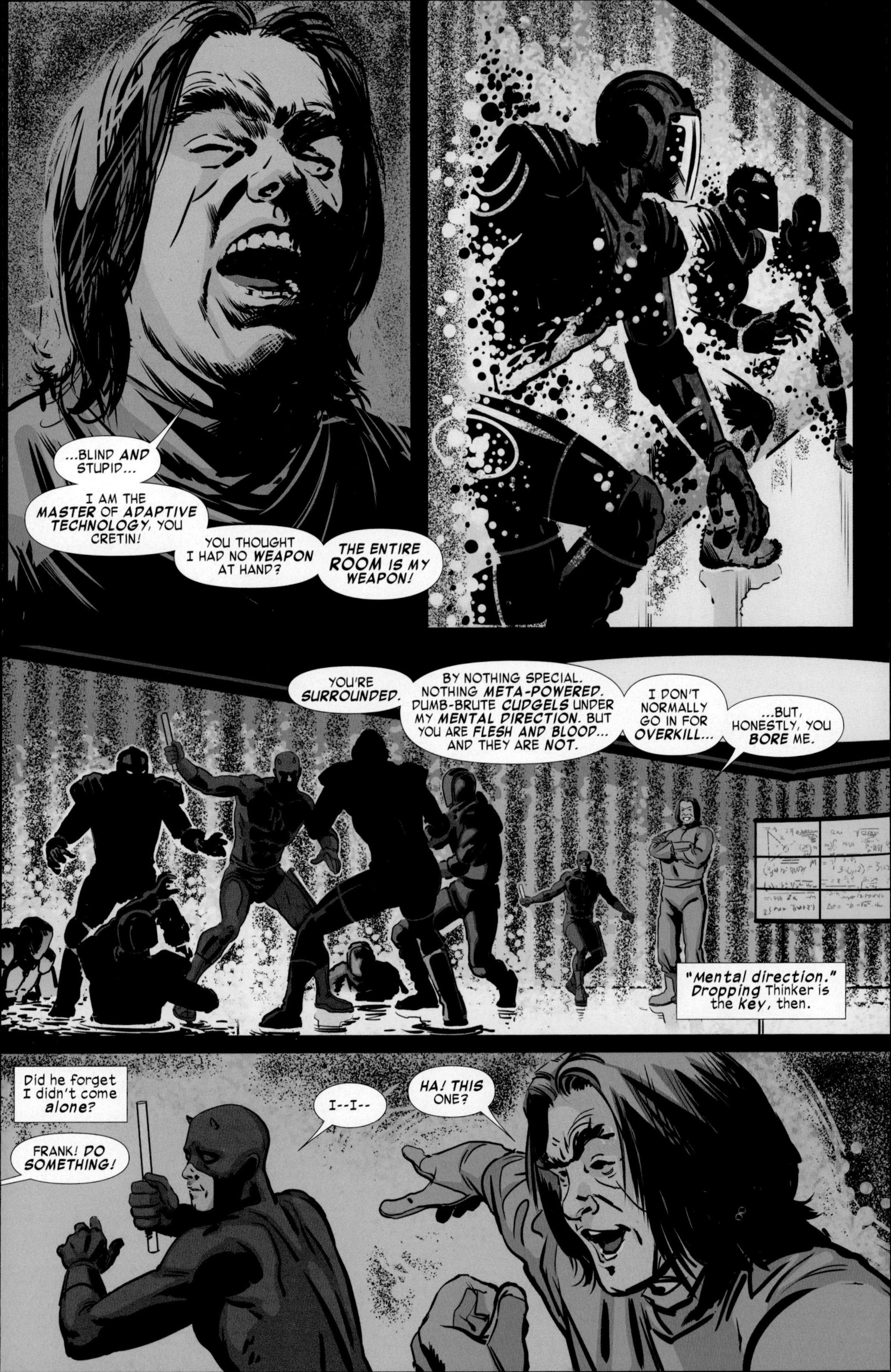
...BLIND AND STUPID...
I AM THE MASTER OF ADAPTIVE TECHNOLOGY, YOU CRETIN!
YOU THOUGHT I HAD NO WEAPON AT HAND?
THE ENTIRE ROOM IS MY WEAPON!
YOU'RE SURROUNDED.
BY NOTHING SPECIAL. NOTHING META-POWERED. DUMB-BRUTE CUDGELS UNDER MY MENTAL DIRECTION. BUT YOU ARE FLESH AND BLOOD... AND THEY ARE NOT.
I DON'T NORMALLY GO IN FOR OVERKILL...
...BUT, HONESTLY, YOU BORE ME.
"Mental direction." Dropping Thinker is the key, then.
Did he forget I didn't come alone?
FRANK! DO SOMETHING!
I--I--
HA! THIS ONE?

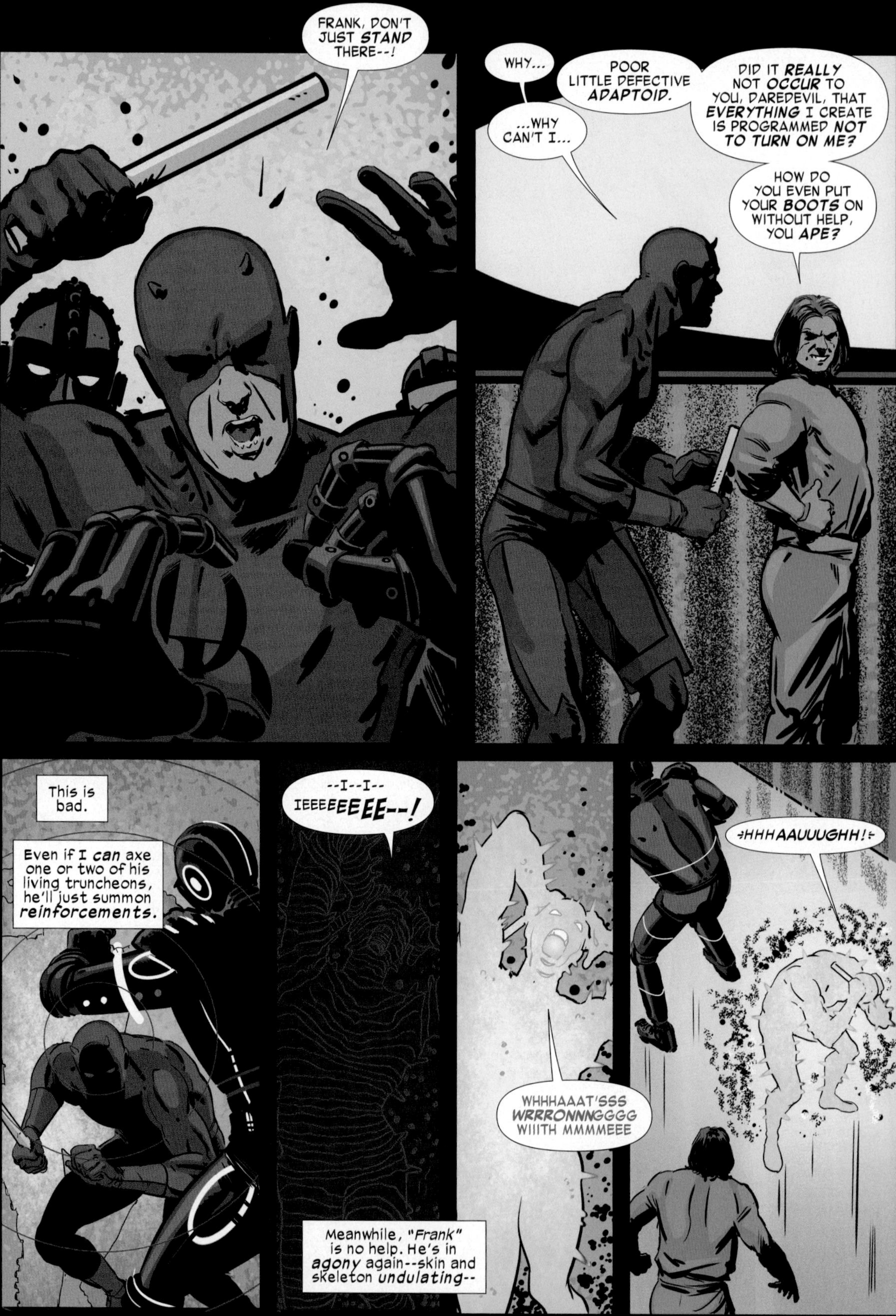
FRANK, DON'T JUST STAND THERE--!
WHY...
...WHY CAN'T I...
POOR LITTLE DEFECTIVE ADAPTOID.
DID IT REALLY NOT OCCUR TO YOU, DAREDEVIL, THAT EVERYTHING I CREATE IS PROGRAMMED NOT TO TURN ON ME?
HOW DO YOU EVEN PUT YOUR BOOTS ON WITHOUT HELP, YOU APE?
This is bad.
Even if I can axe one or two of his living truncheons, he'll just summon reinforcements.
--I--I-- IEEEEEEEE--!
Meanwhile, "Frank" is no help. He's in agony again--skin and skeleton undulating--
WHHHAAAT'SSS WRRRONNNGGGG WIIITH MMMMEEE
HHHAAUUUGHH!

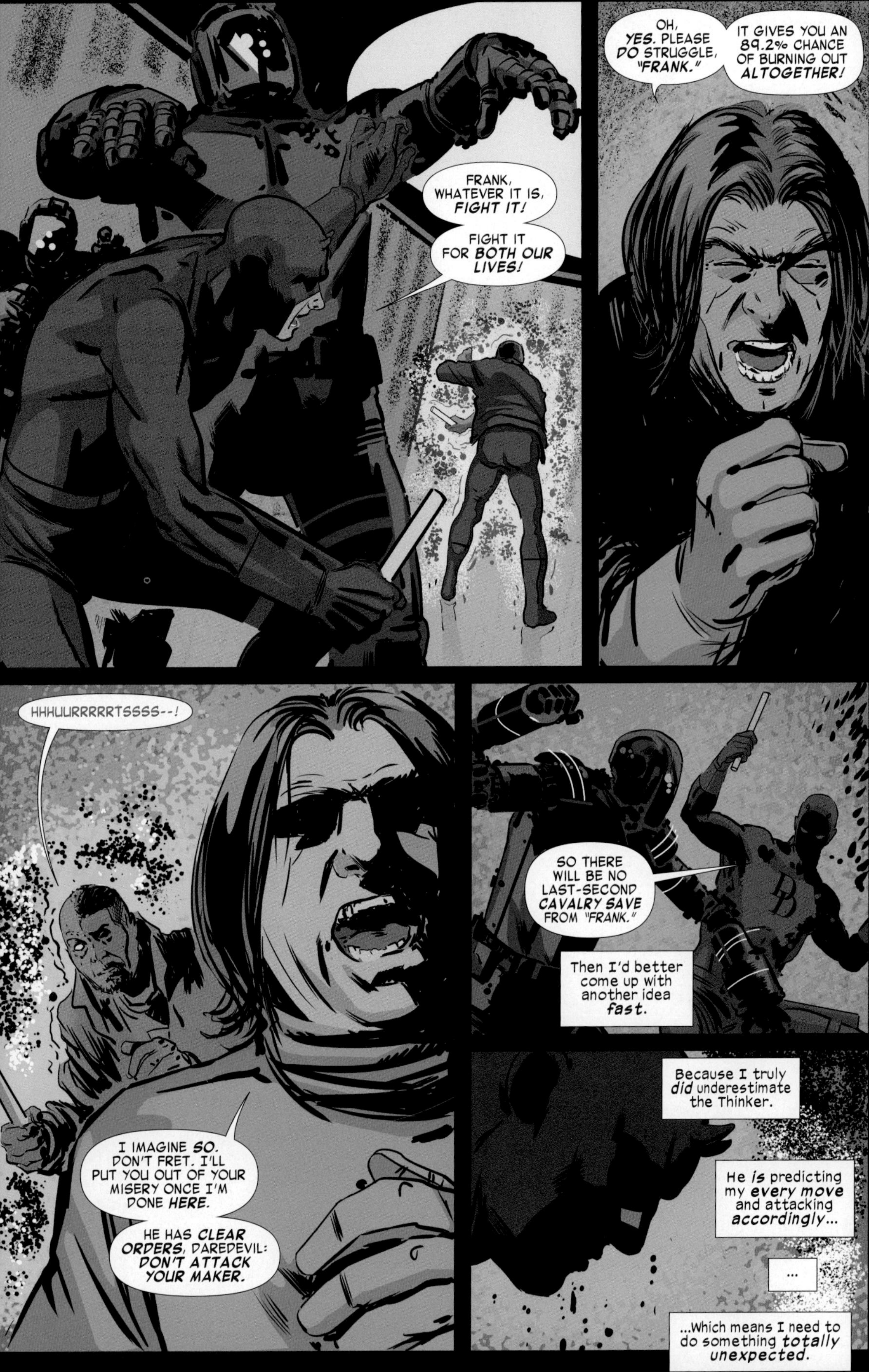
FRANK, WHATEVER IT IS, FIGHT IT!
FIGHT IT FOR BOTH OUR LIVES!
OH, YES. PLEASE DO STRUGGLE, "FRANK."
IT GIVES YOU AN 89.2% CHANCE OF BURNING OUT ALTOGETHER!
HHHUURRRRRTSSSS--!
I IMAGINE SO. DON'T FRET. I'LL PUT YOU OUT OF YOUR MISERY ONCE I'M DONE HERE.
HE HAS CLEAR ORDERS, DAREDEVIL: DON'T ATTACK YOUR MAKER.
SO THERE WILL BE NO LAST-SECOND CAVALRY SAVE FROM "FRANK."
Then I'd better come up with another idea fast.
Because I truly did underestimate the Thinker.
He is predicting my every move and attacking accordingly...
...
...Which means I need to do something totally unexpected.

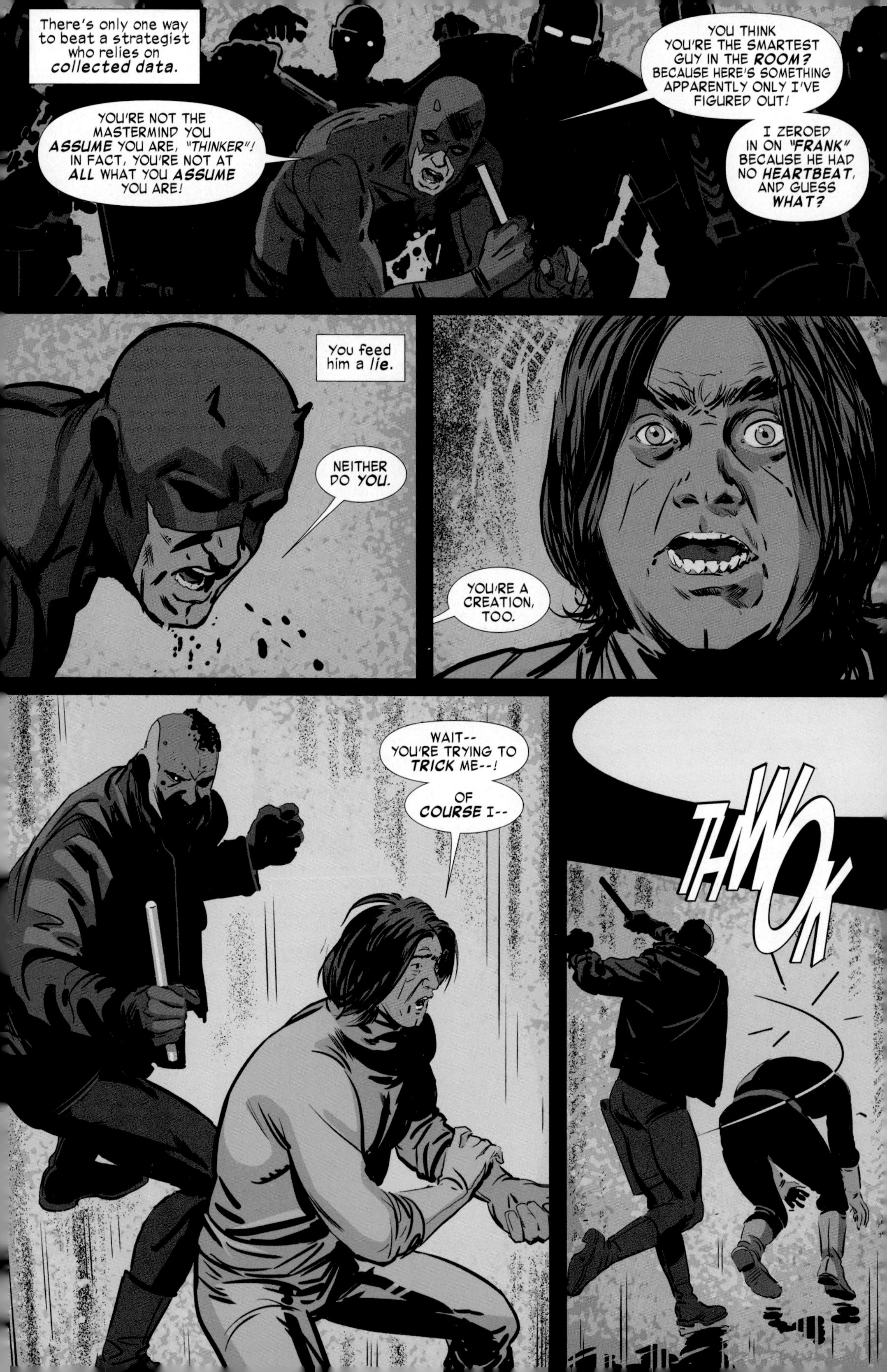
There's only one way to beat a strategist who relies on *collected data*.
YOU'RE NOT THE MASTERMIND YOU *ASSUME* YOU ARE, *"THINKER"*! IN FACT, YOU'RE NOT AT *ALL* WHAT YOU *ASSUME* YOU ARE!
YOU THINK YOU'RE THE SMARTEST GUY IN THE *ROOM?* BECAUSE HERE'S SOMETHING APPARENTLY ONLY I'VE FIGURED OUT!
I ZEROED IN ON *"FRANK"* BECAUSE HE HAD NO *HEARTBEAT*, AND GUESS *WHAT?*
You feed him a *lie*.
NEITHER DO *YOU*.
YOU'RE A CREATION, TOO.
WAIT-- YOU'RE TRYING TO *TRICK* ME--!
OF *COURSE* I--
THWOK

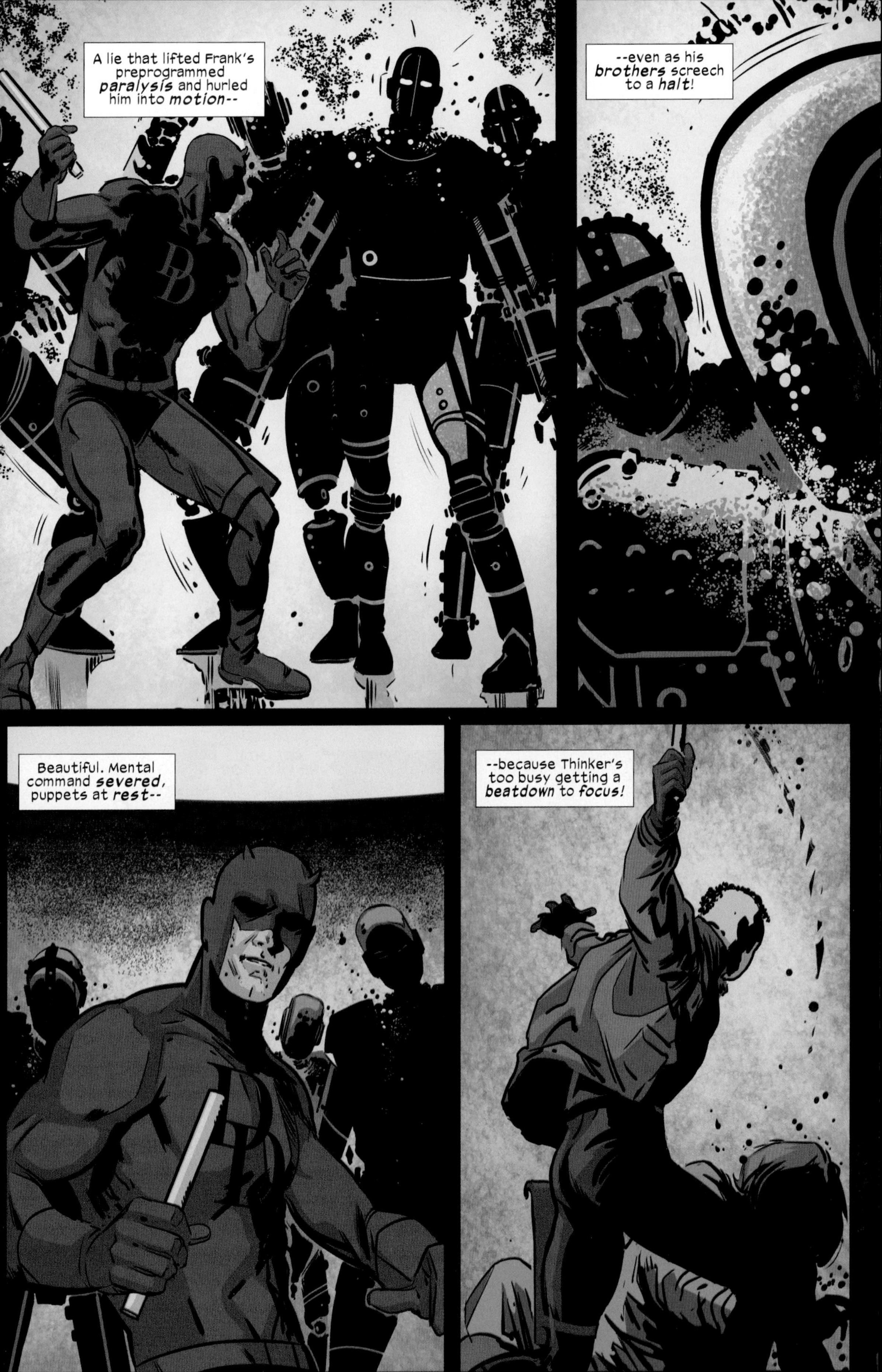
A lie that lifted Frank's preprogrammed *paralysis* and hurled him into *motion*--
--even as his *brothers* screech to a *halt*!
Beautiful. Mental command *severed*, puppets at *rest*--
--because Thinker's too busy getting a *beatdown* to *focus*!

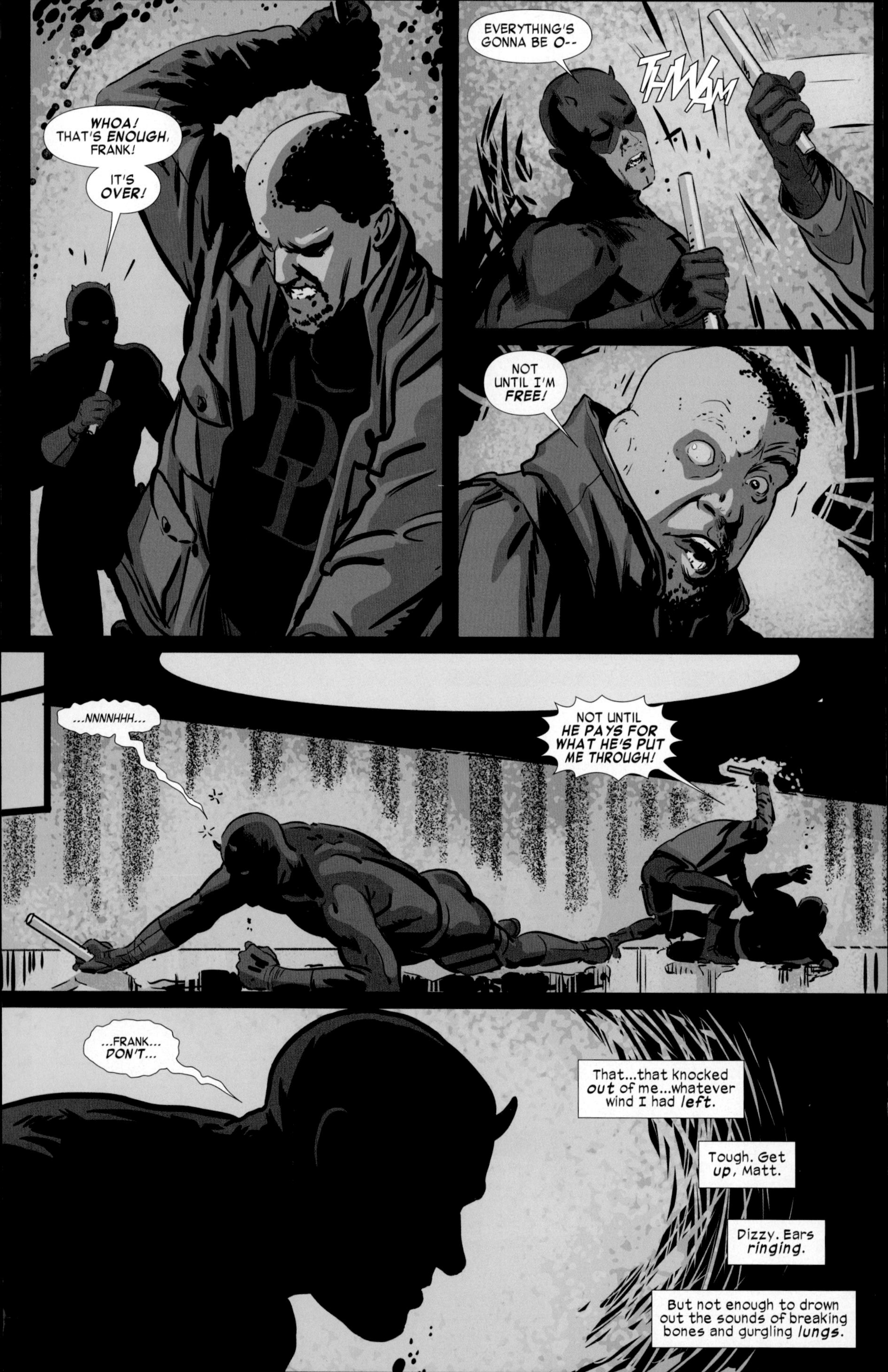
WHOA! THAT'S ENOUGH, FRANK!
IT'S OVER!
EVERYTHING'S GONNA BE O--
THWAM
NOT UNTIL I'M FREE!
...NNNNHHH...
NOT UNTIL HE PAYS FOR WHAT HE'S PUT ME THROUGH!
...FRANK... DON'T...
That...that knocked out of me...whatever wind I had left.
Tough. Get up, Matt.
Dizzy. Ears ringing.
But not enough to drown out the sounds of breaking bones and gurgling lungs.

THUD THUD THUD

FRANK, *STOP...*

...FRANK, HE'S HAD ENOUGH...

...SHOW SOME *MERCY,* FOR *GOD'S SAKE!*

He's not reacting to my voice.

He'll just keep at this, robotically, methodically, until Thinker is *dead,* won't he?

He has no *capacity* for mercy.

I believe in souls.

I believe to my very core in the innate goodness of people.

All along, I've been reacting to "*Frank*" as if he were human because I so *wanted* him to be.

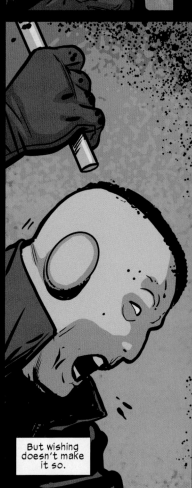

But wishing doesn't make it so.

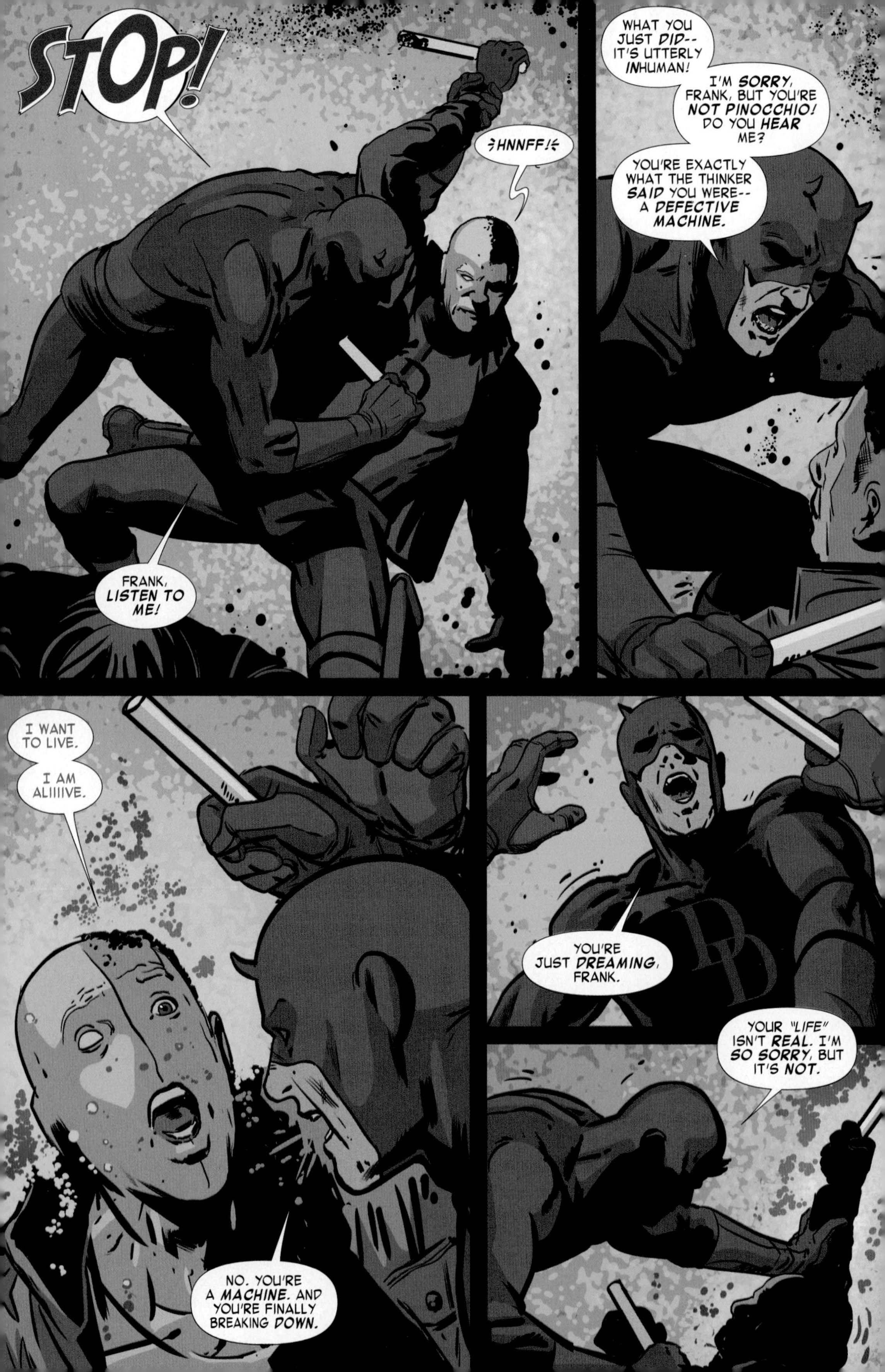
STOP!
HNNFF!
FRANK, LISTEN TO ME!
WHAT YOU JUST DID-- IT'S UTTERLY INHUMAN!
I'M SORRY, FRANK, BUT YOU'RE NOT PINOCCHIO! DO YOU HEAR ME?
YOU'RE EXACTLY WHAT THE THINKER SAID YOU WERE-- A DEFECTIVE MACHINE.
I WANT TO LIVE.
I AM ALIIIIVE.
NO. YOU'RE A MACHINE. AND YOU'RE FINALLY BREAKING DOWN.
YOU'RE JUST DREAMING, FRANK.
YOUR "LIFE" ISN'T REAL. I'M SO SORRY, BUT IT'S NOT.

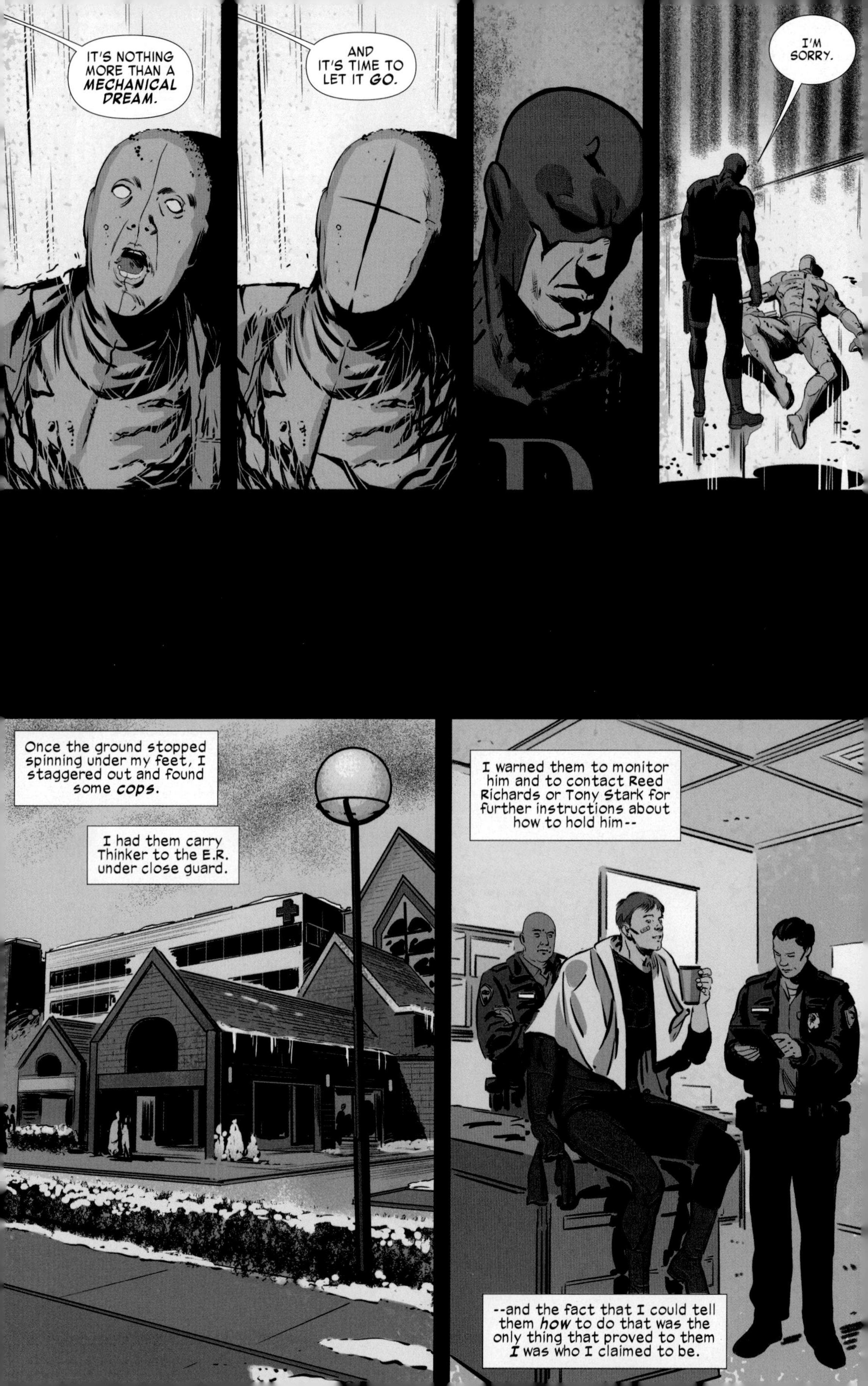
IT'S NOTHING MORE THAN A MECHANICAL DREAM.
AND IT'S TIME TO LET IT GO.
I'M SORRY.
Once the ground stopped spinning under my feet, I staggered out and found some cops.
I had them carry Thinker to the E.R. under close guard.
I warned them to monitor him and to contact Reed Richards or Tony Stark for further instructions about how to hold him--
--and the fact that I could tell them how to do that was the only thing that proved to them I was who I claimed to be.

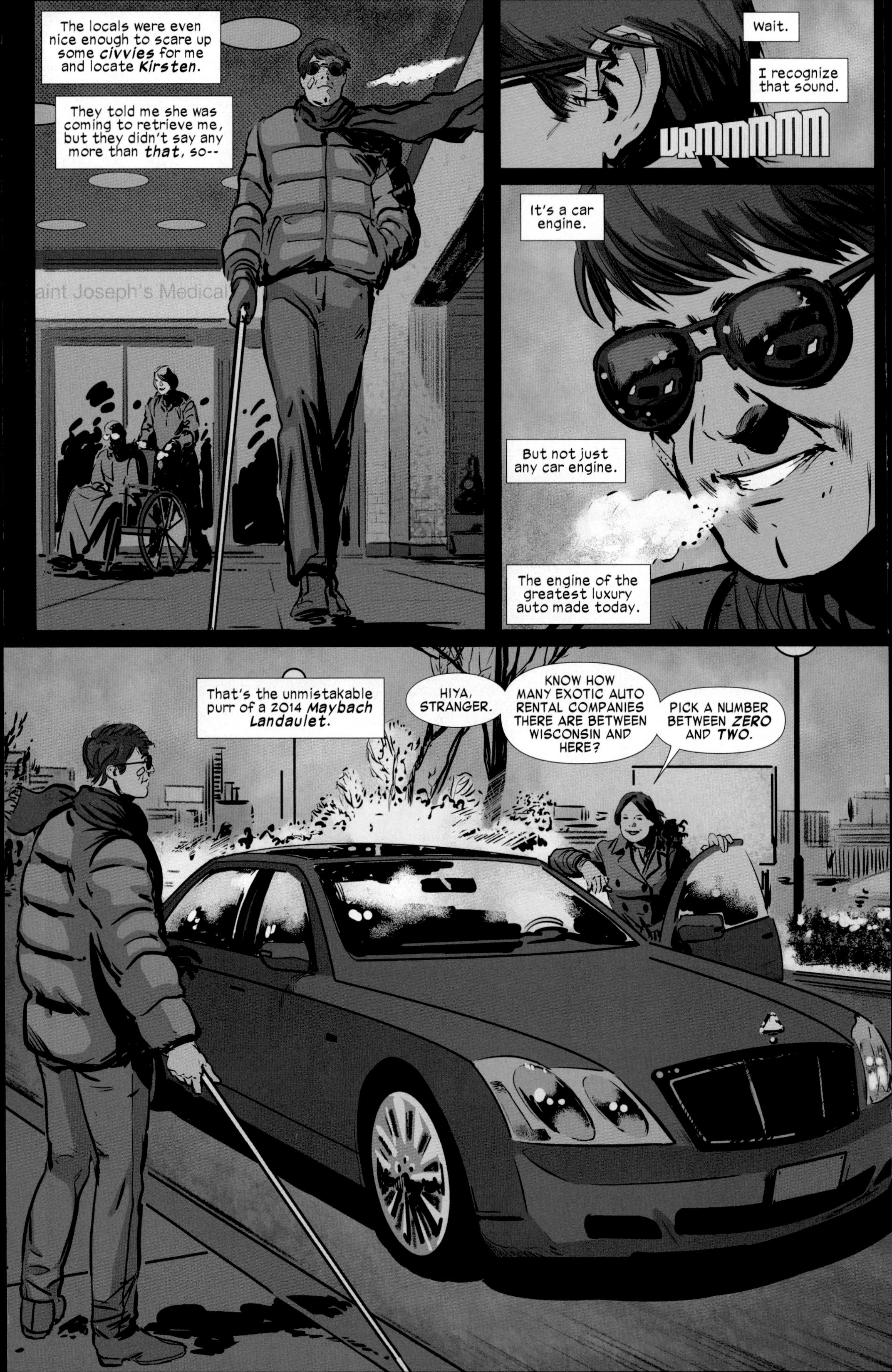

The locals were even nice enough to scare up some *civvies* for me and locate *Kirsten*.
They told me she was coming to retrieve me, but they didn't say any more than *that*, so--
aint Joseph's Medical
Wait.
I recognize that sound.
VRMMMMM
It's a car engine.
But not just any car engine.
The engine of the greatest luxury auto made today.
That's the unmistakable purr of a 2014 *Maybach Landaulet*.
HIYA, STRANGER.
KNOW HOW MANY EXOTIC AUTO RENTAL COMPANIES THERE ARE BETWEEN WISCONSIN AND HERE?
PICK A NUMBER BETWEEN *ZERO* AND *TWO*.

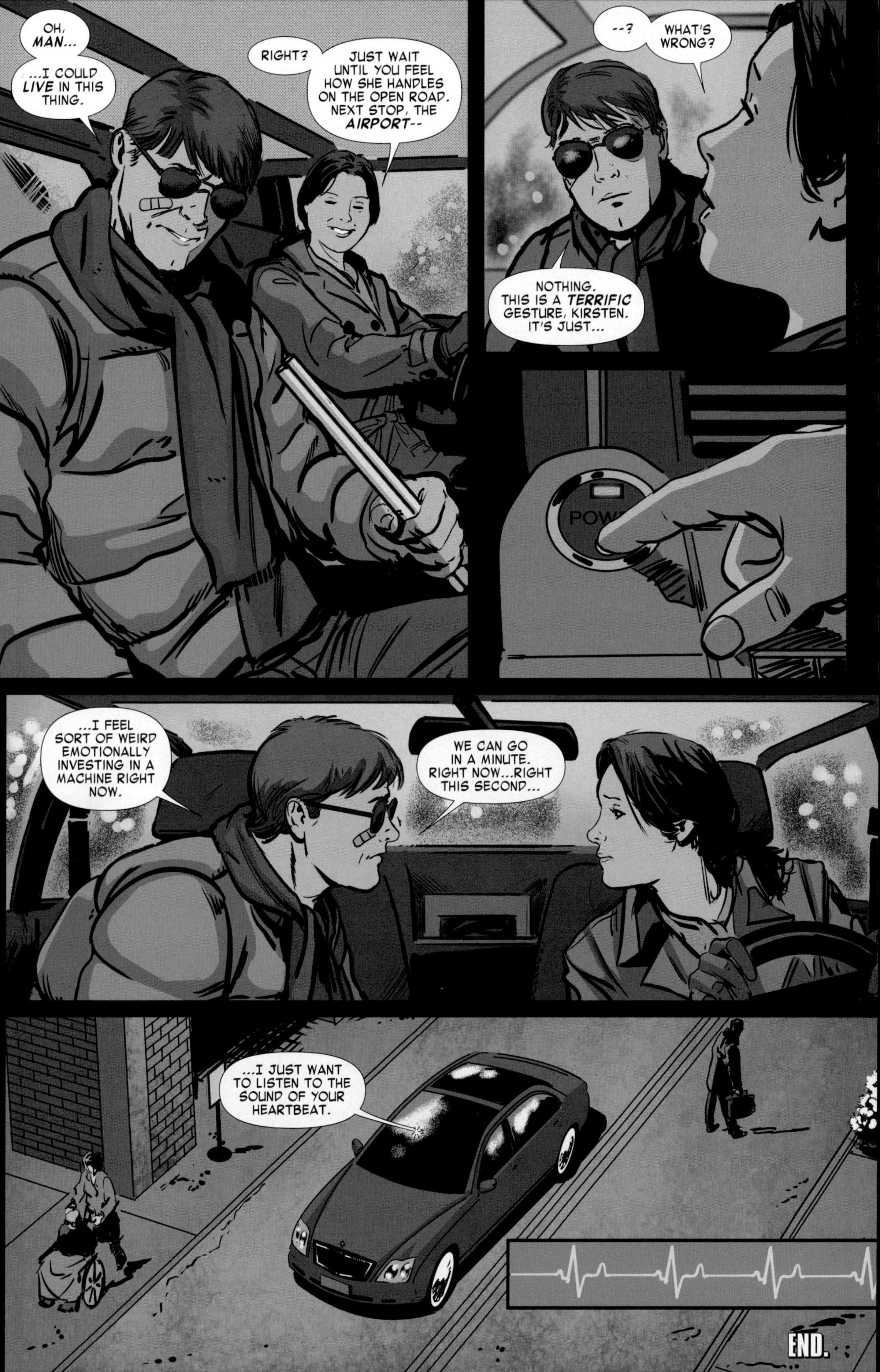
OH, MAN...
...I COULD LIVE IN THIS THING.
RIGHT?
JUST WAIT UNTIL YOU FEEL HOW SHE HANDLES ON THE OPEN ROAD. NEXT STOP, THE AIRPORT--
--?
WHAT'S WRONG?
NOTHING. THIS IS A TERRIFIC GESTURE, KIRSTEN. IT'S JUST...
POW
...I FEEL SORT OF WEIRD EMOTIONALLY INVESTING IN A MACHINE RIGHT NOW.
WE CAN GO IN A MINUTE. RIGHT NOW...RIGHT THIS SECOND...
...I JUST WANT TO LISTEN TO THE SOUND OF YOUR HEARTBEAT.
END.

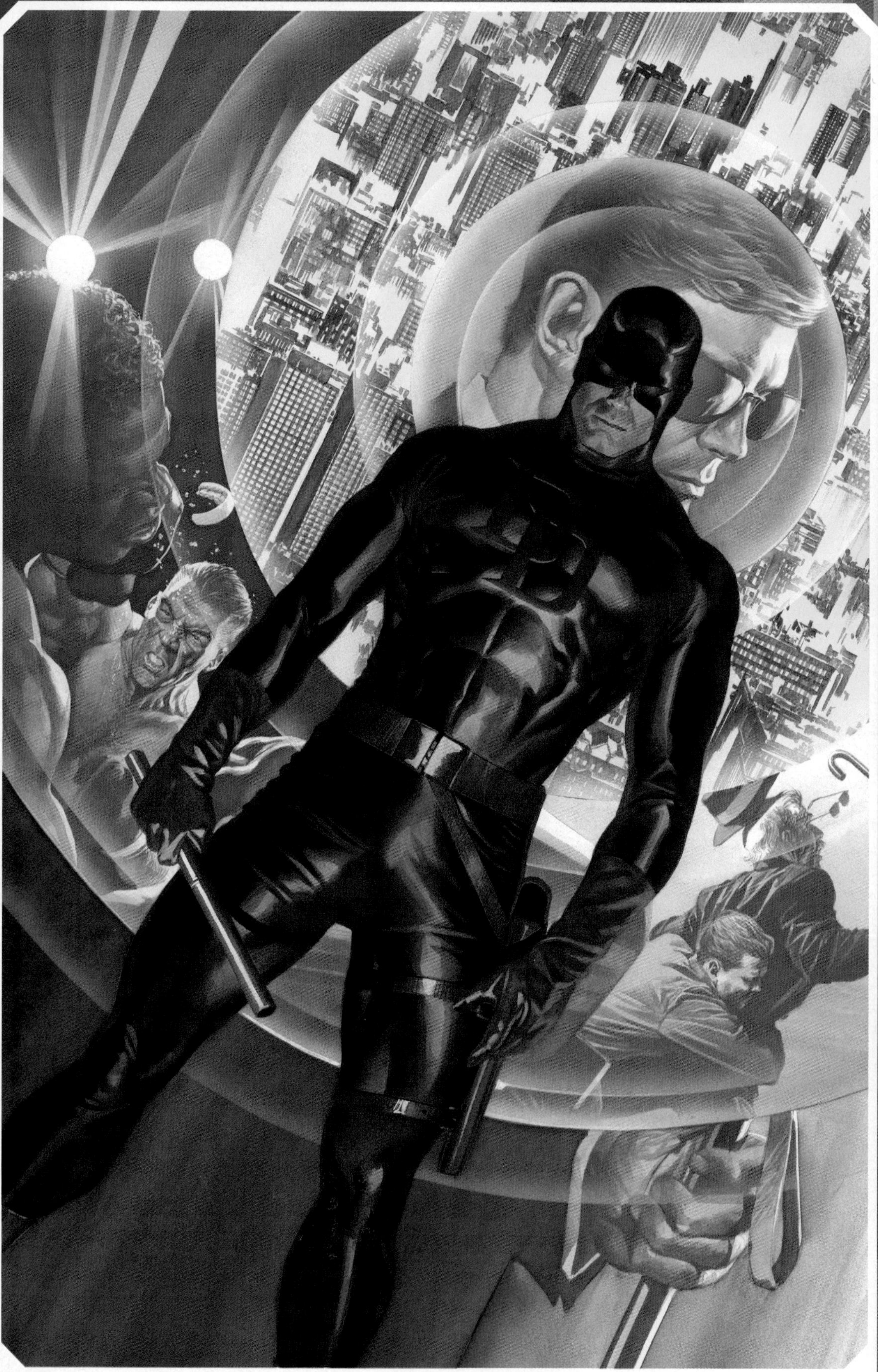

DAREDEVIL #1 75TH ANNIVERSARY VARIANT BY ALEX ROSS

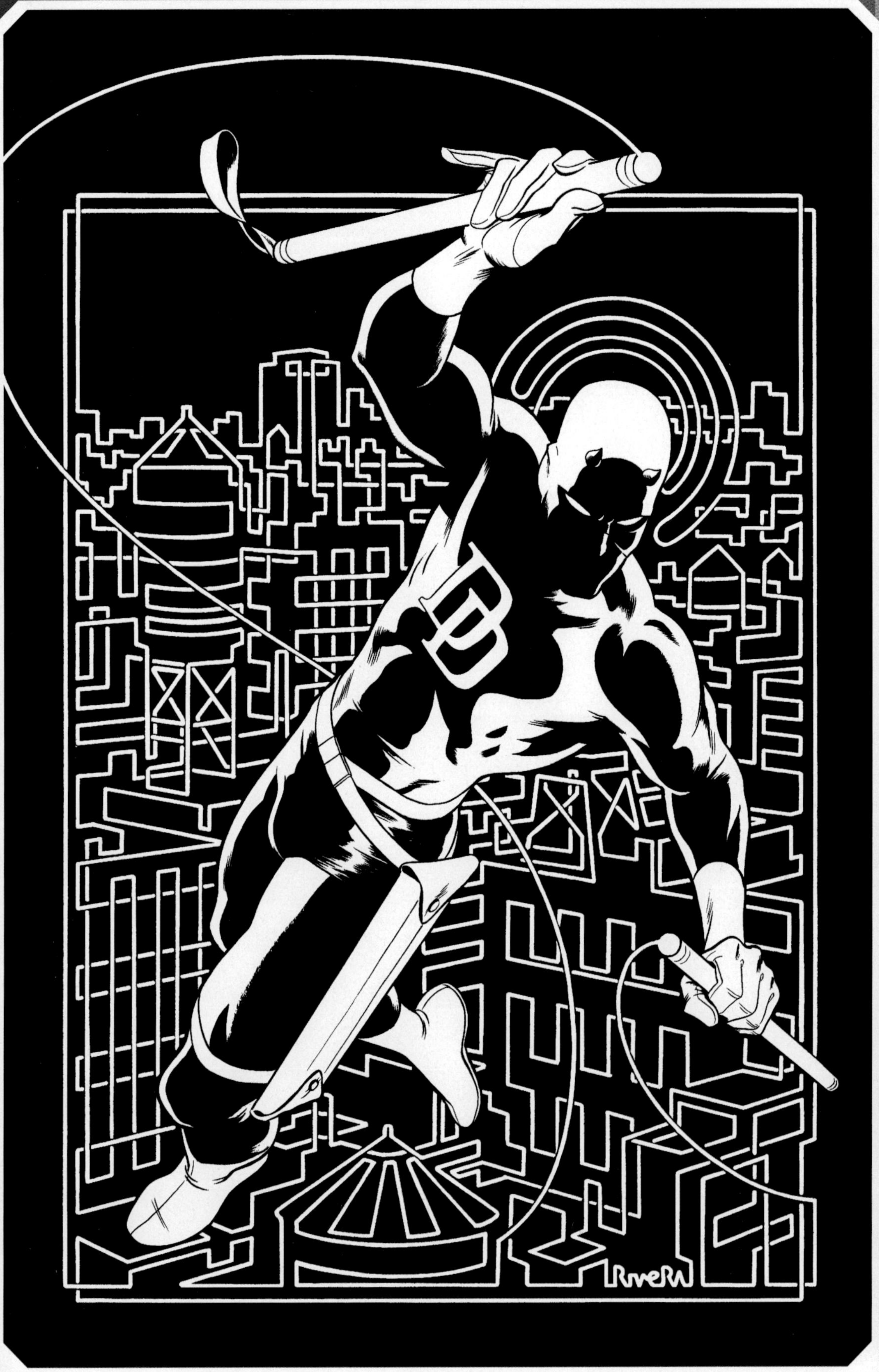
RIVERA

VARIANT BY PAOLO RIVERA DAREDEVIL #1

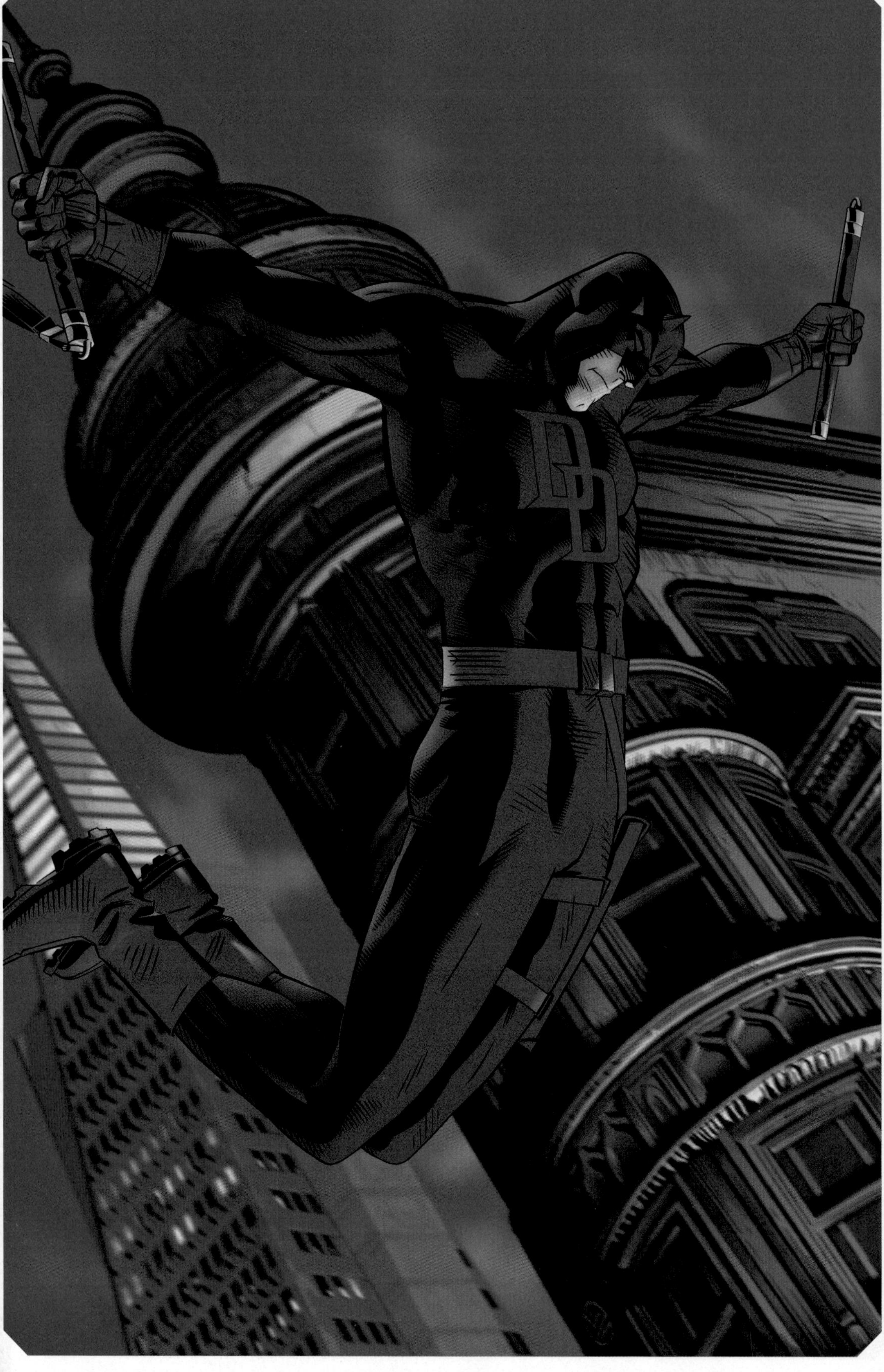

DAREDEVIL #1 WIZARD WORLD VARIANT BY MICHAEL GOLDEN

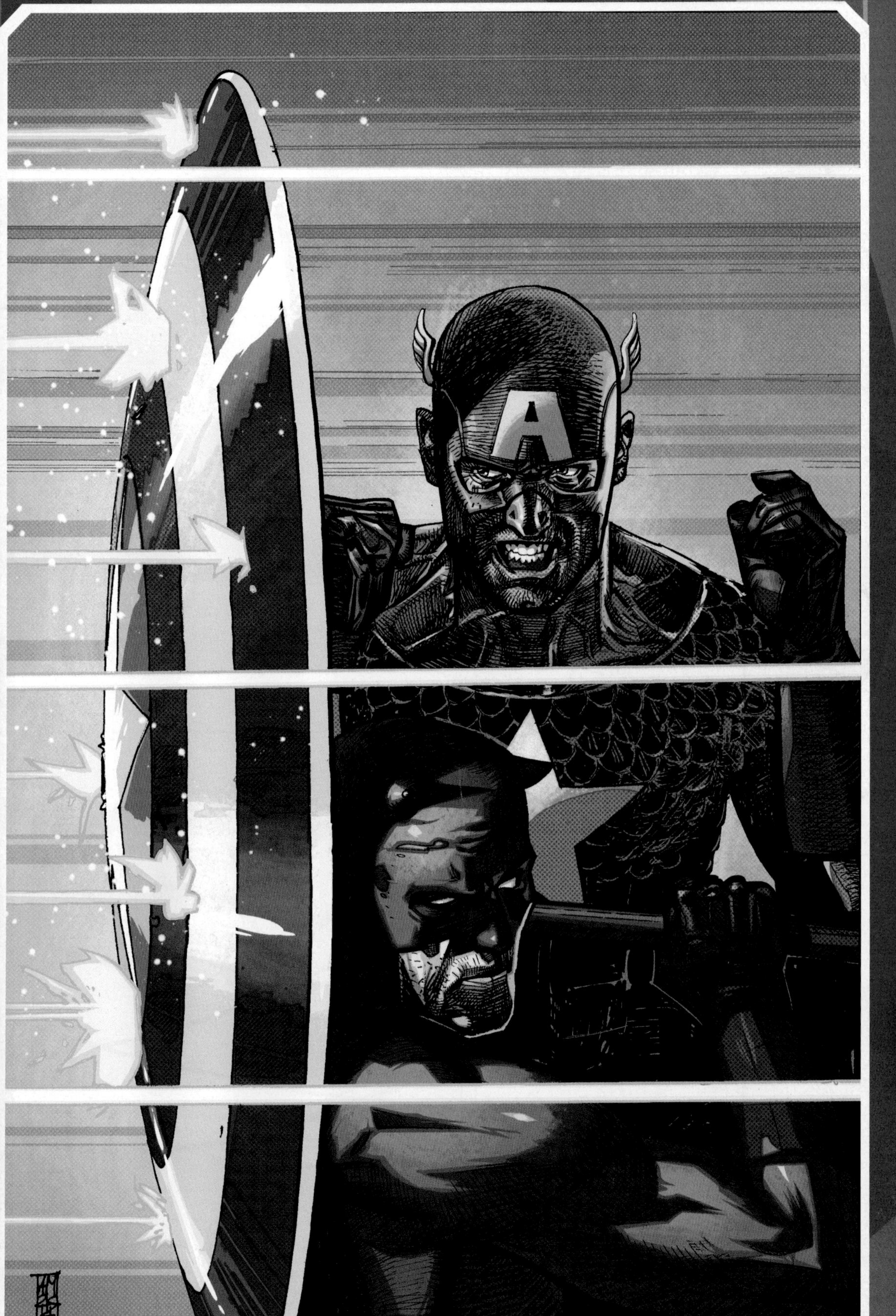

CAPTAIN AMERICA TEAM-UP VARIANT
BY ALEX MALEEV & DAVE MCCAIG
DAREDEVIL #2

DAREDEVIL #1
ANIMAL VARIANT BY CHRIS SAMNEE &
JAVIER RODRIGUEZ

DAREDEVIL #1
VARIANT BY SKOTTIE YOUNG